DATE DUE

NOV - 8 1993	
NOV 22 1993	
APR 8 1994	
APR 21 1994	
FEB - 2 1995	
FEB 16 1995	
FEB 23 1995	
MAR 10 1995	
APR - 9 1996	
FEB 13 1997	
FEB 29 2000	
MAY 1 2003	

THE UNRESOLVED QUESTION

I understand, though I do not approve, the proceedings of poor Wolfe Tone and his confederates. They wished to make a complete separation between Great Britain and Ireland. They wished to establish a Hibernian republic. Their plan was a very bad one; but, to do them justice, it was perfectly consistent; and an ingenious man might defend it by some plausible arguments.

> Thomas Babington Macaulay
> in the House of Commons,
> 6 February 1833

. . . we hereby proclaim the Irish Republic as a Sovereign Independent State . . .

> The Provisional Government of the Irish
> Republic to the people of Ireland,
> Easter Monday 1916

THE UNRESOLVED QUESTION

THE ANGLO-IRISH SETTLEMENT AND ITS UNDOING 1912–72

NICHOLAS MANSERGH

YALE UNIVERSITY PRESS
NEW HAVEN AND LONDON 1991

Copyright © 1991 by Yale University

All rights reserved. This book may not be reproduced in whole or in part,
in any form (beyond that copying permitted by Sections 107 and 108
of the U.S. Copyright Law and except by reviewers for the public press),
without written permission from the publishers.

Designed by John Nicoll

Set in Linotron Bembo by Best-set Typesetters Ltd, Hong Kong
Printed and bound at The Bath Press, Avon, Great Britain

ISBN 0-300-05069-0

Library of Congress Cataloging-in-Publication Data
Mansergh, Nicholas.
The unresolved question: the Anglo-Irish settlement and its
undoing, 1912-72/Nicholas Mansergh.
p. cm.
Includes references and index.
ISBN 0-300-05069-0
1. Ireland—Politics and government—20th century. 2. Northern
Ireland—Politics and government. 3. Irish unification question.
4. Irish question. I. Title.
DA963.M28 1991   941.5082—dc20   91-50587 CIP

TO GREGOR

TABLE OF CONTENTS

PREFACE

The author was indebted during the early 1980s, while he was preparing to write this book, to the Public Record Offices in London and Northern Ireland, to the National Library and the State Paper Office in Dublin, to the House of Lords Record Office and the British Museum, to the Archives Departments of University College and Trinity College, Dublin, to the Bodleian Library, Oxford, the Library of the Royal Commonwealth Society and of the University of Birmingham. He was also grateful to the State Department, Washington, for access to material in their archives. Much more recently the author was indebted to the Franciscan Friars in Killiney, who hold the de Valera papers. The author owed a special debt of gratitude to Mrs Sally French of Fulbourn, who typed almost all the book with much patience and efficiency.

INTRODUCTION

In constitutional terms the parameters of the Anglo-Irish settlement 1920–25 may be readily defined. They were determined by, and rested upon, a threefold statutory foundation. The first of these was the Government of Ireland Act 1920,[1] which made provision for the division of Ireland into two parts; one part consisted of the twenty-six counties of what was described as Southern Ireland, even though it included the most northerly of Irish counties. The other consisted of the six counties of Northern Ireland. Each part was to acquire a limited measure of self-government exercisable through local parliamentary institutions. Next came the Anglo-Irish Treaty (or more strictly, the Articles of Agreement for a Treaty between Great Britain and Ireland), 1921.[2] On ratification by procedures the Treaty itself prescribed, this gave British and Irish statutory sanction for the bringing into existence, in place of the Northern and Southern Ireland provided for in the Act of 1920, of an Irish Free State as a Dominion within the British Commonwealth of Nations embracing the whole of Ireland, but from which, however, Northern Ireland, as defined in the Act of 1920, might and did opt out. Finally, there was the Agreement of 1925[3] which disposed of certain outstanding issues relating to finance and the delimitation of the boundary between the two parts into which Ireland was by then divided.

The settlement was formulated, as the recital records, within the years 1920–25, but the period is in other respects too restrictive to provide a satisfying basis for historical enquiry. Too much was derivative at the outset and too inconclusive at the close for that to be so. Moreover, it is not period, but theme – the making, working and final dismantling of the 1920–25 Settlement – that has determined the range of this essay in historical reconstruction. The book is neither a narrative history, though it is for the most part arranged in chronological sequence, nor a constitutional treatise, but rather an essay or series of essays in politico-historical analysis, concerned with unravelling the origins of the settlement; the interplay of concepts, interests and personalities which finally shaped it; the nature and purposes it was intended to serve; the measure of its success or failure in achieving them and the circumstances of its undoing. As with *The Irish Question 1840–1920*,[4] to which this book may be regarded in some sort as a sequel in more than chronological terms, concern is with problems rather than the period in which they fell. With regard to the Treaty, in his classic study, *Peace by Ordeal*,[5] Pakenham's interest was on the men who made the Treaty; in this study mine is on the Treaty that they made.

The opening, with regrettable exceptions, in recent years of official records and also of private papers is to be welcomed, the more so in that it has made possible the writing of a range of special studies and monographs which have greatly enriched our knowledge of modern Irish history, and progressively widened the range of scholarly enquiry. The opening of the archives, paradoxical as it may seem, tends to enhance the value of what has long been accessible. House of Commons Debates in the pre- and immediate post-war years and the Dáil Debates from 1919 onwards have rather more to convey to us of what happened and why, when read in the knowledge of what political leaders wrote to one another in private correspondence, or a Prime Minister in notes composed at Cabinet meetings to entertain a friend. But in the background there lies the interesting and at times perplexing question of a right balance to strike.

In diplomatic history, study of dispatches, minutes, conference and other official records is essential to understanding, but if diplomacy be defined for our purpose as dialogue between states, then the history of the Irish settlement and its aftermath is not adequately so described. Its range is wider. The negotiations which led to the Treaty of 1921 might indeed be characterised as quasi-diplomatic in that the Irish party to them were the representatives of an embryonic, albeit as yet unrecognised, state. But in overall perspective, a principal feature was the broad sweep of continuing exchanges, as between peoples, parties and communities, all seeking to realise their aspirations or safeguard interests within whatever new political and institutional framework might emerge. That was not destined to be determined by dialectics alone. Behind the words lay the weapons. While the precise role of force in the shaping of the settlement remains to be reviewed, it is not in question that the threat and then the use of force was fundamental to the unfolding Anglo-Irish drama.

It is not the purpose of this book, as it has been of others, to describe the armed counterpart to the political struggle, but to analyse the new balance it helped to create. Yet the deployment of force as a basic reality must needs be kept in mind, if any just balance between high-level political developments, of which record is made, and unrecorded and often cruel realities that provided the setting to them, is to be preserved.

On 6 February 1833, Thomas Babington Macaulay told the House of Commons that 'much rather would I have lived on the line of march of the Pretender's army in 1745 than in Tipperary now'.[6] Some at Westminster may well have entertained such passing thoughts between 1919 and 1922. The author was in Tipperary at that time and recalls, among other happenings of those troubled years, his boyhood recollections of how the familiar morning and afternoon sound of blasting at the stone quarry at Soloheadbeg, two miles away, acquired – on 21 January 1919 – a new significance by reason of its association with the shooting of two policemen* stationed at the barracks in Tipperary town. Armed with loaded carbines, they were guarding gelignite on its way by horse and cart to the quarry. The author may perhaps be relied upon to think of the events of those days as near realities, not as distant phenomena or as issues in high politics with but remote regard (such as is evident in records of many Cabinet deliberations) to how and why they had arisen or what they meant to those who experienced them. History was forged in sudden death on a Tipperary by-road as surely as ever it was in meetings at Downing Street or for that matter at the Mansion House in Dublin, where the Dáil met coincidentally but fortuitously for the first time that same day, 21 January 1919. Even though it was not immediately apparent, that event signalled the opening of the guerrilla fighting, retrospectively known as the Anglo-Irish war or the War of Independence. This lasted until the truce in 1921 and, in proportion as it was sustained against great odds, it came increasingly to invest the protagonists of physical force with a popular appeal denied in the immediately preceding years to their constitutional predecessors, vainly seeking concrete concessions from one of the more dilatory and then from the most politically agile of British Prime Ministers. For the policemen who died at Soloheadbeg there was reserved the melancholy fate of having fallen on the wrong side of history. 'Where Tipperary leads, Ireland follows' was a saying of which the Archdeacon reminded his congregation at mass on Sunday, 29 January, adding, 'God help poor Ireland if she follows this lead of blood'.[7] Follow it she did. Sixty years later, the shots that rang out on that winter's day at Soloheadbeg had come to be spoken of as the first fired in the War of Independence. How better to convey the sanction of posterity? Yet even successful national revolutions exact a price, the nature of which later generations find it hard to remember and contemporaries impossible to forget.

The interplay of force on the ground and high politics at the centre which led to the radical reshaping of Anglo-Irish relations, was important in itself and in this book is studied for itself. But the Anglo-Irish Settlement 1920–25 touched upon history at many points. While before 1914 the pervading atmosphere predisposed political leaders to violent

---

*On a Sunday afternoon some months previously, two Abbey schoolboys had asked members of the RIC, also from Tipperary, at the Grenane crossroads if they were not now fearful of going around on patrol. The reply was 'very possibly' had they been stationed in County Clare but not in County Tipperary.

speech and a threat of violent action, the basic fact remained that a principal but not the only source of it was the Irish question. This had entered, as the passage through parliament of Lloyd George's budget, 1909, and of the Parliament Act 1911 testified, into the mainstream of British politics, with the result that Irish antagonisms spilled over into English political debate in a period that came to be marked by extreme alienation of Conservative from Liberal forces. After the war that question re-emerged, different in many of its manifestations, but still retaining much of its power to disrupt and divide. 'The event was fatal to the Prime Minister', noted Churchill,[8] of Lloyd George's negotiation of the Anglo-Irish Treaty and it was a major factor that led on to the downfall of the coalition and the realignment of English party politics. In signing the Treaty, Michael Collins foresaw that he was signing his own death warrant, but not perhaps that he was setting the pattern of Irish politics for more than two generations. Other countries – Canada, Cyprus, Nigeria and South Africa – were to have their 'Ulsters', potential or actual, whilst in pre-independence India, Jawaharlal Nehru had nightmares of multiple fragmentation on the Ulster model. That, too, was a twentieth-century phenomenon, associated with the ending of empires, where earlier Irish experience warned of the price of a partition, without offering assured guidance on how to avoid incurring it.

In all of these things there was, over and above the clash of vivid personalities who have received full or, proportionately, overmuch attention, a concurrence of circumstances themselves in significant measure determining developments affecting Irish, British, Commonwealth and world politics, that may be identified in the language of the *Annaliste* School as a *conjoncture* and be studied, as is attempted here, not in isolation, but related to their wider background. In less than three decades, one integral part of the settlement was undone with Irish secession from the Commonwealth in 1949. In a little more than half a century, the other with the local parliamentary institutions in Northern Ireland, which Ulster Unionists in 1920–21 had regarded as a guarantee of a 'final settlement', was dismantled – ironically, by the heirs of the English Unionist party which had played a decisive part in bringing them into being. That marked the end of the settlement in formal terms and the two phases in which the ending came about provide the climax to this book. The fashioning of a new relationship is for another time, and another pen.

PART I

THE HISTORICAL BACKGROUND

CHAPTER 1

College Green, Dublin Castle and Westminster: The Institutional Factor

The Imagery of the Past

The Cardinal de Retz, theorist of revolution and practitioner of faction in mid-seventeenth-century France, reflected in his *Memoirs*[1] 'that examples of times past move men beyond comparison more than those of their own times. We accustom ourselves to what we see . . . ' – even, he surmised, to a phenomenon so remarkable as Caligula's horse as Consul had it held office in our time. But the impact of past examples cannot be blunted by such familiarity. On the contrary, it is likely to have gained rather than lost in emotional force with the passage of the years – so much so, that given a similar conjunction of circumstances, it may have a determining influence on people's reactions to later events. It is as well to keep this in mind. The implications of words or gestures or most of all the unspoken assumptions behind them, may be missed if judged on their own and without regard to 'examples' drawn from earlier times, such as have conditioned the thinking and outlook of later generations.

In late nineteenth- and early twentieth-century Ireland the revolutionary sequence was so well known that it sufficed to 'speak of ninety-eight', to allude to Emmet, to Mitchel, to Smith O'Brien, to John O'Leary and the Fenians to conjure up examples from each succeeding generation that in Irish minds pointed forward to the awe-inspiring climacteric that was 1916. Thus in 1880 Parnell in the United States had spoken of paving the way for Ireland 'to take her place among the nations of the earth'. There was no specific reference to Emmet and the symbolic rising in 1803 but, writes Professor MacDonagh,[2] 'no Irish-American audience of the day would fail to catch and develop the revolutionary resonance of these words'. Over the doorway lintel to the Widow MacCormack's house on a lonely hilltop near Ballingarry in County Tipperary there hangs a plaque with the injunction 'Remember '48'. Likewise, it suffices to recall another gesture – they were little more – this time in Europe's Year of Revolution.

While the imagery of rebellion dominated the people's mind, it did not stand alone. Beside the politico-insurrectionist tradition there was a

constitutional-parliamentary heritage. At the heart of it was the Irish
Parliament (1782–1800) – Parliament House in College Green known
by the name of the most illustrious of the 'Patriot' leaders as Grattan's
parliament. It was an ascendancy body with a place in popular memory
for two reasons, one creditable, the other shameful – it *was* an Irish
parliament, it was also one whose members colluded with the English
administration in bringing about its own demise. Both merit illustration.

On the evening of 5 September 1844, Daniel O'Connell the Liberator,
freed after sentence for his campaign for the Repeal of the Act of Union
was acclaimed by a procession 200,000 strong and six miles long, stopping
opposite the Parliament House in College Green, where he removed his
cap and 'pointed with his finger to the noble edifice, which he hoped to
reanimate with the soul of national life; and turning slowly round, gazed
silently into the faces of the people'. It was a dramatic episode – that silent
gesture, eloquent of the national hopes and aspirations – and thunderous
cheers greeted it.

In 1890, Parnell, at the nadir of his fortunes and returning to Dublin
from a disastrous defeat in a by-election at Kilkenny, a bandage covering
an injured eye, his hair and beard awry, had only to fling out his arm and
without speaking to point, as he passed the old Houses of Parliament,
for the crowd to roar its applause.[3] What need of words? Recollection
of Grattan's parliament, which had once assembled and debated there,
symbolised the Irish demand for restitution of a parliament that had an
appeal at once traditionalist – what had been should be again – and
revolutionary – a 'political' new departure.

A generation later, however, in the Treaty Debate in December 1921,
the note was not one of acclaim – far from it – but of admonition.
President de Valera, recalling the sorry ending of Grattan's parliament,
warned deputies not to tread in the footsteps of the 'ignominious House
that voted away the Colonial Parliament that was in Ireland in 1800',
while later in that same debate those who voted for the Treaty were
stigmatised by Miss MacSwiney as having been guilty of 'a betrayal worse
than Castlereagh's'.[4]

All were 'examples' from times past, which conjured up emotive
images well calculated to excite, to discourage, or to discredit, this last
by cruel association with the name of the Chief Secretary, himself an
Irishman – principally responsible by influence of office, supplemented
by distribution of honours and assurances of patronage, for persuading
members of the Irish Parliament to vote away its existence in 1800.

College Green

That Grattan's parliament should have meant so much either way to later
generations is understandable. In the eighteenth century as in preceding

centuries, there was an Irish parliament. Its subordination to parliament at Westminster was not in doubt, only its extent. Until 1720 that was left decently veiled; but in that year, affronted by questioning of its ultimate authority, parliament at Westminster enacted the 'Sixth of George I', a statute little noted in English but filling a much resented page in Irish history. The Act declared that the English Parliament had full authority to make laws 'of sufficient force and validity to bind the Kingdom and people of Ireland' and further denied all appellate jurisdiction – the question which had brought matters to a head – to the Irish House of Lords.

Half a century later, with the revolt of the American colonies, the situation looked very different, both in theory and practice. In respect of the former, concentration of power in one imperial legislature was no longer unquestioned: on the contrary it was increasingly deemed 'pernicious': in respect of the latter, Ireland, denuded of British troops needed for North America, had for its protection Irish Volunteers formed in 1778 to resist rumoured French invasion of an island otherwise well-nigh defenceless. The Volunteers, armed at their own expense, and therefore outside direct government control, were a force to be reckoned with; although at that time predominantly an ascendancy body loyal to Britain, they were also for the most part settlers by origin, and as such excited by the revolt of the American colonists and sympathetic to their aims. When on 19 April 1780, Grattan, assured of the backing of the Volunteers, moved a resolution in the Irish House of Commons that the King, and the Lords and Commons of Ireland 'are the only power competent to make laws to bind Ireland', he was in a position to command attention.[5]

Two years later, on 15 February 1782, the Volunteers at a convention at Dungannon resolved that 'a claim of any body of men, other than the King, Lords and Commons of Ireland, to make laws to bind this kingdom, is unconstitutional and a grievance'. The resolution was taken up in the Irish Parliament and an Address forwarded to the King.[6] The Rockingham Whigs, now in office, were already committed to concession, Charles James Fox, their principal spokesman, being predisposed, if the matter were pressed, to separation with a treaty as against continued English resistance to Irish demands. In this favourable climate the statutory restrictions upon the Irish Parliament were repealed on 16 April 1782. Grattan declaimed: 'I am now to address a free people; ages have passed away, and this is the first moment in which you could be distinguished by that appellation. . . . Spirit of Swift! spirit of Molyneux! your genius has prevailed! Ireland is now a nation! In that new character I hail her! and bowing to her august presence, I say, *esto perpetua*.' Here was a note that might strike a chord that would sound across the gulf dividing the Protestant ascendancy and the Catholic 'hidden nation'.

There followed, in 1783, a Renunciation Act, deemed superfluous by Grattan but insisted upon by Henry Flood, second only to Grattan among

the 'Patriot' leaders, on the ground that no possibility of infringing the
new constitution should be left open – 'other Straffords may arise'. The
Act explicitly reaffirmed the right of the people of Ireland to be bound
only by the laws 'enacted by His Majesty and the Parliament of that
kingdom in all cases whatever . . . for ever'.

It was all very moving. But Grattan's eloquence could not disguise, still
less dispel, uncomfortable realities. The exercise of legislative independence was in the hands of a Protestant parliament[7] representative only of
a Protestant 'nation', and with Dissenters outside, not all of that. Neither
the qualified enlightenment nor the oratorical flourishes of members
stirred by the rhetoric and elated by the outcome of the American War
of Independence could disguise the hollow ring to their pretensions. In
principle, they might claim the title of 'Nation' as much as the American
colonists, but in practice they lacked the cohesion, numbers and resources
to sustain it.

The outcome was that after 1782 there were two independent parliaments, but they were under the one Crown, in whose name all executive
functions were discharged. The system could work so long, but only
so long, as important measures passed concurrently through the two
parliaments.[8]

But in the short term it was neither the institutional imperfections,
nor minority concern for its own future, but rather the external menace
of revolutionary France, with its challenge to the existing social order
throughout Europe, that sealed the fate of the 1782 experiment. In its early
days the revolution, with its precepts of civil and religious liberty, was
acclaimed by the 'Patriots' or their successors as heralding 'glad, confident
morning'. However, liberty, equality and fraternity might be politically
welcome in the abstract, but not if they stimulated an upsurge of agrarian
revolt or French revolutionary republicanism as translated into Irish terms
by societies of United Irishmen – the first of which was founded in Belfast
in 1791 – or by Theobald Wolfe Tone, the Protestant Secretary of the
Catholic Committee who had helped to found it and who made no secret
of his aim to unite all Irishmen in the cause of religious equality. Many of
the Patriot leaders, Grattan among them, championed that cause: others
did not. The latter were prompted chiefly by consideration of the long-
term implications of its attainment for them and their descendants.

In 1793 a Catholic Relief Act, passed at the instance of Parliament
at Westminster, had enfranchised forty-shilling freeholders. Catholic
emancipation seemed bound to follow. If it did, the Protestant 'nation'
would become a small minority politically as well as demographically. If,
however, the British Isles were to be reconstituted as a single polity, that
minority would have an assured future existence as part of an overall
religious majority. Pitt, on 18 November 1792, had put the point con-
cisely in an oft quoted letter to the Lord-Lieutenant, Lord Westmoreland.

With Union, he wrote, 'the Protestant interest in point of power, property and Church Establishment, would be secure, because the decided majority of the supreme legislature would necessarily be Protestant, and the great ground of argument on the part of the Catholics would be done away with, as, compared with the rest of the Empire,* they would become a minority'.[9]

For his part Pitt had reached the conclusion before 1798 that separation should be superseded by Union, but rebellion, followed by the French landing at Killala in September that year, seemed to him to provide conclusive security reason for putting into effect forthwith a change of course upon which he had already decided. Ireland, the argument ran, was 'like a ship on fire': it must either 'be extinguished or cut adrift' and extinction, that is Union in parliamentary terms, had thus become 'an imperial necessity'. Grattan's parliament, the by-product of one revolution, the American, was in short-term perspective the victim of another, the French. The manner in which a majority of its members colluded in its dissolution affords a melancholy contrast to the fine professions which had characterised its coming into being. The first settlement of Anglo-Irish relations in modern terms had ended in failure. Yet no later settlement could discount, still less disregard, its history and the causes over a broad front of its undoing.

The Union

The historiography of the Act of Union would make an interesting study: here it suffices to indicate some features that loomed large in subsequent debate. In 1843, Count Cavour, the later architect of a united Italy, noted that there could be 'but one voice in condemning to infamy those who made traffic of the independence of their country',[10] though in his case it was coupled with the view that he formed in pre-famine travels that Union had been beneficial to Ireland. Others discounted any such counterweight. 'If ever a statute has lacked moral validity', wrote the youthful G.P. Gooch (who, as a Liberal, was to contribute to debates on Irish affairs in the 1906 House of Commons), 'it is the Act of Union of 1800 . . . the methods by which a majority was secured form, perhaps, the most disgraceful chapter in the modern history of Great Britain. . . . The union was a settlement by compulsion, not consent, a war measure standing in the same relation to ordinary legislation as martial law bears to civil justice.'[11]

---

*In late eighteenth-century usage, Empire meant the place where authority and power resided, in this case the British Isles, not as later the subject territories. Cf. R. Koebner and H.D. Schmidt, *Imperialism. The Story and Significance of a Political Word 1840–1940* (Cambridge, 1964), pp. 252–75.

Irish nationalist denunciation of the Union, however, was disposed to distinguish between two facets: the means by which the passage of the Act of Union through the Irish Houses of Parliament was ensured and the constitutionality, or otherwise, of its enactment. Both were spelled out by Arthur Griffith, the founder of Sinn Féin, in his work *The Resurrection of Hungary*, which in its various manifestations provided the blueprint for Sinn Féin activism from its publication in 1905 until 1919. The tone was polemical. Amongst the artificers of Union, Griffith denounced Pitt as Ireland's enemy – 'a deadlier enemy than Cromwell'; Fitzgibbon, Lord Chancellor of Ireland from 1789, as an Irishman who had furthered Pitt's Unionist policies and as 'the darkest Irish figure in Irish affairs since Mac Murrogh' 'who brought the Norman o'er' and Castlereagh, to whom Griffith attributed a principal responsibility for effecting Union with an appearance of Irish consent.[12]

Griffith did not believe that the means employed, however reprehensible, were of fundamental importance. 'We need not', he wrote, 'call into question the validity of the "Act" of Union on the ground that it was carried by corruption and intimidation of the vilest type . . . The "Act" of Union was never valid.' The contention was based on the argument that the representatives of a people were not entitled to vote away that people's independence. It was a view that had been eloquently advanced in College Green at the time of decision. Would the members of the Irish Parliament, it was asked, be exceeding their own legislative competence were they to approve the Bill? William Cunningham Plunket advised that they would be: ' . . . if', he declaimed, 'you pass this act, it will be a nullity . . . you have not been elected for this purpose – you are appointed to make laws and not legislatures . . . you are appointed to act under the constitution, not to alter it . . . you are appointed to exercise the functions of legislators and not to transfer them and if you do so, your act is a dissolution of the government . . . '.[13] Grattan also held this view, but in Griffith's dismissive opinion, 'having salved his conscience by saying so . . . he [Grattan] returned to his favourite occupation of making eloquent speeches',[14] as, indeed, Irish parliamentarians continued to do down the years. 'The position that Ireland takes up, and has always taken up for 112 years', said Sir Thomas Esmonde on the introduction of the Third Home Rule Bill in 1912, is this: 'That this Parliament [Westminster] has no right to make laws for Ireland. The Irish people have always held that the only power competent to make laws for Ireland is a Parliament of Ireland.'[15] It was a view at no time upheld in British courts.

The historiography of Grattan's parliament reflects the ambiguities implicit in its existence, the manner of its dissolution and the ambivalences in Irish attitudes towards it. Beyond dispute it was a Protestant parliament, representative only of a minority, and not all of that, and as such, exposed to D.P. Moran's contemptuous dismissal of it as 'an ascendancy charade'. But *per contra*, it had come into existence on a surge of colonial nationalism; it was associated with an idealised concept of an independent Irish legislature in a continuing imperial setting and its leaders, touched by the eighteenth-century enlightenment, showed themselves for the greater part not insensitive to the claims of the majority to civil and religious emancipation. For a century or more the colonial parliament of 1782 served as a symbol of what had been, and what might be again. Despite its limitations, it was an all-Ireland parliament. On 16 April 1982, the Taoiseach, C.J. Haughey, at a reception in the old Irish House of Lords to mark the bicentenary of the concession of legislative independence, noted that the best of Grattan's contemporaries were 'for that time remarkably free of prejudice' and that Grattan's parliament provided 'a brave attempt to balance conflicting aspirations' which 'were and still are on the one hand for national independence and on the other for the maintenance of links with Great Britain'.[16]

The Government of Ireland Act 1920 (section 66) was to provide that should the government of Southern Ireland decide to acquire for the use of the Parliament of Southern Ireland the premises of the Bank of Ireland situated in or near College Green, they would be entitled to do so on payment of compensation to the Bank. That parliament died at birth, and it was not thither that the Dáil repaired in 1919, but to the Mansion House and then to the town house of the Dukes of Leinster, thereby with deliberate intent repudiating association with College Green. But there was no repudiation, rather assumption that an Irish parliament there would be at the heart of any later settlement. In that respect, the precedent of 1782–1800 served as a beacon casting light to the more distant goal. There was long to wait. Meanwhile

> Here, where old Freedom was wont to wait
> Her darling Grattan nightly at the gate,
> Now little clerks in hall and colonnade
> Tot the poor items of provincial trade.

Dublin Castle: Government under the Union

The preamble to the Act of Union made recital of how the Parliaments of Great Britain and Ireland 'severally agreed and resolved that in order to promote and secure the essential interests of Great Britain and Ireland and to consolidate the strength, power and resources of the British Empire, it will be advisable to concur in such measures as may best tend to unite the two Kingdoms of Great Britain and Ireland in one Kingdom. . .'. The plurality of parliaments and kingdoms reflected the immediate past, the singular, one kingdom, foreshadowed the future with the first article of the Act affirming that 'the said Kingdoms of Great Britain and Ireland

being upon the first day of January 1801 and for ever after united into one
Kingdom, by the name of the United Kingdom of Great Britain and
Ireland'. This last proved to be an overstatement. The Union lasted 120
years in full force and effect. For that period, all-Ireland was part of the
United Kingdom. It was not, however, in the terminology of a later time,
an integrated part. It is true there was one parliament for the United
Kingdom, to which 103 members were returned by Irish constituencies
throughout the whole period – though on a basis of population, it should
have been twice that number at the outset and some two-thirds of it at
its close.* Irish representation at Westminster, irrespective of scale, was
consistent with the concept of a United Kingdom. But there was no such
positive application of principle in respect of government. In that domain,
there was no attempt at incorporation in the United Kingdom system, nor
indeed any sustained attempt at anything in respect of administration. In
its way that was not surprising. At the time, politicians were concerned
with the enactment of Union and its manifold repercussions, not with the
machinery for the administration of one part of the United Kingdom. The
Act of Union itself had made no provision for that, not even to the extent
of outlining its form. Some three years elapsed before it was decided to
have a Lord-Lieutenant, or Viceroy, residing in Phoenix Park, at its head,
with a Chief Secretary in Dublin Castle presiding over departments and,
as the years went by, a multiplicity of boards also Dublin-based, many
of them brought into existence haphazardly as need arose or political
pressures demanded.

The office of Lord-Lieutenant, once established, and that of Chief
Secretary, survived throughout the period of Union, though hardly
anyone who considered the matter with detachment failed to conclude
that one or other was superfluous. It was customary for either the Lord-
Lieutenant or the Chief Secretary to be a member of the Cabinet – in 1919
exceptionally both were included in Lloyd George's post-war Coalition
Cabinet, but for the rest in the later years of Union, the Chief Secretary
served alone. That meant responsibility was effectively vested in his
hands. In reply to an enquiry from John Morley, Balfour[17] remarked in
the course of the debate on the 1904–5 'devolution' crisis that when the
Chief Secretary 'is in the Cabinet, and the Lord-Lieutenant is not, the
Lord-Lieutenant is not, in any true sense of the word, the head of the Irish
administration'. Lord Wimborne, who filled the office in 1916, found that
the Under-Secretary in Dublin Castle held 'the doctrine of the Lord-
Lieutenant's total irresponsibility',[18] a notion to which the files recording

---

*Isaac Butt at the Home Rule Conference assembled in the Rotunda in 1873
calculated that it should then have been 112 (Redmond Papers, 15102). In 1919, the
Irish Committee of the Cabinet reckoned on around 60.

the Lord-Lieutenant's activities lends credibility.[19] Yet the Chief Secretary, if in the Cabinet, in addition to his responsibilities as head of the Irish administration had to answer for it in parliament and, when a member, in Cabinet also. As a result, the Chief Secretary spent much time travelling to and from Dublin on the Holyhead–Kingstown boat, which for a bad sailor was exacting at best and something of an ordeal for Augustine Birrell, who held the office longer than anyone else in this period.[20]

The Chief Secretary further served as the principal channel of communication between the Irish party's leadership on the one hand and Cabinet and Prime Minister on the other. Important in any circumstances, this was doubly so when party leadership and members, under edict of Parnell, deliberately isolated themselves from social contact with members of English parties. None the less, despite the variety of their duties, Chief Secretaries, though exposed to danger in troubled times, gave little impression of being overworked and in Birrell's case, it was his manifest indolence that drew fire.

The most lasting impression of Castle administration was of structural confusion. Under pressure from Irish members, or from famine or other catastrophe or evidence of inadequacy or negligence, remedies were improvised, reforms effected – but in part, never as a whole. The upshot was a series of inconsequential actions. Departments were created and boards or commissions appointed according to the real or alleged needs of the time, but never in relation to some overall structural design. By no means all deficiencies, however, were to be attributed to ill-devised machinery of government. The calibre of those who administered it has also to be taken into the reckoning.

Both administrators and administration have been fortunate in their historian, Dr R.B. McDowell, first in respect of his patient unravelling of a ramshackle machine, inherited and adapted from pre-Union days and, secondly, in respect of his restraint in judgement on those who worked it. These included conscientious administrators, some of whom rendered lasting service to Ireland. Yet there are not, one suspects, many historians who would have written so appreciatively of the qualities, so entertainingly of the idiosyncracies, so gently of the failings of this particular cadre of administrators.* It is not easy to judge an administration in isolation, but Dr McDowell has not failed to note that two distinguished officials from India, Sir Joseph West-Ridgeway and Sir Antony MacDonnell, who transferred to Dublin Castle, were highly critical of what they found there

---

* Dr McDowell is especially lenient in judgement on those who neglected their duties in order to have more time for composing Greek verse or other literary pursuits. Those dependent on state action would hardly have thought this a valid plea in mitigation.

– the former asserting that 'nothing could be more chaotic and effete than the present system of government by boards', which worked smoothly only under a strong Chief Secretary or when a common danger threatened the existence of the Castle; the other seeking to introduce a measure of rationalisation. In both cases, reforming zeal led, though for different reasons, to frustration and disillusion. Certainly the laxities and irregularities of which Dr McDowell writes, would not have been tolerated in the Governor-General's Secretariat in Calcutta. George Wyndham, when Chief Secretary, spoke of the government of Ireland being conducted 'only by continuous conversation', most of it lost in the smoking rooms of the St Stephen's Green Clubs.[21]

In judging the quality of the Irish administration, it is as well to keep certain political considerations in mind. One is that Unionists at all times had a vested interest in defending, Liberals, once converted to Home Rule, in criticising, and Nationalists in deriding it. The last named did not want a good administration; it was a point of principle that they would not seek to improve what existed and in practice the more open it was to criticism, the better the Home Rule cause was served. 'Bad' not 'good' government was the theme. On this score, Nationalists had little cause for complaint. On 21 February 1905, Campbell-Bannerman commented,[22] 'Of the existing government in Ireland no defence can be found that I know of.' In the Devolution (1904) and Irish Council (1907) debates, none of weight was adduced. Balfour resorted to flippancy – if the domicile of the Irish administration were not in a Castle, it would be impossible, he opined, for literary orators talking about gloomy portals to 'raise a sort of prejudice that medieval practices prevail', such as would be discounted by a more prosaic name.[23] But generally Liberal and even Nationalist presumptions of the inadequacy of the administration elicited little contradiction. The reason was not hard to find. 'So far from Irish government working smoothly', noted G.P. Gooch, 'it does not work at all'.[24] That sometimes seems to have been precisely true. What was the number of boards administering services in Dublin? Wyndham in 1905, as Chief Secretary, said 42; Birrell, in 1907, also as Chief Secretary, said he had been supplied with a list of 45, but he was not sure; Balfour, an ex-Chief Secretary, opted for 47.[25] What is one to think of an administration incapable of precision on a central feature in its own organisation? 'We are governed', Redmond had earlier protested, 'by a network of public boards – the Education Board, the Board of Public Works, the Local Government Board, the Congested Districts Board . . . and I know not how many other Boards, all of which are nominated by Dublin Castle'. The Chief Secretary presided but what knowledge did he acquire? There had been 53 Chief Secretaries since Union, 27 in the half-century since 1855, and no Irishman since 1871. 'The permanent, centralised, nominated, semi-independent boards', Redmond further complained, 'stuffed full of the members of the ascendancy Party, have been omnipotent in the Government of Ireland.'[26] But, and here was the rub, short of Home Rule, the party was not prepared to associate itself with remedial measures. After the success – as he saw it – of the Land Conference in 1903, William O'Brien might be convinced, or convince himself, that 'conference plus business' was the road to travel, but John Dillon, sensitive to the pulses of nationalist opinion and fearful of the consequences of collaboration, was moving the other way. 'Every day', he noted, 'I grow more strongly convinced that the [Land] Conference and its result was a mortal blunder'. Beware of doctrines of conciliation was his theme. Carried to its logical conclusion the argument ran that the land question, being a weapon in nationalist hands, 'to settle it finally would be to risk Home Rule, which otherwise *must* come'.[27] The cause of Home Rule would not be advanced by improving Dublin Castle administration, still less by cooperating with it, but only by its root and branch elimination.[28]

It was an indication at once of the variety of the interests at stake and the sensitivities, which possible reorganisation of the administration touched upon, that the proposals for a measure of devolution published in 1904 provoked reactions of 'crisis' proportions, once it became known that the Under-Secretary at the Irish Office, Sir Antony MacDonnell, had had rather more than a hand in its drafting. MacDonnell, who carried over the soubriquet of 'the Bengal Tiger' from his Indian days, was a Catholic and a Home Ruler who had abandoned his career in India at the invitation of the Chief Secretary, George Wyndham, on the assurance that he would be allowed to 'compass the objects he held to be of primary importance'. In effect, the devolution scheme he propounded was an essay in administrative rationalisation, a principal feature of which was to be the creation of financial and legislative councils to coordinate the work of the forty or so boards in existence and thus effect a degree of centralisation in place of the existing absence of effective coordinating authority. Initial Nationalist reactions were disparate. Redmond contented himself with dismissing the proposals as an irrelevance: 'for us there is no such thing as an alternative policy to Home Rule. If your Government in Ireland were as good as it is notoriously . . . bad, we would be still Home Rulers'.[29] Dillon's reaction, in keeping with his deep-seated mistrust of Dunraven and other landlords active in the Reform Association, was one of forthright hostility.[30] In this he was at one with the Ulster Unionists who bayed for MacDonnell's blood, Charles Craig denouncing him as 'their worst enemy in Ireland', one who was 'opposed to their ideas in every direction in Irish politics, and furthermore, placed in a position where he could be an injury to the cause of the Union.' The scheme from the Unionist point of view was 'nothing but a step towards Home Rule'.[31] It is possible that both MacDonnell and Craig were right. A measure of efficient government *might* have detracted from the urgency of the demand for Home Rule and, with greater semblance of possibility, at the same time have strengthened the case for unitary government under Home Rule.

That a scheme with such implications should have been formulated with the known assistance of the Under-Secretary of the Irish Office was not the principal ground of Nationalist repudiation. On the contrary it rested on principle – no cooperation with British-controlled government in Dublin. Nationalist reaction to the devolution proposals in 1904–5 was the first, their rejection of the Irish Council's bill three years later the second indicator that the Dublin Castle administration was likely to survive unreformed to the end of the Union. The choice before the Irish people was not therefore likely to be one between good government and national government, but between bad government and national government. To sustain that judgement it is not necessary to accept uncritically Liberal aspersions or Nationalist polemics – there suffices the devastating judgement of the Permanent Under-Secretary of the Treasury, Head of the British Civil Service, Sir Warren Fisher: 'The Castle Administration does not administer.'[32]

Westminster

Repeal of the Union had been the theme of Daniel O'Connell's campaign. If interpreted literally, Repeal implied a return to the *status quo ante*. But that, to quote Professor MacDonagh, was 'politically nonsensical'. The conditions on which Grattan's parliament rested 'lay in that overflowing receptacle, the dustbin of history'. Repeal had, however, great attraction by reason of its very ambivalence. It was not intended 'as a specific proposition' but rather as 'an attempt to *elicit* a proposition from the British government'.[33] Home Rule which, on the failure of Repeal and after a lapse of years, succeeded it as the embodiment of immediate constitutional Irish nationalist aims, was, on the contrary, specific. That indeed was part of its attraction for Gladstone. 'I do not think', he wrote to Hartington on 18 November 1885, in the hope, vain as it proved, of enlisting his support for Home Rule, 'that . . . sufficient allowance has been made for the *enormous* advantage we derive from the change in the form of the Nationalist demand from Repeal of the Union (which would reinstate a parliament having *original* authority) to the form of a Bill for a derivative Chamber acting under imperial authority. The whole basis of the proceeding is hereby changed.'[34] The point it may be thought was well taken. Yet such was the place of a parliament in Irish thinking that for nationalists the great essential was embraced in Repeal and Home Rule alike. Either would result in the reconstitution of an Irish parliament. At root it was the institutions, not the source or the extent of its powers that mattered. Beyond that there was a larger ambivalence. That parliament might be represented either as an end in itself or as a stepping stone. This was a theme on which Parnell knew well how to ring the changes. While professing that Home Rule with an Irish parliament was his aim, he also declared in the 1885 election that the party was fighting on 'a platform with one plank, Irish independence'.

In its diluted Home Rule guise, this was the assignment John Redmond, elected chairman of a once more united party in 1900, inherited at a remove of ten years, from the 'Chief' whose memory he revered. Eighteen years later, John Dillon, who in 1900 had stood aside to open the way to Redmond's election (despite misgivings about Redmond's capacity for the task) and the reunion of the party, said at Redmond's graveside that most men thought Redmond had faced a task 'beyond human powers'.[35] What was it about the task that prompted such reflection?

In its immediate form, the task was the achievement of Home Rule for all-Ireland by conditionally peaceful – Parnell was well aware as in his last electoral campaign of the dividends that might accrue from threats of violence, not always decently veiled – parliamentary means. The tactical guidelines had been laid down by Parnell; simply stated, they were the deployment of the votes of an independent, united, disciplined and oathbound Irish party in the House of Commons, now on one side and now on the other to make and, even more important, to threaten to unmake, governments until either by newly found conviction or more likely in despair, one or other or both of the English parties agreed to Home Rule for Ireland. It was a tactic forged for a parliamentary situation such as existed in the early 1880s – that is to say, on a balance, or near-balance, between the two great English parties, neither of them as yet committed on this issue. But did it remain well suited to the parliamentary situation in the early years of the new century? This was an important question, but one to which Redmond does not appear to have addressed himself. He was perhaps too loyal to do so. Yet in retrospect it can be seen more clearly than by contemporaries that some important elements in the situation had changed. The effectiveness of the tactic had at all times depended less upon the numerical strength of the Irish Nationalist party than upon the relative strength of the English parties. As Redmond himself argued, what mattered was not the number of seats the Irish party won but whether it held the balance. 'I care not', he said before the first of the two elections of that year, if the number returned was not 86 or 76 or 66 so long as the party 'was absolutely united with the Nationalists obtaining that position of absolute dictatorship which has always been the objective of Nationalist strategy'. But even the holding of the balance by itself in these later days only questionably sufficed. Leadership with capacity and readiness to contemplate ruthless action, together with ability to convey more than a hint of menace – or political blackmail – was also needed to give the semblance of reality to the implicit threat. Parnell had both: Redmond neither. He lacked the personality and the base in popular, national standing alike. In the place of an uncrowned king, there was in more than name only a party chairman. Though a firm upholder of party unity, that unity throughout Redmond's period of leadership was frayed at the edges, there was 'all for Ireland' William O'Brien, there was Tim Healy, there were others campaigning or skirmishing, certainly in the Home Rule cause, though by no means necessarily in the party's interest. Such freelance activity weakened, if only marginally, the party's impact in the House of Commons.

More important was familiarity. With the efflux of time, the psychological impact of the Irish vote had weakened. In the 1880s it was great, partly because it was novel. Twenty years later there had come a cooler appreciation of its limitations. The two English parties had taken up position on the Irish question. The Conservative party, on the accession of the Liberal Unionists to their banner, had become the Unionist party, the new designation indicating a fundamental allegiance to Union. The Liberal party's commitment to Home Rule was claimed at the least to be a matter of principle: Home Rule remained the Party's goal, though timing significantly was reserved as a matter for a Liberal government when in office. Shortly after Campbell-Bannerman's election to the leadership in February 1899, he made both points explicit, declaring that while the Liberal party remained the only English party attached to the principle of Irish self-government, they claimed the right, as practical men, to say when in office how and when they should apply it. 'I repudiate', he remarked a few days later, 'the necessity, the expediency, aye, and the possibility, of any such promise', that is about timing.[36] Such affirmation of entitlement to freedom of manoeuvre in respect of timing was a point of concern to the Irish but, despite Liberal-Imperialist wavering, by 1905 the party's commitment to Home Rule was not in serious question. So it was that for the flexibility of the early 1880s there was substituted the rigidities of the new century.

In a sense progressive crystallisation of English party attitudes on Home Rule increased the difficulties of Redmond's situation. On the one hand, the firmer the Liberal commitment in principle to Home Rule, the more difficult for the Irish to vote them out of office; on the other, Unionist fundamentalism seemingly destroyed all prospect of a deal with them. What then became of Parnell's tactical concept? In 1910, the year of the two elections, not once but twice the Parnellite concept of balance was realised, but what was the point of throwing out the Liberals if the Unionists declined to qualify their allegiance to Union as a basic party tenet? That was a question from which Redmond shied away except briefly in 1909–10 when he threatened to, but did not in the end, deploy the Irish vote against the Liberals, not, be it noted, on the major Home Rule issue but because of the incidence of the liquor taxes imposed on Irish brewers, distillers and publicans in Lloyd George's budget of that year.

Thereafter the Liberals pursued their own course on Home Rule much as though concessions might be urged upon Redmond with little or no fear that he would ultimately make rejoinder 'enough is enough'. To threaten and then conform (67 Irish members voted for the Budget in the end) was ill advised.

Redmond was a shrewd parliamentarian and he may rightly have judged that as between risks, it was wiser to underplay rather than over-play his hand. It was not as though the English parties for their part were altogether without options. Lord Hartington had reflected as early as 29 August 1885:

> His [Parnell's] action may result in a series of short Governments; it may result in some uncertainty and change of policy. . . . But the time will come, after these inconveniences have been endured for a time, when, in consequence of such actions of the Irish party, minor political differences which may exist among the parties in this country will be comparatively obliterated, and means will be found by which a practically united parliamentary representation . . . will impose a firm and decided veto upon proposals which are in their opinion so fatal and so mischievous.[37]

That was one possibility, or, as Hartington was seeking to persuade Gladstone, a probability. There was another associated with it: that the leaders of the two English parties might reach agreement to dispose of Home Rule in a way acceptable to them, irrespective of Nationalist party opinion. Though the second was the subject of cross-party negotiation in 1910, neither was realised until 1919–21, when a Coalition government, under Liberal leadership but dependent on Unionist votes, propounded a new settlement. Nevertheless, both were latent throughout the period.

Historians nowadays are apt to write of a Liberal–Nationalist alliance at Westminster as from 1905.[38] An alliance, however, customarily rests upon the assumption of formal, written obligations by the parties to it. By such criteria, no alliance existed. There were presumptions of joint action to advance a particular aim, Home Rule, which amounted to an *entente*. But even then it was not '*cordiale*'. The differences between Liberal non-conformity and Irish Catholicism on a whole range of issues from temperance to education, from pensions to liquor taxes, were in any case too wide for that. There was common ground between Nationalists and the more radical Liberals as with Lloyd George on the anti-colonial front, but with this difference – the Nationalists welcomed early Boer victories, Lloyd George and the Radicals for the most part did not.

Over and above the distancing which was a natural product of such differences, there was further the alienation of nationalists from those who sustained British rule in Ireland, whether themselves British by origin or West British by inclination, 'Castle' Catholics being held in particular disesteem as collaborators, who had every reason to know better and to act otherwise. Members of the administration, Liberal as well as Unionist, as a result were socially confined within a restricted circle and at all times likely to be reminded of the barriers actual, over and above pyschological, between them and the people for whose government they exercised responsibility. Yeats, a somewhat surprising figure in this context, when invited to assist with a *tableau* of *The Countess Cathleen* at the Chief Secretary's Lodge indicated that he could not go near the Lodge because of his nationalist convictions, acceptance of such an invitation being in his view tantamount to collaboration and, accordingly, to be declined on principle. T.W. Rolleston, however, did agree to play the part of First Demon in the performance and for that Yeats never forgave him, the more so since acceptance was followed by Rolleston's appointment to a post in the Department of Agriculture.[39] In general, a boycott of Castle or Castle-associated functions was a symbolic gesture reflecting nationalist resentment at the very existence of a Castle administration.

More important politically was the veto rigorously enforced by Parnell on social intercourse by Irish members with British parliamentarians and officials. It applied to Lords-Lieutenant – which was of little or no moment – and also to Chief Secretaries. It was only 'as a great concession to years of friendship', noted Lady Bryce in 1907, 'that John Dillon consented to dine with us privately at the [Chief Secretary's] Lodge just before we left for the United States'. Redmond visited Birrell in his office in Dublin Castle on 16 October 1913, for the first time.[40] The case for the imposition of such a veto was well grounded in Irish thinking and experience. In the debate on Union in the Irish House of Commons on 5–6 February 1800, Grattan had voiced a fear for the future which in the earlier years of Union had been in more than part realised. Irish members residing in England, he had forecast, 'will be nominally Irish representatives; but they will cease to be Irish men'.[41] It was against this that Parnell by his edict desired to guard. No one should dismiss such fears as groundless. Nor were they confined to Irishmen. Mackenzie King, who served as Prime Minister longer than anyone else in Canadian or Commonwealth history, 'trembled' to think what would have happened to Canadian interests had not someone of his courage (again his own word) been in London at imperial conferences to resist social devices and other attentions 'to influence one's mind even against one's better judgement'. Had not Asquith himself once remarked that John Bright was the only man in public life who had risen to eminence without being corrupted by London society? And he did not get to the top!

But there was also a price to be paid once the Irish members were associated with the Liberals in seeking to enact Home Rule legislation, not briefly as in 1886 but for an extended period. In place of informal gatherings and a meeting of minds traditional under a parliamentary system, there tended to be formal communications and representations. The Irish in that sense were in the House of Commons but not of it. Even their leaders, as there will be occasion to note, were apt to be inaccessible when Parliament was in recess, Redmond at Aughavanagh without telephone and with unpredictable post; Dillon at Ballaghaderrin in County Mayo, with his own overriding preoccupation with land reform. Once again this might have weighed little a quarter of a century earlier when Gladstone was driven on by his own missionary spirit. But Asquith was notably lacking in crusading zeal and it was out of respect for past commitment and consideration of present advantage that he kept to the Liberal party course. Such enthusiasm as he might otherwise have felt was damped by a sense of *déjà vu* shared by the older generation on both sides of the House, A.V. Dicey doubting 'whether human ingenuity could now produce on Irish Home Rule either a new argument or a new fallacy'.[42] All of these, it may be urged, were matters of incidental importance and intrinsically this indeed is so. But in a period that has with some justice been described as being peculiarly one of élitist politics, with power concentrated in the hands of party leaders, might not the Irish party have influenced not only the course but also the outcome of events by taking advantage of opportunities of informally expounding their views to ministers? As it was, they kept their distance, more fearful of the risk of being influenced than concerned to influence. It was the prescribed course, and they were not venturesome men.

Such speculation should not deflect attention from the fundamental disadvantage under which the Irish party laboured at Westminster. Again Grattan had had perception of it. In that same debate on Union on 5–6 February 1800, he noted that the Act of Union would reduce the membership of the Irish House of Commons to one-third, and would transfer that one-third to another country where it would be merged and lost in the superior numbers of that country.[43] Was not this the fundamental factor – that the ground on which the Irish party had to fight placed them at too great a disadvantage? Was Westminster the right milieu for the attainment of Irish aspirations? Arthur Griffith was convinced it was not. In 1910 he noted in the *United Irishmen* that the 103 Irishmen in the House of Commons were faced with 567 foreigners and forecast that 'ten years from now the majority of Irishmen will marvel that they once believed the proper battleground for Irish freedom was one chosen and filled by Ireland's enemies'. Did not Griffith's contention, despite overstatement – Ireland had some good friends in the House – represent the hard core of reality? If it did, was Parnell's strategy on the longer term likely, or even certain, to prove inadequate? Or to put the point in its setting, did Redmond, did the party, fail because of lack of flexibility or skill in their use of parliamentary tactics or did they fail because success could not be achieved on terrain so unfavourable to them as that at Westminster? This is a point that touches closely on Redmond's reputation.[44] As it stands, he is apt to be dismissed as a leader in a 'mendicant' nationalist tradition guilty of grave errors of judgement, as a result of his over-conciliatory attitudes. But if Griffith were right, then the true indictment is quite otherwise and failure is to be attributed to persistence in a misconceived strategy.

Griffith argued not only that Westminster was an impossible battle-ground: he offered an alternative. The alternative was abstention. In his judgement it was warranted not only on national but also on constitutional grounds. Grattan's parliament in his view, as already noted, had acted unconstitutionally, beyond its legitimate authority, in subscribing to its own dissolution. The reconstitution of an Irish parliament would therefore be a return to constitutionality. The simplest way to effect it would be to summon Irish members of parliament to reconvene in College Green. This was what Griffith advocated. True they numbered only 103, of whom 80 at most would be likely to attend. But they could be reinforced by representatives of local authorities and others: indeed he attached much importance to the bringing in of elected local representatives. It would be a revolutionary step but one that could be defended as being designed to restore the constitution. True, that argument could not be successfully sustained in the courts, given the acceptance of Coke, Blackstone and Dicey's assertion of the transcendent competence of parliament.[45] But while Griffith's contention was likely to receive scant consideration under English law, there was a continental precedent, the relevance of which Griffith with remorselessness pressed upon his readers. It was provided by the reaction of Magyar nationalists to the loss of constitutional rights, conceded to them by the Austrian Empire in its hour of weakness, in 1848, but withdrawn after the Magyar revolt had been suppressed with Russian aid and great brutality the following year.[46] Under the leadership of Francis Déak, the Magyars thereafter pursued a policy of passive resist-ance and non-cooperation, steadfastly refusing to be moved by imperial threats or seduced by imperial blandishments. Nothing, they maintained, could be considered unless and until their constitutional rights were restored.

The aspect of the Magyar contention that was of particular moment to Griffith was their rejection of all invitations or commands to send deputies to the Imperial Parliament in Vienna where, they felt, they would be at a great disadvantage both in numbers and in debate, the latter because among Magyars German was spoken fluently chiefly by those whose nationalist sentiments were likely to be at best Laodicean. With Austria's defeat in Italy in 1859, followed seven years later by their crushing reverse at Sadowa which sealed the loss of hegemony in Germany to Prussia,

Magyar persistence, based upon the twofold principle of Déak's policy, no deployment of force and no participation in the deliberations of the Imperial Parliament, achieved its purpose. An agreement, the *Ausgleich*, was reached in 1867. Henceforward the link between Austria and Hungary was to be a personal one, the compromise itself being in the form not of an arrangement between two governments and peoples, but of two contracts entered into separately with the House of Habsburg. Francis Joseph remained Emperor in his Austrian dominions, but in Hungary he was crowned and anointed King. As for the parliaments, they remained wholly separate and common business was conducted by delegations sitting alternately in Vienna and Pest. Responsibility for foreign affairs, peace and war, rested with the Emperor and while each of the partners had a local military force, the army was that of *Kaiser und König* (*K und K*). Of greater importance to Griffith was the concession of fiscal autonomy. The Magyar leaders were disciples, as was Griffith, of Friedrich List and his gospel of protectionism and when the time came for the negotiation of an Irish settlement, Griffith, mindful of Magyar precedent, sought to insist on a similar concession to Ireland.

The overall originality of Griffith's contribution lay not in conception – Gladstone in the debate on the first Home Rule Bill had alluded to the possible relevance of 'the altogether new experience of Austro-Hungary'[47] – but in consideration of the inferences to be drawn from it. Stripped to essentials the argument itself at the least had relevance.[48] It purported to show how a people who had risen in rebellion, been crushed, had eschewed violence and yet by resolute refusal to contemplate cooperation without prior restoration of what they deemed to be their constitutional rights, had in fact achieved their ends.

There were criticisms of two kinds. It was argued in the first instance that the equivalent of the Magyars were not the Irish but the Anglo-Irish,[49] likewise a dominant race. But there was this crucial difference. Magyars, according to the 1910 census, constituted a small majority, not a small minority, in the eastern half of the Empire, 11 to 9 being the conventional calculation, and, more important in the context, the association in Austria-Hungary was not of one people with its colonists, but of two nationalities, or indeed two races from different continents, the Teutonic Aryans and the Magyars who had migrated westward from the Russian steppes. The analogy subsumed not only conflict but also a measure of common interest between nationality and Empire; otherwise independence rather than dualism would have been the logical goal. This was a second source of criticism. D.P. Moran denounced Griffith and his 'Green Hungarian Band' for having a misconceived order of priorities. They had nailed their flag to the masthead not of a separatist Gaelic republic, but to the monarchical 1782 constitution which 'had sent us adrift in a new world which persuaded Irishmen to make the greatest sacrifice in our power – the sacrifice of our national character'. He meant the Gaelic language, for him the essence of nationhood – something which 'mere political independence, a parliament in College Green . . . will not necessarily bestow.'[50]

Whatever the merits of the *Ausgleich*, assuredly it was not in a republican but in the monarchical tradition, while with regard to method, passive resistance and abstention were weapons in the armoury of a parliamentary party, not of a revolutionary movement. The threat of withdrawal of Irish members from Westminster on grounds of principle might consistently with his own principles have been deployed by Redmond against Asquith. But that was not Redmond's way. Until it was too late for him and for the party, he kept to the path Parnell had marked out, without consideration of new devices to meet the challenge of new circumstances. Ireland, wrote Griffith, needed its Francis Déak. But Redmond thought in terms of an Irish Botha – which carried as will be seen quite different connotations. In the event, he assumed the mantle of neither: he remained John Redmond, a master of parliamentary procedure more loyal to Westminster than Westminster was to prove to him. That was his tragedy. As for Griffith, a man of influence in other countries as well as his own,* he lived to see the application of the abstentionism he had advocated in association with the force he had repudiated, bringing about part fulfilment of his aims.

---

* Griffith's exposition of the Sinn Féin programme was widely publicised in South Africa, where he had worked as a journalist from 1896 to 1898 and more importantly in India. There his work and writings were frequently referred to in the Indian press and by Indian nationalist leaders.

CHAPTER 2

Home Rule: One Step or Two? The Liberal-Nationalist Dichotomy 1905–11

Liberal Tactics and Irish Expectations

In May 1902, Asquith in a much quoted statement of Liberal policy on Ireland enunciated two principles: the maintenance of the supremacy of the Imperial Parliament and as liberal a devolution of local powers and responsibilities as could be attained by methods which would carry with them, step by step, the sanction and sympathy of British opinion.[1] The second, in the light of previous experience, was bound to be an important consideration, Home Rule increasingly being reckoned an electoral liability at constituency level. The party had a distinctive programme to put through on social issues and many in their ranks feared that if a third Home Rule Bill were sent up to the Lords (who in 1893 had unceremoniously, and without perceptible rebound on themselves, thrown out the second by 419 votes to 41), it would be rejected out of hand and another election, with Home Rule the dominant issue, would necessarily follow. When Morley demanded that Home Rule should be put into the forefront of the party programme, Asquith reacted by telling Herbert Gladstone that if this received any countenance from Campbell-Bannerman it would do 'incalculable and perhaps fatal mischief'.[2] A majority at the forthcoming election, Asquith argued, could be obtained only if it were made clear that a Liberal government would *not* introduce a Home Rule Bill in the next parliament; if they did, it would, as he put it, be 'chucked out by the H. of L. and . . . wreck the fortunes of the party for another twenty years'.

Campbell-Bannerman was sceptical. On 26 October 1905 he replied to Herbert Gladstone (who had conveyed these views to him),

> If I were to be critical, I think he [Asquith] and John M[orley] have been a little too emphatic and peremptory. It was surely unnecessary (and may be inconvenient) to declare absolutely that nothing in the way of Home Rule should be attempted in the whole of the next Parliament. That there would be time or opportunity for anything like a full-blown H.R. Bill is utterly unlikely, but we do not know how circumstances

may change and I doubt the wisdom of precluding any approach to it being made. It would not be very difficult to frame a 'formula' . . . before the election expressive of our attitude.

There may be some insincere and even hostile feeling about Home Rule in some so-called Liberal quarters . . . and if such people are sensitive and suspicious we may lose their votes – but they would be a mere flea bite compared to the loss of belief in our sincerity on the part of the mass of real Liberals.

We have come through it before, by being straight and direct and we can do it again.[3]

The letter was posted from Merano in the South Tirol whither Campbell-Bannerman had moved from Marienbad, where invitations to share about half his meals with King Edward VII, while welcome from the point of view of a Prime Minister in waiting, had been 'to the great detriment' of his cure.[4] A consequence of Campbell-Bannerman's migration was that the Irish were unable to find him, T.P. O'Connor reporting to Redmond on 30 October 'C.B. is not in London: I believe he is not even in England yet; the last heard of him was from Vienna.'[5] This uncertainty about his whereabouts was not fortuitous – Campbell-Bannerman having deliberately prolonged his stay abroad so as to defer, among other things, an exchange of views with the Irish leaders until the Balfour administration had moved into the last phase of disintegration. As a result, it was not until 14 November that John Redmond, with T.P. O'Connor, met Campbell-Bannerman over breakfast in London. 'He s'd', Redmond's longhand note records, 'he was stronger than ever for Home Rule. It was only a question how far they cd. go in the next Parlmnt. His own impression was that it wd *not* be possible to pass full Home Rule, but he hoped to be able to pass some serious measure wh wd be consistent with and wd lead up to the other. He wd say nothing, however, to withdraw the larger measure from the Electors.'[6]

At Stirling on 23 November, Campbell-Bannerman duly reaffirmed that any Liberal initiative must be consistent with and lead up to the wider Home Rule policy. The point was therefore not only privately but also publicly on record. But that makes the more remarkable an apparent omission in Redmond's breakfast conversation. Did he really neglect to enquire on the morrow of the 'Devolution crisis' what sort of 'serious measure' Campbell-Bannerman had in mind? If it was an oversight, it was of a kind that changes the course of politics. There was a common interest on both sides in understanding of intent and the highest priority might be expected to have been given to consideration of the nature of the contemplated step towards Home Rule. Without it, there was a grave risk of alienation between two parties brought together for one purpose and, that purpose apart, not natural allies. But other evidence suggests it may not have been oversight but miscalculation that led Redmond to leave the matter unexplored. The explanation in that case was almost certainly that he was proceeding on the assumption that the party would hold the balance in the new parliament. Dillon assuredly was. 'If the Liberals quarrel with us after the election', he had earlier written to Redmond, 'we shall have it in our power to make their position an impossible one'.[7] On 26 December Redmond exchanged views with Keir Hardie on the likely outcome of the forthcoming election. Redmond, given the Parnellite concept of parliamentary strategy, was bound to wish, as he did, for a small Liberal majority, but Keir Hardie* on the other hand, hoped for a large one in the belief that the Liberal party in office 'would go to pieces sooner with a large than a small majority', adding perceptively that the Liberal party either way was 'a decaying quantity'.[8] Redmond, on this reckoning, would seem to have allowed a wish to acquire semblance of reality, fostering the illusion that after the elections he could lay down his own conditions. In the event, Hardie's prognosis was to be tested and the realisation of Redmond's hopes deferred for a further four years.

Balfour resigned on 4 December 1905 but did not dissolve Parliament, thereby confronting the Liberal leadership with the choice, hazardous as it was widely deemed to be, of forming a government before an election or of cravenly declining the opportunity. C.B. took a robust line. 'Many people', he wrote to Ripon, 'seem impressed with the disadvantage of accepting office after resignation. Anyone can see there would be inconvenience and that as a mere move in the party game it would be clever to refuse.' But it would have a 'damping effect' on supporters who 'know nothing of tricks and pedantries and judge by facts'.[9] Campbell-Bannerman likewise strongly repudiated the notion that the Liberals after an election should not accept office unless they had a majority independent of the Irish, though in 1901 Asquith had entertained that opinion, and Haldane continued to do so.

The general election took place in January 1906 and the Liberals won 377 seats, obtaining a majority of 84 over all other parties combined. It was a landslide victory without parallel in English politics until the Labour triumph in 1945. The Nationalists held 83 seats, which was satisfying but marginally relevant. They did not hold a balance. There was no balance to be held. The assumption Dillon entertained and from which Redmond at the least did not dissent thus proved unfounded. The party was left with a generally well-disposed government to work with, but one also without a specific commitment on the step or steps to be taken towards Home Rule.

---

*Hardie was concerned to avoid even the appearance of friction between the forces of Labour and Nationalism; Redmond was detached (Redmond Papers 15193(8)).

A small incident may suffice to indicate the post-election power relationship. Redmond desired an amendment to that part of the King's speech opening the new parliament which referred to the repeal of the Coercion Act. He pressed strongly for it. There were delays, and finally from the new Chief Secretary, James Bryce, came a note worthy of so eminent a jurist. 'Apart from other difficulties', wrote Bryce, 'it [the speech] will have been before now submitted to him from whom it is deemed to emanate.'[10] Alteration was thereby precluded. *Roma locuta est: causa finita est*. The Liberal position was as yet far from vulnerable.

The Liberal Government and the Irish Party Relationship: The Role of Chief Secretaries

Yet while the Liberal government's independence of the Irish vote determined the nature of their relationship with the Irish party, there is insufficient evidence to sustain the allegation that this was exploited by them to retract from their pre-election policy statements on Home Rule. Campbell-Bannerman in November 1905 had after all advised Redmond that a Home Rule Bill was an objective to be attained by stages or 'step by step', as the policy was described in the election campaign. Yet the time involved in the taking two (or more) steps was bound to, and did, create resentment in Ireland where nationalist opinion, after past disappointments, could hardly be expected to be understanding of the tactical considerations behind it. It was a responsibility of the leadership on both sides to ensure that no serious division, such as would prejudice the attainment of their common Home Rule goal, should arise as a result between Liberals and Nationalists on the important, certainly, but none the less subsidiary, questions of procedure and timing. In the discharge of this responsibility, that is of harmonising Liberal and Nationalist opinion, a great deal depended upon the relationship established between the Chief Secretary, Augustine Birrell, on the one hand and Redmond and Dillon on the other.

In April 1921 Lord Midleton, a leader of the Southern Unionists and Secretary of State for India 1903–5, was to write to Austen Chamberlain alleging, 'For fifteen years since we left office in 1906 [*sic*] no first class man, perhaps hardly a good second-rate politician, has governed Ireland, and from absolute peace the country has degenerated to a condition in which I suppose no part of the British Isles has been in since the Civil War.'[11] No first-class man? With the name of James Bryce, the author of *The Holy Roman Empire* first on the list of Chief Secretaries? Yet Midleton had a point. Bryce had academic virtues which were political liabilities. Not only did he see both sides of the question, but having outlined proposals, he was apt then to set out the objections to them. This was not a rewarding tactic in House of Commons debates. Nor was Bryce a good House of Commons man. After taking part in debate he did not repair to the smoking room but hurried off to resume the writing of the next chapter of a book. He was undeviating in his support for Home Rule – in 1893 in Florence as Minister in attendance on Queen Victoria, he had even tried to talk things over quietly with her only to find 'the pitch had been queered by Mr. Gladstone's sermonising'. But he gave the impression of being 'a Home Ruler *in despair*, adopting it as the least of a choice of evils'.[12] More important, Bryce as Chief Secretary did not succeed in getting *en rapport* with Irish leaders, nor they with him. They found his enquiries into fauna and flora in the west of Ireland tedious,[13] his interest in and encouragement for the language an irrelevance. When Bryce was assailed in Griffith's paper, only one man, and he of no influence, felt moved to pen a word on his behalf. 'We said – and we repeat', wrote Patrick Pearse, 'that Gaels will retain kindly memories of the official who, in spite of all the forces against him . . . ' has given 'practical support to the Irish language.'[14] For the rest, there was relief on both sides when in order to serve as British Ambassador in Washington Bryce relinquished an appointment which from the outset he had regarded as an experiment. If it is difficult to apportion responsibility at this failure to establish mutual understanding and respect, there is little doubt it was prejudicial to prospects of any step-by-step policy. There had been neither exchange of confidences nor meeting of minds, only frustration, with Bryce said to be 'in despair' about the failure to reconcile views on the draft proposals for an Irish Council. Were it not that Bryce's successor was Augustine Birrell, one might even be tempted to say that Bryce was too serious minded.

Birrell was no doubt much in Midleton's mind. He was a gifted littérateur. His touch was light: so was his political weight. In the old parliamentary phrase, he lacked 'bottom'. Nor did he take kindly to Ireland and its climate. 'We are having beastly weather', he wrote to Herbert Gladstone in December 1907 from his Norfolk home, 'but as it is not Ireland, it is paradise.' His letters, difficult to decipher, relied upon length and underlining for driving home an argument. A six-page letter of 30 October 1907 surveying the Irish scene had 110 single and two double underlinings. Of Campbell-Bannerman it is difficult to judge, but neither was to prove effective with Asquith who was to be a principal recipient after 1908. Prime Ministers generally welcome brevity and Asquith was predisposed to the unemphatic. As intermediary between Redmond on the one hand and the Prime Minister and the Cabinet on the other, Birrell's tone became concerned, at times plaintive, with his representations correspondingly little heeded. The *Leader*'s shafts – 'The Bristol Buffoon' or 'London's Leading Liberal Light Comedian'[15] were merciless. Yet who can doubt that the Home Rule cause, not least at the outset, would have been better served by a less agreeable and more ruthless personality?

The Irish Council Bill: a Tentative First Step

With the Liberals established in office, what was central to their Irish policy was the possibility, or otherwise, of reaching an understanding with the Irish on the step towards Home Rule that would conform to the Liberal tactic of not forthwith exposing a flank to the Lords. This had its difficulties. With the rank and file of the Nationalist party already resentful at the prospect of delay, any such less than half measure ran the risk of being regarded with a jaundiced eye. The leadership were familiar with Liberal reasoning but highly sensitive, especially Dillon as we have seen, to the danger of the party's being outbid at home by dissident Nationalists, while impairing their independence at Westminster through association with interim measures. The twofold risk made the leadership wary. 'A very good thing,' T.P. O'Connor wrote to Redmond in Ireland on 28 January 1906, 'if you and Dillon could come here for the next fortnight.' In the interval before the meeting of parliament 'an enormous amount of good could be done', while 'ministers are crystallising their projects and could be influenced'. But Redmond and Dillon were not to be persuaded to participate in more than minimal exchanges of view. When Lloyd George later that year outlined Liberal tactics and sought to elicit comment from Redmond, Redmond, as he himself recorded, 'expressed no opinion'.[16] There were detailed discussions about the interim measure that emerged as the Irish Council Bill, but no meeting of minds. Perhaps there could not have been, given lack of Liberal conviction on other than tactical advantage and Irish ambivalence about whether any such measure was a good idea or not. For them much appeared at risk. In January 1907 Dillon wrote that they must make sure 'that it shall be no Greek horse introduced into our camp, and that under the cloak of a measure of devolution no audacious attempt shall be made to break up' the Home Rule party.[17] Did that mean they were to reject all concession of self-government short of Home Rule out of hand, on the ground that it would divide the party and prejudice the prospect of Home Rule? Or were they, being a constitutional party, to seek by acceptance of less than palatable proposals to establish themselves as an element in the government of their country and so lay a more secure foundation on which full self-government could later be built? That was the issue before them in 1907.

In May the Liberals announced a measure which, despite all the differences at the drafting stage, they hoped the Nationalists might regard as a step forward, whilst they themselves disclaimed that it represented any movement at all towards Home Rule. The measure was entitled 'an Irish Council Bill'. The essence of it was to be found in the proposed constitution of a partly nominated and in larger part representative body to oversee the work of eight of the more important boards among which responsibility for the administration of Irish services was divided. The chosen eight included Local Government, Poor Law, Agriculture and, above all, Education. The function of the Council was to control and coordinate existing activities: there was to be no extension of them.

The government spoke of their own proposals with becoming diffidence. Birrell, in moving the first reading on 7 May 1907, alluded to 'humble dimensions' and a lesser occasion than historic Home Rule precursors. He further remarked that the Bill 'does not contain a touch or a trace, a hint or a suggestion of any new legislative power or authority'. If it were a success, it might, however, 'pave the way to Home Rule'.[18] Campbell-Bannerman described the Bill as a 'little, modest, shy, humble effort to give administrative powers to the Irish people'.[19] Balfour commented, not unreasonably it may be thought, that the Chief Secretary had brought in a Bill in which he did not believe.[20] What mattered, however, was whether the Irish believed in it. Initially Redmond had been receptive, and had spent time with Liberal ministers seeking to improve the Bill technically.[21] But his attitude underwent a sharp change when he was faced with what he had been most concerned to avoid, a hostile reaction at home. He then came out strongly against acceptance at a meeting of the National Convention of the United Irish League at which the measure was formally rejected. Without Irish endorsement, or at least acquiescence, there was no alternative to its withdrawal. This was announced on 29 July. Birrell, who thought 'our mistake was ever to have touched Devolution at all', had already offered to resign.[22] Campbell-Bannerman had insisted that he should stay. That was another mistake. Birrell was henceforward associated with miscalculation and consequent failure. Neither were of much moment. A decision, greater perhaps than they themselves realised, had been taken by the leaders of the Irish party.

With signs of uncertainty and irresolution, the Irish party had in 1907 reached a decision in principle, namely that a gradualist approach to Home Rule would prejudice its attainment. After the withdrawal of the Bill they underlined this by pressing for a resolution committing the government to the principle of Home Rule. Since their request was acceded to, subject to verbal amendments by Campbell-Bannerman,[23] the question of whether or not a measure of devolution would have diminished Home Rule prospects was to remain untested. Historians generally have accepted the party's view that it would have done so. But other possibilities are not to be altogether discounted. G.P. Gooch, serving as Parliamentary Private Secretary to the Chief Secretary, placed the Bill in another, a neutral so far as Home Rule was concerned, context: that the Bill offered an instalment of good government but left Home Rule 'exactly where it was before'.[24] The altogether opposite view was that the party's rejection of the Irish Council proposal outright was an error of judgement on the part of a constitutional party and that far from prejudicing the prospect of early Home Rule it would have enhanced it by giving Irishmen experience of

government, however limited, and by its very existence have attracted
the transfer of more power if only on grounds of administrative convenience. This view may merit rather more consideration than it has
received. Given watchful Unionist scrutiny, such an outcome might seem
improbable, though not impossible in view of the strength of the government's position in the House. What remains rather more within the
bounds of possibility is that the Council, if established, through the
exercise of strictly coordinating functions would have strengthened Irish
administration on an all-Ireland basis. That particular possibility went
by default. Its doing so did not exclude the passage of beneficial reforms
in other fields, notably the Irish Universities Act and the Land Act 1909,[25]
both of importance (though outside the scope of this work); it carried
implications only in respect of future administrative organisation. Unity
was a consideration foremost in the minds of those who did *not* want it.
For the rest the Nationalist position received authentic expression in a
phrase – 'concessions be damned: we want our country'.

The 1910 Elections: the Irish Party Holding the Balance

Campbell-Bannerman died on 22 April 1908. Irish parliamentarians,
Dillon excepted, held him in affectionate esteem: Irish historians, with
reservations about the strength of his Home Rule convictions, allowed
that he had caught the imagination of subject peoples within the Empire
by his restoration of self-government to the Transvaal on 6 December
1906. Contemporaries, Indian even more than Irish, regarded and continued to regard this as a 'magnanimous gesture', and moderates in both
countries asked for no more than a comparable concession to their own.[26]
That would have placed Ireland on the same footing as the colonies of
settlement, becoming known as Dominions. 'What we mean by Home
Rule,' said Redmond on 7 May 1907,[27] 'is that in the management of all
exclusively Irish affairs, Irish public opinion shall be as powerful as the
public opinion of Canada or Australia is in the management of Canadian
or Australian affairs'. It had, however, been open to the government to
restore self-government to the Transvaal by administrative action, that
is by letters patent without reference to the Lords, whereas to concede
Home Rule to Ireland required legislation and that in turn was conditional
upon the assent of the Lords over and above the approval of the Commons. None the less, henceforward colonial and especially South African
precedents★ continued to be an element in British and Irish parliamentary
thinking down to and after the negotiation of the Treaty in 1921.

★ R.C.K. Ensor, *England 1870–1914* (London, 1936), p. 423, comments on the
influence of what he calls 'the Botha–Redmond conjuncture' in 1910, the year in
which the South Africa Act 1909, took effect and when Redmond's parliamentary
standing was at its zenith.

Campbell-Bannerman's successor, Herbert Henry Asquith, was not predisposed to the making of gestures and with his accession to office relations followed an eventful, certainly, yet readily definable course. With rejection of the Irish Council's bill and a step-by-step policy discarded, attention was concentrated on the introduction of a Home Rule Bill without preliminary or precursor. But while that left the Irish party, untrammelled as they were now to be by interim constitutional proposals, free to concentrate on a single objective, it was apparent that the neutralisation of the House of Lords was a condition of its attainment. Redmond had, therefore, to secure a firm commitment by the Liberals to introduce a Home Rule Bill with a measure which would render the Lords' veto subject to limitation in time. Both were achieved in circumstances which realised the hopes of the party's leadership.

In the early years of the Liberal administration, Irish expectations of the Unionist mutilation or outright rejection of Liberal measures in the Upper House were more than fulfilled. A Land Valuation Bill, an Education Bill, a Licensing Bill, which would have involved the suppression of 30,000 licensed premises over fourteen years and which was not popular with the Irish party, were all thrown out. The government, in Tory phraseology, were reduced to 'ploughing of the sand', while Liberal strategy remained that of allowing the account between peers and people to mount up until 'the cup was full' and an appeal could be made with confidence to the people themselves.

Against all conceivable calculations of self-interest, the Lords themselves threw down the challenge on an issue on which by established convention they had no standing. Provoked by the impositions introduced by the Chancellor, David Lloyd George, in his 1909 'people's budget', which was regarded as at once a pioneering essay in welfare legislation and a frontal attack on wealth, the landed interest being the principal target, they rejected it. The Irish party, while generally welcoming the welfare element, especially the introduction of old age pensions, despite anxiety as to how the cost would be met under Home Rule, were dismayed by other features, which provoked a storm of protest in Ireland. Chief among them were new liquor licensing arrangements and a tax on spirits, which in conjunction affected distillers, brewers and publicans[28] from whom the party drew electoral support, as well as financial sustenance on a significant scale. In return they expected the party to protect their interests. This confronted the party leadership with a dilemma: if the party did not measure up to such expectations, there were others only too ready to do so. Yet if the party carried opposition à l'outrance they would risk alienating Liberal leaders, not least the Chancellor whose budget it was. The initial reaction was to incur the risk. Against past insistence on the absolute primacy for Home Rule, the party accordingly went to great lengths in pressing for concessions on the incidence of liquor taxation in Ireland. The government, assailed by the Tories over a broad front, was little disposed to make them. The outcome was not accord, but the first misunderstanding between Redmond and Dillon on the one hand and Lloyd George on the other. It was about the more arcane features of liquor taxation relating to valuation of licensed premises and the minimum rate and resulted in an appeal to Asquith. On 1 October he replied suavely that there was no ground for charging Lloyd George with breach of faith and expressed regrets for any misunderstanding. Redmond rejoined next day that there was 'no misunderstanding in the matter whatever'. But Asquith was not prepared to make concessions. 'I expect', he wrote, 'any hardship that may result from the Budget proposals to the small brewers, whether in England and Ireland, and I see no sufficient ground for differentiating in this matter between the case of the two countries, will be slight . . . '. 'My belief', he added later, 'is that their apprehensions are greatly exaggerated.'[29]

Irish resentment, fanned by representations from the grass roots, persuaded the party to go so far as to vote against the second reading but on the crucial third reading on 4 November 1909, sensitive to the incongruity of Irish nationalists voting on the same side as the diehard Unionists, they decided to abstain. The budget was carried by 379 votes to 149. The Lords, disregarding the opinion of the more moderate Tory leaders thereupon decided to follow Lord Milner's advice, to reject it – which they did no 30 November by 350 votes to 75 – and 'to damn the consequences'. The Liberals dissolved. For the Irish party, the Lords' vote was an uncovenanted mercy, since it opened a way to an end: the curbing of the powers of the Upper House on other than Irish issues. That the Unionists should have acted thus with such a prospect before them defies credibility to this day.

Redmond's first concern in this new situation was to obtain assurances from Liberal leaders of their intention to introduce a Home Rule Bill, if returned to power. Their replies were judged not unsatisfactory,[30] Lord Loreburn, a veteran Home Ruler, said that he would always do his utmost to place Home Rule on the Statute Book, while on 6 December John Morley, the doyen of Home Rulers, fully conscious of the gravity of the consequences of an inadequate or halting declaration, professed himself entirely satisfied about the sincerity of the Cabinet. In a speech in the Albert Hall on 10 December 1909, Asquith publicly acceded to the Irish request; 'the solution of the problem can be found only in one way [cries of "Home Rule" and loud cheers] by a policy which, while explicitly safeguarding the supremacy and indefeasible authority of the Imperial Parliament, will set up in Ireland a system of full self-government [loud cheers] in regard to purely Irish affairs. There is not and cannot be, any question of separation . . . '.[31] The emphasis was on Liberal concepts of consolidation by timely concessions leading to better government with explicit repudiation of a step in the onward march of a nation. Yet the

Liberal commitment represented a notable success for Redmond's leadership. He was at the pinnacle of his power and reputation.

The outcome of the first (January) 1910 election fulfilled Redmond's highest hopes. The result was Liberals 275 seats, Unionists 273, Labour 40 and Irish Nationalists 82. The Liberals thus were returned with a small majority over the Unionists. There followed a perceptible stiffening in Redmond's attitude. Asquith, at their first meeting after the election, found Redmond 'cold and critical if not avowedly hostile' but consoled himself with the thought that between the unpopularity of the Budget in Ireland and the O'Brien party on his flank, Redmond was 'not altogether his own master'. He was less sanguine by 25 February when 'the exorbitant demands' of the Nationalists and the impossibility in existing circumstances of counting on a stable majority had persuaded some of his colleagues, so he told the King, 'that the wisest and most dignified course for Ministers was at once to tender their resignation to your Majesty'.[32] But ministerial resolution was soon restored.

The government had initially to determine questions of procedure in view of the difference in priorities between Liberals and Nationalists: Redmond's first concern was the ending of the Lords' unqualified (in time) veto: Asquith's to dispose of the Budget. Should the Unionists not accept the verdict of the election, Asquith would have had to count upon the King's willingness to create a sufficient number of peers to ensure the passage through the Upper House of a measure curtailing its own powers. Asquith was unable to inform the leader of the opposition until 20 July 1910 that the King, George V, had signified that he would consider it his duty to act on advice if tendered to this end. In the Commons, the government were dependent at the least on Irish abstention. The Cabinet, however, were also resolved that there should be no bargaining. The Budget, as submitted to the House after the election, must in essentials be the same as that submitted before it. This led once more to strained relations. In order to reassure Redmond who, fearing lest the Budget once through the Commons with Irish support, or acquiescence, confrontation with the Lords might be sidestepped or delayed, took the line 'no veto, no budget'. By way of counter, the government on 29 March laid before the House three resolutions embodying the principles of the Parliament Act that was to be.[33] They were severally voted upon and approved on 14 April and the Budget reintroduced and then finally passed on 27 April by the Commons,[34] with 67 Irish members voting in favour, and then without a division by the Lords. But with the question of the Lords' delaying power outstanding, fate intervened. On 6 May, King Edward VII died.

The King's death exposed the vulnerability of the Irish party even when holding the balance in the event of one little considered and, as it proved, unrealised eventuality – that of a *rapprochement*, such as Hartington had

envisaged in 1885, [35] between the English party leaders on fundamental
issues, Home Rule chief among them. In the early summer of 1910 the
prospect was not hypothetical. On 18 May Asquith assured the new King
that, irrespective of Redmond's views, he would explore the possibility of
some understanding with the opposition to avoid another general election.
On 6 June Asquith found in the Cabinet a 'practically unanimous desire' to
hold such discussions. In June accordingly, following upon 'the lamented
demise of the Crown' and acting on the new King's suggestion, Asquith
invited Balfour and his principal colleagues, Lansdowne among them,
to talks on the possibility of interparty agreement on constitutional questions, including relations between the two Houses. Redmond was neither
informed nor consulted, even though Birrell, one of the Liberal representatives, was incorrectly believed to have provided a liaison with him.[36]
T.P. O'Connor wrote to Redmond of 'a general feeling of uneasiness', of
'all kinds of rumours' going round, while assuming the Liberals 'would
not act without consulting you'. He urged Redmond that it was 'desirable
– more, necessary' for him and Dillon to come to London, but without
avail.[37]

   In the event, while there was some progress at the conference on other
issues, the Liberals declined to make a concession such as would allow
Home Rule to be placed in a special category of 'organic' or 'structural',
change to be dealt with by special (and delaying) process of referendum or
otherwise. In November the talks finally petered out in failure. R.C.K.
Ensor surmised 'that had a leader less inelastic on this subject' (Home
Rule) than Lansdowne 'been in charge, the conference would have succeeded'.[38] If indeed this were so, it renders the failure of the talks a matter
of moment. With agreement, then Griffith's scenario of 103 Irish members
faced with 567 foreigners would indeed have acquired outward semblance
of verisimilitude.

The Implications of the Enactment of the Parliament Bill

In June the Parliament Bill was introduced in the House of Lords. It
provided that Bills, passed by the Commons in three successive sessions
and rejected each time by the Lords, should become law, provided two
years had elapsed between the second and third readings in the House of
Commons. The Upper House accordingly would be able to delay, but no
longer to veto, Home Rule. With regard to the former, two years in
politics as Redmond was to learn the hard way, could be a long time. In
the Lords, however, consideration of the Bill was deferred while counter-
proposals for their own reform were formulated, along with other devices
to deflect the government from its purpose, or at the least to confuse the
electorate about what was at issue in rival schemes. Asquith reacted

sharply, dissolving parliament on 18 November and calling for an election in December. This time round, the principal issue was not in question. It was Home Rule. The outcome was all that Redmond could reasonably have wished. The Liberals and Unionists tied with 272 seats each, Labour returning 42 and the Irish 84 members. On 21 February 1911 the Parliament Bill, identical in every respect with that which had been read a first time in April 1910, was reintroduced in the Commons: on 23 May it reached the Lords and on 10 August the 'diehards' made their last reckless but unsuccessful bid to defeat it.[39]

Over and against the attainment of a major objective, on which all further progress was dependent, there were some entries to be made on the debit side, not least the alienation of Nationalists from Liberals over the Budget. That left its scars.[40] As a result the *entente*, let alone any notion of alliance, was wearing thin with the Liberals, who were in fact almost as resentful at Irish reactions as the Irish were known to be at some of the Budget impositions. A letter from Lloyd George to Redmond some months after the Budget had been passed reflected the changed relationship. On 6 November 1910, the day on which the Cabinet concurred in the Prime Minister's intention to advise a dissolution, Lloyd George replied to representations from Dillon in terms which conveyed only exasperation. 'I have been so busy fighting for Home Rule in the [Constitutional] Conference that I have had no time to attend to the imaginary grievances of the Irish publicans. *We* – the entire Liberal force – are fighting a desperate battle for your national cause and staking all on our absolute loyalty to it.'[41] And then a familiar refrain – 'As great things are to be decided in the next few days, it is a pity you cannot be within reach of consultation.' How irked the tone by comparison with that at Campbell-Bannerman's breakfast table five years earlier! Yet on matters of substance the balance had come down heavily on the credit side for the Irish.

By the end of 1910 Redmond had almost every cause for satisfaction. Consider the record. The Parliament Act had put a term to the delaying power of the Lords; a Liberal government pledged to carry Home Rule was confirmed in office and, last but not least, that government remained negatively dependent on Irish votes. What more favourable combination of circumstances could be looked for? Did it not, moreover, prove near-conclusive evidence that the tactical concentration on one step, not two, had been correct? And even in respect of interparty relations, coolness in the higher echelons was counterbalanced by livelier support for Home Rule among the rank and file of the Liberal party. Where they had been comparatively apathetic in 1906, a new feeling was said now to pervade their ranks. Ensor attributed this 'to the brilliant success' of Campbell-Bannerman's policy of restoring self-government to the Transvaal. 'Their slogan', Ensor writes, 'now was to make Redmond the Irish Botha'.

Redmond was judged to have had many qualities for the part and had the Liberal hand 'been extended to him, as it was to the Boer leader, he would have grasped it in the same spirit'. But there was one flaw in the prospect, as was soon to become only too apparent.[42]

PART II

THE SHAPING OF THE SETTLEMENT

If you mean to please any people, you must give them the boon which they ask: not what you think better for them but of a kind totally different.

Edmund Burke, Speech on Conciliation with America, 22 March 1775

CHAPTER 3

The Unionist Dimension 1912–14:
One Nation or Two?

The Third Party: Identity and Aspiration

In April 1902 President Steyn of the Orange Free State, seeking to dissuade Kitchener from imposing British rule upon the defeated Boer Republics, warned him: 'The conditions in Ireland had arisen mainly from the fact that Ireland was a conquered country.'[1] So indeed at that time it must have seemed to observers in distant places. But ten years later, no one could have confined himself, even allowing for the 'mainly', to so simple and single an explanation. By then it was apparent that the conditions in Ireland derived from the fact that Ireland was a conquered and in part a settled country. Had she been only the first, no doubt independence, given Ireland's geographical position, would not have been won without force – after all, the Unionist party had come into existence in 1886 not to save Ulster but, as its name indicated, to preserve the Union – and only by stages dominion and then a republican status, within or conceivably outside the Commonwealth, would have followed for Ireland as a whole. It was the identification of a third party in terms of polity over and above community, and the widening scope for manoeuvre that a triangular political situation affords, that made such an outcome, not unrealisable, but altogether more difficult to realise.

The third party was composed of the descendants of mainly Scottish settlers in the province of Ulster, six of whose counties (not the same six as later constituted Northern Ireland)* had been planted in the reign of James I. That they came to form a distinct community is not in question; one has only to read the testimony of nineteenth-century travellers or rely on one's own twentieth-century observation to be persuaded of that. In 1833, Macaulay, who, if the Union were to be repealed, preferred separation to any intermediate course, contended that 'every argument

---

*Antrim and Down, both included in Northern Ireland, were not 'planted' by James I, while Cavan and Donegal were planted but not included in Northern Ireland.

which has been urged for the purpose of showing that Great Britain and Ireland ought to have two distinct parliaments may be urged with far greater force for the purpose of showing that the north of Ireland and the south of Ireland ought to have two distinct parliaments', chiefly, though not only, because 'theological antipathies are stronger in Ireland than here'.[2] Nassau Senior, the first professor of Political Economy at Oxford, returning from his Irish travels ten years later, in 1843, went as far, or further, in concluding that Ulster was to be thought of as a different country, because with few exceptions the state of the population there was 'not merely dissimilar but opposed' to that in the rest of Ireland.[3] Did such differences, he asked himself, cumulatively amount to a case for separate political treatment? The Act of Union had made no such provision, the whole of Ireland being governed (or misgoverned) from Dublin Castle, but Nassau Senior concluded that this – that is the establishment of a single government to administer two countries (as he termed them) with such divergent social organisation – was the underlying weakness of the Union settlement. But so long as the whole of Ireland remained within the polity of the United Kingdom, no separate administration for the northern counties was either contemplated or still less proposed. It was only with the possibility, imminent as it had seemingly become by 1886, of retraction of imperial control by the concession of Home Rule that the fundamentals of the situation were deemed by the opponents of Home Rule to be about to change in such a way as to require bifurcation of Irish government in order to protect the minority. Had they a valid case? And if so, what form should such bifurcation take?

It is frequently alleged that the Liberals in general, and Gladstone in particular on his sudden conversion to Home Rule, were guilty of grievous miscalculation by their discounting of the fears of Ulster Protestants, to whom the name of Gladstone soon became and long remained anathema, at the prospect of being placed under a Home Rule government which they were convinced would be tantamount to Rome rule. But is this a true indictment? Gladstone, in introducing the First Home Rule Bill, made two points: first, that he could not 'allow it to be said that a Protestant minority in Ulster . . . is to rule the question [i.e. Home Rule] at large for Ireland. I am aware of no Constitutional doctrine tolerable on which such a conclusion could be adopted or justified.' And, secondly, that he was prepared to give 'the most favourable consideration, with every disposition to do what equity may appear to recommend' to schemes, 'short of refusing the demand of Ireland at large', for the exclusion of 'Ulster itself, or, perhaps with more appearance of reason, a portion of Ulster' if 'recommended by a general or predominating approval'.[4] Though not without its characteristic Gladstonian ambiguities (as in the last phrase 'approval' of whom?) was not that a reasonable approach? After all, Ulster in 1886 was a subordinate issue, Chamberlain himself making plain that his intent was 'to kill Home Rule not to exclude some Ulster counties from it, and his tactic to deploy the Ulster question for that purpose. One of the great difficulties of this problem was, as he remarked with a hint of menace, 'that Ireland is not a homogeneous community – that it consists of two nations . . . and I ask how are you going to enforce the provisions of your statutory Parliament?'[5]

A quarter of a century later, Chamberlain's hint was in process of transformation into flamboyant and challenging assertion. How and why remains a large and hitherto not satisfactorily resolved question. Time for opposition to crystallise was no doubt a conditioning factor. More certainly the seeming imminence of Home Rule was the precipitating factor. It was that which introduced the 'now or never' edge of reality into the rhetoric of resistance. But rhetoric as well there had to be: it was a condition of organised resistance. The rhetoricians for their part could rely upon an authentic emotional response from traditional grassroots Protestant sentiment in the northern counties. That was not in doubt. But resistance to what? To Home Rule for Ireland? Or to the inclusion of Ulster in a Home Rule polity? These were different aims and pursuit of the former might well, by virtue of its overreach, prejudice attainment of the latter. After all it was the English electorate that would ultimately decide and the alienation of that electorate on the longer term could not be to the advantage of Ulster Unionists. But on the shorter, the combination of strong language with concealment of purpose, as between defeat of Home Rule or Ulster exclusion from it, offered tempting tactical advantages.

The New Unionist Leaders – Carson and Bonar Law Come; Balfour Goes

It is a matter for consideration whether Edward Carson was elected to succeed Walter Long as leader of the Ulster Unionist Parliamentary party on 21 February 1910 and Andrew Bonar Law to succeed A.J. Balfour as leader of the Unionist party on 13 November 1911, because they best reflected the impassioned temper of their respective followers or whether *per contra* by virtue of their election they became principally responsible for stirring it up over and above giving it free expression. On the first hypothesis the leadership elections were of interest; on the second they were of historical moment.

The new Unionist leaders were drawn from outside their respective natural bailiwicks, Bonar Law being a New Brunswicker by birth and early education and Carson not an Ulster, but a southern Unionist, educated at Portarlington School and Trinity College, Dublin, which, in its Dublin University manifestation, he represented in the House of Commons from 1892 to 1918. The choice of Carson, which came first in time, implied that resistance to Home Rule rather than safeguards for Ulster was to be the aim, if only because concentration on Ulster would necessarily indicate readiness to think of Southern Unionists, of which Carson was one, as being in the last resort expendable. On this assumption Carson had the right credentials. He had been appointed Junior Counsel to the Attorney-General for Ireland in 1887 and in that capacity had prosecuted for the Crown for offences under the Crimes Act. Then in 1892 Balfour, impressed by his courage and the quality of his advocacy, appointed him Solicitor-General for Ireland.[6] In 1900 he became Solicitor-General in Britain. There was no doubt about the all-Ireland basis of his Unionism. 'From the day I first entered Parliament', Carson recalled in later years, 'devotion to the Union has been the guiding star of my political life'.[7] But was there not ambivalence between the challenging words and tactical dispositions?

In reply to a proposal for a separate Ulster parliament put to a meeting of the National Unionist and Conservative Associations on 17 November 1910, Carson said Ulster would never be a party to any separate treatment. But on 31 January 1911, presiding over the Ulster Unionist Council he identified the design to place them (the Ulster Unionists) under a Nationalist government – a tyranny to which we 'never can and never will submit' – as the crucial issue. After the enactment of the Parliament Bill on 18 August 1911 the emphasis was on Ulster alone. On 25 September 1911 at the end of a tumultuous protest meeting at Craigavon, at which Carson's flair for theatrical demonstration coupled with resounding eloquence made a tremendous impression, he announced the intention of the Ulster Unionist Council (which had been called into existence in 1904–5,[8] in reaction against the devolution proposals) to set up a provisional government to take charge of the province when a third Home Rule Bill was enacted.[9] Did not this indicate that the Southern Unionists were deemed to be expendable? Clearly that was far from his intention. He did not credit the notional existence of two nations in Ireland; he believed there was only one in the British Isles. His aim was accordingly to preserve the Union; Ulster was to be the means. The misgivings of Southern Unionists were unfounded. On 10 October 1911, at a meeting at the Rotunda, Carson told them what they wished to hear. 'You need fear', he said, 'no action of Ulster which would be in the nature of a desertion of the Southern Provinces'. And then came the statement which his biographers call 'the core of his policy, what was for him its purpose and justification'[10] – 'if Ulster succeeds, Home Rule is dead. Home Rule is impossible for Ireland without Belfast and the surrounding parts.' Did Carson believe it or was it rather something he wished to believe, because the alternative was too painful for a Southern Unionist to contemplate? In any event, it proved a great miscalculation – and one not made by the leader of the Unionist party, A.J. Balfour.

Balfour's days as leader, however, were almost numbered. He was said to be depressed by the prospect of resumed party conflict and disillusioned with politics. From *Der Kaiserhof*, Bad Gadstein, he replied in August 1910 to an enquiry from Austen Chamberlain about a meeting with the Liberal leaders in discouraged and discouraging terms:

> Let me shelter myself behind the plausible evasions supplied by the fact that it is August, that I am abroad and that I am doing a cure . . . put the whole thing off till November, especially as the King has bitten another slice out of my home time by bidding me to Balmoral.
>
> I had almost forgotten that there is such a thing as politics . . . . The weather is beautiful, the scenery fine and I know no one here. What more can a tired politician want?[11]

On 2 September Lansdowne reported: 'I hear A.J.B. has returned very well and in good spirits.'[12] But he did not remain so for long. He made no secret of his alienation from the 'last ditchers' who could not be dissuaded from pursuing what Balfour regarded as an 'essentially theatrical' policy of resistance to the Parliament Bill to a final vote. Thereafter, smarting from the humiliating defeat that followed in August 1911, the diehards turned against their leader and adopted the B.M.G. (Balfour must go) slogan first coined by the tariff reformers. On 11 November 1911 Balfour resigned. His resignation had momentous consequences in Anglo-Irish politics, partly because it removed from the leadership (though not from later Cabinet membership)[13] a man who was intellectually convinced that the alternative to Union was separation of those who wished to separate and still more because his resignation opened the way for the election of a successor who was by descent and continuing family ties associated with Protestant, or to be precise, Presbyterian Ulster.

The advice of one Canadian, Max Aitken, to another, Andrew Bonar Law, on their way to the Carlton Club for the election to the leadership on 13 November 1911, was to 'remember you are a great man now'. 'If I am a great man', replied Bonar Law, 'then a good many great men must have been frauds'.[14] There were two favoured candidates, Austen Chamberlain and Walter Long, both of whom had backed the 'ditchers' as against the 'hedgers' in the debates on the Parliament Bill and, more immediately relevant, both of whom were steeped in Irish politics. On Home Rule, Chamberlain stood where his father had stood when he 'killed' Gladstone's first Bill but, in sharp contrast to his father, he lacked political ruthlessness in such marked degree as to invite the Churchillian quip that he always played the game and he always lost it.* As for his principal rival, Walter

---

* This is by no means incompatible with Oliver St John Gogarty's later description of Chamberlain as 'one of the grandest human beings I ever have met'. *As I was going down Sackville Street* (London, 1937), p. 236.

Long, he was, and in a secondary chairman of committee role he remained, close to the heart of Irish policy-making throughout the period.
The link had been forged in 1905 when, on Wyndham's resignation,
Balfour had written to Long inviting him to serve as Chief Secretary: 'I do
not *ask* you to go to Ireland; but if you accept the office of chief secretary
you will be doing me a great service and rendering a still greater one to
your country'.[15] Though Long held the office only for nine months, he
further commended himself to Irish Unionist opinion as member for
South County Dublin 1906–10. Neither Long nor Chamberlain became
leader of the Unionist party in 1911: that lot fell, in the familiar pattern
of triangular contests, to Bonar Law, the compromise candidate, who
himself lacked all disposition to compromise on Irish affairs.

Andrew Bonar Law was not a Canadian *tout simple*: he was a Canadian
of Ulster Presbyterian descent. While his father, a minister of the Free
Church of Scotland, had been born in Coleraine and had returned on
retirement in 1877 to his native Ulster, his son, Richard, in the fullness of
time became ennobled as Lord Coleraine. Andrew Bonar Law completed
his schooling in Glasgow and entered business there as an iron merchant,
frequently visiting Ulster while his father lived. Not surprisingly, once
established in politics, Bonar Law came, so his biographer tells us, to feel
'more strongly about the Ulster question than anything else in politics at
this time'.[16] On election as leader of the Unionist party he committed
himself with no apparent hesitation to an extreme course in support of
Ulster Unionism.

There is one aspect of Bonar Law's concept of his role, not, it is true,
without precedent in Disraelian times but which, by reason of its Irish
policy implications, merits comment here. He took, or professed to take,
the view that the leadership of the party was an actively shared responsibility, his associate in it being Lansdowne by virtue of the latter's leadership of the Unionists in the Upper House. 'Leadership of our party is
shared', Bonar Law told Asquith in October 1913, and in December that
year he remarked in a letter to Lansdowne: 'I think we are a curious pair of
leaders, for it is evident you are not enjoying it and at this moment I
would give a good deal to be out of it too.'[17] They were 'a curious', in the
sense of an improbable, pair in other ways – the Glasgow ironmaster with
his austere early upbringing in the manse on the one hand and, on the
other, a great landowner moving from Bowood in Wiltshire to his estate
in Scotland, to Derreen in County Kerry, and one who was descended on
his father's side from Lord Shelburne, the eighteenth-century Prime
Minister, and on his mother's from Talleyrand, through Talleyrand's
natural son, the Comte de Flahault. Their correspondence when
Lansdowne was away for the recess at Bowood or Derreen, was generally
more understanding than might be expected, given a fundamental difference in approach to Home Rule. While professing concurrence, it disclosed differences in their priorities in an Irish settlement. Lansdowne was

not so uniformly inflexible as is sometimes supposed – he was ready to support the Irish Council Bill in 1907 had it reached the Lords[18] – but he was wholly at one with Bonar Law in wishing to defeat Home Rule. When the differences papered over arose beyond that simple but questionably realisable purpose, should the Unionists refuse to negotiate or should they concentrate their resistance on Ulster? Bonar Law favoured the first, Lansdowne the second. This was the more important because Bonar Law consistently emphasised Lansdowne's co-leadership status and paid deference to his opinions, even when he did not share them.

Lord Blake takes the view that the question of a separate treatment for Ulster had not been seriously suggested before the autumn of 1913.[19] If this is limited to formal proposals, accepted by Cabinet or advanced by opposition, it is so. But such a possibility had been seriously entertained not least by Bonar Law. 'Probably', he wrote in studied understatement to Lansdowne in early October 1913, 'I have looked upon the solution of leaving Ulster out much more favourably than you have for I have had the idea for very many years that that might perhaps in the end be a right way of dealing with the situation only as a last resort.' He was opposed, however, to any public disclosure of this since 'nothing would seem more foolish than to give the enemy the idea that we were not only ready but anxious for a settlement on these lines'.[20] Lansdowne in any case was neither. For him sentiment strongly reinforced by self-interest rendered anything in the nature of partition if not a last, then a second-last resort. His known opposition to it, coupled with the erroneous notion that behind him in the South and West there was a 'solid body of Unionists'[21] was a factor delaying public Unionist party acquiescence in a solution on such terms.

The Third Home Rule Bill

The Parliament Act on the Statute Book, the government turned its attention to the preparation of a Home Rule Bill which would settle the Irish question. It was decided that the Bill of 1893 should serve as a model and a committee of seven ministers was appointed by the Cabinet in January 1912 to draft one accordingly. The committee met intermittently, and, even when pressed by the Cabinet and by time, produced no complete draft until a few weeks before the Bill was to be introduced. Little attention was given to the signs of incipient revolt in Ulster. Dr Jalland goes so far as to assert that as a result most ministers remained 'sublimely ignorant that Ulster might wreck their bill'.[22] As against this Asquith, so his biographers tell us, was only too well aware that Ulster would be his most formidable difficulty, but, as on other issues, he showed no disposition to take the initiative, preferring to leave that to the Unionists. The wisdom of so passive a course did not pass unchallenged.

On 6 February 1912 Lloyd George and Churchill formally proposed in Cabinet that Ulster, or those counties in which Protestants were in a clear majority, should be given an option to contract out of the Bill as introduced. The Cabinet, brought face to face with the implications of Ulster Unionist resistance, 'anxiously' and at 'great length', as the Prime Minister reported to the King, debated not the principle of such concession which, it was accepted, might have to be made, but its timing. Should such an option be given at the outset, or should it be withheld as a concession to be made, should circumstances so require, as an amendment at some later stage? The conclusion, which had the support of a large majority of the Cabinet including the Prime Minister, was that the Bill as introduced should be for the whole of Ireland but with the rider, as Asquith also reported to the King, that the Irish leaders should be warned 'that the Government held themselves free to make . . . changes, if . . . it becomes clear as the Bill proceeds that some special treatment must be provided for the Ulster counties . . . '.[23] Asquith's policy was accordingly one for all-Ireland, without special concession to Ulster in the first instance, on the ground that any such concession would be tantamount to an admission that the government had been unable to formulate a policy for all-Ireland, and therefore at variance with Asquith's view that Ireland, as he put it later in Dublin was 'a nation, not two nations, but one nation'.[24]

Lloyd George and Churchill remained dissatisfied and continued to think the Cabinet's failure to take the initiative at the outset a mistake. Lloyd George was later to remind Redmond that he had no part in it and Churchill to complain that 'We had been met by the baffling argument that such a concession might well be made as the final means of securing a settlement, but would be fruitless till then.'[25] Asquith's biographers, Spender and Asquith and Jenkins concur in this judgement, as does Dr Jalland,[26] who focuses attention on it as an error of an historic order of magnitude. This conclusion rests on the argument that an initial concession of county or other option allowing for exclusion would have indirectly imposed restraint on the Ulster Unionists' opposition to the Home Rule Bill. This is because the grounds for Ulster resistance would have been rendered that much the less persuasive, and therefore English Unionist support for the Ulster Unionist cause would have been qualified. It is a nice point. But on balance, is it not equally, if not more, likely that while still denouncing Home Rule in any form, the Ulster Unionists would have been outraged at the prospect of exclusion, not of Ulster but of only four and a half counties, and paid scant regard then as later to modification in English Unionist views? After all Carson was announcing plans for a Provisional Government for Ulster at Craigavon some months before the contents of the Bill were known. The target might have been different, the goal and the tactic surely the same. In the light of a long sequel is it not beyond the bounds of credibility to suppose they would show sensitivity to English notions of how they should react? Nor are likely Nationalist reactions to be overlooked. Even as it was, Redmond was much taken aback on being told of Cabinet willingness to contemplate such concessions at a later stage: the actuality at the outset would have affronted him beyond measure. No adjustment in presentation would have made up for later lack of resolution in the execution of policy.

The Government of Ireland Bill was introduced on 11 April 1912, with Asquith unequivocally reaffirming the government's commitment to Home Rule on an all-Ireland basis. 'Throughout the welter and confusion, amid all the varying phases and fields of our electoral and Parliamentary campaigns', he said, 'one thing has remained constant, subject neither to eclipse nor wane, the insistence and persistence of the Irish demand. It remains today, in April 1912, what it was in January 1886, and what in the interval it has never ceased to be: a demand preferred by four-fifths of the elected representatives of the Irish people.' As for Ulster, the province as a whole was represented by 'seventeen Unionists and sixteen Home Rulers . . . Have you any answer to the demand of Ireland [Hon. Members "Yes"] beyond the naked veto of an irreconcilable minority?'[27] There was little or nothing more to be said. Yet one wonders whether behind the measured phrases, there was understanding of all they might mean – 'persistence', of Irish demand, 'irreconcilable' minority opposed to its acceptance.

There was one innovation in the Bill intermittently alluded to in the Irish debates of succeeding years. Asquith, who did not presume 'to bend the bow of Ulysses', addressed himself with a semblance of seriousness to federalist proposals (Home Rule-all-round), with Ireland coming separately and first before Scotland or Wales but not to remain on its own – the explanation given for this departure being that because of the burden of business in the Imperial Parliament, Home Rule, in that larger sense, '. . . rested upon the necessities, is demanded by the responsibilities and is indeed due to the honour of the Imperial Parliament'.[28] In fact the suggestion was made in the hope, illusory as it proved, of enlisting the support of federalists who had persuaded themselves that the distinctively nationalist element in the Irish demand might be diluted by equation with generally neutral opinion in Scotland and Wales. As one federalist put it, the upshot would be an Ireland in the role, not of a dominion like Canada or Australia, but rather of a province like Ontario or Quebec.[29] Deflation by association was the aim.

'The cardinal principle' on which the Bill proceeded was stated in express terms in its first clause: 'Notwithstanding the establishment of an Irish Parliament . . . the supreme power and authority of Parliament in the United Kingdom shall remain unaffected and undiminished over all persons, matters, and things within His Majesty's Dominions.'[30] Specifically, the authority of the Imperial Parliament was to remain unimpaired in questions of peace and war, treaties, the levying of new customs duties, coinage, postal services outside Ireland and, for a period of six years, control of the police. Furthermore the Irish Parliament was debarred from the endowment of religion or the imposition of religious disabilities and its taxing authority was limited so that *inter alia* it could not add more than 10 per cent to the rate of income tax or of death duties. Irish membership in the Imperial House of Commons was retained by way of counter to charges of a separatist measure, but reduced from 103 to 42, leaving the 42, contrary to earlier proposals, at liberty to speak on all subjects. There were few new thoughts and no daring departures here; the emphasis throughout was on reservation and safeguards. Yet the Bill earned the welcome accorded to it by John Redmond[31] and members of the party, on one ground and one only – it proposed to reconstitute a parliament for Ireland, all-Ireland, that would have power 'to make laws for the peace, order and good government of Ireland'. For them it was the 'example' of College Green that counted, not the powers or the lack of them to be vested in it. Once a parliament was restored much else would be added and the psychological gain would more than compensate for restrictions that were little short of humiliating.

The introduction of the Bill gave a foretaste of the dialectical confrontation that was to come, the Prime Minister's exposition of its content and purposes being interrupted by Bonar Law and Craig with allegations that he had no convictions or, if he had, that he had sold them to Redmond in order to stay in office, while Carson concluded with a tremendous climax of denunciation: 'We believe it to be an unnecessary Bill. We believe it to be a fatal Bill for our country, and an equally fatal Bill for yours, and, above all things, we believe it to be involved in the greatest series of dishonourable transactions that have ever disgraced any country.'[32] (The last once again an allusion to Asquith's alleged subservience to the Irish Nationalist Party.) Unionists were at one against Home Rule in principle, Bonar Law and James Craig being, as Craig declared, with Carson against the Bill – against 'every clause, every line, and every word in it on behalf of those not only in Ulster, but in all parts of Ireland who have been the friends of this country in the past'.[33] That certainly implied that the defeat of Home Rule, not simply the safeguarding of Ulster, continued to be the Unionist aim.

Exploring the Dimensions of the Ulster Question

On 11 June, opinion was tested by an amendment moved by a back-bench Liberal, J. Agar-Robartes, to approve the Bill, subject to the counties of Antrim, Armagh, Down and Londonderry being excluded from its provisions. Agar-Robartes maintained that his amendment would remove one of the chief obstacles to Home Rule, his contention being that Ireland consisted of two nations but was being treated as one in the Bill. The amendment was an embarrassment to government and opposition alike. Bonar Law said he would vote for it but not for a moment would it weaken his opposition to Home Rule:[34] Walter Long that he could not vote against a proposal which offered to give Ulster a portion of what she wanted.[35] As for Carson, the amendment implied compromise but, he declared, 'There is no compromise possible'. And even as a compromise it was inadequate – he would never leave out Fermanagh and Tyrone. Lloyd George, who exercised economy in public expression of his views on Home Rule controversies at this time, as he was later to remind his colleagues, rejected the amendment but on the specific grounds that if four counties were to be excluded 'there ought to be an overwhelming demand for it' and clear agreement about the counties that were to be excluded. He saw no evidence of either. As Asquith had already underlined and as the amendment itself implied, it was not a case of a united and homogeneous province, a Quebec, resisting Home Rule; it was of some part of it and that part, argued Lloyd George, variable and indeterminate. Surely the Unionists, if they were in earnest, should be specific and ask for whatever it was they wanted? It was not a theoretic enquiry. Even if the area were limited to the four north-eastern counties, the respective populations showed a substantial minority of Roman Catholics, namely, 315,404 to 729,624 Protestants. But the Unionists' claim was for the nine counties comprising the whole province of Ulster in which population and representation (18 Nationalists to 17 Unionists in the House of Commons) was nearly evenly divided. Did that warrant special treatment and if so, in what form? 'Home Rule within Home Rule'? Or actual exclusion from the jurisdiction of a Home Rule parliament?[36] The amendment was lost: the questions remained. Relating as they did to the principle of exclusion and the extent of any area to be excluded, the answers given to them were bound to be at the heart of any settlement based on partition.

Outside parliament there were longer-range dialectical exchanges in which the Unionist leadership held to the initiative. Two days before the introduction of the Bill in the House, on 9 April 1912, Bonar Law with Carson beside him had addressed a huge demonstration of Ulster Unionists at Balmoral, Belfast,[37] with what was said to be the largest Union Jack ever woven, flying above the platform.* His theme was 'you will save yourselves by your exertions and you will save the Empire by your example'. This was followed at Blenheim on 12 July by Bonar

---

* 'In the centre of the enclosure there was a tower with a 90' high flagstaff on which was broken, at the instant of passing the resolution against home rule, a giant Union Jack.' P. Buckland, *Irish Unionism 1885–1922* (Belfast, 1973), pp. 217–18.

Law's oft quoted verbal onslaught on the Liberal government. They were likened to 'Gadarene swine' going down the steep places into the sea: they were charged, by virtue of their enactment of the Parliament Act, with having destroyed the balance of the constitution and having become as a result no longer a legitimate government, but 'a revolutionary committee that had seized by fraud upon despotic powers'. More ominous was an allusion to things that were 'stronger than parliamentary majorities'. Asquith in reply coined memorable phrases with which to pour scorn upon the 'reckless rodomontade at Blenheim' which furnished for the future 'a complete Grammar of anarchy'.[38] But did phrases suffice?

Despite the flamboyant flourishes of the new Ulster-oriented leadership of the Unionist party, there remained the now familiar ambivalence in motivation due to different priorities. Balmoral and Blenheim were conceptually some distance apart, the former being first concerned with measures to protect Ulster from 'Rome' rule, the latter with Ulster as the focal point of a campaign to save the Union by destroying the credibility and undermining the authority of the government.

Traditionalist supporters of the Union were apt to deprecate the note of militant defiance on Ulster. 'I feel just as strongly as Bonar Law about Ulster', wrote Lansdowne to Chamberlain on 22 August 1912 from Derreen, 'although I should personally have used language less suggestive of readiness to carry a rifle in her defence'. In replying four days later, Austen Chamberlain took the opportunity of denying reports that he differed from Bonar Law on Ulster, though he allowed that with Lansdowne he would have expressed himself differently. Ulster, he believed, would be right to resist and if 'hard but cold as steel, government cannot go on'.[39] If that indeed were to be so, then Unionists had no need to decide where they stood – whether on Union or Ulster: but if not, the day must come when they would perforce have to make, for many of them in likely Border areas, a painful decision.

The choice had conceptual over and above political complications. In 1886 some Unionists, Joseph Chamberlain and Salisbury among them, had countered Home Rule by asserting that there were two nations in Ireland and that they could not be associated in one polity; once Home Rule had been defeated, however, Unionist policy rested on an entirely different premiss – that there was no such thing as an authentic Irish nationality. Home Rule might be killed by kindness because, and only because, Irish discontents were social. If Unionists were to credit, as for the most part they did not, the authenticity of Irish nationality, then as Balfour argued, the logical solution would be not a half-way Home Rule house but separation. Given, however, the majority Unionist premiss that there was no such thing as a distinct Irish nation, a shift from opposition to Home Rule in any shape or form to Home Rule for Ireland with exclusion for Ulster, or some part of it, required at least qualified recognition of Irish separatism.[40] But that in turn carried the further implication that if there were two nations in Ireland, English Unionists in upholding the Union against 'nationalist' Irish wishes were committing themselves to repression of a nationality, and incidentally, as it were, but by necessary consequence, conceding that their earlier policy of killing Home Rule by kindness rested upon a fundamental misconception. The new militancy obscured such conceptual differences, but did not dispel the confusion deriving from them.

The Cabinet's warning of 6 February 1912 to the Irish leaders to the effect that ministers would feel free to make changes by way of amendment of the Home Rule Bill or not pressing on with it under the Parliament Act if it became clear that special treatment should be provided for the Ulster Unionists, moved quickly from the realm of possibility to that of probability. This was the product of principle and political pressures. On the first, members of the Cabinet once persuaded of the authenticity of the minority demand, felt committed on liberal principles to give due consideration to minority representations, while keeping in the forefront of their minds the claims of the majority, who for nearly thirty years had pressed their demand for a measure of Irish self-government by constitutional means. It was at this point that political pressure was sharpest. Safeguards for the minority consistent with the unitary aspirations of the majority would have to be devised, if Asquith's professed determination not to allow 'the naked veto of an irreconcilable minority'[41] to block the road the majority wished to travel were to be upheld. It was a formidable assignment and one Asquith was not well qualified to discharge. What was lacking was not so much resolution as the appearance of resolution. To live up to his profession in the face of combined English and Ulster Unionist provocation called for a more menacing stance than came naturally to him. 'We had better wait and see',[42] Asquith had admonished his opponents in the House for the first time on 3 March in the debate on the reintroduction of the Budget after the 1910 January election. Thereafter he developed an unfortunate addiction to a phrase which was derided as expressive of proclivity to procrastination. It was not only in this respect that Asquith's qualities of balance and intellect were at a discount. He could be relied upon to sustain a cause, but less certainly to advance it. As Lloyd George in cross-party correspondence with Austen Chamberlain in 1914 was to underline, it was important for him [Chamberlain] to understand not only the Liberal point of view, but more especially the fact that 'the P.M. is under an obligation of honour to the elected representatives of the Irish people to do his best to place Home Rule on the Statute Book'.[43] This was true, but in a sense irrelevant. It was not Asquith's sense of obligation or commitment that caused concern to his Irish allies so much as his notion of what giving of his best required of him. As one of his biographers has remarked, Asquith was a man 'without initiative in ideas and in policy'.[44] Nor was he given to heartwarming words or inspiring gestures such as might have come from Campbell-Bannerman. This lack of political creativity or psychological stimulus was the more important, if, as Churchill was to remark to Austen Chamberlain in November 1913, Asquith was 'supreme' in Cabinet. 'He holds the casting vote and he thinks it unfair to use it till all have spoken.'[45] This placed the onus on consensus, not leadership and often induced uncertainty on the part of the Chief Secretary as to what should be conveyed to Redmond, or had been decided. Finally Asquith was indolent. He dealt with problems – and people – that came his way but did not seek them out. This last applied to Redmond whom he saw only rarely and then in the later phase of the developing crisis, not for an exchange of view so much as the delivery of admonition. Tactical reasons have been advanced to explain this measured distancing, but one suspects they served chiefly to provide a rationale such as Asquith desired for his every action. The cumulative effect was to make Redmond's reliance on Birrell almost complete at a time when Birrell's taste for Irish politics, never pronounced, was in perceptible decline and his oft professed wish, from which each time he was dissuaded by Asquith, was to resign.

While ultimate responsibility rested with the Prime Minister, it cannot be said that he was well served by his Chief Secretary or realistically briefed by the Irish leadership in this crisis of his Irish policies. Birrell to his credit frankly acknowledged his own inability to get inside the Ulster Unionist mind; as to what the Unionists would actually do, he remained as a result an agnostic. Redmond for his part strengthened Asquith's reluctance to steer a resolute course by affirming, as late as October 1913, that 'all the extravagant action, all the bombastic threats, are but indications that the battle is over',[46] when in fact there had been only preliminary skirmishing, while Dillon, his biographer tells us, was 'obsessed'[47] at this time, the late summer and autumn of 1913, with the theme that the Ulster Unionists were bluffing, pouring scorn on Ulster threats of civil war and saying that if they did set up their Provisional government they would soon come begging to be taken over by the Irish government proper. But such contemptuous dismissals satisfied only those who had reason to wish it to be so. Others, more perceptive than Birrell, or Redmond, or for that matter than Dillon, have failed down to this day to produce conclusive evidence of the degree to which the Orangemen with their proclamations and their demonstrations, their volunteers and their Provisional government were or were not bluffing. 'I can call spirits from the vasty deep', claimed Glendower seeking to commend himself as an ally to Hotspur, who in a rare moment of common sense, rejoined, 'Why, so can I, or so can any man; But will they come . . . ?'[48] To this day, in the case of Ulster, there is no certain answer and there can never be because circumstances for which resistance was planned, that is enforcement of a Home Rule settlement, never arose.

Redmond's belief that the Orangemen were bluffing *tout simple* was not credited by the government. To demonstrate that the Ulster Unionists overplayed their hand in extravagant gestures and blustering threats was not tantamount, though some cherished the notion, to saying that they had no hand to play. Ministers conceded that behind the histrionics there were factors of strength in the Ulster Unionist position. It was not in question that, as foreshadowed by Carson, they had made preparations for resistance. From 31 January 1913 they had the Ulster Volunteers to give point to their protest and from 17 September that year, plans for the setting up of a Provisional government to take over responsibility for the government of the province, the day the Home Rule Act was inscribed in the Statute Book. They could make an effective appeal to a wide section of the electorate by claiming they had organised resistance only because they wished to remain a part of the United Kingdom. In their stand they had the assured support of the Unionist party and its leadership.

Could the government enforce the Act against a community thus entrenched, given that military enforcement, as was widely suspected, might be resisted or subverted by Ulster Unionists' friends with hands on the levers of power, Major-General Sir Henry Wilson, Director of Military Operations at the War Office 1910–14, not least among them? The answer was surely in the affirmative. What was at issue was the question of price. That price might range from coping effectively with localised protest to civil war (not necessarily confined to Ulster). The range was important. One factor likely to go far in determining it at the moment of decision was the degree of resolution – this was a constant and a conditional factor – with which the Liberal government advanced toward their Home Rule goal and a mirror image to this, the extent to which Bonar Law, who was himself coming to speak and write of civil war in an alarmingly matter-of-fact way, was or was not prepared or able to exercise some restraining influence on the diehards. These included many unusual and some formidable figures. One of them was Lord Willoughby de Broke – who told Austen Chamberlain,[49] 'my heart sinks at the idea of being asked to abandon the Act of Union, which by common consent had given so much peace and happiness' and to avert such a frightful calamity the price to be paid for peace 'may be too great'. They also included the Cecil family, and Milner[50] who had come to entertain nothing but contempt for the 'rotten' system of parliamentary government and had launched a campaign to raise funds to promote resistance should Home Rule reach the Statute Book; he was associated with the Imperial Federationists and those Round Tablers who persisted in the notion that the distinctive Irish national claim could be submerged in an amorphous, unsought British Isles Federation.[51] Also among them was that most gifted, if also impetuous member of a younger generation, F.E. Smith, who in 1913 acted as Carson's 'galloper' at a review of the Ulster Volunteers. Most of them were anxious to pledge English conservatives to forceful, if need be, backing of an Ulster, as distinct from a Unionist (in the traditional sense), cause. The mind of the leadership was not immediately apparent: it unfolded from the autumn onwards of 1913 as the cohesion of the Liberal – Nationalist front was probed and the resolution of the Prime Minister in the face of threatened resistance was put to the ultimate test.

Party Manoeuvres on Ulster

The Ulster question acquired a sharper edge in the late summer of 1913 for the good and sufficient reason that the Home Rule Bill had completed its first two circuits under the Parliament Act, having been twice passed by the Commons and twice defeated by the Lords, the relevant dates and votes being as follows: on 16 January 1913 the Bill was carried in the House of Commons on its third reading by 367 to 257 votes and defeated in the Lords by 326 votes to 69; on 7 July 1913, at the end of its second circuit, it was again carried by the Commons and rejected a week later by the Lords. Even then Asquith continued to contend that if the Bill were to be amended, it was for the opposition, not the government, to make proposals. This the opposition was not prepared to do, basically because of indecision and divided counsel on where to take their stand. The King was anxious lest his own position be prejudiced while his ministers, as he complained to Birrell on 24 July, were 'drifting'. Nor was he content with complaint; he took the initiative and asked Bonar Law and Lansdowne, as leaders of the opposition, for their views. They responded with a memorandum on 31 July.[52] Its principal theme was the need for a dissolution before the Home Rule Bill was enacted. They contended that in the circumstances this might be effected by exercise of the royal prerogative, the King withholding the Royal Assent until he had ascertained whether it would be possible to appoint other ministers, who would advise him to allow the question to be decided at a general election. Professor A.V. Dicey lent his weighty sanction to the constitutional propriety of such a course. Asquith, however, on being consulted, gave short shrift to a proposition well calculated, in his view, to drag the sovereign into the arena of party politics and so bring about 'a constitutional catastrophe'.[53] Yet the fact that such a notion had been advanced had its importance in respect of Liberal–Nationalist relations. Asquith could, and did at a time he deemed appropriate, outline this fearful prospect to Redmond by way of extracting concessions from him. After all, an election won, despite what Bonar Law was to say, might not mean Unionist acquiescence in Home Rule, while an election lost would imperil Redmond's political existence.

The first open move as the Home Rule Bill entered its last phase came on 11 September 1913. Lord Loreburn, who had resigned as Lord

Chancellor in 1912 and until his resignation was known to have been with John Morley, one of the two members of the Cabinet most strongly committed to Home Rule, wrote a letter to *The Times* followed by a memorandum for circulation to the Cabinet, which suggested the calling of a conference of party leaders to explore the possibility of 'cooperation for the good of Ireland'. The proposal carried overtones of the abortive 1910 interparty coalition – slanted conversations designed to open the way to interparty understanding on Ireland. Loreburn himself in the memorandum alluded to the possibility of employing federal or devolutionary devices to provide safeguards for four counties. Loreburn's intervention struck a sympathetic chord in high places, but stirred Irish suspicions, in fact unfounded, of the ex-Lord Chancellor's collusion with former colleagues on motive and timing.

Politically Loreburn judged the key to be 'largely in Lansdowne's hands'.[54] In that he was mistaken. It was in those of Bonar Law, who on 18 September reported to Carson and Lansdowne separately and in slightly differing terms, on the substance of a conversation he had had with Churchill at Balmoral. In the course of it, Bonar Law said he had warned Churchill that the government's programme was impossible of fulfilment without civil war, that the Unionists would be driven by their action to make government, including government in the House of Commons, impossible and that the moment the Home Rule Bill was passed Carson would not only set up a Provisional government, but would further allow only forces controlled by that government to operate in the area. He had warned him that in England also there would be no half measures, should the Unionist party say that Ulster was right and that they should support them. He foreshadowed a situation in which the Army 'encouraged by us' would not obey orders to use force in Ulster, in which case, 'we should regard it as civil war and should urge the officers of the Army not to regard them [the Liberals] as a real government but to ignore their orders'.[55]

Asquith had few illusions about Loreburn's contemplated conference. It overlooked the fact that there was 'a deep and hitherto unbridgeable chasm of *principle*' between government and opposition on Home Rule. Should the Unionists continue to give unqualified support to the Ulster Unionists, that left as bleak alternatives abandonment of the principle of unity by the 'veiled'* or 'naked' exclusion of Ulster (or some part of it) or enforcement of that principle at the risk, in Asquith's view, of 'organised disorder' though not of civil war. The first, partition however disguised,

* In a letter to Balfour of 7 January 1914, Bonar Law recorded Asquith's use of the phrase 'the veiled exclusion of Ulster' with the implication that Asquith had coined it and that he (Bonar Law) had not heard it before. If so, its use here may be premature. See Bonar Law Papers, 34/1/8.

was 'anathema' to Redmond, the second, civil war apart, had to be faced. If the Bill were amended so as to become inadequate or postponed, the prospect was infinitely more grave. 'If the ship after so many stormy voyages', Asquith wrote, 'were now to be wrecked in sight of port, it is difficult to over-rate the shock or its consequences.' Ireland would 'become ungovernable'.[56]

The King, much worried over the situation, as Churchill reported to Asquith on 21 September, 'at which I do not wonder', favoured a conference such as Loreburn had suggested. If that were not to be and there were no settlement, he thought there should be a dissolution before the Bill was presented for the Royal Assent. Churchill indicated his dissent with vigour, outlining the likely consequences: 'an infuriated Nationalist Ireland under a Unionist coercive government which had just been organising rebellion and had got power by such means'.[57] To Asquith on 22 September the King conjured up an almost equally disturbing alternative – that of armed struggle constituting civil war between the forces of an Irish Home Rule executive and the Ulster Unionists reinforced from England, Wales, Scotland and even the colonies.[58] The essential thing was some move that might open a way out of the Irish impasse.

T.P. O'Connor, who alone of the Nationalist leadership was in London, sensed that the situation was full of disturbing possibilities. As in 1910, what confidence could they entertain that, if interparty talks there were, the Liberals could be relied upon not to respond to suggestions for compromise until after consultation and agreement with them? In the event, Lloyd George on behalf of Asquith sent for O'Connor so that he might learn of Irish reactions to Loreburn's letter – a particular possibility being that the Unionists might enter a conference if Ulster counties were to be given the option of deciding their future by plebiscite. O'Connor, who had not himself been briefed, could indulge only in speculation. Redmond at Aughavanagh on being apprised of the situation felt there was no sufficient reason for him to leave its leafy glades, while Dillon,[59] at Ballaghaderrin and much concerned with the labour disputes in Dublin, remarked that for him 'The Ulster question and the Cabinet appear dim and distant and of minor importance.' He did, however, recognise that concession of Home Rule at the price of option 'for the four counties' would make 'our position a very difficult one'.[60] Redmond's public reaction did not come until 12 October when, in a speech at Limerick, he claimed that all the argumentative opposition to Home Rule was dead. This showed an alarming complacency. On the other hand, his warning that Irish Nationalists could 'never be parties to the mutilation of the Irish nation' was a timely reminder to Liberals who were beginning to think of possible compromise in precisely that way. Redmond, also, had a memorable phrase: 'The two-nation theory is to us an abomination and a blasphemy.'[61]

Asquith–Bonar Law Talks, October–December 1913

On 8 October, Asquith, deciding a conference of leaders was out of the question in existing circumstances, proposed informal consultations between them to Bonar Law. Law assented. On 14 October 1913 the two leaders had the first of three secret meetings – the second was to be on 6 November and the third on 10 December – of which both participants left accounts substantially in accord, but with some revealing differences in presentation.[62]

On Bonar Law's account, two possibilities were explored at the first meeting – a general election on Home Rule, as the Unionists demanded, and the exclusion of Ulster from the jurisdiction of a Home Rule parliament. Asquith dismissed the first – what purpose would be served by it when Carson had stated that Ulster would resist whatever the outcome? To this Bonar Law replied that while the Unionist party was pledged 'to support Ulster to the utmost if there were no Election, that pledge was contingent, and if an Election took place and the Government won, our support would be withdrawn'. And he added a point of long-term significance: 'Mr. Asquith must understand as well as I did that this made all the difference, and that it was really the certainty of British support which made the strength of the Ulster resistance.' Nor did he refrain once again from indicating to Asquith the lengths to which the Unionist party would go, ranging from the possibility of disorder in parliament and 'as a result of all this of his [Bonar Law] finding that the Army would not obey orders'. At this, Asquith, according to Bonar Law's account, evinced mild surprise that 'we had pledged ourselves definitely to support Ulster in resistance'. Neither professed to be happy about 'exclusion', Bonar Law frankly admitting that if the question of Ulster were removed 'one of the strongest points in our favour in an election would be gone and our chance of winning it would . . . be diminished'. He was, however, willing to throw the Southern Unionists 'to the Wolves' unless there was a general outcry led by Lansdowne; if they were unanimous in regarding this as a betrayal that 'would make any action on our part impossible'. Asquith indicated greater readiness to distance himself from his Irish allies. The government, he said, was by no means absolutely dependent on the Nationalists. Unionists 'were in the habit of speaking of him as absolutely dependent on the Irish, but as a matter of fact, it was really the other way; that the Nationalists without the support of the Liberal Party were powerless, and that if . . . the Government decided on any course which commanded the support of their own party the Nationalists would have no choice but to accept it.'

These were pointers to consideration of a deal on the basis of exclusion of Ulster coupled with concession of Home Rule for the rest of Ireland. But while there was a sense almost of convergence in principle, this did not extend to the question of the area to be excluded. Asquith spoke of 'the North-east counties'. Bonar Law noted that 'it was quite evident . . . that he had in his mind only the four counties' but 'I was afraid of that line of discussion' and 'I passed from that subject without going into it at all'. Why, Bonar Law explained in his covering letter to Lansdowne. He deduced that Asquith's next move would be to sound the Nationalists and with their acquiescence secured, there would then be 'a very great danger' that the Unionists would be invited to a conference and be confronted with a proposal to exclude Ulster 'reasonable' in definition: four counties remaining in the Union and a plebiscite in the two doubtful ones, all of which Carson could not possibly accept as a solution and 'yet it is so reasonable that we would . . . be in a hopeless position if we had to refuse it'. The best thing that could happen, therefore, was that Asquith should find the Nationalists 'irreconcilable' and that as a result there would be no conference.

Asquith's account of the talk has the merit of giving greater precision to the definition of the principal issues at stake. According to it, he put the following points to Bonar Law for elucidation. First he asked him whether he was prepared to throw the Unionist minority in the South and West to the wolves? To this Bonar Law's reply was 'yes', unless a substantial minority of the sheep were found to protest. Then Asquith asked what did Bonar Law mean by Ulster? The whole province? The four north-eastern counties? The four north-eastern counties plus perhaps Tyrone and one other? The reply was that this might be left over, but Bonar Law thought the whole province in the first instance. To the last question, on whether exclusion was to be permanent or subject from the outset to an option of inclusion, the answer was in favour of the latter.

In an agreed summary of the first Asquith–Bonar Law exchange of view, it was recorded that while the Unionist party continued to have the defeat of Home Rule as its first priority, its leaders were agreed that if there were not a general outcry in the South and West, and if Ulster (undefined in respect of area and called X) were left out of the Bill, then they would not feel bound to prevent the granting of Home Rule to the rest of Ireland. While, therefore, the Unionist party had not abandoned its nominal first priority, the defeat of Home Rule, dwindling hopes of realising it were bringing the secondary purpose of safeguarding Ulster into first place and with it the need to define the area referred to as X in Bonar Law's report. This indeed was becoming the crucial issue. Austen Chamberlain, a good barometer of Unionist opinion, commented on 2 November in a letter to Lansdowne:

I assume that Carson could not touch anything short of the exclusion of six counties and that nothing less than this would avert civil strife; and though I think that to carry this Bill with this change only . . . would be little short of disastrous, I do not hesitate to say that it would be infinitely better than the Bill as it stands not only for Ulster but also for Southern Loyalists and for the United Kingdom . . . .[63]

Why it would be better for the Southern Loyalists he did not explain, no doubt realising it was a useful but groundless assertion.

The Asquith–Bonar Law meeting on 6 November, its importance discounted by the latter, served to bring one point into sharper focus. If there were to be a compromise, both party leaders were agreed that it would be the Nationalists who would have to make the necessary concessions. The two were, furthermore, nearer agreement on what those concessions should be. Bonar Law's theme was that if there were to be any suggestion of a settlement at all 'it was utterly useless' unless and until the Ulstermen were satisfied that after any new settlement they would be left in precisely the same position as the people of England and Scotland. That meant leaving Ulster as part of the United Kingdom. And what was meant by Ulster? Carson spoke of the whole province, but when Asquith put it to Bonar Law that it would be impossible to include essentially nationalist counties, Bonar Law cautiously rejoined that Carson might be so persuaded, but unquestionably the very minimum Carson would accept would be the six plantation counties. For the rest of the conversation, recorded Bonar Law, it was assumed, though Asquith had withheld specific concurrence, that by Ulster was meant the six counties. If this indeed were so, and other evidence bears out the impression, then this was the moment when the debate on area was lost and won. Bonar Law for his part took out a reinsurance policy as well. He said that in no circumstances would the Unionist party accept responsibility for a settlement on the basis of the exclusion of the six counties for a period to be terminable only at the wish of the people of Ulster expressed in a plebiscite. But the most they might say was that much as they disliked it, they were willing 'to submit to it rather than face civil war'. Both leaders agreed that a necessary condition would be an undertaking by Lord Lansdowne to ease the passage of any such amendment to the Home Rule Bill through the Lords. As to the Nationalists, Asquith reflected: 'Redmond and the "Old Guard" realise that this is their last chance, and that they must choose between such a settlement and nothing.' Bonar Law, however, subsequently confided to Balfour that if Asquith could not bring the Nationalists into line he would be 'in a very bad way, while we shall be in a very good position'.[64]

Bonar Law asked Asquith 'what is the next step?' Asquith replied that it was for him (Asquith) to lay a proposal before the Cabinet. In the event it was formulated not by Asquith but by Lloyd George at a Cabinet meeting on 13 November. As Asquith reported with studied detachment to the King, Lloyd George suggested amendment of the Bill so as to concede temporary exclusion, but with automatic inclusion after a period of three years. This, Lloyd George had contended, had two distinct advantages: (1) no one could support or sympathise with the violent resistance of Ulster to a change which would in no way affect them for some years to come, and (2) before the automatic inclusion of Ulster took place, there would be two general elections, which would give the British electorate experience of the actual working of Home Rule in the rest of Ireland.[65]

His calculation was that the Ulstermen could not mobilise their forces in 1914 against a situation that would not come into existence until 1917 or even 1919, by which time hopefully their organisation would be in the process of disintegration. Nothing in retrospect seems more improbable. Who, on a moment's reflection, could think of the Ulster Unionists peacefully surrendering what they had been authorised to hold, irrespective of whether that was for three, five or six years?

Asquith took soundings of Redmond on 17 November 1913.[66] His theme was the likelihood, in the event of no agreement and given the escalating preparations for resistance in Ulster, of a 'bloody prologue' to Home Rule. How was it to be averted or at least delayed? By the exclusion of Ulster for five or six years and then for it to be automatically included? Redmond was alarmed. He could conceive of no proposal which would array against it a more united body of sentiment in Ireland, both North and South. Yet he made one ill-advised concession. If the proposal was put forward by Bonar Law, he might look at it – otherwise he could not entertain it for a moment: it would split the party from top to bottom.

On 24 November Redmond further indicated in a letter to Asquith his anxieties on these or similar tactical moves. Exclusion, 'apart from its mutilation of Ireland would', he told Asquith, 'expose our people in Ulster to intolerable oppression'. Bonar Law, he believed, could have been forced to make an offer but for the 'unfortunate intervention of well-intentioned mediators'. Asquith, after consulting the Cabinet, replied that there was no question 'at this stage of our making any "offer" or "proposal"' but adding, 'We must, of course, keep our hands free . . . to take such a course as then in all the circumstances seems best calculated to safeguard the fortunes of Home Rule.'[67]

On 27 November Churchill sounded out Chamberlain on board the yacht *Enchantress* about the basis of any possible compromise.[68] Churchill stated, correctly as the Prime Minister's record of the Cabinet meeting on 6 February 1912 testified, that he had never ruled out the possibility of exclusion – *never*. 'Of course Redmond hated it, but they were not absolutely bound to Redmond. . . . They would not allow Ulster to veto Home Rule but they had never excluded the possibility of separate treatment for Ulster.' There were, he went on, three ways of dealing with Ulster: (1) Home Rule within Home Rule; (2) exclusion for a fixed term, say, two general elections must have intervened and then inclusion if parliament had not otherwise decided in the mean time; (3) exclusion till Ulster voted herself in with provision for a vote in five or ten years. Chamberlain replied that it was useless to enter into discussion other than on the basis of the third course listed above: 'exclusion until Ulster voted for inclusion'. This was tantamount to a demand for partition in perpetuity. 'My root objection', Chamberlain told Churchill, 'is to the idea of Ireland a Nation. That was separatism and must end in separation.' Churchill countered by saying that in turn was tantamount to denying to Irish sentiment any sense of national satisfaction in the enjoyment of its parliament and would be a mistake. Chamberlain's impression was that Churchill, like Lloyd George, Grey and Asquith, wanted a settlement but 'as to the means they have no clear ideas'.

On 10 December Asquith conveyed to Bonar Law the news that the proposal favoured by the Cabinet was that Ulster should be excluded for a definite term of years and come in automatically at the end of it. Bonar Law dismissed this out of hand as unacceptable and 'hopeless'. There was no possibility except on the basis of the exclusion of Ulster full stop. There followed some weeks of playing for position with Asquith and, more forcefully, Lloyd George seeking to soften up Redmond, chiefly by reference to the growing concern of the King about the risk of civil war in Ulster.[69] Yet the most disquieting thing left on Redmond's mind was that Lloyd George thought that in the last resort 'we would agree to anything rather than face the break up of the government'. Redmond was especially fearful of a formal government initiative that would stir deep resentment at home, and then be spurned by Carson and Bonar Law. If offered exclusion of counties by plebiscite for a period of three years, would they not reject it scornfully with a demand for six, but if six were offered, would not the nine be claimed and with no time limit, if Ulster were offered, why then would they not fall back on the sanctity of the Union, a position which had never been explicitly abandoned?

Exclusion in any form, as Redmond well knew, would be bitterly resented by party members, while Unionist acquiescence in Home Rule remained ostensibly conditional, so far as the English Unionist party was concerned, on Bonar Law's being ready to 'ditch' his co-leader Lansdowne whose Unionism, tinctured with anti-Belfast bourgeois/working-class sentiment, was increasingly marked by pronounced anti-partitionist views. What merit had safeguards in Antrim for a landowner in Kerry? Moreover were the prospects of a package on these lines – exclusion with Home Rule – to become known, there would be, so Bonar Law had advised Stamfordham in October, 'a wild outburst of resentment against us in the South of Ireland which would be reflected with almost equal violence in England', while Lloyd George told Redmond that Carson and Craig had warned Bonar Law that if anything of the kind became known 'it would raise hell in Ulster and destroy every chance of success'.[70] That suggested, since secrecy on such a matter could hardly be preserved, that notions of a *quid pro quo* were as likely as not to result in yet more uncompromising confrontation. What then remained as seen from Westminster?

The members of the Cabinet were not so much divided as uncertain in their own minds about the nature and extent of any offer that should be made to secure Unionist acquiescence in Home Rule – or, failing that, such as would spike Unionist electoral guns by depriving them of a reasonable case on which to fight the election which they so vociferously demanded. Should it be made conditional upon Nationalist party acquiescence? If that were forthcoming, or indeed in any event, should the offer be made formally in the House on the second reading or should it be negotiated first behind the scenes? And what should be the substance of the offer? It seemed of little use, in view of Unionists' outright rejection as posited by Bonar Law and Chamberlain, to proceed with Home Rule within Home Rule, that is devolution of authority from Dublin to a subordinate administration in Belfast, despite its appeal to Nationalists. That left the alternatives of exclusion of an area yet to be determined from the jurisdiction of a Home Rule parliament for a period of years, that period to be of three, five or six years' duration, with inclusion at the end of it or inclusion for a period likewise yet to be determined with the option of exclusion at the end of it. Should the area to be excluded be determined by the wishes of the electorate or should parliament decide upon a unit, whether four counties or six or the whole province of Ulster to be excluded *en bloc* as Carson was known to favour? In sum, there were many possible concessions and their variety gave tempting scope for manoeuvre and deferment of decision. Nor was it an abstract question of which of the options might be deemed the most fitting in the interests of the population: it was rather a question of which reflected most nearly the balance of complex forces, and a right judgement on the weight to be attached to threats of force almost daily uttered in the marketplace.

As an organised body the Ulster Defence Force dated from 31 January 1913: Professor Eoin MacNeill's article 'The North Began' urging the formation of a national counterpart was published on 1 November that year. On 25 November the Irish Volunteers were formed with the Ulster Volunteers as the model. Redmond did not, however, welcome the creation of this nationalist counterpart on general as well as particular grounds. His biographer tells us he distrusted every sort of spontaneous political organisation, while at the deeper level of principle he remained committed to the constitutional course long since charted. Nevertheless he had become vulnerable to initiatives north or south by those whose allegiance to constitutional practice at least was qualified, at most non-existent. The foundations of Redmond's leadership were thus being eroded from within as well as without, at a time when decisions that would go far to shape any new settlement could not for long be deferred, with the Home Rule Bill scheduled to complete its third and last parliamentary circuit before enactment by late summer of 1914.

Pressure for Concessions by Redmond

Anyone disposed to think that the Asquith–Law talks or Lloyd George's procrastinating propositions had served a moderating purpose would do well to glance at Bonar Law's letter to Stamfordham of 26 January 1914. 'In our belief', he wrote, 'there are now only two courses open to the Government – either they must submit their Bill to the judgement of the people or prepare for the consequences of civil war'. He added a shaft aimed at Asquith to the effect that it would be a great misfortune if the government were led to believe there was any hope of the dangers threatening the country being removed by delay. On the first of these two courses, the government were under strong counter-pressure from among their own ranks, concerned lest the intentions of the Parliament Act be flouted by the calling of yet another election: on the second, in so far as ministers credited the threat of civil war, they believed it might be averted not indeed by procrastination but by concessions. To be effective, it was thought that such concessions would have to be substantial and explicit. In late January 1914 the King, restating his view that the Ulster Unionists would never send representatives to a Dublin parliament whatever the safeguards, pointed to the disturbing effect of making concessions allegedly final which did not take account of this.[71] In conjunction these representations from opposition and monarch, near-coincidental in time, at the least impressed on the government the need to ensure their freedom of action by obtaining concessions from Redmond. How they were to be obtained may best be judged from Redmond's record of what the Prime Minister conveyed to him on 2 February, the eve of the new parliamentary session. What a change in relationship since 1910 is there disclosed!

Redmond's memorandum reads:[72]

> Mr. Asquith told me that he desired to let me know everything that had occurred since his interview with me last November. He said he had had repeated interviews with Mr. Bonar Law, and three interviews with Sir Edward Carson; that of the two he had found Sir Edward Carson much the most [sic] satisfactory to deal with.* These gentlemen

---

* Asquith had already been reported by Churchill as finding Bonar Law easier to deal with than Balfour. If therefore this were a mathematical proposition, one would expect him to find Carson even more satisfactory to deal with than Balfour. But he did not and one suspects that after Carson's 'stay of execution' speech the following month, Asquith was likely to have adjusted his opinion of dealing with Carson sharply downwards.

maintained their position obstinately that nothing short of the total exclusion of Ulster from the Home Rule Bill could lead to a settlement by consent.

Mr. Asquith informed me that he and his colleagues were all firmly opposed to the exclusion of Ulster, or any part of Ulster even temporarily. They had come to the conclusion that a temporary exclusion on the part of Ulster would have the most disastrous results on Ireland. He informed me that he had made no offer to Messrs Bonar Law and Carson, but that he had tentatively made suggestions to them, none of which they seriously discussed.

He informed me that the general situation had undergone a very unfavourable change since he saw me in November, and that it would be necessary for him when challenged, as he was sure he would be in the debate on the Address, to announce what concessions the government were willing to offer Ulster in exchange for a settlement by consent. He began by assuring me that the government had no intention of hauling down the flag or of abandoning their determination to pass the Home Rule Bill, but he felt it his duty to point out to me explicitly the grave danger which menaced the government. He told me a very serious crisis had arisen with regard to the Navy Estimates. . . .

[Still more serious was the position that had arisen with regard to the attitude of the King.★ He assured me that the King was not in the smallest degree hostile to Home Rule, and had repeatedly stated so, and that no one would be more delighted than the King would be if the matter could be arranged by consent. The King however has become thoroughly convinced of the reality of the Civil War threat, and has pressed the Government very hard for a General Election before the commencement of this Session.

The King admits that Home Rule was before the Electors at the last Election, but says that at that election no one believed for a moment that Home Rule could cause Civil War, or anything approaching to it, and that if they had known what has since occurred, they might have voted differently. He argued that before making himself responsible for the passage of Home Rule, he must be assured that he had his people behind him. The King never contemplated, and does not contemplate,

---

★ This and part of the following paragraph on the King's attitude are omitted from Denis Gwynn, *The Life of John Redmond* (London, 1932), pp. 250–2 without indication of any such omission. This has led to the assertion that the memorandum is reproduced in full. The point is of some importance; for Asquith the concern of the King was an integral part in the softening-up process of 2 February. It was Asquith's bombshell. King George V was alive and Gwynn may have felt precluded from reproducing this reference to his views, in accord with rules then prevailing.

refusing the Royal Assent to the Home Rule Bill, if passed through the House of Commons the third time under the Parliament Act, but he clearly intimated that he considered his power of dismissing his Minister[s] as was done in 1834, as a course open to him, and one which he might feel called upon to adopt. Mr Asquith said that he would not himself have been astonished if the King had taken this course before the opening of Parliament, but he took it for granted that he would not do so now. Contingencies may arise, however, and in Mr Asquith's opinion were likely to arise in which it was quite conceivable that the King would dismiss his Ministers and send for the Leaders of the Unionist Party to form a Government. This of course would lead to an immediate dissolution, but the serious thing would be that, even if the Liberals were elected again at the General Election, the sequence of the Parliament Act would have been broken, the last two years would have been wasted, and the work would have to be begun all over again. This the government was determined to avert by every means in their power.]† Mr. Asquith said he had reason to believe that the crisis might arise on the Army Annual Bill. This Bill must be passed into law by a certain date in March or April, otherwise the Army is disbanded, and there is no power to pay it or continue it in existence. He expects the Opposition in the House of Commons will take up the position that they won't sanction the Army Bill until they know how the Army is going to be used in Ulster. He thinks they will fight the Army Bill in the House of Commons, and possibly resort to extreme disorder of such a character that, [probably with the connivance of the Speaker,] the whole business of the House will be held up. [In such an event, he believes the King would act in the manner indicated. Further than this, even if the Army Bill were passed through the House of Commons, it would be open to the House of Lords to reject it, a course they would be very likely to pursue, in which case the King would probably meet the deadlock in the manner already indicated.]

These considerations have led Mr. Asquith to the conclusion that for the safety of Home Rule it is essential that he should make an offer to Ulster of such a character that in the event of their refusal of it, and he thinks at this stage any offer he makes short of the exclusion of Ulster would be rejected, it would deprive them of all moral force, [and would avert any action by the King.]

The offer Asquith had in mind contemplated local administrative control in Ulster and a right of appeal on the part of the majority of its members to the Imperial Parliament against the application of legislation passed by the Irish Parliament on subjects to be defined. Redmond placed

† Passages in brackets not reprinted in Gwynn, *op.cit.*

his surprise and dismay on record. He had contemplated large concessions in an agreed Bill, so long as they were consistent with the creation of an Irish Parliament.

Asquith wrote to Venetia Stanley the next day: 'I had Birrell with me at the Leviathan interview. I developed the situation with such art as I could muster, until the psychological moment arrived for discharging my bomb [reference to a possible Lords' amendment to the Army Act so as to force a dissolution or leave the government without military presence]. My visitor shivered visibly and was a good deal perturbed . . . '.[73] Well he might be! On 5 February he replied not without dignity but from a position of manifest weakness reaffirming his conviction first that the risk of civil war in Ulster had been gravely exaggerated and second that any announcement of concessions would have a disastrous effect on the position of the Nationalist party and would be regarded as a 'betrayal of the Nationalists of Ulster'. He then reiterated his readiness to consider all proposals consistent 'with an Irish Parliament, an Irish Executive, and the integrity of Ireland'.[74] But while his reply was to the point, as Asquith acknowledged, Birrell noted that Redmond was shaken. Nor was the news Birrell later conveyed on the wisdom or otherwise of a detailed statement on concessions of a reassuring character. He reported with familiar emphasis, '*Great difference of opinion disclosed*' in Cabinet.[75] The immediate outcome, however, was as Redmond wished.

In the debate on the Address, no concessions were offered by the government but Bonar Law restated the minimal Unionist demand which, if met, would remove the resistance of Ulster, in the concluding sentence of his speech in reply. It was either exclusion or an election.[76] The Prime Minister conceded neither, but gave an undertaking to table definite suggestions for meeting the case of Ulster. This undertaking was conditional upon the extraction of concrete concessions from Redmond forthwith, the more so because of the King's positive reaffirmation of his view that Ulster could in no circumstances be placed under a Dublin parliament.[77] Asquith was thus faced with the question once put to Job: 'Canst thou draw out Leviathan with an hook?'

Concessions and their Rejection

The first move was made by Lloyd George. He was of the opinion that any concession must have two essential characteristics: (1) it must be an offer the rejection of which would put the Unionists in the wrong as far as British public opinion was concerned; and (2) it must not involve any alteration in the scheme of the Bill. In Lloyd George's view only one suggestion would meet these two desiderata – his own of November 1913. This would allow any county that desired to contract out to do so by plebiscite for a period of years as yet indeterminate, but necessarily beyond the next election, which in peacetime conditions could not have been later than December 1915.[78] On 2 March, Redmond responded with a statement of Irish views. The party, he said, was ready 'to take considerable risks' in allowing forward for discussion proposals that they knew 'will be both unwelcome and disappointing' to their people. Of the solutions that had been suggested, Redmond felt that Home Rule within Home Rule which he greatly preferred having been ruled out, a plan proposed by Sir Horace Plunkett, the essential feature of which was that the Ulster counties should be in at the outset but be allowed to vote themselves *out* of the jurisdiction of a Home Rule parliament after ten years would, if it could be carried by consent, be 'far and away the best of the suggested settlements'. But it had not got under way and they were left with the third possibility, that of conceding the right of any county in Ulster to vote itself temporarily out of the jurisdiction of the Irish Parliament. This was urged upon them as 'best suited to the existing situation, and as offering the best tactical advantages'. In Redmond's view the option should be limited to three years, during which time a general election would take place and should be given effect by a suspensory clause providing that the Bill should not apply to the counties contracting out, but should otherwise remain unaltered. 'To sum up', read the crucial sentence, 'we are ready to give our acquiescence to the solution – of the standing out for three years by option of the counties of Ulster and to recommend it as the price of peace to our people'. In return for readiness to make this concession, Redmond asked for an assurance that 'this will be the last word of the Government'.[79]

The Cabinet met on 4 March and Asquith gave Redmond the assurance he asked for 'without tying our hands in regard to matters of detail, which might reasonably form the subject and accommodation of further negotiations'.[80] The King, who had earlier observed that Home Rule within Home Rule would not suffice to satisfy the Ulstermen, now indicated his grave fears 'that the proposed limit of three years will not be acceptable to Ulster'.[81] He thought that would also be Carson's view. Asquith thereupon deputed Birrell to explain to Redmond that he (Asquith) had difficulty in making his argument complete unless the limit of three years on exclusion were extended. 'Any extension of these years' (the three), replied Redmond on 6 March, 'about which we thought we had come to an understanding, will very much increase our difficulties and cause the deepest disappointment. Of course, we regard it as absolutely essential that a definite period should be fixed and that there should be an understanding that that period should not be extended under any circumstances.' Asquith replied with some bland observations on the lack of close scrutiny of the timetable for elections which had resulted in insufficiently grounded calculations. 'It is essential', he now wrote to that argument to show that such an Election *must* (not only may) intervene before the expiration of the term. The following table of extreme, but possible, dates shows that no term of less than six years would satisfy this condition:

Home Rule Bill becomes an Act	June 1914
Irish Parlt meets	June 1915
Dissoln of present U.K. Parlt	October 1915
Dissoln of following U.K. Parlt	October 1920
6 years expires	June 1921

A term of five years would (or *might*) expire in June 1920, i.e. before the General Election in the United Kingdom.[82]

A period first indeterminate, then formulated as three, had been thus lengthened to five and now at the last to six years.

On 9 March, when moving for the third time the second reading of the Home Rule Bill, Asquith announced the government's concession under which any county might by a majority of its electors vote itself out of the jurisdiction of a Home Rule parliament for six years,[83] at the expiry of which it would come in unless the Imperial Parliament otherwise decided. 'There was', Asquith told Venetia Stanley, 'a huge crowd, but I did not count to excite them: so I adopted a rather funereal tone'.[84] If this was intended to keep the temperature low, it failed signally. Asquith's olive branch – 'the very extremest limit of concession' as Redmond described it – was rejected with contempt. 'We do not want sentence', declaimed Carson in one of the memorable phrases in debates not lacking in oratorical purple, 'with a stay of execution for six years'. And for good measure, he discounted all prospect of settlement on the basis of Home Rule for the rest of Ireland as against concession for Ulster – 'we will never agree to the sacrifice of the people of the south and west, whatever may be the benefits which may be offered to Ulster'.[85] At a more prosaic level, he commented on an administrative problem in the scheme which had been insufficiently, if at all, regarded by others. It was, he said, fantastic to think of setting up a whole system of government for Ulster for a period of six years and then dismantling it with uncertainty clouding the intervening period. But, of course, the timetable was at no point a serious proposition. Carson need not worry, said Tim Healy, 'having allowed themselves to be hustled and bustled all along the line . . . having "swallowed" so much, the government will not hesitate now to take the last jump or the final gulp'.[86] That other Nationalist freelance, William O'Brien,[87] claimed that Bonar Law had emerged triumphant in what Redmond had called 'a gigantic game of bluff' in securing 'the official recognition of his new Orange Free State'. Was O'Brien right? Asquith's assurances of 'temporary amputation' (a less than felicitous choice of words)* not permanent mutilation, carried no more conviction in politics than in medicine. After two years of political probing and manoeuvre what was really at issue was the nature of exclusion: whether naked or veiled, whether four, six or nine counties to be determined by county option or *en bloc* by government decree – for good or for a fixed period of three, five or six years, with Carson's 'stay of execution'. Asquith's offer of county option, however much the Unionists might declaim against it in parliament, was the concession which Bonar Law had earlier feared, because it might commend itself to the British electorate. That, by March 1914, was a cause for yet more vehement denunciation. The Covenanters' campaign could not be allowed to peter out by democratic process in a four-county enclave. Only, therefore, if the government were prepared and in a position to use force could such a compromise be envisaged.

The King had entertained, and Bonar Law voiced with some frequency, doubts about the Army's readiness to use force against Ulstermen protesting against the imposition of Home Rule upon those who wished only to remain citizens in all respects equal and at one with those in Scotland, Wales or England. The events that have gone down to history as the Curragh 'Mutiny' cast further doubt upon the resolution of a government which had only imperfect control of the Army. As a result, soon after the humiliations of debate – one has only to peruse those on the second reading of the Bill in March, disregarding the misleading gloss supplied in Asquith's letters to Venetia Stanley, to sense them – came a loss of credibility in capacity to govern such as governments rarely survive. In Ireland with the Curragh incident, framed against an already manifest and continuing inequality of treatment as between Ulster and National Volunteers in respect of the import of arms, it was destined never to be restored. For that first responsibility rests with the government and secondary responsibility with Sir Edward Carson, widely admired and then imitated in the most reckless of his gestures. The realities behind them, however, still remained untested.

In June Augustine Birrell visited Ulster and made further appraisal of opinion there. He noted the conviction of Unionists everywhere in Ireland that there would have to be a general election before anything of any real political consequence happened in respect of Home Rule. This was

---

* In October 1913 Redmond had given a hostage to fortune in declaring that 'Irish Nationalists can never be assenting parties to the mutilation of the Irish nation.'

a matter of political instinct reinforced by English Unionist assurances
that electoral victory would get rid of Home Rule altogether. Until this
contingency was removed from the realm of probability it was, in Birrell's
opinion, impossible to measure the full fighting force of the Covenanters.
There could be no question about their courage, their being well armed
and well drilled, but save among 'the most furious "No Popery" men . . .
the feeling is universal throughout Ireland that the exclusion of any part of
Ulster is both hateful and impossible, and I am certain that, but for the
belief that a general election may get rid of the Home Rule Bill altogether,
this opinion would in Ulster itself have been publicly and vehemently
expressed'. Birrell believed that the government's concessions offered no
solution to the difficulties of the situation. As and when the Bill became
law 'the Carsonite leaders would find it very difficult . . . to postpone
doing something', but what their particular sort of rebellion would prove
to be 'nobody I met knew'. But unless there was agreement on a dissolution 'I am certain that Sir Edward Carson will be compelled . . . to raise
the flag somehow or another in Belfast whenever the unamended Home
Rule Bill becomes law'.[88]

The Buckingham Palace Conference and the Pre-war Balance

The summer sequel to the March debates and the Curragh incident provided the epilogue to the legislative history of Home Rule. There was no
progress on substantive issues but in May, Asquith came to an under-
standing with Bonar Law on procedure. They agreed that any changes to
be made in the Home Rule Bill should be made, not by amendment to the
Bill, but by incorporation in a separate amending Bill to receive the Royal
Assent on the same day as the Home Rule Bill. Accordingly, on 23 June a
Government of Ireland (Amendment) Bill was introduced in the House of
Lords by Lord Crewe, Lord Privy Seal[89] on the lines indicated by the
Prime Minister on 9 March[90] – that is by temporarily excluding an area in
Ulster to be determined by county option from the jurisdiction of a Home
Rule government. It had a rough reception. On 8 July an amendment to
the Amending Bill was moved by Lord Lansdowne. He desired to see the
Irish nation one and undivided under the British flag and found exclu-
sion wholly bad and detestable, but rather less bad and detestable than it
would be without the amendment standing in his name, making exclusion
permanent for all nine counties of Ulster without plebiscite or timetable.[91]
This was duly passed. Government tactics had failed ignominiously.
The alternatives remained, as before, enforcement, further concession or
dissolution of parliament, no longer inconceivably through the exercise
of the royal prerogative, leaving the Liberals to fight an election at a
time when by-elections indicated their fortunes were in decline. On the
King's initiative, a conference was called. It was designed to serve a time-

honoured purpose of conferences and committees – that of delaying the day of decision. So much it achieved – and no more.

Two representatives of each party attended the Buckingham Palace Conference which opened on 21 July – Asquith and Lloyd George (the latter included in place of Crewe at the instance of the Irish) for the government, Bonar Law and Lansdowne for the Unionists, Redmond and Dillon for the Nationalists, Carson and Craig for the Ulster Unionists. There was no secretariat and no official minutes were drafted. But two members of the conference, Bonar Law and Redmond, made personal records,[92] which in essentials are in agreement. Of the two, Redmond's is the fuller and more formal, Bonar Law's the better at recapturing illuminating incident. Asquith's impressions may be gleaned from his letters to Venetia Stanley. It appears it was the first time he had fully grasped the significance of Tyrone, 'that most damnable creation of the perverted ingenuity of man'. 'I have rarely felt more hopeless in any practical affair' was Asquith's conclusion.

At the outset of the conference, Asquith identified the two outstanding points as area and time limit for exclusion. Area, the Unionists dissenting, was taken first: time limit touched upon but never considered. Carson pressed for the exclusion of all Ulster and when Redmond said that was 'quite impossible', he demanded 'a clean cut' excluding a *block* consisting of the six counties of Antrim, Down, Armagh, Derry, Tyrone and Fermanagh, including Derry City and Belfast, all to vote as one unit, to remain under the Imperial Parliament but to have administrative responsibility for their own affairs. Redmond said that this could not be seriously considered. Any area to be excluded could only be on the basis of the people's wishes. He submitted a detailed breakdown of community allegiance based on detailed delimitation by district. In a memorandum circulated to the conference, the Irish party's view, if partition there should be, was that the only principle of division was that 'those districts should be excluded in which the population was predominantly Unionist, and those districts should be included in which the population was predominantly Nationalist'. In principle, this was unacceptable to Carson who had earlier and rhetorically enquired whether Ulster Protestants were going to abandon men 'in another county just because there may be a majority here or a majority there'. To take out districts, he told the conference, would be 'absurd'. The people of Ulster would not control Catholics: they would remain under the jurisdiction of Westminster. A change in government would be justifiable only 'where the difference of population was absolutely preponderating'. His solution was the exclusion of the whole province and then in a reasonable period of time Ulster was more likely to be willing to come into a United Ireland.

According to Bonar Law's account, Redmond and Dillon admitted that if they were free agents that was a plan they would adopt – but they were not and it was absolutely out of the question. Lloyd George suggested the division of Tyrone. Both the Irish parties found this unacceptable. On the assumption that everything else was settled the Speaker proposed that Tyrone be excluded for two years and then its future decided in a plebiscite. At this, according to Bonar Law's account, 'we looked at each other in silence for some time', all perhaps that an uncomprehending English intervention merited. Time limit was not discussed but, according to Bonar Law, Redmond and Dillon implied that they would give way on it but would not say so unless agreement was reached on area. Asquith advised the King to the same effect, that is that the government was going ahead with county option but with the omission of automatic inclusion after a term of years. 'The Irish,' Churchill had added, 'acquiesced in this reluctantly'.[93] For them that was becoming only too familiar – but if partition there was to be, they were not to do as well again.

On the same day, 24 July, Austria's ultimatum to Serbia was delivered. Was there a hint of relief in Asquith's comment? 'We are within measurable or unimaginable distance of a real Armageddon which would dwarf the Ulster and Nationalist Volunteers to their true proportions.'[94] On 30 July, in view of the deteriorating international situation, Craig suggested to Carson that an offer to postpone the Amending Bill would be most patriotic and might greatly disconcert the Nationalists. Bonar Law concurred, the Prime Minister was hurriedly invited to Bonar Law's detached Bayswater villa (where he speculated on the possibility of his being kidnapped by Ulster Volunteers) and later, after consultation with his colleagues, accepted the Unionist offer. Accordingly, consideration of the Lords' Amendment was not proceeded with, though desultory attempts at compromise continued on familiar lines. 'Evidently Asquith', wrote Selborne on 12 August 1914, 'is going to try once more to persuade Redmond to agree to the complete exclusion of the six counties before 28 August' (when parliament would rise). But as Selborne himself allowed, this was impossible for Redmond. Perhaps another conference, he reflected, might reach a settlement on the basis of Redmond being given his Act but with the six counties excluded as a temporary measure though 'the exclusion of the six counties would be statutorily no more temporary than the Act'.[95] The King, wrote Lord Stamfordham on 14 August,[96] feels it will be nothing short of 'a national disaster' if agreement is not arrived at. 'Would Ulster', he enquired, 'accept the Exclusion of the four counties plus half of Fermanagh and the whole of Tyrone?' Two days later, he reverted to the point. Should not the opposition, he enquired, 'try and decide upon a *minimum* which would be acceptable to them as excluded territories? . . . $5\frac{1}{2}$ would that not be acceptable?' The answer was in the negative. On 11 August the Colonial Secretary, Lewis Harcourt, ruled out settlement on the basis of exclusion of the six counties as 'not humanly possible' and, as the only solution envisaged, enactment of the Home Rule

Bill with operation postponed for say a year, on the argument that that was what would have happened but for the war.[97] Agreement on the fate of the Bill was as hard to come by as agreement on its content.

In Ireland, with the onset of war, the balance had moved perceptibly to the Ulster Unionist side. In the pre-war years they had seized the initiative in organisation of volunteers, importation of arms, planning for a Provisional Government. The Nationalists had admiringly followed in the case of the first two, but without benefit of the turning of a blind British eye in respect of the second. The consequence of that unequal start was that attention was progressively focused on what the Ulster Unionists might accept, rather than on what the Nationalists would, or might reasonably be expected to, concede. In politico-constitutional terms this imbalance is reflected in the two or more years' retreat from the unitary Home Rule settlement of the Irish question formulated in the Home Rule Bill as introduced in April 1912, to consideration of its amendement. First this was so as to exclude four counties from its operation, then to exclude an area as yet undefined with a time limit, then the tacit discounting of the time limit. Finally, immediately pre-war by way of counter to the Liberal–Nationalist concession of county option, there was the exclusion of six counties as a block, with no plebiscitary determination of boundary and without assurance that the demand for the exclusion of the whole nine counties of Ulster had been discarded. How had this come about?

The answer of the revisionist school of historians is by a combination on the one hand of miscalculations by the Liberal government, chief among them being their failure to outline the concessions they were prepared to make in the Bill when introduced, coupled with their overall infirmity of purpose under pressure and on the other, the readiness of the Ulster Unionists to resist the imposition of Home Rule on Ulster by organised force. Such assessment presupposes that the Ulstermen were not 'bluffing', at any rate in the sense that the Nationalist party leadership alleged. But if so much be allowed, is the overall emphasis right? Bonar Law would not have thought so. In September 1913 he told Churchill 'it is certain we would stick at nothing if it came to the point'. There would be a Provisional government in Belfast and 'here in England there would be no half measures'. On 14 October, as will also be recalled, he told the Prime Minister 'Mr Asquith must understand as well as I did that ... it was really the certainty of British support which made the strength of the Ulster resistance'. This and the language he used about civil war invite the question, was Bonar Law bluffing? If he was not, as the evidence suggests, then it was his Ulster commitment rather than Ulster Unionist preparations that decided how the balance would fall. Far more important than the timing of Liberal concessions, whether in April 1912 or March 1914, was the Unionist party leadership election in 1911. It is inconceivable that Long or Chamberlain would have entered into an open-ended commitment to Carson and the Ulster Unionists, let alone assail the government in such strident tones. The temper of the opposition would have been different. If, therefore, there was one crucial moment on the road to partition, it was at the Carlton Club on 13 November 1911. But in part consequential upon it there may be discerned another in respect of the area to be excluded. That was in October 1913 when at the first of the three Asquith–Bonar Law meetings Asquith entered into a preliminary exchange of views about the exclusion of Ulster or some part of it without stating categorically then (or later) that it would be a condition of any consideration of the area to be excluded that it would be determined in accord with clearly defined and defensible liberal principles. It was then that the Unionists were let off the hook. As for the rest, it may be remarked in anticipation that, while most of the features of the 1920–25 Settlement were foreshadowed in the acrimonious Third Home Rule debates of 1912–14, dominion status and the republic were not.

CHAPTER 4
The War Years 1914–19; Parliamentary Epilogue, Revolutionary Prologue

The First World War conjures up in the minds of an older generation of Irishmen images of Redmond's gesture, of Belgium overrun, of Home Rule deferred, of division in the ranks of the Volunteers, of lengthening casualty lists from the Western Front, of recruiting campaigns, of the Easter Rising and the long-drawn-out executions, of Lloyd George's negotiating finesse, of the swing to Sinn Féin violently accelerated by the threat of conscription and of the Parliamentary party jostled by erstwhile supporters along the road to political oblivion. Of these, two, Redmond's gesture, or more particularly the sequel to it, and the threat of conscription had an alienating and never to be forgotten impact on Anglo-Irish relations in the run-up to the settlement; a further two, the Easter Rising, and the negotiations that followed (and failed) fixed the parameters of the 1920–1 Settlement. As the negotiations that preceded the Treaty are bereft of much of their meaning viewed apart from the Proclamation of the Republic in 1916, so also are the deliberations and political manoeuvres in Cabinet and committee without close regard to the 1916 post-Rebellion Lloyd George negotiations. At issue in the one was status: in the other, partition: that is to say, in the context of this study and in chronological order the second and the first parts of the settlement. A matter for some surprise is that the great body of Irishmen, some 200,000 who fought on the Western Front, of whom 49,400 died,★ alone of the men and events that once loomed large, had no perceptible bearing on the settlement: like the Habsburg armies on some forgotten eastern front they were fighting in a cause and for an Empire their fellow-countrymen, and for that matter not a few among themselves, came to repudiate.

Questions of Perspective

The erosion of respect for the parliamentary process became a by-product of the Home Rule struggle of the pre-war years. On the arguments that

---

★ The Memorial to them on the banks of the Liffey in Dublin at Islandbridge, long neglected, was in part restored in 1987–8.

the balance of the constitution was being disturbed by the passage of the Parliament Bill, that an organic part of the constitution, the Act of Union, was threatened and that the Prime Minister had become corruptly sub-servient to a minority party, the Unionists contended that the 'authority' of the government might properly be resisted unless and until reaffirmed in a further election or a plebiscite; some made preparations to do so. The leader of the opposition alluded with frequency to the alternative of civil war and wrote of political opponents, Liberal and Nationalist separately and jointly, as 'the enemy'; the King was encouraged to consider the exercise of a long disused royal prerogative, and towards the end was himself perturbed lest the Army could not be counted upon to support the application of Home Rule, if enacted in Ulster, by force or by show of it. The most vulnerable to the atmosphere of impending violence were among the least responsible for creating it, namely, the Irish party. They were vulnerable because their support at grass roots was conditional upon their ability to satisfy their militant supporters that there was a reasonable prospect that they might achieve their aims by constitutional means. If parliamentary majorities were to determine action, those aims were on the point of fulfilment in August 1914: but if they did not suffice, then the party had reached the dangerous point at which anticipated attainment of a long-sought goal was to be denied them and even their most loyal followers, sensing that was in prospect, moved to ask whether the party had a continuing *raison d'être*. Historians indeed have generally subscribed to the view that the point of no return had been reached by August 1914.

Substantial reasons can be adduced to sustain this judgement, chief among them that war or no war, Liberal–Nationalist Home Rule aims, resting on the assumption of one nation, had been finally frustrated with-out an acceptable alternative in view. Asquith for his part seems to have felt as much, as did a number of his colleagues. How otherwise to account for their retrospectively less than edifying expressions of relief on the imminence of a greater conflict which would afford them an honourable way out of the Irish *impasse*?[1] Yet – and this also has to be taken into the reckoning – contemporaries generally did not for the most part see it quite that way. There is little or no reason for surprise that a minority in Ireland, nurtured in the Fenian tradition and sceptical even in Parnell's heyday of the likely efficacy of parliamentary methods, should have turned in anger to thoughts of rebellion. What is surprising is that at this time of humiliating loss of face for constitutional nationalists, there should have been at the outset so widespread a response by the majority, possibly the great majority, in Ireland to the appeals of Nationalist leaders for cooperation with Britain in the war. Never had the conquest of Ireland by England seemed more complete, wrote Piaras Béaslaí in his biography of Michael Collins, while a correspondent writing to Bonar Law from

Killarney on 10 August 1914 remarked that he had been very much struck by the great change in attitude since Redmond's speech of 3 August pledging Irish support in war. On all sides, the correspondent said he had sensed enthusiastic support for the British Empire – but he added a caution for the future, 'the right thing had to be done'.[2] Both suggest that alienation from the party came less with the shelving of Home Rule than the manner of it and as much or more than either, because the 'right thing' was not done after the outbreak of war.

The subsequent and progressive alienation of Irish opinion from the party is not in doubt, but the timing and causes of it at grass roots have not received systematic or satisfying explanation, maybe because historians with others have been blinded by the light of the sequel. Between Irishmen whose thoughts were moulded in the pre-war years and the generations who came after, there was the interposition of 1916, effecting a psychological transformation so considerable as to constitute a near unbridgeable gulf in outlook and understanding between the generations. Even in times of comparative continuity, few generations survive the critical scrutiny of their successors with motivation understood, let alone reputation unimpaired: in time of revolutionary change when the angle of vision itself is altered, judgement on what went before is likely to have an added element of incomprehension. Looking back upon the 'terrible beauty' that was 1916, Yeats described himself and his companions living till then but 'where motley is worn'.[3] But at the time – and historians are concerned with the reconstruction of the past – psychologically as well as circumstantially there is little evidence that Irishmen were thinking of themselves as living in a fool's paradise.

In retrospect assurances of Irish cooperation in the war coupled with insistence on the enactment, albeit with simultaneous suspension, of the Home Rule Bill, which constituted the twofold response of the Nationalist party to the outbreak of war are deemed symbolic of the ignominious failure of the constitutional movement to achieve its ends or even to understand the deeper impulses of Irish nationalism. Yet again there is little to suggest that they so appeared to the Irish people, other than those schooled in the physical force tradition, at the time. There was disappointment and a sense of having been misled, but not of failure of so cataclysmic a kind as to demand recourse to other than parliamentary methods. The sequel was not foreseen. One cannot remind oneself too often that the Easter Rising came as a great surprise. The blindness of Birrell is a commonplace, but it is apt to be insufficiently pondered how many on all sides shared it. The Irish party, while fully aware of the revolutionary forces on their flank and sensitive to the fact that their own image was tarnished, none the less saw insufficient reason to depart from the tactics they had hitherto employed. On the contrary, the leadership, much as their actions may now seem an essay in self-deception, kept to the same course, in particular redoubling their efforts to get Home Rule on the Statute Book.

Redmond's Unrequited Assurances

On 3 August 1914, the phrase 'the one bright spot' was twice used – by Asquith, who privately so described 'the settlement of Irish strife' as a result of the outbreak of war in Europe, adding 'God moves in a mysterious way his wonders to perform',[4] and then by Sir Edward Grey in the House of Commons, 'the one bright spot in a very dreadful situation is Ireland. The position in Ireland – and this I should like to be clearly understood abroad – is not a consideration among the things we have to take into account now.' To this Redmond responded with reference to eighteenth-century precedents, recalling that 'in 1778 at the end of the disastrous American War when . . . the military power of this country was almost at its lowest ebb, and when the shores of Ireland were threatened with foreign invasion, a body of 100,000 Irish Volunteers sprang into existence for the purpose of defending her shores', And, he went on, 'May history repeat itself . . . I say to the Government that they may tomorrow withdraw every one of their troops from Ireland. I say that the coast of Ireland will be defended from foreign invasion by her armed sons, and for this purpose armed Nationalist Catholics in the South will be only too glad to join arms with the armed Protestant Ulstermen in the North.'[5] It was a dramatic and, in parliamentary terms, a well-timed and telling intervention, its impact deepened by its being delivered immediately following upon the speeches of Grey and Bonar Law.

In giving assurances, which it is to be noted related only to the defence of Ireland, Redmond was greatly influenced by the impending German invasion of Belgium – Belgium had refused passage to the German armies but had not been invaded when he spoke – though later, in September, he was to be warm also in his allusions to France, 'the old friend of Ireland'[6] and in expression of Irish sympathies with France's 'rightful claims' to Alsace. But most of all he reverted to the image of himself, Home Rule enacted, as at one with Botha and Smuts, also able to say that in Ireland, as in South Africa, the concession of free institutions 'has changed the men who ten years ago were your bitter enemies into your loyal comrades . . .'. In this it was not his representation of the state of Irish opinion so much as his tactics, or rather his lack of them, that left him without convincing counter to criticisms, that were at once personally wounding and when framed in the imagery of the past, politically damaging – *Irish Freedom*, the voice of the Irish Republican Brotherhood arraigning nationalist leaders 'before the bar of history . . . as Traitors and Renegades worse than Castlereagh' because of their support for the war effort. Redmond, who had neither exacted conditions from the Prime Minister, still less from the War Office, nor consulted his colleagues – Dillon it seems clear would have warned against precipitate commitment at the time as he did retrospectively,[7] but as so often, he was elsewhere – had left himself exposed and vulnerable. When Redmond sought to repair the omission, he found the doors were closing against him. That from the British point of view was singularly ill advised. But, apart from some Liberals, British opinion gave little indication of warming to the notion of a Botha on the doorstep.

The War Office, that great Unionist stronghold, trusted neither Redmond nor his Volunteers. They rebuffed proposals he made for an Irish Division, to be largely manned by National Volunteers with its own officers and badges, but accepted proposals for an Ulster Division based on the Ulster Volunteer Force. Recommendations for commissions were turned down. Kitchener, under the impression that he was Irish, which at least was a proposition of some plausibility since he had been born at Ballylongford and was thereby qualified to pronounce upon Irish affairs,★ was resolute in vetoing everything put up, while Lloyd George, though expressing dismay, focused his energies on securing Kitchener's acquiescence in plans for a Welsh Division. By 8 August 1914, Redmond, already disquieted, protested to Asquith that Kitchener was contemplating simply an appeal for recruits from Ireland and the taking of no immediate steps to direct it to the Volunteers, still less to entrust the defence of Ireland to them or pay regard to Irish sentiments. He warned the Prime Minister that if none of these things were done, it would all end not in boundless enthusiasm but in 'a sense of affront, disheartenment and hurt by the people generally'.

It was not done and all that Redmond forecast came about. 'From the very first hour', he was to complain in October 1916,[8] 'our efforts were thwarted, ignored, and snubbed. . . . Everything, almost, that we asked for was refused, and everything, almost, that we protested against was done.' Asquith allowed that this was so. He spoke of 'dreadful mistakes and most regrettable blunders'; Lloyd George of 'stupidities' perpetrated at the outset of the war that 'almost look like malignancy' and were 'beyond belief'. Redmond, though there is no evidence that the precedent was in his mind, may be thought of as having followed much the same course as Cavour, who had sent Piedmontese troops to fight in the Crimea on the side of England and France in the hope, well grounded as it proved, of enlisting their backing in due course for the unification of Italy under the

---

★ His first discussion with Carson at the War Office ran as follows: 'Surely you are not going to hold out for Tyrone and Fermanagh?' he asked, to which Carson replied, 'You're a damned clever fellow telling me what I ought to be doing.' (Colvin, *Life of Lord Carson*, London, 1936, Vol. III, p. 27 and M. and E. Brock (eds) *H.H. Asquith, Letters to Venetia Stanley*, Oxford, 1982, p. 166, fn. 4.)

House of Savoy. But in Ireland, a comparable gesture availed only to discredit its sponsor and in the longer term to harden sentiment in favour of insistence on a right to neutrality when Britain was at war. In 1939 it was by no means only Eamon de Valera who remembered the disastrous consequences of cooperation for Redmond. No Irish leader would lightly travel that road again.

Home Rule Enacted and Suspended

In August–September 1914, Redmond had another and overriding preoccupation – to get the Home Rule Bill on the Statute Book. The achievement of that end in one step had been the goal of Nationalist policy in three parliaments, the way to it had been opened by the passage of the Parliament Act in 1911 and now, in August 1914, the Home Rule Bill, having completed its third parliamentary circuit, awaited the Speaker's certificate and the Royal Assent before the end of the session. The Unionists continued to demand and the King remained predisposed to yet one more election before enactment but, while Asquith no longer excluded such a possibility – Grey was known to favour it – the rank and file of the Liberal party felt it would make a nonsense of the Parliament Act. The Irish, moreover, were vehement in their insistence that whatever wartime moratorium might be placed on its operation, the Bill should be enacted; as Asquith noted, 'to both Irish and Welsh* to have their Bills *law*, however long their operation is postponed, is everything'.[9] If it were not enacted, Redmond threatened there would be no more recruits from nationalist Ireland. Enactment was achieved, but not with goodwill.

The party leaders had agreed that consideration of controversial measures should be deferred for the period of the war. Did the Home Rule Bill come within this category?[10] That it was controversial went without saying but it could be, and was, contended by Asquith that all stages having been or being about to be completed, it was no longer actively so. From this view, the Unionists dissented, alleging – and they had a case – breach of understanding. The Prime Minister, under strong pressure from his back-benchers and threatened withdrawal of support by Redmond, stood his debatable ground. As a result, the goal was achieved and on 18 September the Clerk of the Crown at the bar of the House duly announced the Royal Assent 'Le Roy le veult.' There followed scenes of wild rejoicing among Nationalist and Liberal Members[11] (the Unionists having left the House in a body) which have carried an ironic echo down the years.

* The Welsh Church Disestablishment Bill.

Associated with the Home Rule Act was an Act suspending its operation not 'indefinitely' as Churchill and others have written,[12] but – a very
different thing – until a date to be determined 'not being later than the end
of the present war', that is the signing of the peace treaties, and with a
pledge that parliament would then have an opportunity of passing an
Amending Bill making special provision for Ulster. Home Rule, therefore,
had reached the Statute Book 'in one step' as the Irish party leadership had
envisaged, but at the price of deferred application and acquiescence in the
prospect of two polities in Ireland. Yet though painful the price, there was
from the Irish Nationalist point of view one positive gain – a flicker of
light in a darkening sky. With the Act and the time limit on the Statute
Book, there could not be, as some more ardent Unionists desired, another
post-1886 experiment in killing Home Rule by kindness – one to be
embarked upon in the spirit, 'we have done it before: we can do it again'.
On that Redmond had closed the door: it was his most enduring achievement. By reason of his insistence on a time limit expiring at the end of the
war, an Irish settlement there would have to be. Even for Unionists the
days of Union were numbered.

What of Ulster? Her future was left unresolved with Asquith on 25
July advising the King of the government's intention of proceeding with
county option but without timetable. As against such uncertain intention
the Ulster Unionists now had the statutory assurance that parliament
would have an opportunity of making provision for Ulster by special
amending legislation before the Home Rule Act came into effect. This in
itself indicated that the balance had tilted the Ulster way. Furthermore, it
was to the advantage of the Ulster Unionists that not county option but
exclusion of a 'clean-cut' six-county block was immediately at issue when
debate left off before the war. It created a presumption that debate would
be resumed on that point. Finally, in September 1914, what had been
implicit since the Curragh incident was made explicit in assurances the
Prime Minister gave to opposition leaders. 'Under the [wartime] conditions which now exist...', Asquith told the House, 'the employment of
force, any kind of force, for what you [Bonar Law] call the coercion of
Ulster, is an absolutely unthinkable thing... a thing which we would
never countenance or consent to....'.[13] Although his assurance altogether
failed to placate the opposition, it carried, despite the wartime qualification, an unmistakable ring of finality. There would be no coercion of
Ulster, with the Ulster Unionists in effect left to decide what was coercion. To that the government was now pledged.

Overall, despite Redmond's parliamentary triumph, and the party
exhilaration at Home Rule enactment, the events of July–September 1914
sowed the seed of proximate disillusion with the constitutional programme. There is no doubt about the fundamental factor that tarnished
wartime gesture and Home Rule enactment alike: it was the prospective

partition of Ireland, no longer 'veiled' by distance, but rather advancing in
naked reality, unadorned even by the consoling part-delusions of time
limit, or plebiscite. 'Ireland without Ulster is Ireland with its head off, and
although Thomas Carlyle had heard of an Irish saint who swam the
channel with his head under one arm,★ an Ireland beheaded is impossible,
is unnatural, and *shall not be*. A Conference at Buckingham Palace to
delimit Ireland, to mark off Ulster and say "This is where England begins"
is a fitting end to what has been called constitutional agitation in Ireland.'
Thus wrote *Irish Freedom*, the voice of a small minority, yet in this almost
certainly expressing the reactions of the majority – Redmondite as well as
republican – and leading inexorably towards the thought that one method
having failed, it remained to try another, well grounded in Irish tradition
and nourished down the years by the blood of martyrs. That tradition, the
Fenian tradition, though it was there before the Fenian formulation of it,
was a physical force tradition. It was also a republican tradition; Wolfe
Tone, not Parnell, was its prophet and Tone, Edward Fitzgerald, Robert
Emmet were in its roll of martyrs. It had its origins in time of one great
war: might not another afford a chance of its realisation?

Redmond continued blindly dismissive of what alone could save him,
namely, getting his hands on the levers of power. Thus in the course of
the debate on the Suspensory Bill on 15 September, he spoke of establishing a Home Rule administration in terms of astonishing negation, saying
that with an army being created 'the idea is absurd that under these
circumstances a new Government and a new Parliament could be erected
in Ireland'.[14] With Home Rule in prospect since 1912, was this not a confession of near-total failure to prepare for the assumption of the responsibilities of government? And does it not once again cast a questioning
light on the rejection of the Irish Council Bill in 1907? Might not the
existence of a cadre of administrators experienced in coordination of the
work of a variety of bodies have formed the nucleus of an organisation,
the existence of which would have constituted an argument for some
transfer of powers and on an all-Ireland basis? The Ulster Volunteers had
their imitators in the South – indeed, on the view of *Irish Freedom*, rather
more than that, for when Dillon claimed that the 'Party' were responsible
for the Volunteers it noted 'We tell Mr. Dillon that the man responsible
for the starting of the Volunteers was Sir Edward Carson, the only Irish
Member of Parliament who has any backbone . . .'.[15] Might it not have
been to the advantage of the Nationalists had the embryonic Ulster Provisional government also had its 'mirror image' in the South?

The parliamentarians were at a disadvantage on another front, their

---

★ As is also said of St Denis who likewise carried his head from the Seine to the site
of the Abbey where the French kings are buried.

own parliamentary front. The Irish question was on ice for the duration: after September 1914 there were no great debates, no dramatic moves. Under such conditions, contacts between Nationalists and Liberals diminished and relations, never close, perceptibly and progressively distanced. In late 1914 the incoming Viceroy, Lord Wimborne, in 'a very sanguine frame of mind' entertained thoughts of improving them. Birrell was discouraging, advising him that he was not the least likely to see Dillon and Redmond and Devlin with their 'feet under his mahogany' at the Viceregal Lodge and 'quaffing his mellow wines'.[16] Then on a more important matter, the principle of avoidance of association with government in Dublin was deemed to apply with even greater rigour to participation in government in London. When in May 1915 Asquith perforce reconstituted his government to form the first wartime coalition, he issued a twice repeated invitation to Redmond to accept office in it. Redmond rejected all of them out of hand. Acceptance, in his view, was 'an absolute impossibility'.[17] No doubt this may have been so but here again there remains an impression of a conclusion easily reached on the assumption that no thought need be given to the possibilities of a conditional answer, seeking assurance before any commitment that the government stood by the notion of county option and would not concede more. In view of the subsequent 1916 negotiations, it would have been a point worth having on record. It would have required persuasive leadership to have influenced Irish opinion even to the point of sceptical acquiescence. Yet Unionists, English and Ulster, had good reason to welcome Redmond's refusal. The price of rejection, given Carson's inclusion in the Cabinet, could only be to tip the balance further against the Nationalist party and to deprive Redmond of a weapon, either in the form of conditional acceptance or resignation on a well-chosen issue or exchange of view on essentials – all three of which might have been deployed with effect. If, as in 1907 and again in 1915, such openings were foreclosed, did not a parliamentary party remain at a disadvantage being in but not of the system? Why then remain?

The replacement of a Liberal by a Coalition Cabinet, irrespective of Nationalist representation, brought disadvantage to the Nationalist cause. With Bonar Law, Lansdowne, Balfour and Carson serving in the Cabinet, albeit not in posts of the highest importance – Bonar Law was Secretary of State for the Colonies, Carson, Attorney-General – the shelving of Irish issues was a condition of its survival. Even so, cooperation did not come easily. Birrell had reason to feel more keenly than anyone except the Prime Minister himself the humiliation of having to take counsel with those who so recently had flaunted their contempt for 'enemies' in the Liberal and Irish parties. 'It is all very dark to me', Birrell bewailed on 26 May to the Under-Secretary at the Chief Secretary's Office, Sir Matthew Nathan, Nathan 'the unwise' as he called him, still not knowing what was going to

happen to the Irish administration. When by 29 May he knew it was to
carry on unchanged, he protested that he could not 'bear the thought of
physical contact in No. 10 with these fellows' about whom he had used
language which he quite thought might secure '*my immediate release*'. A
man of resigning mind, he never found the moment right to resign; his
reasons this time being twofold: loyalty to Asquith, 'a man in great straits
who has always treated me as a brother' and to his colleagues.[18] On the
wider front, with a Cabinet psychologically, over and above politically, so
deeply divided, Irish policy could only be bipartisan. That meant there
was none. The Liberals had lost the initiative on Irish policy – for all time
as it proved.

The Easter Rising

When in 1914 the Irish question was placed on ice, the widespread assumption was that the war would not be of long duration. Once the
Western Front was stabilised and prospects of early victory faded, the
insufficiency of what was thought of as a comparatively short-term device
became apparent. To existing division between minority and majority in
respect of Home Rule were added division within the nationalist ranks on
the nature of Ireland's participation in the war. It surfaced following upon
a speech by Redmond on 20 September 1914, at Woodenbridge in County
Wicklow in which he appealed to the Irish Volunteers to serve 'not only in
Ireland itself, but wherever the firing line extends, in defence of right,
of freedom and religion . . . '. Members of the original committee of
the Volunteers led by Eoin MacNeill thereupon repudiated Redmond's
leadership. This was duly noted and reported upon by Birrell in a paper
circulated to the Cabinet in November.[19] It was reassuring in its conde-
scension. He was aware there were 'dogs', he assumed they were at any
rate half asleep and he deliberately decided to let them lie. His correspondence as Easter 1916 approached shows that he was aware, too, that
there were risks of sporadic outrage, that Ireland was once more 'a *seething
pot*', but he remained none the less strongly opposed to coercion on the
evidence before him. His attention was focused rather on the struggle for
power in London, which he viewed with fastidious distaste. On 12 April
1916 he wrote from the House of Commons: 'The P.M. is at the moment
the *Top Dog* but over what *Body* is he to preside is the question. Damn all
their Politics.' On 18 April he wrote, again to Nathan and again from
London, 'I have no desire to be on the spot in such times as these and in
County Mayo or Achill I shall breathe easier than in this hotbed of
dishonourable intrigue.' On Saturday, 22 April, he wrote, 'Here I am, not
in Achill as I hoped to be but in St. James's Street. . . . In the meantime my
relations with Redmond and Dillon are broken off. I hear they have taken
to their tents . . .'. On Easter Sunday, 23 April, he added,[20] 'Redmond and

Dillon are very much out of temper just now', and he thought Redmond might take advantage of the Cabinet crisis to seek to recover 'his lost authority in Ireland' by a 'violent speech'. On 24 April came news from another source of more than a violent speech: 'Insurrection broke out at noon today in Dublin when attack made on Dublin Castle but not pressed home.'[21]

Birrell moved off the stage with criticisms of his neglect of his responsibilities. On 5 May the *Freeman's Journal* once again reflected on how very different things would have been had Redmond, like Botha, been Prime Minister in his own country, and on the same day a leading article in the Southern Unionist *Irish Times*, was also ringing in his ears.[22] 'Mr. Birrell's resignation of the Chief Secretaryship', it pronounced, 'like so many acts of the present government has come too late. It is a public blessing but it has been purchased at terrible cost to Ireland. Mr. Birrell is witty, eloquent and learned. Unfortunately, he was sent here not to teach literature but to rule Ireland. . . . He has been the most mischievous Chief Secretary whom Ireland ever knew.'* As he was leaving, Birrell remarked, not without insight: 'It is not an Irish rebellion and it would be a pity if it became one.' The execution of the leaders, however, ensured that it did, though the inference that this was because of their number and the period of time over which they took place needs to be treated with reserve. However few and summary they had been, the imagery of the past would have led to a revulsion of feeling in favour of the rebels – what might have been mitigated was the measure of the alienation of Irish from British that ensued. Nor is it clear that it was an error in judgement that was chiefly responsible, as against tardiness in assertion of judgement. Most of the evidence indicates awareness on the British side of the long-term damage that was being done by the military, but no corresponding sense of urgency in seeking to impose a limit to it.[23] On 27 April the Cabinet, on deciding that martial law should be proclaimed over the whole of Ireland, had given General Maxwell plenary powers to administer it. But not until 6 May was instruction sent that the death penalty was not to be inflicted except upon ringleaders and that it was desirable to bring the executions to a close as soon as possible. In fact they continued until 12 May. Lloyd George told Dillon that he had written 'a very strong letter' to the Prime Minister on the military administration which he described as 'stupid', with the rumoured arrest of the Bishop of Limerick as 'too fatuous even

---

* Denis Gwynn told the author that, when writing his biography of Redmond, he had come across a further bunch of Birrell's letters likely to provoke yet more criticism of his regime. He enquired tentatively of Birrell if he might make use of them. Birrell replied telling him to make what use of them he wished. As for himself he would soon be beyond the reach of historians. It is pleasant to recall something much to his credit.

for Maxwell'.[24] But when did he write? On 10 June, the damage by then was beyond repair.

The military had no responsibility for the execution of Sir Roger Casement. Acting virtually on his own, Casement had sought (and failed) to persuade Irish prisoners of war to enlist in an Irish brigade and to seek German aid in fitting out an expedition to support the Rebellion – than which few things were better calculated to stir antagonism in Britain, and above all, in Ulster. What was at issue was not sentence, which was accepted as inevitable, but reprieve. There were representations from many quarters, from Dillon, from the United States Senate, from James Bryce who, as former Chief Secretary and former Ambassador to Washington, might have been expected to carry weight, but all to no avail. 'There can be few other examples', Roy Jenkins has commented, 'of a Cabinet devoting large parts of four separate meetings to considering an individual sentence – and then arriving at the wrong decision'.[25] And so, with the fifteen men there was also 'the ghost of Roger Casement . . . beating on the door'.[26] If it be accepted that atmosphere is an ingredient in most successful negotiations, it could now be assumed on every side that it would not be favourable for long years to come.

Asquith's Memorandum

The principal victims of the Rising were the members of the parliamentary party. 'Home Rule', declared Redmond on 3 May, 'has not been destroyed: it remains indestructible'. But he was mistaken. Home Rule and Union alike had been destroyed. What was to replace them immediately and in the longer term? To this there was a paradoxical answer. The Rising indicated more than ever the need for an early settlement and at the same time its suppression left no one for the British to settle with. The result was an attempt to reach a settlement with a party and a leadership discredited beyond hope of rehabilitation in popular esteem. Asquith, whose courage is to be applauded but whose dilatoriness is to be deplored, decided to form his own impressions by visiting Ireland.[27] This he did, on 11–19 May. On his return he wrote a memorandum which formed the basis of a further attempt to unravel the Irish question.

The memorandum that Asquith submitted to the Cabinet was in two parts, dated respectivly 19 and 21 May 1916.[28] On his visit, he had formed two distinct impressions. The first was that despite the prudence and discretion of the military command, there had been incidents* which had

* Chief among them was the murder of Francis Sheehy-Skeffington, a well-known and well-loved Dublin eccentric. He was a pacifist opposed to the Rising though sympathetic to its aims. Asquith described it as 'the worst blot' upon the proceedings of the military.

aroused 'a good deal of uneasiness and sympathy in many people in
Dublin and elsewhere in Ireland who lent no countenance to the outbreak'
with the rebels and the second that there did not seem to be 'any general
or widespread feeling of bitterness between the civil population and the
soldiers'. He himself 'went one day on foot partly through a considerable
crowd and was received, not only without disrespect, but with remarkable
warmth'. These impressions would seem to have reinforced his natural
predisposition to think yet again in terms of the classical Liberal solution
of self-government as a step which, by removing sources of friction,
would lead on to more harmonious relations.

But classical Liberal solvents of imperial–national relations were apt to
presume that if there were majority–minority tensions, they too, were
susceptible to similar panaceas. In Belfast, Asquith was reminded that
there existed quite different possibilities. The Lord Mayor of Belfast, 'a
level headed and public spirited man', told him that during the early
autumn of 1915 'a sort of atmospheric wave' overspread Protestant Ulster.
'We had sent' (such was or became the prevailing opinion)

> the best of our manhood to the front; the Catholic[s] of the South and
> West have contributed substantially less; if we were now to allow what
> remains of our available men to recruit, we shall be left defenceless
> against a possible, even probable, Nationalist invasion of our province;
> and our wives, our children, our homes, our industry, our religion will
> be at the mercy of our hereditary foes. From that day to this recruiting
> in Ulster has practically ceased; and so long as this belief, and the
> temper which it engenders, persists, not only will there be no effective
> recruiting for the Army, but there will be a determined resistance to
> any attempt on the part of the State to disarm those who remain at
> home.

Ulster leaders confirmed to the Prime Minister that what he had been
told was a correct interpretation of the state of mind of the vast majority
of the Protestant population of Belfast and industrial Ulster and that
nothing could dislodge such feelings from their minds. Those feelings
rendered domestic disarmament, however desirable, impracticable. What
then remained? One or two repeated to Asquith the old formula of
resolute government but the large majority 'were clearly of [the] opinion
that the only way to escape was by prompt settlement of the whole
problem . . .'. It was, said Campbell, the Attorney-General, 'a case of now
or never'. But what did such a settlement require? The answer came clear
– Home Rule with an amendment of the Home Rule Act 1914, such as
would adequately safeguard the future of the Ulster Protestants. That was
intended and understood to mean exclusion.

The Prime Minister acquiesced, albeit reluctantly. It appeared to him to
be 'the duty of the Government to do everything in their power to force a

general settlement'. By that means alone could arms be controlled and it was all-important that this should be so, lest otherwise the two armies of North and South should be held in leash 'for a final spring at one another's throats when peace was declared'. To the obvious objection that prospects of a settlement on such lines had foundered two years earlier on the area to be excluded, Asquith countered by saying he was by no means sure that the Nationalists (apart from the O'Brienites in Cork from whom he had received a deputation) would not 'be disposed to prefer the total exclusion (for the time being at any rate) of Ulster' to the continued withholding of Home Rule from the rest of Ireland. If, however, the ultimate solution was to be thought of on Home Rule cum partition lines, there had to be wartime transitional arrangements. In respect of these Asquith contemplated the disappearance 'of the fiction' of a Chief Secretary, the appointment of no successor to the Lord-Lieutenant – the Viceroyalty having become 'a costly and futile anachronism' – and single British ministerial control of Irish administration operating with the help of an Irish advisory council.

The Lloyd George Negotiations

The Asquith memorandum prepared the way for negotiations. Asquith spoke in the House of Commons of a bold effort on fresh lines that might lead to an agreed settlement between those representing different interests and parties in Ireland and he told members that the Minister of Munitions, Lloyd George, at the unanimous request of his colleagues had undertaken to devote his energies to the task.[29] But while there may have been occasion for boldness, there was little scope for freshness. By way of substitute, Lloyd George sought to render not unacceptable proposals, rejected in earlier but different circumstances. He had, or considered that he had, a free hand in the conduct of negotiations and, unlike Cripps on his Indian mission in 1942, Lloyd George was bound by no Cabinet declaration, for the good reason that the Coalition Cabinet in 1916 would have been unable to reach agreement upon its content. Yet the lack of a Cabinet directive inevitably gave rise, as reports and rumours multiplied, to concern about what Lloyd George might regard as within the range of the negotiable. On the Unionist side, the understanding was that there was a 'blue print for negotiations', namely Asquith's memorandum. Thus Lansdowne, in a paper circulated to the Cabinet on 21 June,[30] observed retrospectively that 'while it would have been unwise to fetter Lloyd George with meticulous restrictions', it had been understood in Cabinet that Lloyd George would not go beyond the lines of the memorandum. He (Lansdowne) had accordingly no idea that anything so far-reaching as the terms of Lloyd George's reported discussions with Irish leaders was in mind. In particular, Asquith had concluded that the Home Rule Act could not take effect till after the War and by implication, so Lansdowne considered, this conclusion had received public affirmation in the Prime Minister's speech at Ladybank on 14 June, when Asquith had said that at the end of the war 'the fabric of the Empire will have been refashioned, and the relations not only between Great Britain and Ireland but also between the United Kingdom and our Dominions will of necessity be brought under close and connected review'. In reply Lloyd George conceded that he had not been authorised to bind the Cabinet, but equally he had felt entitled to convey to the Irish leaders the impression that he was not merely, in Lansdowne's phrase, 'gathering up' their opinions, but was in a position to and had in fact made them a firm offer on the assumption *inter alia* that Home Rule might be brought into immediate operation.

On 23 June Long echoed Lansdowne's complaints about the scope of the discussions. The Irish business was, he wrote, 'unhappily involved in mystery and the consequence is that a great deal of deplorable misapprehension has arisen'. Both Carson and Redmond appeared to have misinterpreted the Prime Minister's reference to the breakdown of the existing machinery of Irish government, as meaning that the whole form of government under the Union had failed and that Home Rule was the only alternative. But in his memorandum the Prime Minister had written that the Home Rule Act could not come into force until the end of the war. Moreover, alleged Long, Lloyd George had been commissioned to undertake *confidential* negotiations and to report results to the Cabinet before any public announcement was made. The first was obviously unrealistic, since Irish leaders had to consult and persuade their respective supporters, and that made the second difficult. Lansdowne complained in the House of Lords on 29 June that members of the Cabinet were still insufficiently seized of all the points involved in the negotiations.[31]

Unionists' sense of grievance about the conduct of negotiations stemmed from their concern first about the probable and then the actual outcome. Asquith had written *inter alia* of the need for 'a prompt' settlement: in that Lloyd George did not fail him. On the contrary he moved with remarkable speed towards a provisional settlement. The basis of it was the application as soon as might be of the Home Rule Act modified in accord with Nationalist representations so as to keep the number of Irish members at Westminster unaltered at 103 instead of reduced, as contemplated in the 1914 Act, to 42, and in accordance with Unionist demands so as to exclude the six 'plantation' counties of the north-east from the jurisdiction of the Home Rule Parliament for the period of the war, for which time they would be directly administered by a Secretary of State responsible to the Imperial Parliament. The longer-term resolution of the Irish question was to be referred to a post-war Imperial conference.

The negotiation of the settlement, it soon emerged, had been conditional upon ambiguity in presentation. Lloyd George obtained the con-

currence of Redmond and Carson in separate bilateral exchanges at which
the assurances given to the one were not consistent with those given to the
other. By flagrant use of this device, Carson was induced to use his
prestige and powerful advocacy to persuade the Ulster Unionist Council
first that as regards Home Rule the 'game was up', and secondly, that the
area to be excluded should not be the nine counties of Ulster but six –
the representatives of Donegal, Cavan and Monaghan being invited to
sacrifice themselves in the interests of the security that would be given by
a majority of nearly two to one (825,000 to 430,000) in the six counties, as
against one of nine to seven (900,000 to 700,000) in the nine. Redmond
and Dillon were likewise induced to try to persuade their followers,
especially the nationalist minority in Ulster, to acquiesce in the exclusion
of Fermanagh and Tyrone in addition to Antrim, Armagh, Down and
Derry in return for immediate Home Rule, with Lloyd George, by way of
stimulus to prompt action, warning Dillon that Craig had told him it
would take all Carson's influence to secure the assent of Ulster Unionists
to the sacrifice of the three Ulster counties. So it proved.

'They received me', Carson recalled of the meeting of the standing
Committee of the Ulster Unionist Council, 'as coldly as any audience has
ever received any man who had a proposition to put before them'.[32] His
chief difficulty, Ronald McNeill noted, was to make members 'grasp the
significance of the fact that Home Rule was now actually established by
Act of Parliament', and 'that simple repeal of that Act was not practical
politics'. To questions about getting the Act off the Statute Book, Carson
rejoined 'Do not let us live in a fool's paradise. We are men; we are not
schoolboys.' In the end, members acquiesced.* Why? The assurance of
permanence underwritten by Lloyd George who committed himself in
writing on 29 May 1916 to the statement that once the provisional wartime period was over 'We must make it clear that . . . Ulster [that is the six
counties] does not, whether she wills it or not, merge in the rest of
Ireland.'

---

* The actual phrasing of their resolution was as follows: 'The Standing Committee
of the Ulster Unionist Council, 3 June 1916, resolved:
(1) that as Unionists, proud of our citizenship in the United Kingdom, we reaffirm
our unabated abhorrence of the policy of H.R.
(2) As, however, the Cabinet which is responsible for the government of the
country is of opinion that it will tend to strengthen the Empire and to win the
war . . . if all questions connected with H.R. are settled now instead of as originally
agreed, at the termination of the war; and as these suggestions by the Government
put forward by Sir Edward Carson have been made with that view, we feel, as
loyal citizens, that, in this crisis of the Empire's history, it is our duty to make
sacrifices, and we consequently authorise Sir Edward Carson to continue the
negotiations on the basis (of exclusion of 6 counties plus 2 county boroughs). Mss.
Curtis, Bodleian Library, Oxford. Corr. and papers relating to Ireland.

In his parallel separate discussions with the Nationalist leaders, not only did Lloyd George underline the need for quick decision but further dwelt upon the risks of a settlement delayed until after the war. 'Heaven knows what will happen then.' But essentially he won their agreement by persuading them, and through them the party, that the arrangements in respect of the Ulster counties would be temporary. The nature of this assurance merits scrutiny in view of subsequent controversy about it. As recorded by Redmond in manuscript, it was given verbally at a meeting of Lloyd George with Dillon, Devlin and Redmond. They asked Lloyd George whether, if they obtained the consent of their people, they could rely upon him and the Prime Minister not to tolerate 'any further concessions being thrust upon us'. He gave the most emphatic assurance saying 'he had placed his life upon the table and would stand or fall by the agreement come to. He assured us also that this was the attitude of the Prime Minister. We said on that assurance we would go to Ireland and ask the consent of our people but not otherwise.'* The record, initialled by Dillon and Devlin and in Redmond's handwriting, is now among Redmond's papers.[33] It was not initialled by Lloyd George.

The transaction when, as was inevitable, its self-contradictory nature was disclosed, momentarily associated Redmond and Carson in common and indignant repudiation. Yet the breakdown of the settlement that never was merits some closer examination. Five points may be noted. The first concerns the area of exclusion. While Asquith in 1914 had conceded the time limit, he had not abandoned county option in the face of Carson's assertion that a six-county block was a minimal demand. Nineteen-sixteen changed all that. The basis of the negotiation was exclusion *en bloc* of a six-county area. From that there was to be no retreat. The second is that without Lloyd George's negotiating dexterity, if indeed that be *le mot juste*, there was no prospect whatever of a 'prompt' or indeed any other settlement. The third is that in essence Lloyd George was employing a procrastinating device, since the issue of transient or lasting exclusion would in legislative terms be deferred until the end of the war, and the fourth, that in fact the difference, as Devlin surmised, between temporary and permanent exclusion was, politically as distinct from psychologically, minimal or non-existent, since what the Ulster Unionists had once obtained and enjoyed, they would assuredly not have abandoned after a period of years. The fifth – and this is a tangled skein that needs to be more fully unravelled – is that the Cabinet would have been divided, to the point of disruption, had the attempt been made to give effect to the

_____

*Conference of Representative Nationalists of the six counties held on Friday, 23 June 1916. 'Having considered the proposals of Mr. Lloyd George for the temporary and provisional settlement of the Irish difficulty, is of opinion they should be accepted.' Mss. Curtis, *ibid.*

proposed heads of settlement, not only because of the Ulster question
but also, and because of indignant right-wing opposition to immediate
Home Rule, for the rest of Ireland. Once again, Lansdowne was foremost
in opening debate. 'Is this', he asked, in his memorandum of 21 June,

> the moment for imposing upon the country, in the guise of an interim
> arrangement, a bold and startling scheme which at once concedes in
> principle all that the most extreme Nationalists have been demanding,
> viz the disappearance of Castle Government and the establishment of an
> Irish Parliament with an Irish Executive responsible to it? The triumph
> of lawlessness and disloyalty would be complete. We may delude our-
> selves by saying that this arrangement is purely provisional, but the
> capitulation will be palpable and its significance will not be diminished
> by the exclusion of Ulster or part of the province.

Sinn Féin would not be conciliated and, he proceeded in a passage that
reflected a shift in Southern Unionist thinking, reaffirmed at the Convention a year later: 'I have always thought that any measure of Home Rule
which presented to the World as a new Irish nation, an Ireland from
which Ulster or any part of it was excluded, would be a deplorable and
humiliating confession of failure; and if Home Rule is to come I should
prefer a measure embracing the whole of Ireland, with safeguards for the
minority wherever found.'

On 23 June Long supported Lansdowne in arguing that Home Rule
during the war was not, as claimed by Lloyd George, an imperial necessity
but would prove an imperial disaster. But Unionists opinion was not all
one way. The following day Balfour countered with a memorandum
circulated to the Unionist members of the Cabinet.[34] Balfour argued
that, were Lloyd George's scheme to be carried through, 'the six Ulster
counties would have permanently secured to them – by consent and
without bloodshed – their place in the United Kingdom. Will anybody
assert that, if the settlement of their fate be deferred till peace is declared,
terms equally good could be obtained without a dangerous struggle?' He
had always held that rather than submit to Home Rule, Ulster should fight
and Ulster would be right, but equally he had no illusions about the price
in terms of civilised society and damage to property this would entail.
'Very strong therefore', he continued, 'must be the arguments which
would induce me to run the hazard of civil war, when we have offered to
us voluntarily all that successful civil war could give . . .' and, concluded
Balfour, 'the war supplies no sufficient justification for neglecting the
unique opportunity now offered for settling peacefully and permanently
the problem of Ulster'.

Ironically enough Balfour's memorandum was written the same day as
a report from General Maxwell,[35] circulated to the Cabinet, which might
have been thought to knock from under it the principal prop on which

it rested. People in Ireland, noted Maxwell, 'think Sinn Féinism and patriotism are synonymous terms'. Home Rule was again being discussed and that in itself was evidence that rebellion paid. Redmond and his party were discredited, the North was quiet only because the Unionists had the arms and they knew they could defend themselves, and the only conclusion was that the Irish question would never be settled in Ireland.

Lord Robert Cecil followed with a paper on 26 June,[36] to express disagreement with Balfour partly on these same grounds, but further alleging that none of the triumvirate, by whom a Home Rule administration would be principally directed, would have the authority of popular choice. Sinn Féin, on the other hand would, and its two principal tenets were: (1) 'vehement rejection' of any proposal for the division of Ireland; and (2) profound mistrust of the Irish Parliamentary party. Sinn Féin would not be conciliated by the proposals in debate. To withdraw the offer of Home Rule would be equally dangerous, Carson having warned that to withdraw the proposals now 'would throw Ulster into a ferment and convert the rest of Ireland into "hell"'. So what did Lord Robert suggest? Something perhaps a little devious for so high-minded a man – for the duration of the war, martial law with symbolic Home Rule, that is if the necessary Amending Bill excluding the six counties were passed, a Home Rule parliament could meet, elect a Speaker and then adjourn till the end of the war!

The Cabinet met on 27 June and Asquith reported[37] to the King that, despite the hardly won concurrence of Carson and Redmond to the settlement, Lansdowne on grounds of concession to rebellion and risk of encouraging further rebellion, especially in view of the terms of Maxwell's report, and Long on grounds of lack of a genuine acceptance of the basis of it by the Nationalists, could accept no responsibility for it. Cecil advanced in the English interest his symbolic Home Rule cum suspension of executive power till the end of the war stratagem. Curzon feared defeat in the Lords, with the consequent risk of an election and newly elected fresh members 'of a revolutionary tinge being returned'. But Crewe and Grey on the Liberal side strongly supported the settlement and on the Unionist side, Bonar Law, who wondered what was the alternative to the proposal, said he would recommend his party to ratify it at their meeting the next day. But, according to Asquith, it was Balfour who delivered the most effective pronouncement in the long conclave. He dissociated himself entirely from Lansdowne and Long and far from believing the proposed settlement 'a concession to rebellion', he thought 'it might be far more fairly represented as a Unionist triumph', the exclusion of the six Ulster counties having been the maximum demand of the Unionist leaders at the Buckingham Palace Conference. 'With unanswerable logic', he (Balfour) proceeded to point out the absurdity of the contention that the establishment of a Home Rule Parliament at a distance of six or eight, and more probably twelve or eighteen months could seriously embarrass action in the war, stressed the importance of not alienating United States opinion and declared himself a whole-hearted supporter of the policy of Carson and Bonar Law. The moment of decision was approaching. But before it came, Lloyd George intervened. He suggested the appointment of a small committee of the Cabinet to consider further safeguards, which might avert the resignation of Unionist members of the Cabinet. Curzon and Chamberlain agreed, Lansdowne acquiesced, Long held out to the last. The proposal was adopted and the committee (the Prime Minister, Lloyd George, Cecil and the Attorney-General, F.E. Smith) appointed to consider and formulate such additions as seemed to be necessary. By this means, Asquith observed in his report to the King, a series of resignations, with the consequent possible dissolution of the government, which 'would not only be a national calamity but a national crime', had been averted. A week later, on 5 July – when the Cabinet met to receive the report of the committee it had set up and when Lansdowne spoke of his dilemma and Long described his position as a 'cruel' one – to Asquith's satisfaction both decided to remain and Selborne's was in fact the only resignation.[38] But on 11 July in a speech in the House of Lords, which, as Asquith wrote to Crewe, gave the 'greatest offence to the Irish',[39] who resented its general tone and temper over and above its substance, Lansdowne made brutally clear the basis of his continued membership of the Cabinet: permanent exclusion of the six counties together with continuing British wartime control over defence dispositions in the twenty-six regardless of the existence of a Home Rule administration of which his mistrust was ostentatiously displayed.[40].

The headings of the settlement as outlined by the committee and preliminary to the drafting of legislation, were laid before the Cabinet on 17 July. They provided principally:

1. that the Government of Ireland Act 1914 should be brought into force as soon as possible subject to certain modifications;
2. that the Act was not to apply to an excluded six-counties area, which was to be administered by a Secretary of State;
3. that the Irish representation in the House of Commons was to remain unaltered at 103.

To reassure critics, special safeguards were included to protect British military and naval interests. The Act was to remain in force for twelve months but the period could be extended and a permanent settlement considered after the war at an Imperial conference concerned with closer cooperation of the Dominions with the Imperial Government. It is for particular note that the excluded area was to be administered by a Secretary of State – something which happened but not until more than half a century later.

The submission of the outline of legislation which did not foreclose options on Ulster provoked renewed Unionist opposition. Cecil, Lansdowne and Long all returned to the charge. It was essential, argued Cecil,[41] that exclusion should be definite until the excluded areas wished to return. Equally it was impossible for the Unionist party to support a settlement unless Irish representation at Westminster were diminished – the one boon of Home Rule – since otherwise Ulster would be at the mercy of eighty Irish Nationalist members. Lansdowne argued that the Ulster Unionists had 'notoriously' accepted the settlement only on the assumption of permanent exclusion,[42] while Long, supporting Lansdowne's demand for a structural change in the Home Rule Act to exclude the six counties, enquired further whether it was right to divert attention from the war.[43]

On 19 July Asquith reported to the King that he could not assent to further postponement,[44] but that the Cabinet after much discussion of the draft Bill agreed (1) that Carson's claim for the definitive exclusion of six counties could not be resisted; and (2) that the Nationalists should be told that after the Home Rule Parliament had been set up, Irish representation in the Imperial House of Commons must be reduced, with the proviso that it would be restored when an Amending Irish Bill was introduced. This was to make an already disadvantageous compromise impossible for the Irish Nationalist leaders. When the Bill with such provisions was introduced on 25 July, Redmond declined to support it. Even he sensed it was time to extricate himself finally from this disastrous round of circuitous negotiations. On 27 July, Asquith reported to the King: 'It was agreed [by the Cabinet] that for the immediate future in Ireland the simplest and least objectionable plan would be to revert for a time to the old system of Lord Lieutenant and Chief Secreatary.'[45] What it must have cost him to pen those words!

Why did the negotiations lead to this humiliating end? To argue that it was to be attributed to Lloyd George's dexterity, or duplicity, does no more than push the question back a stage further. Why in the first instance did he feel compelled to resort to a negotiating gamble with the odds on premature and damaging revelation so obviously against him? The answer is surely that in no other way could he hope to take even a first step towards a settlement. But conceding so much, was it none the less because of Lloyd George's conflicting assurances that the settlement collapsed? To this long-standing assumption A.J.P. Taylor gives a categoric negative.[46] The objection, he writes of Lansdowne, Long and other hard-core Unionists, was over Southern Ireland, not over Ulster. The first was certainly so. But it was not their only or principal objection, as emerged very clearly in July with reiterated demands for permanent exclusion of the six counties. Would Asquith indeed have made the concession to a 'little aristocratic clique'[47] had it not been for the additional demands for a

reduction in the number of Irish members and for a structural alteration in
the 1914 Act, voiced publicly by Lansdowne in his speech of 11 July in the
Lords, and both assured of broadly based Unionist support, precisely
because they were designed to safeguard the 'plantation' counties? The
truth would seem to be that while there was strong opposition to wartime
Home Rule in the rest of Ireland, the demands for a reduction of Irish
members and structural amendment of the Home Rule Act indicated that
it was the future of Ulster that was fundamental. Asquith's letter to
Redmond dated 28 July 1916 and marked 'for you *alone*', puts it beyond
doubt.★ Asquith wrote 'I say nothing as to responsibility of this person or
that' (for the breakdown of the negotiations) but 'I am sure that you agree
with me that the actual breaking point was not the figure at which the
Irish members should be retained in the Imperial Parliament. This could
easily be arranged by some form of compromise. . . . The real point is the
future of the Excluded area. Carson (naturally) wants safeguards against
the possibility of "automatic inclusion". You (with equal reason) desire to
keep open, and effectively open, the possibility of revision and review – at
an early date.' That was the point which Asquith felt was 'the crux of the
whole matter'. No one had better cause to know.[48]

The Sinn Féin Factor

The purpose of Asquith's memorandum had been to present a matter-of-
fact account of the Irish situation after the Rising and to offer guidelines
for future policies. It proved more successful in the first than in the
second. Asquith had written of new men and a reconstructed administration, but not of a situation that had been transformed. Yet a new factor
had entered in. The era of Home Rule and Home Rulers was ending and
with that would come an end to the dialectical exchanges of the preceding
thirty years on Irish government. For parliamentary representations on the
Irish side there was to be substituted assertion: the doctrine of natural right
was to replace notions of progress by constitutional evolution. The men
who had deliberately sacrificed their lives on Easter Monday, 1916 did not
do so in order to initiate new debate on lines they deemed at all times
unworthy and were now discredited: they did so to assert Irish rights.
They did not believe those rights to be negotiable; on the contrary, they
proclaimed them to be inalienable and indefeasible. In the language they
used, there was no hint of compromise: 'We declare the right of the people
of Ireland', read the Proclamation affixed that Easter Monday morning to

---

★ The letter in manuscript is in the Redmond archives in the National Library,
Dublin, which may account for the scanty attention paid to it in work on Asquith
and the Liberals in Ireland. No copy appears to be in the Asquith Papers.

the walls of the GPO in Dublin, 'to the unfettered control of Irish destinies to be sovereign and indefeasible. Long usurpation of that right by a foreign people had not extinguished the right.' They reaffirmed it, proclaiming 'the Irish Republic as a Sovereign Independent State'.[49] It was as a sovereign state that they claimed for it the allegiance of all Irishmen and guaranteed equal rights to all its citizens. Its *de jure* being was to be translated into *de facto* existence by force – force organised by the Irish Republican Army, a secret revolutionary organisation supported at home by two open military organisations, the Irish Volunteers and the Citizen Army and hopefully by the securing of diplomatic recognition abroad.

For the British government there was a twofold need: first to make a correct assessment of the measure of popular support for Sinn Féin in Ireland, and secondly to judge aright the likely impact of Proclamation and Rising in the working out of a settlement. The responsibility after 7 December 1916 rested, not with Asquith, but with Lloyd George, who had supplanted him. The Irish leaders knew as well or better than most that the change meant a new style and with it a greater element of unpredictability at the top. In July 1914 they had specially asked that Lloyd George, not Crewe, should be the second government representative at the Buckingham Palace Conference, believing, so Asquith surmised, 'perhaps partly from the experience of victims that his peculiar gifts of blandishment and negotiation would be invaluable'. Since then, their experience of those gifts had been enlarged. But uncertainty about where Lloyd George stood remained. On 21 January 1917 Redmond had a meeting with him at the National Liberal Club.[50] It lasted two hours 'mostly on the Irish question' so Redmond recorded, but was not enlightening. 'I could see immediately', Redmond went on, 'that though he had it on his mind he had not given it any serious attention'. Still more discouraging for Redmond, the Prime Minister's mind remained entirely at the point that some form or other of partition was the only possible solution, Protestant feeling in the North of Ireland remaining in his view irreconcilable with acceptance of a parliament for a united Ireland. The most arresting item in the note was personal. Redmond found Lloyd George quite good humoured, 'simple as ever', his temper 'equable rather than cheerful'. But before the year was out and the Irish Convention in disarray, Redmond was to have reason to reconsider this assessment.

In March 1917 Dr Adams, Gladstone professor of Political Theory and Institutions at the University of Oxford and seconded to serve as adviser to the Prime Minister on Irish affairs, had reported to the Prime Minister on the Irish situation. It was, he wrote, exceedingly critical, three things standing out: (1) the pervasiveness and penetration of Sinn Féin doctrine; (2) the decline in the influence of the Nationalist party; and (3) the hardening opinion in Ulster since the Rising.[51] In a further note on 30 March 1917, Adams commented 'Sinn Féin', a name now applied despite republican reservations to the unified separatist movement, 'is an atmosphere not a party and there are no recognised leaders'.[52] Both at the time he wrote were true; both were clarified when the Sinn Féin Árd-fheis met in October 1917.[53] By then, by-elections in North Roscommon on 5 February, in South Longford on 9 May, in East Clare on 10 July and in Kilkenny City, where W.T. Cosgrave was elected on 10 August, all had been won by Sinn Féin and, of corresponding significance, lost by the Nationalists. In the East Clare by-election, where Eamon de Valera, the last commandant to surrender in the Rising, was returned, the size of his majority marked it out as the herald of a new political configuration. Collectively the by-elections provided incontrovertible evidence, not so much that the Nationalists were a spent force, as that they were no longer a force. By contrast, the time had come for the victors to choose a leader and to formulate a programme.

To the leadership there were two claimants, Griffith and de Valera. In the event Griffith stood aside, much as Dillon had for Redmond in 1900, to avoid division, as in any case it was apparent that the proponent of a dual monarchy and one who was predisposed to non-violent resistance was ideologically unacceptable to republicans. Leadership resolved, programme and procedure therefrom remained to be determined.

The members of the Árd-fheis decided that a first step should be to seek recognition of Ireland as an independent republic from the international community of nations. That being approved the question arose – did the making of representations in the name of the republic imply a final commitment to a republican form of government? Such was not universally desired. There was a search for a compromise formula. De Valera produced one. It stated first that the aim was at securing international recognition of Ireland as an independent Irish republic, and secondly, that being achieved, 'the Irish people may by referendum freely choose their own form of government'. The republic for purposes of international representation was accordingly entrenched for the immediate future and, as for the longer term, inevitably the onus would be on those who wished to have an alternative submitted to the people in a referendum. This would place them at a disadvantage. Names are symbols and in the Irish case the Republic having been proclaimed, the issue may be thought to have been decided by what had happened before it was due to be debated. If one pushed the question further back and enquired why was it a republic that was proclaimed in 1916, Fintan Lalor offered as perceptive an answer as may be given: the republic was 'the banner that floats nearest to the sky'. There were, however, curious consequences. Notions of colonial or dominion status much discussed at the time in Ireland, as Adams reported, represented with their monarchical constitutional structure, a line of advance henceforward ideologically foreclosed. In 1917 this was of no immediate moment, the British for their part excluding altogether all thought of a dominion style transfer of powers – but the time was soon to come when things were to be otherwise. When the Irish wanted colonial, or dominion, status the British were unyielding: when late in the day the British came to sponsor it, the Irish, committed to a republic, were opposed to it.

The Irish Convention

Asquith had told Redmond in his letter of 28 July 1916 that the important thing was to keep the negotiating spirit alive. It was superfluous advice – neither could stop negotiating and in the end it helped to bring disaster to both. Lloyd George was also a negotiator, and he negotiated for appearance as well as for ends. The Irish Convention 1917–18 was a grand essay in the art. First he launched a *ballon d'essai* in a letter to Redmond of 16 May 1917, proposing not a convention but a Home Rule settlement with the exclusion of the six counties, subject to reconsideration by parliament after five years; he also formally proposed a Council of Ireland (the first time that such a body was governmentally contemplated) composed in equal numbers of delegations from the two parts of Ireland with powers to extend or to initiate the ending of an area of exclusion. It was only when these proposals failed to get off the ground that Lloyd George reverted to the South African Convention precedent. His letter to Redmond reinforces other evidence to the effect that within a few months of his accession to the highest office, Lloyd George was probing, as a year earlier, for a solution along the lines of exclusion for the six counties, thought of in quasi-permanent terms and Home Rule for the twenty-six with some link between them. 'I saw Lloyd George two or three times in Paris', wrote T.P. O'Connor, on 10 May 1917; 'so far as I could gather he was still on his absurd "clean cut" proposition'.[54] This was so and it reflected the emphasis he placed at this time on the differences between North and South – the inhabitants of the former being, he had told the House of Commons on 7 March 1917 'as alien in blood, in religious faith, in traditions, in outlook – as alien from the rest of Ireland in this respect as the inhabitants of Fife or Aberdeen'.[55] Yet while Lloyd George's mind might be settling on partition, he had not come down conclusively in favour of such a solution. As late as February 1918, reporting on a meeting with members of the Convention, Lloyd George subscribed with other members of the Cabinet to Adams' view that a settlement in wartime was possible only on the basis of one parliament for the whole of Ireland, customs and police in that event being, however, retained under Westminster control. But all was subject to private assurances to Carson that nothing would be done without his assent.

On 25 July the Irish Convention foregathered in Trinity College, Dublin.[56] For Redmond the occasion was overshadowed by party defeats and the loss of his brother, Major Willie Redmond, said by some to have been the most eloquent speaker of his day in the House of Commons, who had lost the seat of East Clare to Eamon de Valera, the Sinn Féin candidate, in June 1917 and who had been killed in action on the Western Front. In the chair was Sir Horace Plunkett, a pioneer of the Irish Agricultural Cooperative movement, with which Adams had been at one time associated. In one sense, Plunkett was a good choice. Not only had he practical experience of farming, much of it in the United States, but he had also a philosophy of rural life with which he had sought to bring a new outlook and sense of purpose to Irish agriculture through cooperation first of creameries and then more widely. Politically he was a Home Ruler who hated the thought of partition and sought to avert it by extolling the merits of a united Ireland within the self-governing Empire. But he made few converts. Birrell earlier on had thought of him as a man with many ramifications and alliances who turned up everywhere and was admirably fitted for the role of Protestant martyr.[57] That is as may be* – what he was not fitted for was the chairmanship of the amorphous assembly of over 100 strong that was the Irish Convention.

The Convention suffered from two handicaps, either of which would have sufficed to render its proceedings fruitless. The first was not merely the absence, but more than that, the outright hostility of Sinn Féin. This meant that the voice of militant republican nationalism was not to be heard at the Convention, but only from outside it in protest. The second handicap was the presence of Ulster Unionists, there only in order to convey their 'inexorable opposition' – the phrase is their own – to Home Rule or any variant of it. By way of wrecking device, they reverted to their earlier demand that not six but all nine counties of Ulster should be excluded permanently and *en bloc*. Had the Southern Unionists known in advance that such were to be the tactics of the Ulster Unionists, they would, according to Lord Midleton, their principal spokesman, 'never have entered the Convention at all'.[58] As it was, their response was to distance themselves from the Ulster Unionists, whose readiness to disregard the interests of the minority outside the nine or six counties was an occasion for surprise as well as resentment. They had lent credence to the assurances of Bonar Law and Carson in the pre-war years, now they were to learn their error. At the Convention, the Southern Unionists put forward proposals for an all-Ireland legislature which showed on the one hand the measure of their alienation from the Ulster Unionists and on the other commanded a degree of nationalist (Redmondite) support which impressed Adams at the time and some others since – Professor Denis

* Plunkett's house at Kilteragh, Foxrock, was burnt by Irregulars in 1923 and Plunkett left Ireland a disillusioned man.

Gwynn to the borders of the ecstatic.[59] But even if workable, which is debatable, the proposals suffered in the hard world of politics from being the product of a minority which was without influence in high places, now that Lord Lansdowne, as the result of an unwise letter, was in eclipse.

Against this background, there was from the outset no possibility of meeting the Prime Minister's 'essential element of a [wartime] settlement', namely, agreement to establish a single legislature for a united Ireland.[60] To this, there were now not one but two obstacles. As the chairman was to report, they might be summed up in two words: Ulster and customs. The former requires nothing by way of further elaboration, but the coming into prominence of the fiscal question foreshadowed the introduction of an item never deemed quite of first importance, but none the less destined to serve as a bargaining counter in the negotiations leading up to the Treaty. In 1917 nationalists of all shades of opinion took the view that control of fiscal policy was an essential element in self-government. They pointed to the Dominions by way of analogy, but few things were better calculated to disturb Unionists, Southern as well as Northern, not to mention the British Cabinet, than the prospect of transfer to an Irish legislature of control over customs. A compromise, an essential feature of which was free trade between Britain and Ireland, was put forward but did not satisfy the Southern, let alone the Ulster Unionists. Agreement was reached only on postponement of an issue on which differences of interest ran too deep for compromise.

The Command Paper reporting on the Convention's proceedings contained no majority report. In its place there was first an account of the Convention's proceedings as related by a chairman, constrained by the representations of others to employ a more prosaic style than he would himself have wished, which consisted of two minority reports – one from fiscal autonomists and the other from Ulster Unionists – and no less than five separate notes and nineteen appendices. The whole was held together, if at all, by Plunkett's letter to the Prime Minister which prefaced the final publication. In the face of the self-evident disagreement recorded in the reports and notes, Plunkett sought to throw into relief first the intricacy of the Convention's assignment – 'to find a way out of the most complex and anomalous situation to be found in history – I might almost say in fiction' – and secondly, the Convention's achievement in securing compromise (by postponement) on one of two major problems – customs and excise – between Nationalists and Southern Unionists, and agreement, also between Nationalists and Southern Unionists, on a complex scheme of self-government duly outlined. Plunkett called upon the Prime Minister – as members of the Convention had already done – to commit himself to giving effect to the latter. He, with them, called in vain. It could not have been otherwise. The agreement rested upon the qualified backing of politically declining forces in the face of unqualified opposition from the

Ulster Unionists in the Convention and contemptuous hostility of Sinn Féin outside it. Such interest as the Convention possessed lay accordingly not in anything it did, but in what it reflected. It was an open debating forum and the ideas it discussed were in many cases those – for example fiscal autonomy, imperial contribution, defence, safeguards or partition for Ulster Unionists and dominion status – which were to come forward with a sharper edge as the nature of the settlement came to be a matter of direct negotiation.

For Lloyd George the Convention was a qualified disappointment rather than a failure. For him it provided a useful and tolerably effective way of demonstrating to America and the Dominions that an attempt had been made to resolve the Irish question, while yet carrying an inbuilt assurance that nothing would come of it, and that failure would be attributed to the inability of Irishmen to agree among themselves. In other words, it was to Lloyd George much as the Cripps mission to India was to be to Churchill twenty-five years later. If anyone entertains doubts on this score, let him glance at the Lloyd George–Redmond correspondence of November 1917–March 1918,[61] when the Convention under Plunkett's erratic guidance and Redmond's failing physical resources was seeking to dispel a sense of its own futility. On 13 November Redmond wrote that the situation in the Convention had become 'exceedingly grave' because of Ulster Unionist intransigence: Lloyd George replied that although he had been in Italy, immersed in very great and probably far-reaching events, he had none the less been devoting 'some time to the Irish situation' and had spoken to Carson on Ulster's intransigence. Redmond wrote again and at length on 19 November. Lloyd George replied on 23 November, saying he had to go abroad for an international conference, adding in an unhelpful postscript that he could not help thinking 'there was a good deal of misunderstanding which can be cleared up by a talk with the leaders of the various interests'. There followed a meeting at which Lloyd George was evidently developing a cold which later caused a delay, 'most unfortunate and full of risk', according to Redmond in dealing with Convention matters. By 15 December Lloyd George had recovered but he was fully occupied 'with serious and urgent questions arising out of the complex military situation'. He wrote a letter for which Redmond, in the hope of salvaging something from the Convention, had pleaded – that is not too strong a word – but which, however, Redmond candid at the last told him on 15 January, arrived 'entirely too late to be of any use to me whatever'. Within a fortnight Redmond was ill, and on 6 March he died. So low had sunk the reputation of the party and regard for its leader that for fear of demonstrations, his coffin was hurried by night through Dublin on its way to his native Wexford, where esteem for him survived political repudiation. The Convention met for the last time on 5 April and its report was published on 12 April. Its sittings had lasted nearly eight months, Lloyd George showing concern when an earlier demise was threatened. By April, it had served his purpose. Redmond, alas for what remained of his reputation★ had once again heeded only too well Asquith's injunction to keep the negotiating spirit alive.

A Package Deal

In early 1918 two questions compelled attention – the first the follow-up to the Convention and the second, in its Irish context, the manpower shortage. The Coalition Cabinet, aware that these were separate issues, decided to treat them as though they were not and as a result produced a package deal – Home Rule and conscription to be extended to Ireland as near simultaneously as was practicable, on the argument that, since there was no prospect of agreement on either separately, objections to each might cancel out if they were taken in conjunction. The one positive result was that the Cabinet *appeared* to have a policy on Ireland, which was important in its English political context, but which, in its Irish, may well have been worse than having none. Not surprisingly, in such circumstances, the composite policy was pursued with a lack of conviction.

On 28 March 1918, the Cabinet, without waiting for the final report of the Convention, decided to extend conscription to Ireland as soon as that report was received.[62] It was an abrupt decision on a matter long debated in a desultory way and one against the weight of official opinion. Duke, on his appointment as Chief Secretary, had assured Maxwell (in September 1916) that 'from my knowledge of English politics and all I could learn of the Irish situation an extension of the Military Service Act to Ireland must be regarded as impracticable'. Maxwell, in a memorandum circulated to the Cabinet a month later, having questioned whether, in 1916, such a policy were not already too late, added that it would, however 'please militant Sinn Féiners and Unionists, the former because it would play into their hands . . . the latter because they consider what is good enough for England is good for Ireland, but the motive imputed to them would be their desire to kill Home Rule'.[63] Duke reiterated his strong objections to conscription in Ireland on 20 and again on 29 March 1918,[64] that is, immediately after the Cabinet decision. Why then was it taken? The answer is first and fundamentally because of a near-desperate shortage of men on the Western Front, with gloomy forebodings even in the highest circles about the stopping of the German offensive short of Calais; for the same fundamental reason there had been earlier conscription crises in Australia and Canada. Second, the pressure of opinion in parliament and in the country upon the Cabinet demanded equality of sacrifice,

★ The centenary of his birth was marked on a national level.

the more insistently with the age of conscription in Great Britain about to be raised from forty-five to fifty. Further stimulating the demand may have been the feeling, expressed very characteristically by Lansdowne, who in 1916 had forecast that the government would eventually be driven to conscription,[65] that 'nothing in the end would be more beneficial socially to Ireland than to pass the bulk of her young men through the army' since it would mean that they 'would return to ordinary life with ideas of duty and discipline', not otherwise to be acquired. But it was the added inducement of a package deal that persuaded the majority of the Cabinet, including Curzon, Smuts and Lloyd George, whose attitude on Ireland was evidently hardening, as Hankey noted in April 1918, to line up with Milner and Balfour on this issue. Smuts' reasoning is of some interest. In the event of the Convention agreeing on a report, and indeed in any event, he thought the passage of a Home Rule Bill and conscription, while in effect simultaneous, should be so timed that Home Rule would come 'first on the ground that this would remove the Irish sense of historic wrong and satisfy United States and Dominion opinion on Home Rule'. Evidently he attached importance to these, in one respect surely misconceived views, for the record of what he said is amended and extended in his handwriting.

On 3 April there was a full-scale discussion on Ireland at a Cabinet conference at which the Viceroy, Lord Wimborne, Duke and Robinson were present. Wimborne said the enforcement of compulsory service before the Convention reported 'would be to cause an explosion in Ireland'. Milner deprecated 'playing with conscription'; once entered upon it would have to be 'seen through'. The majority, however, remained in favour of taking conscription and political settlement together. Smuts thought now was the right time to do so. Bonar Law, having regard to the danger of an explosion in Ulster, guardedly assented, saying that the government would have to stand or fall by both Bills. Robinson thought firmness essential, since weakness would provoke resistance to the death. While agreeing with Wimborne on the need for contemporaneous action, he none the less expected general opposition from Unionists and Sinn Féin, were the two measures to be introduced in conjunction. 'However strange it might appear', commented Milner, 'an attack from both sides would not be a bad thing'. He also felt that an Irish settlement must needs be imposed. The fundamental point was the war, remarked Balfour in gloomy philosophic reflection, and the question was whether they would be stronger if they got a few men from Ireland at the risk of disturbances, or did nothing. He laid down two policies – all or none. If the second were adopted it would be difficult to persuade England to accept the decision. 'We should have to state', he concluded, 'the naked truth that Ireland is a sheer weakness, but it would be a greater weakness if we did something than it was if we did nothing'.

The package policy was announced in the House of Commons on 9 April[66] with a Military Service Bill on the one hand which, while not extending conscription forthwith to Ireland, empowered the government to do so by Order in Council and an invitation to Parliament to frame a measure of self-government for Ireland. Carson commended conscription but without concession on the ground that it was either good or bad in itself; the Nationalist members were united in passionate protest against it and next day Lloyd George thought the Irish 'were trying to work themselves up into a frenzy'.[67] On 16 April the Military Service Bill passed through the House of Commons and the Irish members as a body withdrew from Westminster, never to return.

Withdrawal from Westminster: the End of the Constitutional Party

The two supreme services which Ireland has rendered Britain, wrote Churchill, are her accession to the Allied cause on the outbreak of the Great War, and her withdrawal from the House of Commons at its close.[68] There was, however, some sacrifice of exactitude as the price of a well-turned phrase. It was the Irish Nationalist members who withdrew, the Ulster Unionists remained. Furthermore, a House with responsibility for the framing of an Irish settlement was likely to find the assignment deceptively easy to discharge with the views of the nationalist majority unheard.

In so far as the withdrawal of the party's members coupled with their subsequent appearance in Dublin on a common anti-conscription platform suggested some wider convergence of views between the parliamentarians and Sinn Féin, it was wholly misleading. There was political warfare à l'outrance between them. The parliamentarians had not abandoned their parliamentary tactics. They had withdrawn in protest on a particular issue. They were not, and did not become, abstentionists in principle. The policy of total abstention, Dillon contended, was 'absolutely insane', one moreover which left the representation of Ireland to Carson and his followers.[69] It was a point on which he and Griffith engaged in rancorous altercation. In November 1918 the voters were to come down conclusively in Griffith's favour. The long day of dialectical parliamentary warfare had in fact drawn to its close in April 1918.

For that conscription provided the occasion but it is not to be identified as its cause. The Parliamentary party were destroyed by their own twofold illusion. They continued to believe that unity, or at least some semblance of it, might yet be preserved by constitutional means and that Home Rule might yet satisfy Irish aspirations. But what had a younger generation, moved and uplifted by the Easter Rising, to say to Dillon or he to say to them? They belonged to different worlds.

There was the stuff of tragedy here epitomised in the divisive conflicts of the last leader's closing years. In his early days Dillon had been devoted, as we have seen, to *la politique du pire*, that is, to a persistent belief that making things worse was the only way of making them better. In application this required good judgement and foresight. The former he possessed, the latter was clouded by his innate pessimism. He was a man who was little disposed to adopt new methods or accept a new order of priorities. The grandson of an evicted tenant, he hated landlords. That hatred, his biographer tells us, 'througout his career provided him with most of his political dynamism'.[70] But what was at the heart of the socio-agrarian problems of the eighties, and what was arguably still a safeguard against compromising collaboration in the period of the Land Conference, the devolution crisis and the Irish Council Bill, later resulted in preoccupation with local land issues in Mayo and later still with exaggerated and distracting, conspiratorial notions of politics.

Dillon was too perspicacious to participate in the Irish Convention but not perspicacious enough to draw the right inferences from its failure. By the time he took over the leadership, the party had lost its hold on Ireland, and with it such influence as it retained at Westminster. Though sometimes alleged against Dillon, as frequently against Redmond, he was emphatically not a leader in a 'mendicant' nationalist tradition (to borrow a phrase from Indian National Congress dialectics of the time). He was a patriot, outspoken and courageous, as his speech in the House of Commons on 11 May on the Rising and the executions amply testified.[71] He had also remained impressively consistent in his idea of a settlement. 'All that we ask', he had told Australians in Adelaide in May 1889, 'is that we in Ireland shall stand in the same relation to the Empire as you in Australia . . .'.[72] In 1918 his thoughts were on Dominion Home Rule. In so far as he believed that it could be extracted from the Coalition Cabinet by parliamentary pressure he was, the records make clear, living in a world of make-believe. Three years later Ireland was to acquire dominion status, not by the constitutional processes to which he had given exacting loyalty, but through physical force, which he had deliberately discarded on grounds not of morality but of *realpolitik*. The attainment of the dominion goal by such means and at the price of partition gave him no satisfaction. He was alienated from his successors by convictions too deep to be discarded and by the generational gap which existed long before a generational theory of politics came to be formulated. So it was that at the end, in Professor Lyons' words, he was 'left alone and disillusioned, presenting to history the spectacle – melancholy but not without nobility – of a fiercely honest man who loved his country, but learned through harsh experience that patriotism was not enough'.[73] But the moral to be drawn was rather, and equally, if not more disturbingly, that in certain political contexts even in traditionally democratic political systems, constitutionalism is not enough.

The Package Deal Undone

Meanwhile the Cabinet appointed another committee on Irish policy. The chairman was Walter Long, and Curzon, Smuts, Cave, H.A.L. Fisher and Duke were among the members. The purpose was to draft another Bill in the Home Rule conscription policy. The first meeting was held on 15 April 1918. On 20 April, Tom Jones, after a long discussion, told Hankey that he thought the government's Irish policy was 'a mad one':[74] on 9 May Chamberlain was contending defensively that 'to withdraw from compulsion was to surrender the unity of the Imperial Government' in face of a challenge from Irish Nationalists and he did not see how the government could remain in office if that were done. Smuts conceded that 'in abstract principle' Chamberlain was right – conscription and Home Rule were 'conjoint, associate measures', but, contrary to his earlier view, he felt that Home Rule might mean 'letting loose forces of Civil War when we are fighting for our life' and should therefore be held over anyway as 'a big imperial question'. Conscription, also carrying its own civil war risk, should be likewise deferred.[75] On 14 June the Irish Committee reported it was impossible to give effect to the dual policy. Conscription was tacitly dropped and, in Churchill's retrospective verdict, the government was left with 'all the resentment against compulsion and in the end no law and no men'.[76]

The constitutional discussions in the Irish Committee, without leading anywhere, were somewhat more illuminating. The committee had one essential purpose – to play for time. But its members were less than content with so self-denying a role. They looked for a more specific *raison d'être* and found it by seeking to fulfil one avowed object of their being: the drafting of a Bill. But they ran into difficulties both of principle and of detail. The chairman wanted a Bill that might pass through parliament, but felt that the only hope of achieving this was by drafting the provisions in such a way that they would be consistent with federation of the British Isles. He had strong initial support from Austen Chamberlain, who had said on 16 April that powers might be given to an Irish parliament in so far as was compatible with an overall federal constitution. 'I do not exclude federal reconstruction of [the] United Kingdom – that is the real test for the Irish Bill.'[77] In May Lord Salisbury, on behalf of right-wing Unionist peers, asked that the Cabinet should not consent to introduce a Home Rule Bill at that time, since the likely consequence would be the destruction of a great party, 'a national disaster', to which Chamberlain replied that with 'new problems of profound gravity the settlement of old problems become more urgent. However tempting putting contentious questions aside might lead us far on the road to revolution.' In July Chamberlain developed the federal argument,[78] contending that all past attempts at Home Rule had failed, not because of the incapacity of governments, but because of the impossibility of finding a solution within the limits they had set themselves. But were the context to be widened the problem would become more manageable. He himself believed that, because of the complexity of the issues and the revolutionary ferment that would arise after the war, it would have to be in any case, since one imperial government and parliament could no longer deal with everything, but would find it necessary to devolve a part of its responsibilities on other bodies to set itself free for the work, which it alone could do. If such a scheme of federal devolution were not applied, he surmised, 'We shall be in grave danger of revolution before many years have passed.' Devolution, therefore, was as necessary in English as in Irish interests and the two problems should be run together. That would change the context of the Irish question because while it would, for example, be possible to think of customs and excise in the hands of a Home Rule government, it would be impossible in a federation to conceive of them except in the hands of the federal government. So the Chamberlainite moral was: cease to think of the Irish question in isolation, but enlarge the setting, bearing in mind that decentralisation of government is a general not a particular problem.

The argument was not without consequence on the longer term, but it carried only modest conviction in a disillusioned committee, from which Cave wished to resign because he thought it was ploughing the sands, and in which Curzon saw no line of advance.[79] An answer of a kind was later given to Chamberlain's contention in a letter from Lord Hugh Cecil. He recognised, even while deploring, the fact of Irish nationality and he argued that federalism and nationality were contradictory and mutually fatal. 'The truth is', he wrote, 'that colouring federalism with nationalism is like painting a rat red; it kills the animal'.[80] From this the conclusion was that nationality and federalism alike having revealed their impracticability, the Irish might eventually be driven towards Union with provincial devolution. Cave was right: it was time to go. The committee was without hope because it was helpless. As Long noted on returning from Ireland in June, the association of Home Rule with conscription would result in the most liberal Home Rule Bill the committee could devise being torn up and treated with contempt by nationalists all over Ireland as well as being vigorously resisted by Unionists.[81]

PART III

THE SETTLEMENT:
THE FIRST PHASE

CHAPTER 5

The Government of Ireland Act 1920: Devolution and Division

The Post-war Environment

In an Anglo-Irish setting, eight years and a whole world passed between the general election of December 1910 and that of December 1918. The first had opend the way to the enactment of Home Rule; the second to its supersession save in the Unionist redoubt in the north-east, in which Unionists had earlier proclaimed their resolve to resist its application by force. But behind apparent inconsistency lay an inner consistency. For nationalist Ireland, not Home Rule, but a republic had become the goal; for Ulster Unionists it was reassurance, that Ulster should remain part of the United Kingdom and apart from the rest of Ireland, even at the price of Home Rule.

The paradox reflects the changes, psychological rather more than political, that took place between 1910 and 1918. They were profound. Churchill would have us believe that, as the deluge subsided and the waters fell after a war in which 'the mode and thought of men, the whole outlook on affairs, the grouping of parties, all have encountered violent and tremendous changes', what was to be seen were 'the dreary steeples of Fermanagh and Tyrone emerging once again. The integrity of their quarrel is one of the few institutions that have been unaltered in the cataclysm which has swept the world.'[1] The point is well made but might not its antithesis be equally or more convincingly argued? At the outbreak of war the central issue was the exclusion of Ulster or some part of it for a period of years or in perpetuity from a Home Rule Ireland; at its close it was how to reconcile Irish republican aspirations with traditional British monarchical sentiment and symbolism, the ultimate destiny of Fermanagh and Tyrone remaining conditional upon the outcome. And what of the mode and thought of men? The generation that discarded the Parliamentary party with contumely and repudiated constitutional means with a calculated disregard for risks or consequences represented a way of thinking and of acting altogether alien to those of Redmond, or Dillon or Devlin. Beside Churchill's 'unaltered' might be put Yeats' 'changed

utterly'.[2] While the contours indeed remained, the elusive spirit of nationalism released by war was at large, to be seen in new and very different
manifestations. Political leaders, Irish as well as British, soaked from their
youth in Home Rule controversies, may be pardoned for having been
slow to recognise how much the substance and temper of Anglo-Irish
politics had changed. Of this, a reminder may suffice. Redmond and
Dillon aspired to , but hardly hoped to attain, dominion self-government
on the Canadian, or even more favoured, the South African model. To
Unionists so large a concession was unthinkable, as indeed in its time it
had been in South Africa, and Liberals regarded it as a distant goal and one
not for contemplation in wartime or post-war conditions. But how slow
they were to grasp that post-war Irish opinion did not want it either!
While the British were catching up, the Irish had moved on. Such was the
measure of change.

The 1918 General Election

On the signing of the Armistice on 11 November 1918 Lloyd George
advised dissolution with an election to take place in December. Sinn
Féin decided to contest it. They issued a manifesto in which their aims
were formulated. First and foremost among them was the establishment of a republic (1) by withdrawing representation from Westminster;
(2) by undermining British power to rule; (3) by calling a constituent
assembly; and (4) by international appeal to the Peace Conference, by
the last of which much store was set. The advancement of these aims,
subversive as they were of British authority, did not exclude the use of
force, one consequence of which was that the manifesto suffered much
from excisions at the hands of the censor. In the following phrases the
words in brackets were deleted: 'Sinn Féin stands (less for a political
party than) for the Nation; it represents the old tradition of nationhood
(handed on from dead generations; it stands by the Proclamation of the
Provisional Government of Easter 1916) reasserting the inalienable right
of the Irish Nation to sovereign independence . . .'.[3] With or without
excisions the message was clear. The aim was independence, it was *not*
Home Rule, party members being collectively dismissed in the manifesto
as 'an obstacle' to be removed – a harsh judgement but not one peculiar to
Sinn Féin: '. . . accredited representatives of Ireland "The Party" can never
be again'. So in 1917 William O'Brien had ended his pamphlet on *'The
Party' who they are and what they have done*, not neglecting to send a
complimentary copy to the party's other unrelenting critic in the wings,
Tim Healy.[4]

    By-election experience earlier in the year had indicated that Sinn Féin
candidates in prison at the least were at no disadvantage against their
opponents in the field – quite the contrary, as Arthur Griffith's victory

over the Parliamentary party candidate in East Cavan on 20 June 1918 strikingly testified. Whether the same factors would apply in a general election was deemed more problematic. In March 1918 Lord Wimborne was succeeded by a 'soldier Lord-Lieutenant', Field-Marshal Lord French, one of the more idiosyncratic figures who stepped on to the Irish stage at this time.[5] With the aim of destroying Sinn Féin, his appointment was quickly followed in a deliberately provocative gesture by wholesale arrests on grounds of alleged treasonable communication with the enemy. Some 115 leaders were deported and some 1,319 others imprisoned, with the result that only 26 Sinn Féin candidates could appear in their constituencies. Yet, as in by-elections, they would seem to have gained rather than lost by such enforced absence.

Sinn Féin's triumph in the general election was almost complete. The Parliamentary party, which had held 68 seats at the dissolution, won only 6 in the election, 4 of them in Ulster, by prior agreement not contested by Sinn Féin. Sinn Féin, which had held 7 at the dissolution, won 73 in the election. In 24 of the 32 counties, only Sinn Féin candidates were elected. The Unionists, who advanced from 19 to 26, carried 4 counties, Down, Antrim, Derry and Armagh, with substantial majorities. But they were in a minority as against the combined Nationalist – Sinn Féin parties in Fermanagh and Tyrone. Overall a high proportion of the electorate did not vote, yet the message of the election was clear. The Unionists were entrenched in 4 counties, Sinn Féin in 26 with the 2 in debate between them, these two Fermanagh and Tyrone, coming down on the Nationalist side.

What the Sinn Féin electoral victory meant was twice writ plain, once politically and once violently for all to read on 21 January 1919. On that day Sinn Féin convened a first meeting of Dáil Éireann at the Mansion House in Dublin. All members elected for Irish constituencies were invited, but the Unionists did not attend on principle and the 34 of the 61 elected Sinn Féin members who were in jail were precluded from doing so in practice. That meant an attendance of 27, though the official record listed 29 by way of providing alibis for Michael Collins and Harry Boland who were contriving de Valera's escape from Lincoln Jail.

At the outset the Dáil thus composed decided that it should itself act as the Constituent Assembly of the Irish nation. In that role, it decreed the establishment of the Irish republic, declared the independence of Ireland and asserted that the elected representatives of the Irish people were alone invested with authority to make laws binding on the Irish people. In accord with Griffith's Sinn Féin programme, a Sinn Féin administration was established, theoretically responsible to the Dáil, though in practice, once conflict was joined with the disintegrating British-controlled government in Dublin Castle, much was decided locally.[6] That was to be the case even more with the direction of the guerrilla warfare which, albeit

fortuitously and on local initiative,* is to be dated from the shooting at
Soloheadbeg, also on 21 January 1919. In sum, Irish nationalism on that
day entered the era of revolutionary action in respect both of government
and the use of military force under its actual or nominal control. Within
little more than a month of the election, therefore, it became apparent that
far from a meeting of minds, there was to be confrontation in the form of
a politico–military challenge to the continuance of British rule.

In England also a new balance of political forces emerged in December
1918.† There the election resulted in an overwhelming victory for the
Coalition, which returned 475 members on the Coalition coupon,‡ no less
than 48 Conservatives without it as against 29 Asquithian Liberals and 59
Labour. The Coalition membership of 475 was made up of 339 Coalition
Unionists, as against 136 Coalition Liberals, generally and less respect-
fully known as 'Coalie Libs' or 'Lloyd George's stage army'.[7] Unionist
predominance in the House was reflected in a Cabinet where Lloyd George
continued as Prime Minister, with immense prestige but no solid party
backing. In the new Coalition Cabinet, formed in January, but not operative till October 1919, Bonar Law was Lord Privy Seal; Balfour, Lord
President; Austen Chamberlain, Chancellor of the Exchequer; Curzon,
Foreign Secretary; Birkenhead, Lord Chancellor; Milner, Colonial Secretary; Montagu at the India Office; Churchill, still a Liberal in party
allegiance, at the War Office and Ian Macpherson also a Liberal, Chief
Secretary, in which office he served for long enough to introduce the
Government of Ireland Bill early in 1920 in a speech which in its lack of
conviction may be thought to foreshadow the disillusion with Lloyd
George's Irish policy that led to his resignation shortly thereafter. The
most important consequence of the election on the Irish front was that it
ensured that the penultimate stages in the negotiation of an Irish settlement
on the English side were to be in the hands of the last of three successive
Coalition Cabinets – those of Asquith, formed in May 1915; of Lloyd
George, formed in December 1916; and Lloyd George again, formed in
January 1919, each increasing in its Unionist as it declined in its Liberal
membership.

* Dan Breen dismissed criticism that he should not have acted 'until the matter had
been solemnly discussed in advance' in Dublin, with the comment, 'we just
listened to all the orations . . . and made up our own minds'. Dan Breen, *My Fight
for Irish Freedom*, new edn (Tralee, 1964) p. 27. In this revised edition, since
reprinted a number of times, a greater degree of self-justification is attempted than
had been evident in the original version in 1924.
† The election was held on 14 December and the results declared on 28 December.
‡ Coupon was the term used to describe a pre-election Liberal–Unionist bargain
providing that up to 150 Liberal candidates would not be opposed by Unionists in
return for their pledge, if elected, to support the Coalition. Cf. Trevor Wilson,
The Downfall of the Liberal Party, 1914–1935 (London, 1968), pp. 135–83.

In the election the Irish question had played a secondary or even lesser part, the campaign being dominated by the release of pent-up wartime emotions finding an outlet in slogans – 'Hang the Kaiser', or, in Auckland Geddes' arresting Cambridge phrase on reparations, 'squeeze the lemon till the pips squeak' – and concern for the welfare of ex-servicemen – 'homes fit for heroes to live in'. But superimposed on pre-war passions on Ireland were newer resentments – in Ireland itself at the 1916 executions and contemplated conscription, and in Britain and more especially in Unionist Ulster, against Irish association with the enemy, the focus being, as Asquith had noted, on Casement's abortive attempt to enlist Irish prisoners of war in German hands in a brigade that would take part in a German-equipped expedition to Kerry. None of these things eased the road to settlement.

The post-election House of Commons may or may not, in the phrase to which J.M. Keynes gave wide currency, have been composed of 'a lot of hard-faced men who look as if they had done very well out of the war' – a study of photographs and a scrutiny of wills might assist judgement – but at the least it was formidable in expressions of rancour.[8] Lloyd George was sensitive to his own vulnerability in the House and felt himself on occasion to be a prisoner of the Coalition. But in the country at large he remained at, or near, the pinnacle of his reputation as the great little man who had won the war. While therefore he had to, and self-evidently did, keep in mind the need for concessions to his Unionist Cabinet colleagues on Irish policy, he had his own base and his own priorities. He desired, of that there can be little doubt, an Irish settlement, but not one at the price of his own and, what had become much the same thing, the Coalition's survival. When that appeared in jeopardy he withdrew, as earlier he had in 1916, and again in 1918, when the extension of conscription was not of his choosing, but pressed upon him. This sensitivity to threats to his own political survival understandably created an impression of inconsistency or even uncertainty about his course of action. Yet while his position induced caution, in one respect it was not as vulnerable as the imbalance in party representation might suggest. While he had always to weigh the chances of any settlement on Ireland being acceptable to the Unionist majority in parliament, there was one countervailing element for which he may have made insufficient allowance – by 1919, if labels be disregarded, not all Home Rulers were on the Liberal side, and with that went a perceptible erosion of uncritical English Unionist backing for the Ulster Unionists.

As to his own predisposition, Lloyd George claimed to be a federalist, professedly prepared to contemplate a federal or devolutionary settlement to the point of its establishing separate legislatures for Wales and Scotland as well as Ireland. The parliamentary Conference on Devolution, set up in 1919 under the chairmanship of Speaker Lowther, lent scant encouragement to thinking on federalist lines.[9] This was crucial, since it was no part of Lloyd George's thinking that concessions be made to Ireland, which would not or could not be made elsewhere. For Ireland alone he favoured, so he told H.A.L. Fisher on 10 April 1919, an all-Ireland parliament with an Ulster committee empowered to protect Ulster's interests, the more so since at that time it had not been dismissed out of hand by either Carson or the Nationalists.[10] Fundamental, however, was Lloyd George's unwillingness to coerce the minority in Ulster. That, according to Tom Jones, was the 'key to his policy'. In his speech to the House (already referred to) of 7 March 1917, he had spoken of Ulster Unionists as being 'as alien from the rest of Ireland . . . as the inhabitants of Fife or Aberdeen. . . . To place them under national rule against their will would be as glaring an outrage on the principles of liberty and self-government, as the denial of self-government would be for the rest of Ireland.' It was this that led to the crystallisation of his aim, instinctive rather than defined, namely, to concede the near equivalent of self-determination to the Ulster minority, and only thereafter, and then within limits, to the rest of Ireland, secure in the knowledge that the force of Unionist objection would have been blunted by meeting their ultimate, non-negotiable demand.

The Formulation of Policy

At this point one may pose neglected questions. What was the government's Irish policy? To what extent had it been formulated or defined? The answers to both questions are set out in a passage devoted to Irish policy in the Coalition's election manifesto of 22 November 1918. It read:

> We regard it as one of the first obligations of British statesmanship to explore all practical paths towards the settlement of this grave and difficult question, on the basis of self-government. But there are two paths which are closed – the one leading to a complete severance of Ireland from the British Empire, and the other to the forcible submission of the six counties of Ulster to a Home Rule Parliament against their will. In imposing these two limitations, we are only acting in accordance with the declared views of all English political leaders.[11]

The passage clearly excluded negotiations on the basis of an Irish republic, since at that time it was inconceivable that a republic should be other than outside the Empire, though the phrasing 'complete' severance might be interpreted as allowing some peripheral flexibility. It also quite explicitly excluded concessions by Ulster to Irish unity extracted by force or the threat of it. Ulster here was defined in terms of a six-county area, not as the whole province demanded by the pre-war Covenanters nor yet as an area to be determined by county option, which was Asquith's final pre-war position. In the intervening years, the 1916 negotiations had left their mark. Yet there was deemed to be some ambiguity as to the degree of persuasion that might be used to bring 'Ulster', thus defined, to accept boundary modification, to cause her to enter into arrangements for joint administration or even consultation on common services – on which the Cabinet Committee on Ireland sought, but did not obtain, clarification. The wording of the manifesto above all reflected the constraints in the formulation of policy for an Irish settlement under the aegis of a Coalition Cabinet, the first commitment of whose Unionist members was to Ulster, and of its Liberal members to a unitary Home Rule state.

The Time Factor

It is no matter for surprise that the Prime Minister and Cabinet showed natural reluctance to make an early move when the new House assembled. Repeated enquiries elicited from Prime Minister and Lord President terse rejoinders to the effect that it was impossible to give any definite date for a statement or a Bill embodying the government's policy. But, while such enquiries received no constructive response, there was a factor that could not be indefinitely disregarded. It was time. The Irish question had been with English statesmen for a long time – 700 years, de Valera was later to explain to Lloyd George, who more than most restricted his interest to the present – but at the end the settlement was hurried. The Home Rule Act was on the Statute Book, and, while suspended for the period of the war, it was scheduled to come into operation automatically when hostilities were formally concluded with the signature of the last of the peace treaties. It was that which provided the necessary incentive for the appointment of a Committee on Ireland in October 1919, its members being reminded when they met that 'the suspension of the operation of the 1914 Home Rule Act will terminate with the ratification of the Treaty of Peace with Turkey'[12] – which, though this could not have been foreseen, was to be delayed until the signing of the Treaty of Lausanne in 1923.

For the Coalition, which could not allow the Home Rule Act to take effect without causing its own disruption, the time factor was tantamount to a time limit, from which there were only two ways of escape – the repeal of the 1914 Act without substitution for it or indefinite extension of the Suspensory Act. With a Coalition government both were deemed impractical and/or ill advised. To the diehard Henry Page-Croft's interjection in the House, 'Repeal', Austen Chamberlain retorted that they might as well be living in the dark ages. 'You cannot safely repeal the Act of 1914. You cannot safely allow it to come into force.' Bonar Law commented that there were two fundamental facts which 'rule the whole situation. The first is that the Home Rule Act is on the Statute Book, and the second is the question of time. We are approaching the period when the last of the Peace Treaties will . . . be ratified, and when that happens, unless something is done, this Act [Home Rule Act 1914] automatically comes into operation.' Even Carson, albeit reluctantly, recognised that this was so, warning Unionists that the Act of 1914 was on the Statute Book and would come into force unless replaced by another statute which *inter alia* repealed it. This in fact is what the Act of 1920 was to do, Section 76(1) reading 'The Government of Ireland Act, 1914, is hereby repealed as from the passing of this Act.' It was, complained T.P. O'Connor, the only effective clause in all its provisions.[13] But it had to be effected in time. The Coalition Cabinet, as its Unionist members had good reason to note, were no longer playing for time, but constricted by time.

The Cabinet's Irish Situation Committee: Appointment and Proceedings

The Cabinet's Irish Situation Committee appointed in October 1919 was to undertake a first consideration of policy. Its chairman once again was to be Walter Long. When in heady pre-war days Long had declared he would not stand idly by while Liberals and Nationalists organised revolution, G.K. Chesterton counselled:

> Walter be wise, avoid the wild and new
> The constitution is the thing for you.

In its Irish aspect that was now his concern! Having lost out on the leadership in 1911, about which he continued to feel aggrieved, he was apt to be sensitive on status and, as 1916 showed, he was not to be discounted on the shaping of Irish policy. Others to serve on the Committee were the Chief Secretary, J.I. Macpherson, his predecessor in that office, Edward Shortt, H.A.L. Fisher, President of the Board of Education and Sir Laming Worthington-Evans, Pensions. Its terms of reference were to make proposals for dealing with the Irish question.[14] What the Unionists stood for was clear enough. What had the Liberals to offer?

A communication circulated to members by Edwin Montagu may serve as *mise-en-scène* for the committee's deliberations as viewed in a Liberal-Home Rule perspective. Montagu put the case for a Home Rule Bill, not of a compromise kind, to be introduced without procrastination in the hope, slender though it might seem, of a constitutional party reappearing in Ireland. Such a measure would, he believed, be acceptable to English opinion given that there were 'far more Home Rulers in England today' than pre-1914. He could not believe there was any real danger of separation, the demand for it in Ireland produced by the denial of self-government being ephemeral. He found it 'impossible to believe that the Irish really want it'. That left Ulster as the one obstacle. The pledge that she should not be coerced, while rightly given, should not be interpreted so as to allow Ulster politicians to reject what to reasonable men seemed reasonable. He believed in one nation; the world was full of cases in which two races had been able to unite. He would give the Irish nation one parliament with powers over the whole of Ireland, but allow to any county at the outset power to vote herself out for a term of years indefinitely renewable. This solution, he felt, would at once give Ireland Home Rule, emphasise Irish nationality as an ideal and allow, to counties that wanted it, temporary union with Britain.[15] In this submission Montagu foreshadowed the Treaty in respect of an all-Ireland framework with acquiescence in exclusion, temporary in name, but allowing for indefinite extension. The whole was vitiated by the notion that the Irish did not want separation. That was the great Liberal illusion.

In its first report dated 4 November 1919,[16] the Cabinet Committee endorsed Montagu's views that the time had come for a comprehensive settlement. In view of the situation in Ireland itself, of public opinion in Great Britain and still more in the Dominions and the United States, they felt they could not recommend the policy of either repealing or postponing the Home Rule Act 1914, and urged the Cabinet to make 'a sincere attempt to deal with the Irish question once and for all'. The committee noted the government's commitment to the preservation of the unity of the Empire, which excluded any proposal allowing Ireland or any part of it to establish an independent republic; past assurances to the Ulster Unionists ruled out their being forced against their will under the rule of an Irish parliament. Given their unwavering and vehement opposition to any such subjection, the establishment by the action of the Imperial Parliament of a single Parliament for all Ireland on the lines of the Home Rule Acts, 1886, 1893 and 1914, was effectively precluded. The starting point for a settlement was no longer to be unity, but division. This was to be the new departure.

Within this context the committee considered three possible courses, in the first two of which deference was paid to the unitary principle. They were:

(a) The establishment of a Home Rule parliament for all Ireland with provision for the exclusion of some part of Ulster by 'clean cut', county option or plebiscite;

(b) A single parliament with safeguards for Ulster;

(c) A parliament of the southern counties and a second parliament for Ulster, together with a council to discharge certain immediate functions, but mainly to promote as rapidly as possible and without further reference to the Imperial Parliament the union of the whole of Ireland under a single legislature.

The discussion on the first proposal was detailed. It was argued that if the policy of exclusion were to be based on county option or some form of plebiscite, as had been under consideration at the Buckingham Palace Conference, the area excluded would almost certainly be administratively unworkable, while the prospect of election or plebiscite would infallibly inflame religious and political passions in Ireland, do more to partition Ireland in spirit and temper than any externally imposed separation and divide Ireland on purely religious lines. On the other hand, exclusion on the basis of province or six-county block would leave large national-ist majorities under British rule and so infringe the principle of self-determination. Finally, in the judgement of the committee, there was one general objection of a most serious kind. Such a solution would involve the retention of British rule in some part of Ireland. That would defeat what they thought of as a principal purpose of the settlement, namely, the getting rid of continued British rule in the domestic affairs of Ireland. That had been the root of the Home Rule movement and if retained in some part of Ireland, it would prove a source of resentment to nationalists and of further criticism from overseas.

The second expedient, in view of the Ulster Unionist hostility, was deemed to be self-evidently a non-starter. The third, however, com-mended itself to the committee in that the creation of two parliaments, one for the North and the other for the South, would get rid of 'the tap root of the Irish difficulty by providing for the complete withdrawal of British rule from the whole of Ireland in the sphere of its domestic government'. By so doing, it would meet 'the fundametal demand of the overwhelming majority of Irishmen ever since the days of O'Connell'; it was 'entirely consistent' with majority resistance in Ulster to rule from Dublin and nationalist resistance in the rest of Ireland to British rule; it was also 'entirely consistent' with the government pledges to Ulster; it would 'enormously minimise' the partition issue, the division of Ireland being a far less serious matter if Home Rule were established in both parts of it and 'all Irishmen' therefore self-governing with 'far the most con-venient dividing line' between the two parts being the historic frontiers of Ulster which, with its comparatively even balance, would minimise the division of Ireland on purely religious lines. To complete the catalogue of merit, there would be a Council of Ireland with members from North and South to keep open the road to unity.

In sum, therefore, the committee's conclusions were first that exclusion from a Home Rule Bill on a basis of county option was unworkable; second, that the idea of an Irish parliament, doubtfully consistent as it was with pledges of non-coercion given by the Prime Minister to the Ulster Unionists, was vitiated, as indeed was county option, by the assump-tion that it was within the power of the Imperial Parliament to 'compel Irishmen to unite'. The third conclusion, which the committee recom-mended to the Cabinet, was the establishment of Home Rule for both parts of Ireland, each with its own parliament, providing for the complete withdrawal of British rule from the whole of Ireland in the sphere of domestic government.

At the Cabinet meeting on 11 November, the committee's conclusions came in for criticism on three points.[17] While it was accepted that the Ulster Unionists could not be coerced and that their separate status should be recognised, it was urged, first, that Ulster Unionists had always taken the standpoint of retaining the same position as Great Britain and not, as the committee contemplated, of being placed under a different regime; second, that the remaining provinces would obtain rather less than under the Home Rule Act and that it was therefore not likely to be acceptable to them, and third, that the three remaining provinces were overwhelmingly in favour of Sinn Féin and that the first action of Sinn Féin in power would be to declare an independent republic unless this was provided against in the Bill in some way. On the other hand it was also accepted that it was impossible to retreat and that a mere repeal of the Home Rule Act or postponement was probably not acceptable to parliament and very undesirable from the point of view of the United States and the Dominions. The committee, taking these views into account, was invited to submit further and more detailed proposals.

The committee's report had provoked particular misgivings in the minds of the Lord Chancellor, Lord Birkenhead, and the Minister of Pensions, Sir Laming Worthington-Evans. In a Joint Note circulated to the Cabinet on 11 November, the day on which the report came forward for first consideration, they advised that no Bill embodying the committee's proposals should be pressed through all its stages in parliament unless the Cabinet became satisfied that responsible people South and North would form the governments necessary to maintain law and order. For their part, they thought it probable that 'the Sinn Féiners will reject the offer with contempt and that the Ulstermen will not welcome it'. None the less they agreed that the proposal should go forward. In a candid postscript Birkenhead added, 'I assent to this proposed Bill as affording an ingenious strengthening of our tactical position before the world. I am absolutely satisfied that the Sinn Féiners will refuse it. Otherwise in the present state of Ireland I could not even be a party to making the offer.'[18] In his concern with the United States and dominion opinion, Birkenhead by no means stood alone.

Were Birkenhead and Worthington-Evans right in thinking the Ulstermen would not welcome the report? That was the crucial question most of all for the Unionist members of the government. The answer was made known when at the committee meeting on 13 November Fisher told members that he had been deputed by the Prime Minister to outline to Sir James Craig how the committee was thinking. In respect of area, Craig had expressed himself against the inclusion of the whole of Ulster in the Northern parliament, believing the six-county area to be preferable.

Protestant representation would thereby be strengthened and, that apart, the six counties would be an easier area to govern. Craig then, contrary to the Lord Chancellor's surmise, expressed his sympathy with the idea of a House of Commons for Ulster and for Dublin, though instead of the Joint Council he preferred a House of Lords for the whole of Ireland 'to arrest legislation'.[19] This was a response on the part of Ulster Unionists that in the end sufficed to determine the parameters of the first phase of the settlement. From the outset they had, through Craig, expressed 'sympathy' with the idea of parliamentary institutions in Belfast despite later disavowals that this was so. For English Unionists also the proposal was welcome in its widening of the range of Ulster options and its opening up of the possibility of a transfer of responsibility for the domestic government of the province (or some part of it) from Westminster to Belfast.

What of the Southern Unionists whose plight under Home Rule elicited professions of concern before the war? The Ulster role at the Irish Convention had already made it abundantly clear that Ulster Unionism was for Ulster and that all that eloquence about Ulster resistance being the means to an end – killing Home Rule – had at last come down to reality – the end was Ulster, and Ulster alone. Southern Unionists, more accommodating than the Ulstermen, had in the mean time become more understanding of national aspirations, as time for them was running out. Implicitly they conceded that the Union could not be maintained in terms of dominion Home Rule. For English Unionists, however, abandonment by Southern Unionists of Union as a lost cause was a liberating factor of greater importance than is apt to be attributed to it. No longer need they, nor did they, feel inhibited in their actions by thoughts of Lansdowne and his supposedly solid body of Unionists in the South and West. As Long was to put it, 'in the old days I felt bound by the just demand of the Unionists, North and South, to be protected by England against the Nationalists' but now that the Southern Unionists had abandoned their old position and were demanding self-government albeit 'in somewhat vague terms' and Ulster was satisfied, 'all we have to consider is how to provide the best machinery for the establishment of a new form of government for Ireland'.[20] Southern Unionists saw things rather differently; it was a case of their being misled and then being abandoned by Unionists in Ulster and England – 'base desertion', Lord Desart described it in a turgid but not unrepresentative communication from Kilkenny circulated to the committee. Southern Unionists, he added,[21] were all opposed to partition – it was politically impossible, impractical in operation; whether Ulster or six counties was the unit there would be continuous agitation by a considerable nationalist and Catholic minority – 'the most bitter and violent in Ireland'. This would react unfavourably upon the minority of the South. But Desart had no alternative to offer – 'I do not believe a scheme imposed by Great Britain will', he remarked, 'in present conditions be accepted here'.

Subsidiary to the larger political questions of area and institutions, the committee was also concerned with making recommendations on the distribution of powers, a matter on which Professor Adams was their mentor, as earlier he had been of the Convention. The basic recommendation of the Bill, which was in the process of being drafted, was that on and after the appointed day there should be established in Ireland, exclusive of Ulster, a parliament to be called the Parliament of Southern Ireland and in Ulster (hereinafter to be called Northern Ireland) a Parliament of Northern Ireland with a Council composed in equal numbers (20) of Members of the two Houses of Parliament 'with a view to bringing about harmonious action . . . to the promotion of mutual intercourse and uniformity in relation to matters affecting the whole of Ireland, and to providing for the administration of services which the two parliaments mutually agree should be administered uniformly throughout the whole of Ireland'.

What, Adams asked, were to be the distinguishing features of the two Irish parliaments? There were, in his opinion, two relevant models: (1) dominion, (2) federal or devolutionary, with fundamental points of difference between them. A Dominion would enjoy almost complete autonomy, with no obligation to make an imperial contribution and having no representation in parliament at Westminster, while under a federal or devolutionary arrangement fiscal powers would be narrowly circumscribed, imcome tax probably, customs and excise certainly being reserved, as also postal services, with a contribution made to imperial expenditure and some limited representation in the Imperial Parliament. Here, he wrote, are two types 'so plainly distinct in their fundamental characteristics that it is vitally important to be clear as to which type is being set up'. The right thing to do, as Adams saw it, was therefore to go frankly for dominion status or, alternatively, to take no step that would prejudice the working of either a federal or devolutionary scheme for the British Isles.[22] The committee found no difficulty in coming down in favour of limited devolution in principle, though members were apt from time to time to be distracted by particular proposals inconsistent with it, for example the transfer of customs and excise, and to debate them in a political context irrespective either of the administrative implications or of consistency. An element of confusion also arose in relation to the Council of Ireland. Was it to be a body to which the parliaments of Southern and Northern Ireland might, as was provided in Section 2 of the draft Bill, transfer powers only by agreement or should it be vested from the outset with some responsibilities of its own? Adams advised that some powers should, immediately on the Act coming into force, be transferred to the Council for a limited period, to ensure that this one all-Ireland institution should at least have a trial. A condition of such trial would, however, be willingness of the future Parliament of Northern Ireland to play their part. Sir Henry Robinson, Vice-President of the Irish Local Government Board, in a paper laid before the committee indicated his belief that it was highly improbable that the Ulstermen would do anything of the kind or that the Parliament of Northern Ireland would delegate any of its powers to the Council of Ireland or even nominate delegates to it, adding for good measure that in the unlikely event of their doing so, the northern delegates would 'find that the anti-English atmosphere of the Council is too strong for them and . . . withdraw'. Clearly, he continued, there was little profit in further discussion unless the government was prepared to constitute a council vested with more than the minimal powers contemplated, namely original jurisdiction in respect of Private Bills, railway matters of common concern, fisheries and control of animal diseases. More than that, Robinson was to explain, would have meant placing the six counties under an outside jurisdiction and this 'cannot be done without the assent of the six counties'.[23] To insist upon a trial fell within the forbidden category of coercion of Ulster.

When the Cabinet met on 3 December the Prime Minister reported on a conversation which he and the Lord Privy Seal, Bonar Law, had had with the Rt Hon. James O'Connor, a Lord Justice of Ireland, who described himself as more of a Catholic than an Irishman, and indicated that he had ascertained the views of the hierarchy on the outline of a settlement in the North.[24] O'Connor favoured county option for Ulster. He believed, however, that it would result in six of the nine counties exercising any such right by voting to remain 'attached' to the United Kingdom, by which he appears to have meant as an integral part of it. Such an arrangement, in his view, was more likely than any other to reunite the six counties with the rest of Ireland, not least as a result of their people being attracted by the almost certainly lower level of taxation under Home Rule. If this were not feasible, he would prefer that a parliament for the north-east of Ireland should be for the six counties rather than for Ulster as a whole. Whatever course the government adopted would be condemned by the Irish people, but he thought that none the less they would be willing to work a scheme providing for a separate six-county parliament. It is clear from later allusions to O'Connor's views in Cabinet and Cabinet Committee, that they were received as reflecting the views of the hierarchy and, as such, carefully weighed, not least O'Connor's expressed preference for the exclusion of the six counties as against that of the province of Ulster.

The Cabinet then resumed discussions on constitution and area in the context of the committee's revised propositions. These were first that there should be a parliament for the South and West of Ireland, with the six counties being allowed to vote in favour of remaining part of the United Kingdom for all purposes; second, that there should be a parliament for the South and West and a parliament for the whole of Ulster and third, that there should be a parliament for the South and West and a parliament for the six counties.[25] In favour of the first proposition, that is, the six counties remaining an undifferentiated part of the United Kingdom, there was said to be a clear basis of principle – that of self-determination to be applied if necessary by plebiscite; against it the assertion that the 'Covenanters' would be opposed, because they had bound themselves to treat Ulster as a unit, that the Nationalists would likewise be opposed and also all moderate elements in the South and West, with the result that the prospect of the eventual unity of Ireland would be thereby 'greatly diminished'. There were practical difficulties as well. Direct rule in the excluded area, by diminishing prospects of Irish unity, would give the impression that partition was the aim of British policy. In respect of some members of the Cabinet, the assumption was well grounded. They were in favour of keeping Ulster, or at any rate the six counties, permanently separate from the rest of Ireland. But the general feeling was that the 'ultimate aim of government policy was a united Ireland with a separate Parliament of its own, bound by the closest ties with Great Britain', something to be attained with the largest possible support and without offending the Protestants in Ulster; or as Sir Edward Carson on another occasion had put it, with Ulster to be won by kindness.

In the light of objections and difficulties, the Cabinet then ruled out the continued inclusion of the six counties for all purposes in the United Kingdom. That brought the related questions of area and government into the forefront. If there were to be a separate parliament, should it be for all nine counties of Ulster or for the six counties?[26] One argument for a six-county area was the already higher rate of increase among Catholics, with the 'danger' that in the course of time the Protestants would be 'swamped' if the whole province were the unit. But like so many demographic forecasts, this was no sooner advanced than it was refuted. Nor has it hitherto been realised. A more substantial argument for the six-county area was the advantage of having people under a Northern Ireland parliament as homogeneous as possible. Against it were the sentiments of the 'Covenanters' for the province of Ulster and also its superiority as an administrative unit. In the upshot, the Cabinet agreed that the Bill should be drafted on the basis of a parliament for Ulster, but reconsidered if it were later found that a six-county area was more acceptable to the Ulster Unionists.

The most important statement in the records of the meeting of 3 December had been the enunciation of ultimate aim – 'a united Ireland with a separate Parliament of its own'. It came in for subsequent questioning. On 10 December 1919, when the draft Bill was before the Cabinet,[27] it was stated that lifelong Unionists would prefer that there should not be a single parliament. But it was reiterated that one of the principal aims of government policy was to produce a good effect in the Dominions as well as the United States and that this object could not be achieved by anything short of a measure paving the way for a single parliament, if and when both the North and South were willing to accept it. The general trend of Cabinet opinion (from which Balfour specifically dissociated himself) remained in favour of adhering to the lines on which the Bill was at present drafted and the original statement of aim.[28] In a predominantly Unionist Cabinet this, with due regard for the reservations, was of importance. At the same time another issue was foreclosing. It was reported that opinion among responsible Ulster politicians was in favour of limiting the excluded area to six counties, 'since the idea of governing the three Ulster counties which had a Nationalist majority was not relished'. It was noted that such a solution would fit in with any scheme for the creation of a federal system in the British Isles.

On 15 December 1919 accounts of further conversations with Ulster leaders on the area to be excluded strengthened doubts as to whether the Northern Parliament would be able effectively to govern the three Ulster counties, where there was a large Nationalist majority.[29] Those leaders, it was reported, 'greatly preferred' that the scheme should be applied only to the six 'Protestant' counties. Sir James Craig had further suggested, in a private conversation with Sir Laming Worthington-Evans, the establishment of a Boundary Commission to examine the distribution of population along the borders of the whole of the six counties and to take a vote in districts on either side of and immediately adjoining that boundary in which there was a doubt whether they would prefer to be included in the Northern or Southern area. This proposal, carefully limited in its application, was commended as being in accord with the practice and principles adopted in the Peace Treaties and was referred to Long's committee for consideration.

When the Cabinet met on 19 December, the Prime Minister reported[30] that he with some colleagues had had a long conference with Sir James Craig that morning and that Craig had again expressed his strong opinion in favour of confining the Northern Ireland parliament to the six counties. He had also expressed himself strongly in favour of the proposed Boundary Commission* in order to define the precise area to be excluded and indicated his readiness to try to work the new parliament. A further discussion on areas followed, in which again it was urged that if the

---

* The traditional view has been that expressed by Denis Gwynn, *The History of Partition 1912–1925* (Dublin 1950), p. 202: 'There had been no question of a Boundary Commission . . . until the suggestion was put forward tentatively to Arthur Griffith by Mr Tom Jones on November 8 [1921]'. Craig is alleged to have found it 'odious'. F.S.L. Lyons, *Ireland since the Famine*, (London, 1971), p. 432. Did no one see fit to remind Craig of its origins?

ultimate aim of the government's policy was a United Ireland, it would be better that the jurisdiction of the Northern Parliament should extend over the whole of Ulster, which included both Roman Catholics and Protestants, both urban and rural districts, and which by its size was more suited to possessing a separate parliament. In favour of the six-county scheme was the knowledge that the Ulster leaders were prepared to work it which in turn might help towards unity with goodwill, while against the all-Ulster scheme was the difficulty for the government of trying to force through something unacceptable to friends and critics alike. It was better, such was the general view, to have something theoretically less perfect, if thereby it would secure more general acceptance. A scheme which was advocated by Craig and by Sir James O'Connor, who as members were reminded could speak for the Irish hierarchy, was likely to meet with a better reception than one they both rejected. The idea of a Boundary Commission to advise immediately on the precise boundary to be included in the Bill met with considerable favour. It was urged, however, that enquiries would produce unrest and the idea was not pursued. The consequences of that omission are with us to this day.

The Cabinet concluded that the Prime Minister in his report to the House of Commons should explain that the following courses were open: (1) to apply the jurisdiction of the Northern Parliament to the whole of Ulster; (2) to apply it only to the six counties; (3) to apply it to the six counties with the exact line of demarcation to be determined by a Boundary Commission. The government inclined towards the six-county solution and were prepared to consider favourably the appointment of a Boundary Commission if generally desired.

The Prime Minister was to move the Resolution in the House on the afternoon of 22 December. Both on 19 December and again on the morning of 22 December the Cabinet was asked to advise him on still outstanding questions bearing on the powers to be transferred to the Irish Parliament.[31] The yardstick was the Home Rule Act 1914 and as measured against it the Bill drafted by the Irish Committee of the Cabinet provided not for an extension but for a retraction of the powers to be devolved. The Cabinet, however, viewing the issue in wider perspective, was divided. The powers in question – customs, excise, posts and telegraphs and transportation – were collectively such as to determine, and be seen to determine, the character of the settlement. Here members of the Cabinet, as earlier in relation to the proposed continued integration of Northern Ireland in the United Kingdom, were sensitive to likely dominion and United States reactions, should the transfer of powers be more limited than in the 1914 Act. But there was an element of complexity not experienced on the earlier occasion. The transfer in 1920 was to be, not to one, but to two parliaments and that being so it was felt that there was a case for continued Imperial control not only as in 1914 of customs and excise, but also of the Post Office on straight administrative grounds. Nor was that all. While two parliaments in Ireland were to come into existence on the appointed day, the Bill envisaged the possibility of a third on an all-Ireland basis, vested with such of the powers of the parliaments of Northern and Southern Ireland as their members by the procedures prescribed in the Bill decided to transfer to it, together with such additional powers as were to be transferred under the Act when that unitary parliament had come into existence. There was here, in this world of make-believe, a further complication which members of the Cabinet found somewhat difficult to resolve. An oft-stated purpose of government legislation was to impress overseas opinion and that was likely to be achieved only by a generous devolution of power to the two parliaments in Belfast and Dublin but, 'the ultimate aim' of British policy being the unity of Ireland, the less that was transferred to the two parliaments and the more that was withheld for transfer conditional upon the coming into existence of an all-Ireland parliament the greater the inducement to unity.

The two strands of debate, the first short-term on presentation and the second on ultimate aim, were not easy to keep separate. The relevance of the analogy of the powers of the states in the USA *vis-à-vis* the federal authority and of the provinces in Canada *vis-à-vis* the Confederation, both of which were now in the Prime Minister's mind – he was to return to them again in negotiations preceding the Treaty – was considered, as was the desirability of the Prime Minister's alluding to it in introducing the resolutions in parliament. After some discussion it was suggested that the Prime Minister's statement should indicate that there had been a clear-cut issue between giving Ireland the powers of a Dominion and the powers of a state in the American Union and that the government had decided on the latter. Ireland would get some of the powers forthwith and, should the two parliaments agree to set up a single parliament, she would get more. The upshot therefore was as follows. Despite fears that control over the Post Office might be dangerous in other than Imperial hands (countered, if not dispelled, by the statement that anyway it was infiltrated by Sinn Féiners already) and despite the point that neither states in the United States nor provinces in Canada had such control, it was agreed that Posts and Telegraphs should, as in the 1914 Act, be handed over to the Irish parliaments.

Of the remaining items, customs and excise, and transportation, the first two were subjected to systematic analysis in a paper by Fisher, who argued the case for the transfer of the entire power over customs and excise after Union as being more likely to enlist support for the Bill and ultimately to promote the principal object of the Bill – reconciliation of the English and Irish races. The Cabinet concluded that the Prime Minister should state that when Ireland was united it would be open to the Imperial Parliament to consider the desirability of giving customs to a united all-

Ireland parliament, but that meanwhile the Cabinet was 'of the opinion that with a divided Ireland it would be quite impracticable to set up a Customs barrier between North and South'. The same applied, but not in such unqualified form, to excise. Transportation, on the other hand, was to be handed over to the Irish parliaments, with particular reference to the possibility of their agreeing to give control to the Council of Ireland at the least in respect of through services.

The Debate on the Resolutions

Lloyd George introduced the Resolutions on 22 December in fine *bravura* style.[32] The first fact, he said, that the House had to notice was that there was a Home Rule Act on the Statute Book. Unless it was postponed, repealed or altered it automatically came into operation the moment the war ceased. When it had been placed on the Statute Book Asquith had given an undertaking that it should not be brought into operation until another Bill dealing with the position of Ulster had been carried. In effect that meant repeal of the Act of 1914 and a new settlement. Here there were two basic facts, neither of them pleasant. The first was that in Ireland alone in Europe, apart from Russia – a tarnishing association in the anti-Bolshevik temper of the time – the classes, elsewhere on the side of law and order, were out of sympathy with the machinery of law and order. This was the more serious because of illusions that had been dispelled. In the past it had been argued that with the improvement in social and economic conditions, coupled with the redress of agrarian grievances bringing a new prosperity, hostility to British rule would vanish. But what had happened? Ireland had 'never been so alienated from British rule as she is today'. The second fact was that a considerable section were 'just as opposed to Irish rule as the majority of Irishmen are to British rule. . . . To force union is to promote disunion.' In addition to these two facts it was a fundamental condition of any settlement that 'Ireland should not be severed from the United Kingdom'. In the war 'a hostile republic there, or even an unfriendly one, might very well have been fatal to the cause of the Allies. I think it is right to say here in the face of the demands which have been put forward from Ireland . . . that any attempt at secession will be fought with the same determination . . . with the same resolve as the Northern States of America put into the fight against the Southern States.' Subject to the two facts and the one condition outlined, the purpose of the government's Resolutions and subsequent legislation was to confer self-government on the whole of Ireland, recognising the opposition of Nationalists to British and Ulster Unionists to Nationalist rule.

The Cabinet had shown concern about the reaction at home and overseas to the Resolutions. This was largely misplaced. What they had to contend with, even in Ireland, was indifference born of a sense of irrelevance outside Ulster. The forecast outline of the Bill, reported Sir David Harrel in a memorandum laid before the committee in January 1920,[33] 'has not received from the Irish press and Public the attention which might have been expected'. That was nicely phrased! For the rest, he observed, the Southern Unionists regarded the establishment of a parliament in Dublin as 'certain to result in disaster for them and ultimately to separation from Great Britain', and the Ulster Unionists were aggrieved at the suggestion that the province be partitioned, the more extreme among them wanting to be left as they were. Surrender of part of the province was not what they had been led to expect. The Nationalists in Ulster objected to the partition of Ireland in any shape or form and particularly to the separation of any of Ulster's counties from the projected Northern government. Yet what would be in prospect, were there to be a separate government for the province as a whole, the population of which under the latest census return was 690,816 Catholics and 836,999 of all other denominations, was factional fighting between the two communities. As for Sinn Féiners outside Ulster, they were bent on resistance to the British government in every shape or form and 'their object is complete separation and the establishment of a Republic'.

The chairman of the Irish Committee also recorded the impressions he had formed on a visit to Ireland in the same month, January 1920,[34] of Irish reactions to the Prime Minister's outline of policy. He, too, was surprised at how little interest was taken, even in Ulster, in the government's proposals. But he noted (1) that Carson's popularity had in no way diminished and that the Ulster Unionist Party would loyally follow his lead; (2) that the main interest was in the boundary, popular Unionist feeling being in favour of the exclusion of the whole province, inner circles that it should be restricted to six counties; (3) that, here at one with Harrel but not O'Connor, Roman Catholics were strongly in favour of exclusion of the whole province, and (4) that Ulster 'will not resist the Bill because the Unionist Party realise that if a settlement can be obtained now, they will secure infinitely better terms than they can hope for from a new Parliament, in which, in all probability the Labour Party would have much stronger representation'.

On 5 February 1920, Walter Long forwarded the revised text of the Government of Ireland Bill to the Cabinet, drawing attention to questions of principle which the committee had reserved for decision by the Cabinet.[35] Among these were the fiscal and related arrangements both in respect of divided Ireland and 'after the date of Irish Union', to quote the chairman's sanguine phrasing, the final determination of the area to come under the jurisdiction of the Northern Parliament. Both were referred to a special meeting of the Irish Committee called for 17 February at the request of the Prime Minister and presided over by Bonar Law.[36]

The debate in the committee on customs and excise had its importance in foreshadowing later Treaty negotiations on the fiscal question, but more immediately an elusive quality which has led to misleading generalisations. Initially the discussion was not, as is apt to be suggested, about the concession of customs and excise to the prospective parliaments of Southern and Northern Ireland, but about their transfer to an Irish parliament *on* Union. The Liberal view, as advanced by H.A.L. Fisher, was that if Ulster ever became reconciled with the South and asked for customs and excise it would have to be given to her. But the heavier guns came down on the side of contingent negation, Bonar Law favouring deferment of consideration till Union took place, Long, ready if he were a private member, to fight any such transfer because it would destroy the federal idea, and, more to the point, because Ulster Unionists did not want customs even on Union and Sinn Féin's hostility to the Bill would not be reduced by offering it; Worthington-Evans because customs meant 'a Customs barrier against this country'. The upshot, Bonar Law reported, was that the Committee desired to make no recommendation on whether customs should be or should not be handed over to a joint parliament after Union. The Cabinet, in turn concerned with the further point, duly noted that any commitment even for that remote contingency would impede the passage of the Bill through parliament.

Bonar Law, in a separate and special report,[37] informed the Cabinet of the outcome of the committee's deliberations on area. It was that the whole province of Ulster be included in the Northern Parliament. And why? Because the committee considered that this was more likely to lead to ultimate Union than an area composed of six counties only. The Cabinet, however, confronted with the renewed expression of reluctance to assume responsibility for the government of the whole province from the Ulster Unionist leadership, ruled otherwise. The area was to be the six counties statutorily defined and without Boundary Commission or plebiscite, Craig's proposals for the former being allowed to lapse; likewise the Liberal case for a plebiscite.

The surprising thing is not the Cabinet's final conclusion, but rather that so crucial an issue remained open so long. Or did it? Once committee and Cabinet had decided in favour of a parliament for the excluded area, had they not foreclosed on their options? It was possible to conceive of Ulster as a whole remaining part of a United Kingdom governed from London, but unrealistic to think of it sustaining a separate parliament on so precarious a balance of political opinion. Equally once the notion of subordinate parliamentary institutions was adopted, it was unrealistic to think of a four-county area sustaining them. There was, therefore, a closer correlation between area and form of government than is apt to be recognised. It was implicit but never made explicit in conceptual form in Cabinet discussions. The Cabinet were in fact confronted by the question in its most practical form. They could devise parliamentary institutions but where did that take them if there was no one willing to work them? To whom could they turn? Not to the Nationalists to whom the idea of a separate parliament in a partitioned island was anathema. Clearly only the Ulster Unionists. But the idea of governing the three Ulster counties Donegal, Cavan and Monaghan, which had Nationalist majorities 'was not relished';* the Unionist leaders 'greatly preferred' as has been noted, the six-county bloc with an assured and lasting majority. Sir James Craig had indicated his own strong opinion in favour of confining the Parliament of Northern Ireland to the six counties, and it is known that this view was shared by Dawson Bates, on whom Craig relied as the surest guide to grassroots Protestant sentiment.[38] The Cabinet, or rather the majority in it, at no point rescinded their views that if the ultimate aim of the government's policies was a united Ireland, then it would be better and more consistent if the jurisdiction of the Northern Parliament extended to the whole of Ulster. Yet without local collaboration, they could not give effect to it. The Cabinet were slow to get the message, but in the end they did; the area to be excluded was determined by the wishes of the only party disposed and in a position to work the institutions contemplated for its governance. In conjunction area and government ensured Unionist predominance for as long as could be foreseen. The Ulster Unionists had moved from threat of rebellion against compliance with the third Home Rule Act to the entrenchment of their political predominance in what was to be in other than name the fourth.

Statutory sanction for both institutions and the area to be excluded was in logic rightly associated in Section 1 of the Government of Ireland Bill 1920.[39] It read:

> On and after the appointed day . . . there shall be established for Northern Ireland a Parliament to be called the Parliament of Northern Ireland consisting of His Majesty, the Senate of Northern Ireland, and the House of Commons of Northern Ireland. For the purpose of this Act, Northern Ireland shall consist of the parliamentary counties of Antrim, Armagh, Down, Fermanagh, Londonderry and Tyrone, and the parliamentary boroughs of Belfast and Londonderry, and Southern Ireland shall consist of so much of Ireland as is not comprised within the said parliamentary counties and boroughs.

The Ulster Unionists had thereby assured to them a lasting overall majority, even though in two of the six counties, Fermanagh and Tyrone,

---

*Captain Craig was to tell the House of Commons on 20 March 1920 that the three excluded counties contained about 70,000 Unionists and 260,000 'Sinn Féiners and Nationalists' and would reduce 'our majority to such a level that no sane man would undertake to carry on a Parliament with it'. H. of C. Deb., Vol. CXXVII, Cols 990–1.

there was not a Unionist majority. There was to be a Protestant parliament but for more than a Protestant people.

There was a further point to be noted and this also was clearly a condition of Cabinet consensus. The partition of Ireland was effected within or upon a concept of continuing unity. The establishment of separate parliaments in Section 1 of the Act was, on paper, in part counterbalanced by the constitution in Section 2 of the Council of Ireland. 'A fleshless and bloodless skeleton', behind which Asquith discerned the spectral figure of an Irish parliament. He appreciated more clearly than any other critic the implications of parity as between North and South, as between minority and majority in the composition of the Council, 'It is left',[40] he said, 'to an Ulster minority for all time to veto, if it pleases, the coming into existence of an Irish Parliament'. None the less such deference to unity was also a condition of Coalition consensus.

The Ulster Unionist Response

In the debate on the second reading of the Bill in late March 1920, Ulster Unionist leaders responded with characteristic differences in emphasis on the outcome. Carson for his part did not lose a last opportunity of denouncing 'the whole policy of Home Rule for Ireland'; desertion of co-religionists in the South 'cuts me to the quick', the truth was there was 'no alternative to the Union unless separation'. But the Act of 1914 was on the Statute Book; if the new Bill were rejected, it would come into force.[41] To that he preferred the new Bill, which at least ensured the six counties did not come under Dublin rule. And then he did not 'look upon a Parliament in Ulster as altogether without a ray of sunshine'.[42] Captain Craig, an Ulster Unionist,* who had earlier allowed that Ulster had been treated generously, saw a veritable shaft, in a Bill which 'practically gives us everything that we fought for'. No longer would the Ulster Unionists be at the mercy of Asquithian Liberal or Labour politicians. 'We see our safety . . . in having a Parliament of our own . . . once a Parliament is set up and working well, as I have no doubt it would in Ulster . . . we feel that we could then be in a position of absolute security', given the six-county area.[43] He noted that Unionist members of the Coalition were prepared to vote for Home Rule. He remarked that it was a very significant fact – Captain Wedgwood Benn alluded to it as 'a most amazing feature in this Debate'.[44] Captain Craig did not perceive its possible remoter import. He thought of the bulwark of local institutions against

---

* Captain Craig was a brother of the Ulster leader, Sir James Craig (afterwards Lord Craigavon) who held junior office in Lloyd George's administration of 1918–21 and therefore felt precluded from speaking.

the left, not foreseeing, as well he might not have, how vulnerable, half a century later, that bulwark might prove in face of repudiation by a disillusioned English Conservative party. Against that the Bill offered no protection. No provision of the Bill was so important as the last – Section 75 – which asserted that the supremacy of the United Kingdom Parliament remained 'unaffected and undiminished over all persons, matters and things in Ireland and every part thereof'. What was about to be launched was an experiment in devolution, not in federalism, and still less in dominion status. In settled times, it was easy to overlook the distinction at Stormont and even at Westminster: 1972 was to provide a sharp reminder.

But if Captain Craig entertained illusions in respect of institutions in the longer run, he had none about unity or of the alleged instruments thereof. 'I would not be fair to the House', he said, 'if I lent the slightest hope of that union [of Ireland] arising within the lifetime of any man in this House. I do not believe it for a moment.'[45] Captain Redmond (a nephew of the former leader of the former parliamentary party) agreed. The Bill had two objects – the repeal of the Home Rule Act and the permanent dismemberment of Ireland. 'The form of partition' had changed from being 'a contracting-out Clause' to a 'Clause erecting in Ireland itself a second nation and a permanent barrier against the unity of the Irish race . . .'. That had not been contemplated even in the 1916 negotiations. 'Upon the very face of the proposals themselves', continued Redmond, 'is written the whole campaign of Unionist Ulster'; and the Bill 'is the price that has been paid to the Right Hon. Member for Duncairn (Sir E. Carson) by the Government which is beholden to him'.[46]

Asquith agreed. To use the term Home Rule of the Bill was 'a manifest and almost aggressive abuse of language', for Home Rule was conceived in terms of unity, if need be to be qualified, but not dualism to be entrenched. The Home Rule Act should not be repealed without the pledge to the majority for a parliament for the whole of Ireland being redeemed. It was a pledge not to a dissentient minority, but to the vast majority. Moreover, only 'clamorous national demand' could warrant the cumbrous duplication of institutions that was contemplated. The Bill started, however, from a foundation not in unity but in dualism. Or as Wedgwood Benn put it more tersely, 'This is a Bill for partition.'[47]

And what was the government's response to such indictment? It was put succinctly by Austen Chamberlain who, conceding that Unionist policy had broken down, 'for one good reason, because our countrymen would not support it . . . for a sufficient length of time', went on to observe of the new Bill: 'It is a paradox of ours that the only hope of union in Ireland is to recognise her present division. It is not we who are dividing Ireland . . . not we who made party coincide with the religious differences . . .'.[48] On this view, Irishmen had self-determined their own division and only they could end it. The Prime Minister developed the

theme.[49] 'Why should we force union upon them when they cannot
establish it themselves?' Ulster he spoke of, not indeed as a second nation
– he put that question on one side and described it as 'an entity to be dealt
with' – but as 'a separate and different part of Ireland'.[50] As for the powers
to be transferred which had been variously described as wretched and
meagre, he spoke of them as 'enormous' and 'gigantic'. It signified little.
The Ulster Unionists would not concede indirectly through a council
what had been successfully resisted for an all-Ireland parliament.

Professor Lyons wrote of the Government of Ireland Bill as 'totally
divorced . . . from the realities of political life in Ireland';[51] A.J.P. Taylor
of Lloyd George having 'devised an arrangement of fantastic complexity, the Government of Ireland Act (1920), the United Kingdom, united
Ireland, a separate Ulster, all mixed together', which 'indirectly . . . ended
the troubles'.[52] They serve to reflect the predominant views of Irish and
English historians respectively. On reconsideration of the records, however, the first appears insufficient and the second in one respect misleading. The insufficiency arises by reason of discounting the Ulster Unionist
dimension. It is true, as we have seen and Professor Lyons reminds us,
that the Bill was received 'grudgingly' by the Ulster Unionists – but
appearance was not reality. Down to this day much has been made of the
point that no one in Ireland wanted the Bill. It was also said at the time.
Birkenhead taxed Carson with fostering such a notion. Carson replied on
20 November 1920, 'May I say, with the full consent of all my colleagues
in Ulster, that this is a fallacy.' Union was 'the soundest policy', but 'we
have made up our minds that in the interests of Ireland, Great Britain and
the Empire, the best and only solution of the question is to accept the
present Bill and to endeavour to work it loyally'.[53] This was another way
of saying that the first part of the Anglo-Irish Settlement coincided with
the realities of Ulster Unionist interests as their leaders conceived them. It
was thus coincidence with political realities in the north-east, associated
with the 'total divorce', to which Professor Lyons rightly alludes, in the
rest of the country, that produced the intractable, albeit secondary to
status, problem of unity.

Few will have read Lloyd George's exposition of the Resolutions that
preceded and the Bill that followed without recognising his dexterity. But
from dexterity in presentation to devising is a long step. Lloyd George
was Prime Minister and Bonar Law the leader of the Unionist Party, the
one without and the other with strong views on Ulster. It was the
conviction of the latter that prevailed. But it is a misconception to think
of the Act of 1920 as a whole as being in any fundamental sense his
achievement or still less the product of Lloyd George's political acumen.
On the contrary it was fashioned in Cabinet committees and carried the
unmistakable imprint of committee search for compromise.[54] It was also
and more importantly the outcome of the continually narrowing range of

choice, which had confronted each successive British government since the outbreak of war. In the broader perspective of Anglo-Irish relations, though apt to be lost sight of in dramatic reconstruction of personal and party in-fighting in the Coalition era, what mattered was the convergence of English political opinion at the highest level upon a particular, and *per se* improbable and, as it proved, inadequate panacea for the problem of Anglo-Irish relations.

PART IV

THE SETTLEMENT:
THE SECOND PHASE

CHAPTER 6
Towards a Dominion Settlement

'I have often wondered', reflected H.A.L. Fisher in a letter to Lloyd George on 19 May 1920,[1] 'where exactly we went wrong in our Irish policy'. For his part he thought 'our great mistake' had been to proscribe Sinn Féin as a whole, on 10 September 1919, with a further Proclamation declaring Dáil Éireann illegal two days later. Surely, he argued, it should have been 'our principal object of policy to attempt to sever the moderate from the extreme elements of that most composite party'. Lloyd George did not dissent. Proscription once decreed was, however, difficult to undo. Fisher's remedy was to have 'the note of conciliation struck again and again. We cannot strike it too often.'[2] But that was not easy to do with conviction. In the summer of 1920 conciliation was not in the air, let alone in the Cabinet, or in Sinn Féin counsels. For that there was one sufficient reason. No military balance had as yet been struck and each side could contemplate a time more favourable to itself for negotiations. The time for conciliation accordingly was not yet.

The Conceptual Divide: 'Rebels from Principle'

'Kings', observed Edmund Burke in his *Reflections on the Revolution in France*, 'will be tyrants from policy when subjects are rebels from principle'.[3] In the years 1916–21, Sinn Féin, to be thought of in this context as a movement rather than a party, were rebels from principle, namely the inalienable right of nations to determine their own destinies. The right was thought of not as something transient but, on the contrary, as timeless and unrelated to circumstances. From that derived much of its force and more of its rigidity. 'The national demand of Ireland', Pearse had written, 'is fixed and determined . . . we of this generation receive it as a trust from our fathers . . . we have not the right to alter it or to abate it by one jot or tittle'.[4] If such were the case before the Rising, how much more so after that sacrificial gesture. On the Sinn Féin view, the Republic had been proclaimed in 1916, mandated by the people in the 1918 election, when the Sinn Féin placards read, 'Vote for the Republic', 'Stand by the men of

1916', and clothed in constitutional form by the First Dáil meeting in January 1919, with deputies pledging themselves the following August 'to support and defend the Irish Republic and the Government of the Irish Republic which is Dáil Éireann against all enemies, foreign and domestic'.[5] The people of Ireland, de Valera was to tell Lloyd George in August 1921,[6] acknowledged no voluntary union with Britain, but on the contrary, claimed as a 'fundamental natural right' the freedom to choose the path they would take to realise their national destiny. They had declared by an overwhelming majority for independence and a republic. Yet, despite the 'notorious' circumstances surrounding Union, Great Britain continued to act 'as though Ireland were bound to her by a contract of union that forbade separation'. There had never been a union – or if there had been, it was, so de Valera told the Dáil, 'severed here on 21 January, 1919'.[7]

Theoretically, the nature of the future constitution was not finally determined at the Sinn Féin 'Árd-fheis' in 1917, but de Valera's compromise formula depicting the war as being waged, not so much for a particular form of government, as for Irish freedom and independence, lost such semblance of reality as it ever had in the process of transition from image to application. The first duty of the Dáil ministry, de Valera asserted, was to translate the concept of a *de jure* into a *de facto* republic. At home this was an end to be achieved by the setting up of a government of the Republic administratively equipped where circumstances allowed to enable its officers on the ground to take over the ordering of affairs, the administration of justice, the collection of taxes and so by degrees to supplant the 'usurping British imperialist regime with an indigenous republican authority'; 'a new polity . . . within the old', as Professor Hancock aptly described it.[8] Abroad recognition for the Republic was sought from foreign governments; though unsuccessful, this served to publicise to the wider world the nature of the Irish objective and its republican foundation, as also to commit Sinn Féin internationally to the republic. If there was seemingly little or no debate among the Sinn Féin leaders about the nature of a settlement they might approve, that was consistent with their emphasis on recognition first. That was the great imperative. Were it to be accorded, all else – unity hopefully included – would follow.

There was in fact no prospect of an Irish abatement of claims other than as a consequence of defeat. That looked unlikely. For the greater part of 1920, the IRA campaign was gathering momentum and the Sinn Féin publicity machine was making significant impact in Britain as well as overseas. In this last the measure of electoral support for Sinn Féin in the local elections in January and June 1920 was the principal factor.

In deciding to contest the elections, Sinn Féin showed itself undeterred by the fact that it was the British government which had introduced proportional representation with the stated purpose of assisting minorities. The outcome confirmed the realism of their assessment. In the Urban District Council elections on 15 January, Sinn Féin secured a majority in 72 out of 127 municipal councils, and in association with the Nationalists in the north-east a further 26. In the County Council and Rural District Council elections in June, they captured 28 out of 33 county councils (Tipperary being divided into two ridings) and 172 out of 206 rural district councils. In three of the four provinces, their control was complete. While allowances may be made for intimidation, the overall inference was not disputable. The Sinn Féin leaders had a mandate as well as elected personnel with which to extend the alternative administration in the critically important local government field and of wider application though somewhat less sure foundation – the elections being local – to substantiate its claim to speak as representative of the national will. While, however, the ballot box was important in the propaganda war overseas, at home it remained subordinate to the military effort. In the last resort, Sinn Féin reposed its faith in physical force. That, sustained over a sufficient period of time, was deemed the recipe for independence. Its effectiveness was associated with singleness of aim, with any hint of dilution in overall republican purpose being likely to occasion or disclose division. So long as Sinn Féin stood firm and united on the rock of the republic, they held the dialectical advantage; only as and when they had to descend from that rock did they have to face dialogue on more nearly equal terms. So long as the British military force could be withstood – and it was an absolute condition – there were therefore practical as well as theoretic grounds for refraining from indicating the nature of a settlement acceptable to them even if only as a basis for negotiations. The British meanwhile scanned the horizon for Sinn Féin moderates who, it was felt, 'must exist': no doubt they did but without judging it timely to show their hand.

Dominion Status Not On Offer

In retrospect, the Anglo-Irish war of 1919–21 is apt to be viewed as a conflict arising from the irreconcilable notions of a possible settlement – a dominion within the Commonwealth on the British and a sovereign republic on the Irish side. This is, however, an oversimplification on the British side. That was neither how it started nor indeed how it continued. Down to May 1921 dominion Home Rule, as it was generally termed, or dominion status was not on offer. It was the slogan of discredited minority groups – Asquithian Liberals, Southern Irish Unionists, Lord Midleton and Horace Plunkett – the last of whom advised H.A.L. Fisher as early as 20 April 1919 of the necessity of announcing forthwith that dominion government would be applied to Ireland.[9] But far from being the goal of British policy, it remained until May 1921 an outcome expressly and repeatedly ruled out of consideration by the Prime Minister and leading members of the Coalition Cabinet.

In November 1919 Adams, as already noted, sought to impress upon the Cabinet's Irish Committee[10] the importance of their coming down clearly on the side either of dominion Home Rule which meant, *inter alia*, fiscal autonomy or of what Adams termed federal devolution. Committee and Cabinet, first by inference and then explicitly,[11] affirmed their stand in favour of devolution and against dominion status. Dominion status was something, as the relevant Cabinet minute of 19 December 1919 duly recorded, that 'had never been contemplated'.[12] In debate, Lloyd George took the dialectical offensive. He taunted Asquith with the question, which allowed of no affirmative answer, of whether anyone in Ireland was in favour of his [Asquith's] 'plan' for dominion status.[13] Labour fared little better. Their theme, it is true, was not dominion status: it was self-determination. But what was meant by self-determination in the Irish context? Not full recognition but rather, J.R. Clynes explained,[14] the *maximum* of national self-government consistent with the unity of the Empire and the safety of the United Kingdom. This the Bill, with its economic and political reservations, and most of all its endorsement of partition, did not supply. It was designed not to concede but to exclude the possibility of national self-government. But when pressed on whether self-determination even with qualifications would not mean a republic, Clynes, with other Labour spokesmen, notably Parkinson and Wedgwood Benn, sought refuge in generalities – Labour could never be a separatist party, rather federalist in the interests of workers in both countries; the problem was to concede a government that would have the good feeling of the majority behind it.

Bonar Law, his words invested with the enhanced authority of the dominion born and destined to be much quoted, copper-fastened dominion status and self-determination by speaking of dominion Home Rule as leaving open the way by two stages to republicanism and secession. 'What', he asked,[15] 'is the essence of Dominion Home Rule?' It was, he said, dominion 'control of their whole destinies'. If the Dominions decided they would no longer make a part of the British Empire, 'We would not try to force them.' Unionists believed him, Sinn Féiners did not. Had it been the other way round, matters might have been readily resolved.

In September 1920 Walter Long, on return from a further visit to Ireland, told Austen Chamberlain that dominion status could not 'be seriously regarded for the simple reason that it was impossible to grant it unless we are prepared to go the whole length and accept the inevitable conclusion, namely practical . . . independence . . . sooner or later, Ireland would demand complete Diminion status . . . and this, I venture to say England could never concede'.[16]

As the sequel showed, not for the first or indeed for the last time, the weighty words of this quintessential Tory, who to his credit was not content to view Irish problems from a comfortable distance, represented views which neither Chamberlain, had he wished, nor Lloyd George could afford to disregard. The upshot was that from the shooting at Soloheadbeg on 21 January 1919, until the negotiations preceding the truce signed on 9 July and coming into force on 11 July 1921, dominion status was not at issue between the Cabinet and Sinn Féin. That can hardly be too strongly emphasised. British policy was embodied in the Government of Ireland Bill, and should that prove unacceptable, provision had been duly made, as Walter Long reflected with a certain relish, not for a forward dominion step, but for a retreat to Crown Colony government. Sinn Féin for their part had no reason to consider what was *not* on offer. Were they to follow their despised and contemned parliamentary precursors in seeking a dominion goal? It was unthinkable!

All in all, the gulf in practice as well as concept between Sinn Féin aspiration and Coalition proposition was therefore, not more bridgeable, but wider than is usually supposed – over and against the Government of Ireland Bill was the Irish demand for recognition of a *de jure* republic. Against such a background, what incentive was there for Sinn Féin to modify a stance which lacked nothing in clarity and all things in compromise? And what inducement was there for the British to try to open negotiations with a political movement which, as they repeatedly complained, had no recognised head and furthermore, was insistent on recognition of a republic, which no British government could accord and survive. Did that mean that guerrilla warfare with a mounting list of casualties and a catalogue of outrage should continue until the British were no longer in a position to maintain their government in Ireland or the Irish capitulated on the symbolic issue which to the majority had come to matter most? Or were the British to modify their stand on the Government of Ireland Bill?

Lloyd George saw little virtue in so doing. Sinn Féin, in their present state of exultation, would not, he felt in March 1920,[17] be prepared to contemplate any retraction of their ideological republican demand. 'If you asked the people of Ireland what plan they would accept', he told the House of Commons, 'they would say "We want independence and an Irish republic". There is absolutely no doubt about that.' Lloyd George therefore wondered whether any useful purpose was to be served by any offer he might make.[18] But in any case, his hands were tied. The first part of the settlement, applying to Ulster, predicated a near coincidental initiative, however otiose it might prove, to give effect to that part of the Government of Ireland Bill that applied to Southern Ireland. That it would prove unacceptable not only to Sinn Féin but to any class in Ireland was well understood. It was not an irreconcilable nationalist, it was Lord Midleton,[19] leader of the Southern Unionists, who described the Bill as a 'red rag to a bull'. The 'really crucial point', however, he advised the

Prime Minister, was among the least considered: finance. The Irish, he forecast, would 'muddle' and 'squander' any surplus, but it would be a 'problem to get any considerable sector of Irishmen to support anything short of complete fiscal autonomy'. On this, and this alone, loyalists and extremists were at one. However, it subsumed dominion status and was inconsistent with devolution. Midleton accordingly believed that something approaching dominion Home Rule afforded a prospect less discouraging than any other; Lloyd George that there was neither occasion nor disposition to consider it.

The accepted interpretation of Lloyd George's overall strategy – disposing first of the Ulster question so that his hands might be free to settle the Irish question in its traditional guise – receives scant support from the records of 1920. Far from taking up Midleton's and others' suggestions of a liberal dominion Home Rule settlement, he remained strongly opposed to it, not least on the fiscal side. He gave little or no impression of a statesman seeing the way opening before him for the implementation of the second phase of a grand design: on the contrary, he was against concession, though not against negotiation. But what about? And with whom?

Few things come over more clearly than uncertainty on the part of many members of the Cabinet, Lloyd George among them, and the Irish executive, about what to do next. They weighed many times the chances of making a successful appeal to moderates within Sinn Féin. But always they came up against the question: did such moderates exist in sufficient numbers and had they sufficient courage to counsel moderation, a course which the American Consul felt carried with it the risk of assassination by extremists? 'If only', bewailed the Chief Secretary, 'moderate opinion in Ireland were definitely on their side,[20] the position of the Irish executive would be quite different'. Indeed – but since beyond doubt it was not, what was the right course to pursue?

The Castle administration favoured a truce, if only so that they might learn in detail what the rebels wanted. Macready favoured it on the ground that the Sinn Féin movement had reached its climax at the general election when they had swept the country, made contact with foreign powers, and appealed to world opinion. Yet nothing, Macready felt, had happened as a result. There was anti–climax and, despite the extremists' claims to the contrary, the people in the majority wanted a truce. The Lord-Lieutenant, while he favoured putting the struggle on a war basis, 'as had been done in the Boer War', did not exclude a truce. And on 1 May with the same end in view, the new (and last) Chief Secretary, a Canadian, Hamar Greenwood, to whose zeal for temperance reform was attributed his decision to join the Liberal party, seized a chance to advise Lloyd George that the moment had come when 'a dramatic turn' in policy might have an instantaneous and lasting effect.[21]

'Chaos in the Castle'

From the British point of view playing for a truce meant playing for time. Viewed in an extended time-scale, it brought to the surface a question long entertained by supporters as well as by critics, namely, was the Dublin Castle administration capable of holding its own against a sustained Sinn Féin challenge? Lloyd George in response to it deputed Warren Fisher, Permanent Under-Secretary at the Treasury, to make enquiry. In a shattering report dated 12 May 1920,[22] Fisher noted that the Castle administration could never have been good and 'is now quite obsolete'. In the critically important sphere (a) of informing and advising the Irish government in relation to policy; and (b) of practical capacity in the application of policy, 'it simply has no existence'. In a note of 15 May supplementing the report, he had more than administrative incompetence to record. With the notable exception of General Macready, 'the Government of Ireland strikes me as almost woodenly stupid and quite devoid of imagination', its members listened solely to the Ascendancy party, they were indiscriminate in their use of the term 'Sinn Féin', so much so that one 'would certainly gather that Sinn Féin and outrage were synonymous'. It served no purpose to point out to them that two-thirds of the Irish people were Sinn Féiners and the murder gang a few hundred. They agreed, but without modifying their attitude, thereby reminding Fisher of 'some people in England – mainly to be found in Clubs and amongst retired warriors and dowager ladies – who spend their time in denunciation of the working classes as "socialists"'. But in Ireland the Sinn Féin party – and here he reverted to the theme his namesake had developed independently – representing the great majority of Irishmen had been proclaimed as an illegal organisation. The fact that Sinn Féin aimed at ultimate separation of Ireland from Great Britain was no argument for withholding recognition from it. It *was* a political party. He recommended therefore that the proscription of Sinn Féin should be publicly abrogated. He also recommended the abolition of the Lord-Lieutenancy 'with its atmosphere of pinchbeck royalty'.[23] To neither was effect given.

Warren Fisher's report elicited the shocked comment from Austen Chamberlain that, prepared though he was for criticism, this was worse than anything he had anticipated. The impression made on the Prime Minister was of 'absolute chaos' in the Castle. Changes in Castle personnel Fisher had recommended were made. Sir John Anderson, an administrator of formidable reputation, later enhanced in India and in Churchill's War Cabinet, was appointed Joint Under-Secretary to the Lord-Lieutenant, while Alfred Cope, an elusive figure who was to play a significant part in the exchanges that preceded truce and Treaty, became assistant Under-Secretary for Ireland. But no such strengthening on the staff side could restore confidence or credibility to the system. The importance of this, as against military factors, is apt to be underestimated. Did not Fisher's report in effect advise temporary measures to sustain a crumbling edifice? When the prospect of talks opened up, the 'official' mind of Dublin Castle came down strongly for a transfer of power. They saw, other things apart, that administratively, there was little or no alternative.

On 31 May Greenwood reported to a conference of ministers with members of the Irish Executive on the impressions he formed on a first visit to Ireland as Chief Secretary. He took the view that the murdering was the work of 'a small gang'. He thought that publicity about government plans was 'rousing' moderate opinion in Ireland as well as in England, but singled out as the big issue 'the inadequacy and sloppiness of the instruments of government'. He drew attention to the longer-term vulnerability of a policy, lack of confidence in which was reflected on resignations from the RIC running at 200 a week as against 25 before the war.[24] Churchill, concurring, alluded by way of counter to the recruiting of a special para-military force – 'a most unappetising prospect', interjected H.A.L. Fisher – to assist the police. On that action was suspended, but not for long. On 27 July such a force, later called the Auxiliary Force – the Auxies – recruited from British Army ex-officers was inaugurated. It was to prove no less 'unappetising' in being than in prospect. Moreover, in so far as its creation eased the British military situation, almost by way of necessary consequence it worsened the political, by consolidating Sinn Féin's national character.

The Coalition Seeks a Way Out

On 23 July 1920 a further Conference of Ministers reinforced by the Viceroy, the principal Dublin Castle officials, J.O. Wylie, Lord Justice to the Government of Ireland 1909–19 and Sir James Craig, held what H.A.L. Fisher reckoned to be the first real discussion in the Cabinet of the Irish question in his time. It was opened with a 'brilliant' speech by Wylie,[25] the theme of which was that the government had been brought to a standstill, that there was no point in relying upon coercion or changes in attitude – 'the murderers are idealists, public opinion absolves them'. He was dead against further exasperation of Irish opinion. The essential thing was to open up contact with Sinn Féin. Provided, Wylie continued, in part confirming Midleton's view that the six counties did not get their parliament, but remained part of Great Britain, Sinn Féin might be interested in an approach that conceded control of customs and excise.

With this analysis Anderson and Cope were in substantial agreement. Lloyd George asked whether anyone had any doubt that, whatever other measures were found, law and the machinery of law must be strengthened. None were expressed but Greenwood again warned that in determining policy it was important to keep in mind the instruments who would have to execute it. On this General Macready interjected, 'Don't lean too hard on the Army.' Macready also again pointed to a sharply increasing number of resignations from the RIC, with the best police officers unable to keep their force together. Balfour agreed that no one could govern with an army as a first line, adding that in his time as Chief Secretary, those responsible for law and order could be trusted and were in earnest. Bonar Law remarked that there had then been no mixture of Home Rulers in the government. Birkenhead insisted the police must be made the first line, the soldiers the second and, with Churchill, he felt it would be necessary to raise the temperature so as to bring about a real trial of strength in order to open up the chance of a wider settlement. Coercion 'full blast' coupled with the Government of Ireland Bill, enacted as soon as might be, was his advice. Bonar Law gave warning that the Bill could not be hurried through parliament. Should there be further fiscal concessions by way of counterpart? Balfour thought this a question that should be considered in the wider setting he proceeded to unfold.

The broad lines of the Irish case, Balfour contended, were 'Ireland a nation'. This was at the back of the growth of the republican party. At the heart of Sinn Féin the ideal was a separate republic. That recognised, no negotiation was possible. Nothing would be got from seeing their leaders other than humiliation. 'It may be you can hold on a little by grasping at one tuft of grass after another in the hope that you will not go over the precipice but over the precipice you will go . . .' Customs and excise on this reckoning would be 'a ruinous concession'. His worst opponents were those 'who hated the idea of dividing Ireland: he liked it'. It was a geographical accident that Ireland was surrounded by sea. That should be ignored and inveterate religious and racial prejudice recognised. Balfour favoured, therefore, proceeding with the enforcement of the settlement embodied in the Bill on Southern Ireland, thereby preserving constitutional parity with the North. On any other lines an Irish settlement was an illusion. He was in favour of fighting disorder and going on with the Bill. So was Craig, who accepted Wylie's diagnosis but not his remedies. Bonar Law was also a hardliner, while Long was horror-struck at the idea of negotiations and threatened that the reaction of the Unionist party in the House would be more determined even than in the case of Amritsar and General Dyer.

The meeting, however, saw the surfacing of other views. Curzon favoured acceding to suggestions from the Dublin Castle administration that the possibility of a pact should be explored. He was himself in favour of getting in touch with responsible leaders in the South to find out what they wanted in a dominion Home Rule context, the price of any such settlement being Ulster 'to be left part of England'. Churchill was not afraid of 'full Dominion Home Rule' except as part of a defeat. Bonar Law said that he would assent if there were an Irish Botha in sight but, as there was not, he left it to be inferred that an unyielding line should be taken. Fisher favoured speedy enactment of the Bill with possible amendment thereafter to concede fiscal autonomy to an Irish parliament, and was convinced that sooner or later 'we should have to deal with the leaders of the South and West'.

As a result of the discussion Tom Jones felt moved to submit a minute to the Prime Minister setting out the advantages of a dominion approach. He thought customs might be included but defence explicity excluded. While the latter was inconsistent with dominion status and a subtraction from it, it might come under dominion Home Rule, that self-contradictory piece of nomenclature much favoured at ministerial conferences, where it served to convey a sense of Home Rule with something added to it, or in other words a conflation of devolution, that is, Home Rule, with dominion status, precisely what Adams had advised against. For the resulting confusion a price was to be paid. The dominion status that Bonar Law had talked about in the House was not the dominion status that was coming under consideration in Cabinet conferences.

Lloyd George brought the 23 July conference to an end with a request that by the next meeting 'definite and final' proposals for the enforcement of law and order should be submitted by the Irish government. That indicated his order of priority. Accordingly there followed in August a Restoration of Order Bill sanctioning the vesting of intensive powers in courts martial in felony cases, and in October military courts of enquiry were authorised in place of inquests. Churchill was later to note that the Coalition had had only two options: 'crush them [Sinn Féin] with iron and unstinted force or try to give them what they want'. 'Unstinted force', despite discussions of a possible basis for negotiations, was the option chosen. As time passed Lloyd George became not less but more firmly convinced that it was the right one. If any doubt is entertained on that score the minutes of a Cabinet conference held on 13 October may serve to dispel them.

The question before the conference was whether there should be further amendment of the Government of Ireland Bill, the possibilities canvassed being the concession of complete fiscal autonomy to both the Irish parliaments and the waiving of the proposed contribution to the cost of imperial services. The principal arguments in favour of such a course were that it would make the Bill more liberal, that it would reduce the continued British presence in Ireland by disposing of the need for British officials to collect customs, excise and income tax there, something certain if retained to act as an irritant, and enable the government to say that this new solution was put forward as a concession designed to settle the question once and for all. As such it would strengthen moderate opinion and so undermine the position of 'the murder gang' and lead to its break-up.

The Prime Minister – and herein lay the chief interest of the discussion

– thought that it would be a mistake to make any such concessions. If the Irish adopted a conciliatory attitude there would be little left with which to negotiate. If, more particularly, the fiscal concessions were made, Ireland could not remain an integral part of the United Kingdom. The retention of customs was the hallmark of unity, as the history of Germany and the United States proved. If that had to be conceded in order to obtain peace it might be considered, but only if it was impossible to get other terms. By giving up these things we should have 'delivered the key of the whole position to Sinn Féin'. It was abundantly clear that they meant to have complete independence and would like nothing less. 'We had got a great inheritance and in a moment of despair must not barter it away to get "Peace in our time, O Lord".' The taxes were weapons he (Lloyd George) was looking forward to using against Sinn Féin. Giving up these taxes with nothing in return 'would be the worst piece of business which this Government had ever done' and he could not face the position. 'If we retained these taxes Sinn Féiners were at our mercy.' The counties in the South must be told they would have to pay for old age pensions, health insurance and other services. The Romans, so he ventured boldly, 'had constantly to do this kind of thing in Sicily'. He was and remained a Gladstonian Home Ruler. He wanted to see Ireland remain an integral part of the United Kingdom. He would stand by the Bill.[26]

Irrespective of the merits of the argument once again, this was not the language of a man who saw dominion status as his goal. Indeed Lloyd George alluded to the possible drafting of an amendment to the Bill, which would enable the British government to retain control of certain parts of Southern Ireland. This was not proceeded with but for the rest it was agreed that there should be no change in the financial provisions. The saga ended on 23 December 1920 when the Bill, unamended in substance, received the Royal Assent.[27]

Northern Ireland: Administrative Preoccupations

The partition, which was the principal feature of the Bill, did not wait upon its enactment. On the contrary the Ulster Unionists, encouraged by Bonar Law proceeded, with Cabinet concurrence, to lay the foundations of devolved government in the six counties in advance. On 8 September 1920, Craig had reported that the situation in Ulster was developing unfavourably 'with great rapidity', and that the loyalists were reacting by threatening an immediate recourse to arms such as would precipitate civil war. He asked for Cabinet approval for the immediate appointment of a civil servant of Deputy Secretary rank with headquarters in Belfast and direct access to the Chief Secretary to assume responsibility for the administration of the six counties and (though this was to be treated with reserve till the Bill became law) to build up an administrative cadre over

against the day of statutory devolution. Likewise Craig asked for parallel
steps to be taken in respect of the armed forces, including the police, with
a commissioner of the RIC to take control in the six counties and a force
of special constables to be locally recruited and organised on military
lines.[28] Balfour felt that in view of the terms of the Bill the government
would be justified in thus hiving off the Ulster administration forthwith
from that of the rest of Ireland.

On 13 October the appointment of the new assistant Under-Secretary,
Sir Ernest Clark, charged with the responsibility of building up the new
administration, was announced. On 1 November the enrolment of recruits
began for a special constabulary force, with an initial strength of up to
3,000 men in three classes: 'A' full-time constables, 'B' part-time and
serving locally, and 'C' an emergency reserve. The organisation of the
pre-war UVF was, so Craig pointed out, there ready to be used in the
creation of the new special constabulary. Formed in the first instance to
frustrate the application of the 1914 Home Rule Act to Ulster, they were
to be reconstituted to make the Act of 1920 effective in part of Ulster
somewhat before its time. What irony was there! Yet, as Dr McColgan
was the first to bring out,[29] on the civilian side the Ulster Unionist
leadership had shown foresight in their grasp of the advantages that would
accrue from the existence of an administrative machine in embryo, ready
to take over the responsibilities of local self-government when the appointed day, 23 December 1920, came. On the military side, they already
had their own organised force. The part-time B Specials, working with
the Royal Ulster Constabulary (whose strength by statute might not
exceed 8,000) and financed by the British government, were drawn almost
exclusively from one section of the community and were soon to acquire
an unenviable reputation in the other.

'War with the utmost violence'

With the recruitment and deployment first of the Black and Tans in
January, and then of the Auxiliary Police in July 1920, Lloyd George to
outward appearance had committed himself, in the Churchillian phrase,[30]
to 'war with the utmost violence' in the rest of Ireland. What was it
intended to achieve? Against whom was the violence to be directed? The
answer to the first question was the restoration of law and order, to be
followed by the application of the Government of Ireland Act 1920 in the
South as well as in the North and, if rejected in the South, to enforce
Crown Colony government. As for force, that was to be directed against
Sinn Féin which, it will be recalled, had been suppressed by British
proclamation in September 1919 as an illegal and unrepresentative terrorist
organisation. Its illegality under British proclamation was indisputable,
but even in a British context its unrepresentative character seemed ques-

tionable. Sinn Féin candidates had swept the twenty-six counties in the general election of 1918. They had assembled to legislate for Ireland as Dáil Éireann in January 1919. The Dáil was banned, its members proscribed. But could that be advanced as evidence that they did not represent popular opinion? Such indeed was the theory. Force was being employed, in Lloyd George's phrase, against 'a small nest of assassins'. It was a 'murder gang' that was to be rounded up. 'We have murder by the throat', he declared at the Guildhall Banquet in November 1920. The British government would not rest, declaimed the Chief Secretary, 'till we have knocked the last revolver from the last assassin's hand'. With King George V, as with many of his subjects, this language carried no great conviction. When, also in November 1920, Greenwood assured the King's private secretary that 'everywhere the move is upward towards improvement', the King felt obliged to question the correctness of his diagnosis and to complain of his oversanguine interpretation of the course of events.[31] In succeeding months public opinion in Britain and in the Dominions overseas was to show signs of mounting revulsion. Was all this concentration of force required to destroy 'a small nest of assassins'? Or did it increasingly look as though it was being applied to keep a small nationality in subjection, at a time when the cause of long suppressed peoples in Central and Eastern Europe was championed in the West? The onus of proof had shifted. Where earlier it had been for Sinn Féin to convince public opinion of the rightness of its cause, now it was for the British to establish good warranty for their actions. The champions of order were coming to be regarded by many of their own people as oppressors of a small nation struggling to be free.

Of immediate moment was the fact that, as the frontiers of policy-making and military execution of policy converged, the British doctrine of the subordination of the military to the political arm was disregarded, and at times flouted, with the soldiers losing what confidence they had in the policy–makers, and the ministers in the professional advice they received from the soldiers – 'unhelpful' was the term Churchill used of their incessant demands for martial law throughout the twenty-six counties.[32] For an authoritative account of these differences and their implications the reader should turn to Dr Charles Townshend's *The British Campaign in Ireland 1919–1921*,[33] where they are unravelled with convincing analysis of the interrelationship of the particular with the personal. What is left is an indelible impression of erosion of standards at the fag end of a terrible war. As much, or more than anything else, that impression derives from policy, or lack of it, on reprisals.

The Chief of Imperial General Staff, Field Marshal Sir Henry Wilson, wanted authorised reprisals.[34] He had no use for the idea of out-terrorising the terrorists, partly because of the effect on the forces employed and partly because the 'Frocks' – the designation denoting his unflattering

opinion of politicians – would let the soldiers down. On 29 September he
had an hour and a half with Lloyd George and Bonar Law. 'I told them
what I thought of reprisals by the "Black and Tans" and how this must
lead to chaos and ruin. . . . It was the business of the Government to
govern. If these people ought to be murdered, then the Government ought
to murder them. Lloyd George danced at all this, said no government
could possibly take this responsibility.'[35] By October, however, he agreed
to shoulder responsibility for reprisals once, in Wilson's terms, these
'cursed elections' (by which he meant the United States presidential) were
over. In December, martial law was proclaimed for four counties, and
extended to four more in January 1921. The soldiers pointed to the
difficulty of martial law in limited areas.[36] On 10 December the Prime
Minister told Macready that the aim was to put the screw on the rebels to
the greatest degree, while army and police went out of their way not to be
disagreeable to the unoffending inhabitants. Macready pointed out that in
Ireland it is very difficult to distinguish between the offending and the
unoffending article. But he gathered that the Prime Minister intended with
one hand to repress outrage, but with the other to wave an olive branch,
and 'so it will be up to us to try and play up to what seems to be a
somewhat complicated policy'. However, the military had won the point
on reprisals: they were to be government authorised. Churchill states this
was welcome to the IRA, but from the republican side that has been
disputed.[37]

By late December 1920 one part of the settlement to which the Coalition was committed was clearly going to be unworkable. By contrast with
the North of Ireland, there was no conceivable collaborating class in the
South to work it. That being so, the proposed settlement was impossible
to apply yet, in view of its duality, difficult to discard. The draft conclusions of the Cabinet meeting on 30 December 1920 noted that the North
of Ireland wanted the 1920 Act to be brought into effect on its own as
soon as possible despite the fact that the South, as it was phrased, 'had no
similar desire'. It was easy to concur in Northern wishes. But what was
the next step in the South? It was one to which governments before and
more especially since have been much predisposed. It was 'the widest
publicity' for the 1920 Act with a 'careful' summary of what to offer,
articles in the press (which might involve payments at advertisement rates)
and posters for priests and schoolmasters.[38] This ludicrous proposition
was coupled with an intention already affirmed that if the Act by these or
other means could not be worked, then Crown Colony government in
one of its manifestations should be applied in the twenty-six counties.

Well-intentioned mediators, Archbishop Clune of Brisbane notable
among them, dismayed by the intensifying conflict, sought at the turn of
the year to find a broader basis for negotiations. They succeeded only
in making even clearer the gulf that lay between the two sides, with

the British *inter alia* insistent on the handing over of arms prior to any truce, Sinn Féin rejecting any such precondition outright. The Coalition resolve to continue with the policy of meeting force with force was itself clearly manifested on New Year's Day 1921, with government-authorised reprisals carried out in Midleton, Co. Cork. But the search for moderates went on, with de Valera, who had returned from his long tour (1 June 1919 to 23 December 1920) of the United States fund-raising and pub-licising the republican cause and who by virtue of his absence had not been directly involved in violence, as more likely than any other of the Sinn Féin leaders to fill a mediatory role. Archbishop Clune, however, reported that he had found Michael Collins the only one of the Irish leaders with whom business could be done. Meanwhile the aim of government re-mained, in the now familiar phrase, 'to crush the murder gang', but now additionally to take any opening for peace that might occur. This reflected a perceptible shift in tactics, though none in purpose.

On 13 January 1921 Lloyd George told Bonar Law that he had received, but mislaid, a letter from de Valera. Auckland Geddes had given him a most gloomy account of opinion in America and he felt that in the interests of peace with America he ought to see de Valera, as de Valera had himself suggested in the missing letter. It seems never to have been found.[39] Had it ever been lost? Anyway it served to encourage exchange of view on how to take advantage of de Valera's return. Bonar Law observed that Geddes was apt to be panicky and what he said ought to be taken with a grain of salt. If we take it with a cellar-full, it was still, urged the Prime Minister, sufficiently serious. But with Bonar Law strongly opposed, nothing was done. He was, Tom Jones thought, one of the most persistent opponents of conciliation, but Anderson, while allowing that Bonar Law was worse than Carson, noted that the Prime Minister was the person really responsible for the policy of reprisals.

On 27 April 1921 the imminence of elections in Ireland under the 1920 Act led to less desultory discussion first on whether in the prevailing disorder the first general election under the 1920 Act should be allowed to go ahead in the South, secondly whether an offer should be made, and thirdly, whether a truce should be negotiated. On the first, opinion came down against postponement, the Prime Minister being persuaded to change his mind; on the second he was not, restating his view that if an offer of dominion Home Rule were made, the Irish would ask 'Will you give us Navy, Army, representation at Washington, the right to impose duties on goods from England', to all of which we would say 'No'. He conceded, however, 'we might discuss where we could not offer'. But he favoured keeping to the Act, pronouncing the judgement that 'with an Act like that on the Statute Book we can beat them'. The options before Sinn Féin – unrestricted warfare or acceptance of an Act less generous than that of 1914 – were hardly such as to induce a favourable reaction. And so despite Liberal demands at least for a concession on customs, the Prime Minister, as in the previous October, was unmoved. His conclusion? 'I am against an offer. It is bad tactics.'[40]

There remained the possibility of a truce. Discussion of it was deferred until 12 May, by which time an isolated event, the significance of which is not easy to assess, had taken place. It was a meeting between de Valera and James Craig.[41]

Craig showed courage in going to the secret IRA rendezvous outside Dublin, while de Valera took a risk that in political terms was real. A principal concern of de Valera's was at all costs to avoid the development of a triangular situation in which Britain would fill the role of arbiter between two warring Irish communities. This meant from a republican point of view that any negotiations must be and must remain bilateral. It was, on this line of reasoning, essential that Ulster should be viewed in the context of a minority community within Ireland, not as a polity apart. With the question of status unapproached, let alone unresolved, de Valera had nothing immediate to say to Craig. According to Lady Craig's graphic account de Valera, gaunt and haggard, had the look of a hunted man (as well he might), and struck Craig as a visionary. He spent the time harping on the grievances of Ireland over the past 700 years. Craig for his part had nothing to say to de Valera except to indicate that he would not budge from the 1920 Act. De Valera conceded nothing of substance on the point he regarded as of critical importance – that any negotiations should be Anglo-Irish, with no Ulster third party. In this though clearly unaware of it, he was to have an ally in an unexpected quarter, Craig, in fact, being more than reluctant to be drawn in in a third-party capacity. The conventional verdict is that the meeting afforded an opportunity, which was not taken, for lessening misunderstanding by personal communication then and later. This has an element of super-ficiality. It is equally, if not more, probable that the better the mutual understanding the wider the gulf between the two leaders would appear.

The resumed debate in Cabinet on a truce was held on 12 May, the eve of the two general elections, one in each part of Ireland to be held under the 1920 Act.[42] While there were no basic changes in approach there were some significant shifts in attitude. The Liberals, Montagu and Fisher, were the principal protagonists of a truce, Fisher arguing that a truce did not necessarily involve concessions, that it might lead to a permanent peace and above all because 'the present situation is degrading to the moral life of the whole country'. They had support on tactical grounds from another Liberal – Churchill. While a truce six months earlier would have been a sign of weakness, he contended that this was no longer so and that it was 'of great public importance to get a respite in Ireland'. Of those against a truce there was Chamberlain, who had changed his mind, there was Balfour who hadn't and admonished his colleagues that a truce would lead in the direction of dominion Home Rule and when that was obtained, the people who wanted a republic would still want it. But of greater significance in the run-up to the settlement, was the Prime Minister. What guarantee, he asked, was there that there would be any response to such a gesture? To base a departure in policy of this kind on the meeting of Craig with de Valera was 'preposterous'. If there was a truce, the price in the negotiations that followed would be too high. Dominion Home Rule was a phrase. If tariffs were conceded, then control over armed forces, then over the western seaports would follow. 'It is the next step I'm frightened at. . . . That means war. . . . People would say, "Why break off the hopeful negotiations". . . I gravely urge that we should not be in a hurry. . . . We've been generous in the Home Rule Act.' Thus Lloyd George remained resolute against a truce, and the reason? It was the likely sequel, a dominion settlement. To that he remained implacably opposed. That mattered. What did not matter, though true, was Lord Fitzalan's coincidental conclusion drawn from a very different premiss that 'you can't make a truce without meeting with Michael Collins. We can't have that.'[43]

Yet while a truce was ruled out, probing for a possible basis for 'a settlement' continued, little affected by the ebb and flow of Cabinet opinion. Also in April the American consul in Dublin commented on the number of emissaries Lloyd George had sent unofficially to Ireland and how they found difficulty in establishing on what terms the Sinn Féin leaders might settle – if indeed they could agree among themselves. Yet the pressures from the countryside remained. That same week, in which the possibility of a truce was debated in Cabinet, the crime statistics in the weekly survey were exceptionally bad – 'no less than 60 attacks on Crown forces' – and the number of military casualties the highest for any week since 1916. It was also said the general public was 'eager for a settlement'.[44] By late May the American Embassy in London reported the Home Secretary and former Chief Secretary, Edward Shortt's conviction that the government 'would have to make peace with those people' (Sinn Féin) and, on the basis of their consular reports from Dublin and Belfast, their own conviction that de Valera was the logical man to lead negotiations on the republican side. The peace idea had grown greatly and it was developing into a trial of strength between the extremists and de Valera. While he was not the leader of the greatest influence in Ireland, his championship of peace would carry the greatest weight in the United States.

The elections were held on 24 May. In the South, 127 Sinn Féin members were returned unopposed; in the North, the Unionists won 40 out of 52 seats. The American Consul in Belfast reported that '24 May witnessed the birth into the world of a Nation as the people of Ulster are fond of phrasing it.' There was, he noted, the greatest enthusiasm but, he

added, 'it strikes one accustomed to American organisation and enterprise
with surprise, that the actual counting of the vote cast . . . should not
begin until ten o'clock . . . the following day' – and to find the voting of
dead men, children and multiplied ballots 'occasion for pleasantries and for
mild boasting'.

The election returns in effect confirmed what was already known,
though not always admitted: the inbuilt strength of the Unionists in the
North and Sinn Féin in the South. So also did the sequel, the Northerners
making preparations for the assembling of their parliament; Sinn Féin to
boycott theirs which, attended only by 4 of the 128 members of the
Southern Irish House of Commons on 28 June, adjourned *sine die*. On the
military side, the position of the British Army as variously reported as
precarious and well-nigh desperate, in a position of stalemate and, probably most reliably, by Colonel Sir Hugh Elles after a tour on 24 June as in
fact 'besieged'.[45] The lines of division were hardening in Ireland and
between Britain and the greater part of Ireland. For the British the time
had come, so Macready advised, when it was a case of 'all out' or 'get
out'.

The prospect of the former looming up in all its potential frightful-
ness provoked initiatives in unexpected quarters. On 18 June Sir John
Anderson, in a courageous departure from the Civil Service convention,
wrote to the Chief Secretary with a request that his letter, which was in
manuscript, be shown to the Prime Minister and the Leader of the House,
Austen Chamberlain.[46] In it Anderson had placed on record his view that
it would be 'the wildest folly' to embark upon 'the very drastic measures'
Macready had outlined without a conviction, which he himself lacked,
that they would command the necessary degree of support in parliament
and country. If the government decided to enforce martial law, they
should, at the same time 'announce the extreme limit of concession to
which they are prepared to go in the direction of Dominion Home Rule'.
With that – which he was convinced would have to be conceded in the end
– there was some hope of the policy succeeding: without it there was
none. Anderson acknowledged that in writing thus he was exceeding his
proper function and expressing views in direct conflict with those of the
Cabinet and above all the Prime Minister. But he was moved to do so
with 'an earnestness and conviction to which I find it difficult to give
adequate expression'.

Anderson's letter is of twofold importance – first in respect of atmosphere and second chronology. The note of near–desperation in a communication from the key figure in the Castle administration provided its
own commentary on the state of mind in that beleaguered outpost. In
itself that must have had its influence on the Prime Minister and the Leader
of the House and through them the Cabinet, where opinion was nicely
balanced between those in favour of concession and those in favour of

persevering for months or years of guerrilla warfare in the cause of the Government of Ireland Act. In that context the date of Anderson's letter, 18 June 1921, is to be noted. Churchill with a fine flourish later recalled that 'no British government in modern times has ever appeared to make so complete and sudden a reversal of policy. . . . In May the whole power of the State and all the influence of the Coalition were used to "hunt down the murder gang"; in June, the goal was "a lasting reconciliation with the Irish people".'[47] The passage might well be foreshortened by substituting 'made' for 'appeared to make'. The precise sequence of events merits recall. On 2 June the Cabinet decided on a date (14 July), on which martial law should come into force, their decision, so Tom Jones judged, registering the high-water mark of repression. On 15 June Macready set out in a memorandum laid before the Irish Situation Committee what war with the utmost violence would mean – the trial of Sinn Féin leaders, de Valera, Griffith, Childers for treason, economic blockade together with martial law as already decided, and Crown Colony government for the South. Even the more right-wing members shrank from the prospect, Balfour advocating transportation as against execution for the leaders. There were therefore signs of an impending reversal of policy when General Smuts lunched with the King on 13 June.[48] Had it not been so the impact Smuts made would hardly have been so marked. The time was ripe, the man was right, but the policy in Lloyd George's view was not quite right.

'Peace with the utmost patience'

Statesmen throughout the Empire had made known their concern with the Anglo-Irish conflict, but among them on such an issue Smuts stood alone. He was not only a Commonwealth leader, he had also served, as had no other, as a member of the British over and above the Imperial War Cabinet. And strange as it may seem to later generations, at the Imperial Conference he represented the Dominion whose reconciliation with Britain was deemed to afford most telling proof of the constructive contribution of Commonwealth to relations between peoples once subject to inperial rule. No one, it was thought, was better fitted, or indeed more ready than he, to extol the virtues of dominion status. For this opportunity was near at hand, with Smuts himself briefed on Irish views before and in the course of his journey to London by Tom Casement.★

The focus was on Northern Ireland. The ground staffing of an administration had not, as has been noted, waited upon passage of the Act, and

★ A brother of Roger Casement. When Smuts' ship called at Madeira he found that Tom Casement had sent him a bulky packet of press cuttings on Ireland. On arrival in London Smuts was kept in touch with Irish views by Art O'Brien.

on 30 May, the elections over and the opening of the Parliament of
Northern Ireland imminent, Craig further asked the British government
to consider favourably requests from the government of Northern Ireland
for civil servants on loan or permanently, with the prudent rider that
secondment to Northern Ireland should not be regarded as a way of
getting rid of the less useful members of the British service. But the
question which immediately preoccupied the Cabinet was whether or not
the King should, as the government of Northern Ireland desired, open the
new parliament.[49] The King wished to do so, and despite misgivings on
grounds of security, the Cabinet approved.

On 13 June Smuts found the King 'anxiously preoccupied' about the
speech he was to make at the opening in the Belfast City Hall. No draft
had been submitted to him by the Irish Office though reputedly a 'blood-
thirsty document' had been composed. Smuts suggested something altogether different. He prepared a draft, of which he sent one copy to the
King and another with a covering letter to Lloyd George. Copies were
circulated to ministers. Neither Balfour nor Austen Chamberlain liked, so
Tom Jones records, 'what they called its "gush", sensing that behind it
all there lurked the innuendo of oppression'.[50] The substance was in
the accompanying letter. In it Smuts spoke of the Irish situation as 'an
unmeasured calamity' and 'a negation of all the principles of government
which we have professed as the basis of Empire, and it must more and
more tend to poison both our Empire relations and our foreign relations'.
He suggested that the King's speech in Belfast should contain a promise of
dominion status for Ireland, a promise which he felt sure would have the
support of all the dominion prime ministers then gathering in London.
But, he warned, 'such a declaration would not be a mere kite but would
have to be adopted by you as your policy . . .'.

The biographers both of Smuts and of King George V believed, in the
words of Professor Hancock, that in the course of a two-hour conversation 'King George V and Smuts broke the Irish log jam'.[51] This is often
taken to mean that Smuts persuaded the King directly and Lloyd George
at one remove to hold out dominion status as the way to settlement. But,
though he may have influenced a change of thinking, that precisely is what
he failed to do. Lloyd George, who alone could tender advice to the King,
was not prepared to endorse Smuts' recommendation of dominion status,
with the result that no such offer was made. This had a significant bearing
on the negotiations that followed. Dominion status was not the starting
point. An explicit offer of it had been the centrepiece of Smuts' (as indeed
of Anderson's) contention. But Lloyd George was not by mid-June 1921
prepared to enter into such a commitment.

The King's speech delivered in Belfast on 22 June contained an anxious
and moving plea for peace and understanding. It made – and on this all
accounts, not least that of the American Consul are agreed – a tremendous

impression in a strife-torn country. On his return, the King urged that the favourable reaction should not be allowed to be dissipated by delay. It was not. On 24 June the Cabinet discussed the opening of negotiations with de Valera.[52] Curzon was a principal spokesman for conciliation. 'At each stage', he said, 'I have been for opening up negotiations with the enemy. I have been more advanced than my colleagues. I view with the intensest satisfaction the step you propose.' When the terms of a draft letter to de Valera were considered, Balfour and Chamberlain once more protested at 'gush'; Curzon with Montagu, however, hoped that 'the Celtic touch might be left in'. The letter of invitation was published on 25 June. On 4 July the American Consul walking round Dublin found that the fervent prayer of all he talked to was peace at almost any price. He also noted that the celebration of Independence Day would not have been exceeded in an American city, but he was uncertain whether de Valera's request to fly the Stars and Stripes was prompted by regard for the US or a desire to annoy the British.[53]

On 5 July Smuts went to Dublin under token disguise as 'Mr Smith'. He went with the concurrence of Lloyd George, but at the invitation of de Valera, who had written of their common anxiety to settle an issue which had embittered Anglo-Irish relations for so long. Griffith, Duggan and Barton, all to serve as delegates to the Treaty negotiations in London later in the year, were present* with de Valera at the talks with Smuts, who reported back to the Cabinet the next day.

Smuts had had two purposes. The first, in which he succeeded, was to persuade the Irish not to refuse Lloyd George's invitation to a conference; the second, in which he failed, was to persuade them of the merits of a dominion settlement. On the first the Irish had contemplated refusal because Ulster had also been invited. The conference was for an Anglo-Irish settlement, and if Ulster were represented the British would exploit the differences between the two Irish parties. Nothing, de Valera insisted, could come from a conference of three parties. Smuts warned them that it would be 'an awful blunder' to refuse to discuss unconditionally the possibilities of settlement. On the second, as one who had the rare distinction of having served as a minister in the old republican government of the Transvaal, as Prime Minister of a Dominion, Smuts was uniquely qualified by first-hand experience to tell the Irish leaders of the case for dominion status as against republicanism. De Valera was impressed but not to the point of concurrence. *No* man, he recalled years later, could have put the case for dominion status more persuasively than Smuts, Lloyd George by comparison appearing superficial, even counterfeit.

---

* According to Smuts, but Duggan was a prisoner in Mountjoy Jail until the truce, so there was presumably some confusion here.

Smuts, however, like Craig, described de Valera as a 'visionary'. When they met, de Valera asserted that there must be a free choice between a republic and a dominion. That would have to be without limitations. Smuts replied, 'The British people will never give you this choice. You are next door to them.' At all costs, he warned, avoid the fate of the Transvaal – a three-year war fought because of limitations on sovereignty and 'my country was reduced to ashes'. De Valera countered by saying that for a republic the Irish would make concessions because a free republic was so great a thing to secure, but for dominion status, none. If the British insisted on dominion status, it should at least not contain irksome limitations inconsistent with that status. They should make 'a great gesture'; the settlement must be 'an everlasting peace'. Churchill when he heard it warmed to the phrase. Ministers agreed upon a truce. It was signed on 9 July and came into force on 11 July.[54]

There remained clarification of Craig's position. At a meeting with the Northern Ireland ministers on 18 June, Lloyd George thought the Cabinet of Northern Ireland should put forward some proposals, the principal reason for this being his reluctance to allow de Valera to claim that the only point of disagreement was on the Ulster question – something which would be less easily explained to the British public than a disagreement on a status issue. To this Craig reacted unfavourably. Northern Ireland had made every concession; there was no way out except that proposed by Balfour, that is every possible concession made to Southern Ireland, Northern Ireland remaining as constituted. He therefore resisted Lloyd George's pressure for further discussion, contending that negotiations were solely between Great Britain and Southern Ireland.

Negotiations

From the outset there were two fundamental issues between British and Irish leaders. The first was partition – de Valera continuously 'harped upon the crime of partition' to Smuts. It was a 'nation' that had been divided and that division had been given British statutory authority. Craig was a minority leader, yet as Prime Minister of Northern Ireland he was treated by the British government as an equal. The other was status. Officials at the outset had put the question: should not the Irish be asked to indicate which were the concrete concessions they would make in return for recognition of a republic? From Smuts' Dublin discussions it was evident that for so great a thing they would have been substantial. But Lloyd George would have none of it. It was a fateful decision. It made clear that from the outset he was negotiating to win on both issues: confirmation of Northern Ireland's area and jurisdiction in the six counties, a 'royal' dominion settlement in the guise of dominion status, but with quite a bit subtracted from it, in the twenty-six. That too was a fateful decision. Cope, who was rather more than a discreet intermediary, later had some understanding words to say. 'It is', he wrote from Dublin on 3 September, 'entirely a question of symbols and people in that revolutionary condition can't give up both their symbols. If you give them independence, they may give up unity; if you give them unity they may give up independence but they must have one or the other.'[55] Lloyd George contemplated otherwise.

The note was struck at the first confrontation with de Valera at No. 10 Downing Street on 14 July. Lloyd George's secretary had never seen him so excited, 'bringing up all his guns', as she put it, with a big map of the British Empire hung on the wall, great blotches of red all over it, and, when de Valera came in, Lloyd George pointed with studied deliberation to the chairs around the table at which the dominion leaders sat – there was Meighen, the representative of English and French united in one dominion; there was Smuts symbolising the reconciliation of Boer and Briton within a Union; and then he looked long and fixedly at the unattributed chair. De Valera remained silent, so it was left to Lloyd George to tell him it was reserved for Ireland. 'All we ask you to do is to take your place in this Sisterhood of free nations'.[56] He then dwelt upon the military resources that would be freed, as the position demanded, for Europe and the Middle East.

Dialectical exchanges, published near contemporaneously, followed upon personal meeting. Lloyd George opened with an offer on 20 July and, as so often happens, this first draft despite objection and criticism remained at the heart of the two months' long contention between the Prime Minister and President.[57] The offer was dominion status with its traditional symbolism: facilities reserved to Britain for naval and air defence and the right, enjoyed by the other Dominions, to impose protective duties or other restrictions upon exchange of goods with Britain withheld, the whole to be embodied in a treaty, which would formally allow for full recognition of the powers and privileges of the government of Northern Ireland, 'which cannot be abrogated except by their own consent'.

Smuts, clearly troubled, set out his reactions at length on 22 July to de Valera hoping that de Valera, did no 'take too gloomy a view of the situation'. Despite the self-evident shortfall of expectations, Smuts made the most of what was there – Irish nationhood recognised and given firm constitutional form in the British League of Nations, a treaty of free trade such as were common between free states, naval stipulations such as those that applied to Simonstown, dominion status which was no static thing and Ireland, as a member of the Imperial Conference, in the great company of Dominions who would ensure that nothing in conflict with Ireland's full rights was asked of her. Irish unity, he felt, required more time and could come in two stages, dominion Home Rule being the first. The Irish state thus constituted would exist within the British Empire. In sum, Smuts' advice to de Valera was to accept what was offered.[58]

De Valera was not to be so easily persuaded. In his reply to Lloyd George on 10 August, he welcomed such recognition of Ireland's right to self-determination as was implied, but commented that the outline of the pact was self-contradictory and the principle on which it rested not easy to determine, 'and a claim advanced by your government to an interference in our affairs . . . we cannot admit. Ireland's right to choose for herself the path she should take to realise her own destiny must be accepted as indefeasible.' Apart from specific limitations, dominion status for Ireland, by reason of her proximity, would be illusory. To counter the consequences of this proximity, the most explicit guarantees would be needed. Since nothing of the kind was forthcoming, the proposals were therefore rejected. But a treaty of free association – this was the first oblique reference to what de Valera had conceived of on 27 July as 'external association' – with the British Commonwealth group, given on the assurance 'that the entry of the nation as a whole into such association would secure for it the allegiance of the present dissenting minority' was a proposition they would have been ready to recommend to the Irish people. 'We cannot admit the right of the British government to mutilate our country, either in its own interest or at the call of any section of our population.' Thus in the opening exchange the conceptual issue was set out – autonomy within the British system coupled with the right of the minority to a separate existence, against the right to a national self-determination, nation being conceived of as coterminous with natural frontiers.

When the Irish reply was handed to Austen Chamberlain (in Lloyd George's absence), in Irish with an English translation, Chamberlain, 'looking more grave than the document itself', remarked that it amounted to a definite rejection of the British proposals. At a subsequent Cabinet meeting over which he presided, Chamberlain restated his opinion that the rejoinder was a specific refusal of dominion status. The Sinn Féin delegates, who had brought the reply over with them, told Tom Jones that Chamberlain's reaction was 'too gloomy a view of the situation'. 'If this means anything', observed Chamberlain in his report to Lloyd George, 'it means they are consciously playing with fire. What a crowd to have the peace of two countries in their hands.' To the King, Chamberlain conveyed his deep regrets that the reply was in the form of an unqualified refusal of the government's proposals.[59] The King, however, while describing de Valera's letter as 'a hopeless document, written by a dreamer and a visionary, with nothing practical about it', not for the first or last time counselled caution and trusted that everything possible would be done to keep the negotiations going.[60]

The Prime Minister himself drafted the rejoinder. 'Nothing', he wrote to de Valera on 13 August, 'is to be gained by prolonging a theoretical discussion of the national status which you may be willing to accept as compared with that of the great self-governing Dominions of the British Commonwealth, but we must direct your attention to one point upon which . . . no British government can compromise, namely, the claim that we should acknowledge the right of Ireland to secede from her allegiance to the King.' And then the conclusive sentence: 'No such right can ever be acknowledged by us.'

On 17 August de Valera judged it wise to report on the exchanges to the Dáil. On dominion Home Rule he restated the argument that because of propinquity Ireland, in the nature of things, could never be offered authentic dominion status as enjoyed by Australia or Canada. As for British rule, 'which is hated by the Irish people to the marrow of their bones', they had one desire – to end it. It was as a separate nation they entered into these negotiations and if they were to be continued, it was as such they must remain.[61]

On 24 August de Valera conveyed news of the Dáil's unanimous rejection of the British proposals to Lloyd George. In a concluding sentence, however, he wrote of 'government by consent of the governed' as the only basis of peace talks. The Prime Minister seized upon it. It had a Commonwealth ring. He sent Tom Jones hurrying to the library of the National Liberal Club, and elsewhere, to find quotations from Irish leaders of other days indicating their willingness to give allegiance to the Crown. Thomas Davis, O'Connell, Butt and even Parnell served their turn.[62] The response from de Valera dated 30 August was dismissive. The most he would do would be to refrain from commenting upon the Prime Minister's 'fallacious historical references'. He was prepared to make no concessions on dominion status. The rejection of the British proposals of 20 July was irrevocable. They were *not* an invitation to enter a free and willing partnership. They were an invitation to enter into an Imperial status. The people of Ireland, exercising a fundamental natural right, had declared for independence and set up a republic.

On 2 September this uncompromising reply reached the Prime Minister on holiday at Gairloch. He called a Cabinet meeting to be held in the Town Hall at Inverness on 7 September, as much to the satisfaction of the Mayor as to the dissatisfaction of Cabinet ministers, Chamberlain complaining of the outrage of being dragged up even further north than Edinburgh. In the Town Hall the Prime Minister reviewed the options before them, starting with agreement to 'an unconditional conference':

Now picture the conference itself. I put forward allegiance to the Crown and membership of the Empire. De Valera says 'Let me see what it all means first.' We would not break off on that. He would then say 'My position is the Republic' . . . So without acceptance of Throne and Empire you march into the bog.

He will ask about powers.

> Next you come to Ulster. He says 'What about Tyrone and Fer-
> managh?' Shall I say 'Tyrone and Fermanagh are already in the Northern
> area?' De Valera says, 'What about your representative principle'. De
> Valera will talk Tyrone and Fermanagh and the break will come on
> forcing those two counties against their will. Men will die for the
> Throne and Empire. I do not know who will die for Tyrone and
> Fermanagh.

If de Valera would not come into a conference 'on the basis of accepting
Crown and Empire, we should have the vast majority of the people
behind us in the overwhelming action which we should have to take . . . I
was greatly relieved to go through the conversations with him without
Tyrone and Fermanagh being raised'. But you could not always count
upon his being a maladroit negotiator.

Inexorably the Prime Minister's argument led to the conclusion that the
British must needs insist upon an advance Irish commitment to Crown
and Empire, with a break on that issue if necessary, and so avoiding
becoming entangled, as would otherwise be inevitable, in the question of
Fermanagh and Tyrone where, as he allowed, 'we had a very weak case'.
As Birkenhead put it, no one would like to lose the opportunity for 'a
good break' on Crown and Commonwealth if there were the chance of a
settlement, but he remained apprehensive that a conference might lead to
'a bad break'. To the surprise of the Prime Minister, the Cabinet evenly
divided, finally came down against an ultimatum. This gave historic
significance to the Cabinet proceedings at Inverness.

There followed the exacting business of composing a draft with one eye
on world and Commonwealth opinion, the other on party and public
feeling at home. There were in effect nine drafts of the letter that was sent
with the heading *Town Hall, Inverness*, foreshortened by the omission of
earlier challenging paragraphs and having a new opening, redrafted by
Chamberlain, stiffening the stand on Commonwealth. It read,

> The principle of government by consent of the governed is the founda-
> tion of British constitutional development but we cannot accept as a
> basis of practical conference an interpretation of that principle which
> would commit us to any demands which you might present – even to
> the extent of setting up a republic and repudiating the Crown. . . .
> Conference on such a basis is impossible. So applied, the principle
> would drive . . . the civilised world back into barbarism.

The letter ended with a request for a reply to the invitation to enter a
conference to ascertain how the association of Ireland with the community
of nations known as the British Empire could best be reconciled with Irish
national aspirations.

The formula had been found but there were to be further flurries as de Valera felt compelled to restate his position, fearing that otherwise Ireland's position would be misunderstood and irreparably prejudiced. The restatement was an essay in semantics – but it was also something more.

Conference

As Lloyd George and de Valera reached agreement on the purpose of the conference, the restatement exposed the impossibility of achieving it without sacrifice of what was deemed fundamental on one side or the other. De Valera, after declaring Irish willingness to enter a conference to ascertain how Ireland's association with the community of nations known as the British Empire might best be reconciled with Irish national aspirations, went on to reaffirm the Irish position. It was only as representative of 'our nation' which 'has formally declared its independence and recognises itself as a sovereign state . . . that we have any authority or powers to act on behalf of our people'. The assertion was backed by reference to the principle of 'government by consent of the governed', with a telling quotation from Lloyd George to give it edge. This was the only thing Lloyd George found to enjoy. On the crucial issue of status he told the Irish emissaries who had travelled to Gairloch to deliver de Valera's letter, that it was absolutely out of the question that he should consent to meet de Valera and his colleagues as representatives of a foreign power like France and Germany. When the Irish delegates alluded to de Valera's difficulties with his own people, Lloyd George retorted that he had shown the greatest consideration for them, that he had wide experience of conferences and negotiations with many different nations, and that he had never met representatives of any nation who were so difficult to negotiate with as de Valera and his colleagues. Their idea of negotiation seemed to be that the other side should make all the concessions, while they simply adhered to their original position.

The Irish are said to have taken these complaints with the utmost good nature.[63] The Irish, however, as the Viceroy on several occasions in his own idiosyncratic style advised Chamberlain, had no intention of breaking off negotiations but, as he put it, at various stages de Valera needed to keep his extremists with him by using 'a lot of nonsensical rhetoric about small nations', being himself ignorant of the effect on the English mind of his intransigent attitude.[64] Fitzalan was right in his latest prognostications. 'There is no doubt', he wrote on 11 September, 'that Sinn Féin are going to accept the conference, the risk being that they might not do it in a properly worded letter'.

De Valera eventually received a reply dated 17 September, from Gairloch, where the Prime Minister had assembled a ministerial conference to agree the terms of a reply and where, according to one of the Cabinet secretaries, it rained from morning till night. The confusion was indescribable, as staff tried to work as at No. 10 in one room with one typist, no telephone, the Post Office with one line being a mile away, and the nearest station 30 miles. (The Prime Minister alone enjoyed it all.) The reply uncompromisingly restated no abandonment, however informal, of allegiance, no recognition of Irish separate statehood.[65] 'We can only recognise ourselves for what we are', rejoined de Valera, thus opening the way to a conference on the basis of statement of respective positions 'to ascertain how the association of Ireland with the community of nations known as the British Empire might best be reconciled with Irish national aspirations'.

The dialectical exchanges of the long summer of 1921 had achieved their purpose. There were to be Anglo-Irish negotiations with a view to a settlement. That apart, they had touched on every issue and resolved none. Little noticed, they recorded the introduction of a new concept in inter-state relations – external association.

CHAPTER 7
Negotiating a Settlement: Issues and Outcome

The most remarkable feature about the Anglo-Irish Treaty negotiations was that they took place when and as they did. Here, in October 1921, two and a half years after the meeting of the first Dáil and the shooting at Soloheadbeg, the 'chosen' leaders of the Irish people were to come to London to play their part in the fashioning of a new settlement of Anglo-Irish relations. South African experience may serve to point the contrast; indeed, it is fitting it should do so. There was to be much reference when the London Conference got under way to what had happened in South Africa some twenty years earlier. Not only did it provide the prototype of recent imperial–colonial confrontation in the field and then in negotiation of a settlement but, further, it came within the first-hand experience not only of Lionel Curtis, the British constitutional adviser, but of one of the principal delegates on either side; Churchill on the British as a war correspondent and Griffith on the Irish side, who had worked for two years in the mining industry. Of others, Lloyd George, bravely denouncing the Chamberlainite war in the Chamberlains' midland stronghold, had narrowly eluded an infuriated mob in Birmingham, while for Austen Chamberlain it suffices to recall that he was the son of the man who had killed Home Rule and engineered the war against the Boer republics. The British C.-in-C. in Ireland 1920–22, Sir Nevil Macready, had served in South Africa for the whole of the war period (1899–1902), while de Valera, once negotiations were contemplated, turned to Smuts as one who had relevant experience of service in President Kruger's republican government, of life under Crown Colony rule and the dominion relationship.

The parallels were arresting; the differences when it came to peacemaking, fundamental. In May 1902, near Vereeniging, in a large tent pitched by command of the British C.-in-C., Lord Kitchener, the sixty representatives of the Boer republics were brought face to face with the bitterness of defeat. Kitchener told them one thing was not open to discussion and that was the continuing independence of the two republics. On 28 June 1919 Botha and Smuts, seated with the victors, remembered as they watched the German surrender at Versailles that they too had felt 'the harrow of defeat'. But the Irish were not defeated. Far from Sir

Nevil Macready as Commander-in-Chief dictating terms to them, the Irish delegates were coming to London to discuss a settlement with the leading members of the British Cabinet, not in a tent but at No. 10 Downing Street. The British were well aware of the implications. It had not been an easy step to take. Later Churchill allowed himself some indulgence – but not much – in writing of the decision to receive the Irish leaders and 'to attempt to form through their agency the government of a civilised state', as being 'one of the most questionable and hazardous experiments upon which a great Empire in the plenitude of its power had ever embarked'.[1]

The calling of the conference may be regarded as the summit of Sinn Féin achievement. They had scaled the negotiating heights: had they the resources to sustain that position? Michael Collins in the disputacious aftermath of treaty-making conceded, 'We had not beaten the enemy out of our country by force of arms.'[2] The phrasing still seems just right. The Irish had not lost the war; equally they had not won it. In the judgement of the military historian of the war, Dr Townshend, 'the Republican guerrilla campaign proved too determined, too resilient, and too resourceful to be put down by the military force which was employed against it'.[3] Yet given time and concentration of purpose, could not Britain have mobilised sufficient resources to achieve at least a temporary subjugation of the country? The crux here was time and attitude. The Anglo-Irish war was at all times psychological over and above military. By the summer of 1921, there was mounting evidence of popular revulsion against its continuance: '. . . it was the revolt of the British conscience', writes Dr Boyce, 'not the defeat of the British army, that obliged Lloyd George to seek terms of peace and settlement with Sinn Féin'.[4] Given the prospect of a quick and decisive outcome and the diminishing demands on British military resources overseas, the British conscience might have been brought to acquiesce in their deployment in Ireland, but not so in the extension of a long-drawn conflict marked by ambush and reprisal. Of that the public were sick and tired.

As for the politicians, there was a discounted factor. Would truce, dialectical exchanges and conference have come in quick succession from midsummer on, had dominion statesman not foregathered for the Imperial Conference on 20 June 1921?[5] Dominion opinion only a little less than American was, as we know from Cabinet records, a cause of much concern in London,[6] and that opinion was now voiced, not at a distance, but on the doorstep. The Dominions stood moreover at the pinnacle of their post-war reputation.[7] British statesmen were concerned to conciliate not to alienate these young nations, standard bearers of the future, and there was also for the Dominions an Irish overseas vote to be lost or won. The setting for the negotiations overall had, therefore, a pronounced Commonwealth flavour.

A transformation in the parameters of Anglo-Irish relations was registered in the invitation issued on 29 September 1921. As defined by Lloyd George in his final letter, the problem was 'ascertaining how the association of Ireland with the community of nations known as the British Empire may best be reconciled with Irish national aspirations'.[8] This was a great departure, the question no longer viewed as in Home Rule days as one of relations within the United Kingdom, but as one within the British Commonwealth of Nations. That marked a 'significant advance' in status, as is generally acknowledged, but, as is not, it also complicated the issue. The obvious course would have been negotiation for a transformation of Anglo-Irish relations, with Dominions involved if at all only at one or more remove. It was British party divisions, not the circumstances of the case, that precluded the following of a natural line of approach. Few could face with equanimity the thought of the Home Rule debate renewed even if at a higher plane. On the credit side, moreover, in British eyes, there was the attraction of Commonwealth, a relationship which had its own foundation in history, laws, conventions and institutions.

In the course of the negotiations much time was spent in elucidating Commonwealth purposes and status implications for the Irish, who had little or no familiarity with them. The British, for example, pointed out that on admission to membership Ireland would be represented at Imperial Conferences. But what did that mean for an Irish Free State in practice? Such questions slanted the negotiations, giving them a radical shift from a British Isles to a British Commonwealth context. To such transformation there was an ironic consequence. None of those taking part in the negotiations had favoured a settlement on Commonwealth lines – all the British delegates until May 1921 having been its committed opponents. Dominion status was a deviation favoured by the dispossessed – Asquithian Liberals, Irish parliamentarians of earlier constitutionalist days, Southern Irish Unionists guided by Midleton who now, as it were overnight, became the lodestar of those under Lloyd George's lead who favoured a settlement under that name, although somewhat short of full measure.

The Delegations

The membership of the delegations to the conference in London was not without surprise. Of the two protagonists in the correspondence,[9] which was deliberately protracted so as to ensure that the Truce was not broken while weather conditions would favour the British, one of them, de Valera, was not a delegate. By his own casting vote, the Dáil Cabinet decided that he, the President, should not go. The matter was discussed in the Dáil on 14 September 1921, the Minister for Local Government, W.T. Cosgrave, observing that it was not usual to leave the ablest player in reserve. Why did de Valera favour this course? Because, so he replied, it was so important to keep the Head of the State and its symbol untouched: 'if he were not the symbol he would go'. On 22 November Arthur Griffith, as leader of the delegation, reopened the question, enquiring of the de Valera whether, with a breakdown of negotiations, which seemed an imminent contingency, he thought 'the time has come for you to come over here,' while on 3 December he was pressed by Barton to do so. On neither of these occasions, as again later, did the suggestion elicit a positive response from de Valera. This was in accord with received diplomatic wisdom, particularly in relation to the weaker party. A prince, Machiavelli advised, should not enter into negotiations in which his emissaries have already failed to achieve their aims.

In the absence of de Valera, the leadership of the Irish delegation devolved upon Arthur Griffith, with Michael Collins as his principal associate. Of the others – Eamon Duggan, Gavan Duffy and Robert Barton – only Barton, as Minister of Economic Affairs, was a member of the Cabinet nominated by de Valera when the Second Dáil met for the first time on 16 August. As important were those who stayed in Dublin – W.T. Cosgrave, Cathal Brugha and Austin Stack. Many years later, as Taoiseach, de Valera would point with a certain satisfaction to four medallions on the wall behind his desk, those of Griffith and Collins on his right and Brugha and Stack to his left. He was *par excellence* the man in, though not necessarily of, the centre. By virtue of his remaining in Dublin, the balance in London was to the right of the Cabinet members. Given especially the presumption reinforced by the antipathy of Brugha, Minister of Defence, to Collins, Minister of Finance, the delegation, inclining right of centre, would not readily identify with the militant revolutionaries in the Cabinet at home. More generally the pressures inseparable from difficult and detailed negotiation would almost inevitably have served to sharpen barely perceptible differences between those who had set off with much the same assumptions. In this case the likelihood was accentuated by the protracted time span, 11 October–6 December, with only intermittent visits by members of the delegation to Dublin in which to repair relationships and restore community of purpose.

The British delegation also had a notable absentee from its ranks: Andrew Bonar Law. He had resigned, temporarily as it proved, from office in March 1921 because of ill health, leaving Austen Chamberlain to succeed him as Lord Privy Seal, leader of the House and of the Unionists in the London negotiations. The last cast Chamberlain in an unenviable role, the son engaged in a plot to barter away the Union his father had saved. Against him the diehard cry of 'traitor' was to be turned, while Bonar Law retained his freedom of action. Birkenhead, although likewise exposed, was altogether less vulnerable. Churchill, also a delegate and foremost exponent of defence requirements, was to leave an account of the proceedings unsurpassed in its sense of historic occasion. Worthington-

Evans, Gordon Hewart, the Solicitor-General, and Hamar Greenwood, the last Chief Secretary whose Canadian origin, according to Tom Jones' surprising verdict, left him among the most understanding of the Irish point of view in the British delegation, made up a team dominated by Lloyd George. He remained sensitive, over-sensitive as now appears, to the political risks of a settlement outside the Union, given the Unionist majority in the House and mindful of the possible emergence of a potential alternative administration under Bonar Law. The last was something that Lloyd George (or rather Tom Jones for him) was to deploy against the Irish – he advised them before pressing Lloyd George to the point of resignation to pause and consider the prospect of a succeeding diehard government. However, what Bonar Law cared about was Ulster and to Ulster's exclusion Lloyd George was committed by his own 1920 enactment and his own oft-stated conviction.[10]

The conference was served by secretaries of unusual calibre and with opinions which they felt little or no need to disguise, but rather a mission to promote. This applied with particular force to Lionel Curtis, the Second Secretary on the British side, an exponent of Commonwealth ideally based upon government of men by themselves, an authority on dominion status and much concerned in the aftermath of the Treaty to ensure due observance of Commonwealth conventions and constitutional procedures designed to preserve imperial symmetry. An article by Curtis on the Irish situation based on impressions formed on a tour of Ireland and published anonymously in the *Round Table*, was thought to have consolidated British ministerial opinion in favour of a dominion settlement. Against Curtis by way of natural counterpart stood Erskine Childers, an Englishman with Irish connections who, despairing of Home Rule, joined the ranks of the republicans, was elected for a Dublin constituency in 1918 and served as Secretary of the Irish delegation.[11] He was as zealous a critic as Curtis was an impassioned believer in Commonwealth. Not for Childers the blurred edges of dominion status. He believed, and was outraged by the thought, that behind a façade of liberal forms they concealed devices to deprive Ireland of rights at last regained. The intensity of his feelings sometimes surfaced in letters to A.D. Lindsay (then an Oxford philosophy don, and later Master of Balliol), who sought to play a reconciling intermediary role. In a pre-conference exchange, Lindsay, while feeling he was stretching beyond the limit of what was realistic, conceded that by way of last resort in a dominion settlement 'secession should be permissible'. Childers' response was swift and sharp. 'Permissible! It is the *sine qua non* . . . not for discussion, but a right'.

Tom Jones was the Principal Secretary to the British delegation. He was unusually well versed in Anglo-Irish affairs over the preceding two years, having served throughout as a secretary to the Cabinet and at discussions at Prime Minister's conferences on Ireland. As secretary, he

kept a *Diary*,★ to which frequent reference has already been made. There is
a certain interest in comparing the formal minutes of Cabinet meetings
with corresponding diary entries. The latter reveal Jones' fascination with
the drama unfolding before him, whether earlier in the shaping of policy
in widely ranging Cabinet or Cabinet Conference discussions, the devices
of ministers to achieve their purposes, the dominating presence of the
Prime Minister throughout, the contributions of emissaries as eminent as
Smuts or of intermediaries as unobtrusive as Cope; the unyielding accents
of Ulster Unionism or the more flexible but peripheral contributions of
the Southern minority; and by way of historic climax, the Sinn Féin
leaders, de Valera first among them negotiating the Truce, and then later
in 1921 for some two months in London the Sinn Féin delegates, de Valera
not among them, at the conference table or less formal, but little less
significant, meetings away from it. Thomas Jones, however, was more
than a compulsive recorder of all matters bearing on Anglo-Irish relations.
His *Diary* entries are more than the notes of an experienced *rapporteur* on
often complex and usually contentious debates. They are the contributions
of a man who himself became emotionally involved and who at a critical
moment on 22 November, by disregarding instructions and communicat-
ing less than he was commissioned to do, probably saved the conference
from disruption.[12] This personal commitment (which it is well to keep in
mind) to a settlement in Ireland on a dominion basis had become something to which he became strongly, almost passionately, predisposed at
the last.[13]

Credentials and Instructions

The formal documents issued to the Irish delegates did not directly convey
a sense of the tightrope walking required of them.[14] After naming the Irish
delegates they spoke of them as 'envoys plenipotentiary from the elected
Government of the Republic of Ireland to negotiate and conclude on
behalf of Ireland, with the representatives of His Britannic Majesty George
V, a treaty or treaties of settlement, association and accommodation
between Ireland and the community of nations known as the British
Commonwealth'. The documents served, however, only a propaganda
purpose since, despite Michael Collins' later assertion to the contrary
when under pressure in the Dáil, they were not formally accepted and
could not have been in the context of the September exchanges without
disbanding the conference at the moment of assembly. It sufficed to say
that they were presented, and that only in a technical sense.

★ Thomas Jones, *Whitehall Diary*, Vol. III, *Ireland 1918–25* groups together a
substantial selection made by Keith Middlemas, editor, of the more interesting
entries relating to Ireland for those years.

With the credentials were associated instructions dated 7 October 1921 in President de Valera's own hand directing the plenipotentiaries to send a dispatch to the Cabinet in Dublin and to await a reply before decisions were finally reached.[15] In the case of a break, the text of the final Irish proposals should be similarly submitted. Credentials and instructions in conjunction presupposed both a republic in being, which was not surprising and also a settlement, if achieved, not with Britain alone, but also with the British Commonwealth. It predetermined the contours of the settlement though dominion governments did not, as the wording might suggest, play any known part in its negotiations.

British and Irish Objectives

The British proposals of 20 July had envisaged a dominion settlement with, it was hoped, the Irish people finding 'as complete an expression of their political and spiritual ideals within the Empire as any of the numerous and varied nations united in allegiance to His Majesty's Throne'.[16] In them, Lloyd George 'spoke from first to last in the language of constitutional monarchy'.[17] The problem, he insisted, was one not of international but of intra-Commonwealth relations. On no other basis was he prepared to enter into discussions. No less than six times he stated that there could be no compromise in respect of the Crown: on that the whole fabric of the Commonwealth rested. De Valera by contrast, though using the adjective 'republican', did not make specific claim to the republic. He felt he could not afford to be provocative on this issue, knowing that the price might be no talks. But the importance he attached to it is evident in his letter to Smuts of 31 July in which he states quite explicitly that for the Irish people the principle of national self-determination, to which they were devotedly attached, found expression in the 'Republic'. In the Dáil in August he spoke of their case resting on the 'fundamental rock of right and justice'. That apart 'we have no case whatsoever . . . and on that rock we shall stand'.[18] Yet he conveyed an impression of a wary readiness to consider adjustment of his stance if, but only if, that would bring in the minority in the North. For the rest, the dilemma confronting him was real enough. While on the one hand 'in recognising ourselves for what we are' he had come close to causing cancellation of the conference, on the other by entering into formal negotiations without explicit affirmation of the existence of the republic, he had left it open for Michael Collins to claim later that it was the acceptance of the invitation that had formed the compromise.[19] Pakenham, sympathetic to de Valera's position, allows that therewith a dominion settlement had become the reasonable, a republic the unreasonable course, to the outside world.[20]

On 11 October the conference met for the first time. In default of an Irish paper – one would like to know more about the reason for this –

members had circulated to them by Tom Jones the British proposals of 20 July. However much amended, the basic paper at any conference is apt to determine the parameters of subsequent discussion. This was to prove no exception. On 11 October Griffith wrote to de Valera: 'Our tactics have been successful up to the present but unless we can get in our Treaty proposals by Monday, the initiative will pass to the British.' To judge by the record, it had already done so. The Irish proposals were a persuasive essay in exposition against the tide of an associate relationship, with Ireland adhering for all purposes of agreed common concern to the British Commonwealth of Nations, with Ireland's freedom and integrity guaranteed and trade and other conventions negotiated on a basis of reciprocity. But the proposals suffered from their delayed submission, being brushed aside as 'too late' by Lloyd George on 24 October. The Irish delegation were put on the defensive. There were excursions, but essentially the debate on status each time returned, or was brought back, to the foundation British document with dominion status subject to six qualifications therein set forth. What were they?

In the aftermath of war, it is not surprising, though still noteworthy, that four of the six conditions listed by the British related to defence. The first was that the Irish should accord such rights and liberties in Irish harbours and on Irish coasts as would enable the Royal Navy in the common interest of both countries to control the seas around them; the second, that the Irish Territorial force should be kept within reasonable limits so that the movement towards limitation of armaments should 'in no way be hampered'; the third, facilities for the Royal Air Force should continue to be normal; the fourth, free recruitment in Ireland to His Majesty's forces should continue; fifth, that there should be no protective duties within the British Isles imposed by either party; and the sixth, that Ireland should assume responsibility for payment of a share of the national debt and the cost of pensions. It was the British intention that the conditions should be embodied in a treaty between the two countries which would define dominion status in so far as that might be thought practicable or desirable. How extraordinary it all was: that which earlier the British had repudiated and the Irish never asked for – dominion status – had become central to the negotiations. Why not an Anglo-Irish Treaty in the strict sense? The short-term answer was that no such treaty could escape from the shadow of Home Rule. It was non-negotiable on both the British and the Irish side. Compare dominion status in South Africa with Home Rule in Ireland. How could anyone opt for the latter, whereas there might be a chance of the former?

To the British view of appropriate setting is to be added the British stance on unity. The form of the settlement, it was set out on 20 July, 'must allow for full recognition of the existing powers and privileges of the Parliament and Government of Northern Ireland which cannot be abrogated except by their own consent'.[21] Here the British were tying their own hands though it may be noted that area was not listed with 'powers and privileges'.

It was the British contention that the conditions listed on 20 July arose from geographical propinquity and other particular circumstances and were consistent with dominion status: it was the Irish contention that they nullified it. In August 1921, de Valera had told the Dáil that dominion status could *never* – the word is his – apply in its overseas form to Ireland.[22] That also was Childers' view. The reason was geographical proximity resulting in a security imperative. Carried to its logical conclusion, it would have rendered all discussion in a dominion context otiose. But neither Griffith nor Collins went so far. Their opening enquiry was on two levels: basically was dominion status conceptually compatible with Irish aspirations and, secondly, were the conditions the British attached consistent with dominion status as practised overseas? Here the ground was tested on particular issues. What of the proposed arrangements for defence? Were they consistent with that status? Given geographical propinquities, could they be? What then were the implications for status?

Churchill sought to equate the conditions laid down on 20 July with those in the British agreement with Canada in respect of naval facilities at Halifax and Esquimault and more especially with those that he had recently negotiated with Smuts on the naval base at Simonstown. Griffith contested the validity of such analogy on the particular ground that while control of Simonstown was being restored to South Africa, the Irish facilities were being acquired. More generally he sought to counteract the Churchillian argument by emphasising that the defence facilities being asked for were different, not merely in scale, but in kind from those in force in the Dominions. They were such as to make Irish neutrality impracticable – no enemy power knowing of the facilities conceded would, or could, afford to respect it. On this point Griffith was emphatic but otherwise defence as such did not rank high in his priorities. It was left for Collins and Childers (who was a full member of the Conference Committee on Defence over which Churchill presided) to contend that what was being asked for was inconsistent with dominion status, as that status applied in the overseas Dominions. An extract from the Defence Committee discussion on 17 October[23] may serve to illustrate conflicting approaches to the debates on defence which necessarily led on to the larger questions at issue.

Mr Churchill, asked whether it was not true that Dominions can remain neutral in time of war, replied,

'Tis not so. In theory when the King declares war, constitutionally all his subjects are at war. In practice, I admit that there has been some

difference of opinion. The claim has been advanced in certain cases that
the Dominions may remain neutral, but the responsible authorities in
these dominions do not hold this opinion and it is not shared by the
British Government.

Mr. Childers – But your responsible Ministers have stated that the
   Dominions may be neutral.

Sir Laming Worthington-Evans – That is a reference to Bonar Law . . .
   You are, if I may say so, over-quoting him.*

Mr. Childers – But the Dominions have a voice in the making of peace
   and war. War is made upon the advice of Dominion ministers.

Mr. Churchill – That is not so.

Mr. Childers – The Treaty of Versailles was separately ratified by the
   Dominion governments . . . It surely follows that they would
   have a voice in the making of war.

Mr. Churchill – One has more time when making peace than when
   making war.

Even if it be allowed that the Irish case was a good one, there was the
irony that it was sustained by arguments resting on grounds not of their
choosing. Arthur Griffith said on 21 October: 'Dominion status is not our
claim.'[24] He noted that the British offer fell short of it in every way.
But to him that was irrelevant. Not only were the Irish unreceptive of
dominion status, they were as a delegation (Griffith possibly excepted)
positively hostile to it. Defence, foreign policy, fiscal autonomy, all were
matters for negotiation,[25] and, as may be judged from the records, the
Irish were ready to consider compromise over a range of matters that
retrospectively may seem remarkable. But to them foreign policy, defence,
trade, however important, were secondary matters – the fundamental
thing was recognition of status as of indefeasible right. The concept of
dominion status with allegiance to the Crown as the essential feature was
not only inconsistent, it was of itself deemed a denial of the notion of a
separate Irish nationality. If there were to be willing compromise it had
therefore to come obliquely by way of recognition of the Crown for
certain purposes from an Irish state outside the British Empire or British
Commonwealth of Nations, as it was in 1921 coming to be known. At
root, it was the British Commonwealth itself that was the difficulty.
When A.D. Lindsay suggested to Childers[26] that his misgivings, lest

---

*Bonar Law was speaking on the Government of Ireland Bill, (H. of C. Deb.,
Vol. CXXVII, Col. 1125, 30 March 1920). The over-quoting arose because Bonar
Law could be taken, according to context, to be arguing on either side of the
question. He was stating, or overstating the autonomy of the Dominions, not to
please the Irish, but to frighten the British out of conceding so much. The Irish,
however, were able to deploy it with effect. See below pp. 290–1.

by reason of proximity and self-interest England would never respect Ireland's dominion status as she did that of Dominions thousands of miles away, might be met by making the Dominions themselves guarantors of Irish rights, Childers professed himself utterly dismayed by Lindsay's misunderstanding of the Irish position. Nothing, he replied, would suffice to ensure an Irish Dominion's treatment on an overseas dominion basis, and at a deeper level such a guarantee would serve only to draw Ireland further into the Commonwealth. If dominion status there had to be, only one thing was tolerable – that that status was on the explicit understanding that it opened the road to secession. As Bonar Law had pronounced, and as Collins has also reminded the conference,[27] the Dominions in practice could vote themselves out of the British Empire.* But what the Irish were looking for was not practice, which they thought would not apply in their case, but recognition in law or convention of entitlement equal to that of Canada on all points as of right. If there were understanding and confidence, then negotiation might prove fruitful. But there was neither. The problem was that there was no blueprint of dominion status, there was no overall correlation between law and practice. There was confusion and an authentic need for elucidation. It was suggested that Childers and Curtis compose a joint memorandum. Sadly, but not surprisingly, the project was abandoned before it took off. Instead there were memoranda by Curtis, which ventured bravely into Irish history and a memorandum by Childers, as well as many other communications, on defence. 'It was a key feature of Childers' arguments on dominion status', writes Dr Hawkins, 'that any settlement along dominion lines must *explicitly* give Ireland the status currently enjoyed by Canada and the other dominions'.[28] That would seem to reflect Childers' approach exactly. He was the most rigorous critic of that status and, as such, he illumined most clearly the price that might be paid for the flexibility which was its outstanding feature.

The distinctive feature of the Irish alternative was association from outside. External association had been conceived by de Valera in July 1921. In later years he liked to recall how the description came to him for the first time one morning while tying up his bootlaces. It seemed to him to crystallise in the two words, external association, all that he wanted to convey. It was at first a concept loosely defined, and then approved (though by some members imperfectly understood) by the Dáil Ministry in the first formulation of Irish notions of an acceptable relationship with the British Commonwealth. It implied a twofold compromise, first be-

---

* In Collins' notes scribbled on scraps of paper at the conference session, there is a reference to Bonar Law and his speech (Rex Taylor, *Michael Collins* (London, 1958), p. 167).

tween Britain and Ireland and then within Ireland, where the more militant
republicans felt that it went as far, if not further, than was right by way of
retreat from the isolated Republic that was their ideal. According to
Collins, the idea was bandied about in Dublin as early as 10 August 1921
with the notion of 'association' with, as against membership of, the
Commonwealth conveyed by the use of that one word in de Valera's reply
to Lloyd George of 10 August. Is was first introduced into the London
discussions by Collins on 21 October when he alluded to a new form of
association. It was laid before delegates on 24 October embodied as Draft
Treaty A in a memorandum,[29] already alluded to, designed *inter alia* to
meet Lloyd George's earlier request for the Irish counter-proposals to
those of 20 July on the British side.

In the secret session of the Dáil on 14 December, that is after the Treaty
had been signed, de Valera was categoric on two points – the first of
timing and the second of formulation. In respect of the first when questioned 'whether we stand for the Republic or not, I said from the start we
stood for external association. I was always for external association. I had
to make up my mind whether we would face war.' On the second the
answer was equally clear: that the status had not been fully formulated,
though there had been exchanges of view and a summary made of what
such a relationship would entail, but there had been no final formulation
before the Treaty was signed.[30] More than anything, these later post-
Treaty exchanges convey a sense of the pressures on leaders new to
negotiating assignment and their secretarial staff. There was no adequate
administrative infrastructure on the Irish side, which over a period must
have placed their delegates at a serious disadvantage as against the British
and the formidable backing on which they could call.

Lloyd George, however, was not prepared to see the basis of discussion
shifted. He desired not to consider a new relationship but to know the
views of the Irish delegation on three points from the old: allegiance to the
Crown; Irish entry into the fraternity of nations known as the British
Commonwealth; and the concession of necessary security facilities. On
allegiance, no reply was vouchsafed, but to the second it was that Ireland
would consent to adhere to the British Commonwealth for all purposes of
agreed common concern. This provided a focus for debate. Did it mean
coming within the Commonwealth like New Zealand or Canada, the
Prime Minister asked? That was not quite the Irish idea of association,
Griffith replied. It was association with Britain and the Dominions from
outside, the Crown being accepted as the bond of association. Such a
relationship would be more than an alliance by reason of its permanence,
and it would allow for representation at an Imperial Council and agreed
common concern in war, peace, trade, and all the large issues. Griffith,
however, stood firm on Ireland's right to neutrality and he 'boggled' (the
word is Lloyd George's) at the thought of Ireland's automatically going to

war in defence of Australia. He did agree to the British use of Irish ports, even if that might mean Irish involvement in war, but envisaged situations in which neutrality could and would be preserved at the discretion of an Irish government. Reciprocal as against common citizenship was contemplated.

Birkenhead reacted to Griffith's exposition by saying these answers had shaken him. And why? Because, so he told his colleagues, the Irish did not accept the Crown. There was the crux. They has some idea of a president. 'They seemed', commented Chamberlain, 'to think of a republic within the Empire'. That precluded settlement. Allegiance was a condition of it. Later the Prime Minister so informed Collins. 'What did allegiance involve?' asked Collins. 'The oath of allegiance', replied the Prime Minister. 'That's a pretty big pill', rejoined Collins. 'Cannot we have an oath to the Constitution?' That indeed was how it was to end up – an oath to the Crown by way of the constitution, not direct allegiance to the King. It served to blunt the resentment of a few and as an emollient for the moderate republican supporters of a Treaty. More, it may be allowed, was beyond the skill of draftsmanship. Hated, the oath was to remain. Were the British then risking sacrifices of substance – agreement on defence, trade, even in some measure foreign policy – by insistence on allegiance and an oath? Was the vaunted flexibility of the Empire such that its fabric would be torn apart were allegiance not enforced? The answer at that time to both questions was in the affirmative.

There was another major issue – unity. This was a question not of seeking to negotiate a new relationship, but rather of reconsidering an arrangement embedded in a British statute the preceding year. 'Unless the North East comes in on some reasonable basis', de Valera told Smuts in his letter of 31 July, 'no further progress can be made. An Ireland in fragments nobody cares about.' The Irish, Griffith told the conference of 14 October, had three objections to what had been done: the division was unnatural, it didn't take away a definite area and it included Tyrone, Fermanagh, Armagh and Derry, all of which would have voted against partition. On two points, Lloyd George was directly challenged, first by Griffith on the abandonment of the principle of unity, to which Liberal governments had been pledged, and then by Michael Collins on a border drawn without respect for the wishes of the inhabitants. To the first, Lloyd George replied as follows:[31]

Attempts have been made to settle the Irish problem since 1886 on the basis of autonomy. Gladstone . . . tried to do it but he came up against Ulster. . . . We tried from 1911–1913. Ulster defeated Gladstone, Ulster would have defeated us. Mr. Churchill and I were for the Bill, Mr. Chamberlain and the Lord Chancellor were opposed. They with the instinct of trained politicians saw that Ulster was the stumbling

block. They got the whole force of the opposition concentrated on
Ulster. Ulster was arming and would fight. We were powerless. It is
no use ignoring facts however unpleasant they may be. . . . You had to
ask the British to use force to put Ulster out of one combination in
which she had been for generations into another combination which she
professed to abhor and did abhor, whether for political or religious
reasons. We could not do it. If we tried, the instrument would have
broken in our hands. Their case was "Let us remain with you". Our
case was "Out you go or we fight you". We could not have done it.
Mr. Churchill and I warned our colleagues. Mr. Gladstone and Mr.
Asquith discovered it. I cannot say I discovered it because I was always
of that opinion. You have got to accept facts. The first axiom is
whatever happened we could not coerce Ulster.

Lloyd George in turn asked Griffith what was his proposition about
Ulster. The answer was 'If you stand aside we will make them a fair
proposal. If you do so, we can probably come to an agreement with
them.' But so long as the British government was behind the Ulster
Unionists, they would be difficult. The British must withdraw – they
were, in Collins' words, giving an unfair advantage to Northern Ireland,
or in Gavan Duffy's 'You are putting a premium upon partition.'
   The large minority within the six-county area was Michael Collins'
more immediate preoccupation. On 14 October he said to Lloyd George
'You and Northern Ireland are faced with the coercion of one-third of
its area.' The allegiance, he proceeded, of the majority in Tyrone and
Fermanagh, more than half Armagh, a great deal of Derry and a strip of
Antrim would be with the authority they preferred, namely, a Dublin
parliament. Lloyd George conceded that if you took a plebiscite of Tyrone
and Fermanagh, there would be a Catholic majority, but contended that
there had to be a new unit and that the six-county area had been acceptable
to the Nationlists as preferable to a new delimitation of Ulster. More than
once Lloyd George in passing mentioned a Boundary Commission.
   In de Valera's mind external association was not an absolute, a good
in itself. It was rather a retreat from what was so conceived namely
the Republic. Its principal virtue, indeed, lay in the fact that it was not
an absolute and would not therefore subtract from republican integrity.
Ideally the Republic would first have come into *de facto* independence
and then, by treaty or otherwise, would enter into association with the
Commonwealth* for particular purposes. Only in that way, as indeed was

---

* As in fact happened on 16 February 1961 when Cyprus, having become a
Republic, immediately thereafter by Resolution of the House of Representatives
decided to join the Commonwealth from outside. See N. Mansergh, *Documents and
Speeches on Commonwealth Affairs, 1952–1962*, (London, 1963), pp. 298–9.

perceived at the time, might arrangement and theory be brought into conformity. This, the status implication, was of moment to many republicans who feared dilution of the republican ideal through any association with the Commonwealth even one from outside it. This meant in turn that for de Valera himself as for a number, as yet to be determined, of his colleagues external association did not provide a basis for further negotiation but represented the limit of negotiation. It was at most as far as they were prepared to go in order to meet Lloyd George on allegiance and to satisfy the minority in the north-east on sentiment.

While external association was advanced initially by the Irish in the context of status, it was also seen, though not by them, as a gesture to Ulster Unionists. There were differences between the two. In the early sessions of the conference, the ground on allegiance had been tested: that on unity only explored. In early November, however, Lloyd George turned his thoughts to the possibility of playing off the one against the other. Might it not be possible, by reducing a manoeuvre complicated by the existence of a third party to its simplest form, to persuade the Irish delegates to compromise on allegiance, in return for assurances of advances towards what Griffith had termed 'essential unity', by which he meant a government in Northern Ireland exercising powers as or more extensive than those devolved under the Act of 1920, but one subordinate conceptually at the least to Dublin. After all, had not Griffith himself linked allegiance and unity in telling Lloyd George and Chamberlain that the only possibility of Ireland considering association of any kind was in exchange for essential unity − association being a concession to Ulster. Griffith so reported in a letter to de Valera of 24 October.[32] In effect, therefore, the Irish delegates could not recommend allegiance to the King unless they got unity.[33] Were there here the ingredients of compromise on the basis of a *quid pro quo* bargain?

The setting was not encouraging. First there was the third party. Chamberlain had earlier suggested taking soundings of Craig. Birkenhead, dissenting, advised the Prime Minister to see Carson: 'Don't send for Craig.' The reason was that Carson was considered less likely to reject the thought of compromise out of hand.[34] Craig, however, was not in person or by office an easy man to circumvent. It was not that he had any wish to be drawn into negotiations on the future of the twenty-six counties. On the contrary, that in his view was an Anglo-Irish affair, with the future of the six counties settled and secure under the terms of the Act of the previous year. He was determined that it should continue to be so.

In the course of the London Conference, Irish views on how unity might be attained underwent change. Initially the view was that the British should quit, leaving the Irish to settle among themselves. But that was superseded by the concept of 'essential unity', to be effected by the power that had brought partition into existence, that is by the British.

This shift in Irish tactics, if anything, enhanced the possibility of a deal. But there remained the two pivotal questions: would the Irish play on allegiance and membership of the British Commonwealth and could the British persuade Northern Ireland to yield sufficient to count as 'essential' unity? At the least, the second meant pressure upon the North. How strong might it be? Austen Chamberlain, as English Unionist leader, while pledged not to coerce Ulster, did not feel precluded from putting on the strongest moral pressure if he felt the settlement was otherwise a good one. Even so, the prospect was bound to arouse misgivings about rank-and-file Unionist reactions on the part of Coalition, let alone non-Coalition, Unionists. But so also would negotiations with Sinn Féin, if much longer protracted.

Lloyd George made the first move. He took soundings of Griffith and Collins. He was successful in persuading the former to write him a letter on 2 November, which was copied to de Valera, to the effect that he had conveyed to Lloyd George Irish willingness to enter into free partnership with the British Commonwealth (later amended to 'the other free states of the British Commonwealth'), such willingness being conditional on essential unity.[35] As Griffith advised de Valera, if the Irish accepted the Crown, the British 'would force Ulster in as I understand'.

Before using this conditional offer as a weapon against Craig, soundings were taken on likely Unionist rank-and-file reactions. Chamberlain enquired of the party whips, Younger and Leslie Wilson, whether if Sinn Féin 'would agree (1) to accept our conditions in relation to the Crown, the Empire, the debt; (2) to join in a guarantee to the Parliament of the North-East, but if that guarantee was made contingent on entry of the North-East into an all-Ireland Parliament, and if Ulster then refused to consent to such inclusion, could we rally the country to support Ulster and for coercion of Southern Ireland?'[36] Younger replied that he didn't think the country would support Ulster in adopting an intractable attitude. Ulster should take some risks. Neither Bonar Law nor Bonar Law with Balfour 'could rekindle the flame which burned so fiercely before 1914. They would delude themselves if they thought so.' Wilson replied to the same effect. There was no possibility of rallying the country in support of Ulster. The present House was very different from that of pre-war years and was elected by an electorate holding very different views. The country wanted a peace settlement. A Unionist Party Conference at Liverpool, the outcome of which Chamberlain viewed with some trepidation, bore out the whips' conclusions and strengthened the resolve of the Unionist members of the Cabinet.

On 10 November Lloyd George wrote to Craig. He conveyed to him his belief that a settlement on the lines of the proposals made on 20 July was not unattainable. Such a settlement would comprise Irish allegiance to the Throne, the government of Northern Ireland would retain all the powers conferred upon it by the 1920 Act, and the unity of Ireland would be recognised by the establishment of an all-Ireland parliament upon which would be devolved the further powers necessary to form the self-governing Irish state. Craig would have needed to read no further! Not all the gloss Lloyd George imparted to following paragraphs on safeguards, on area – 'the creation of an all-Ireland parliament would clearly further the amicable settlement of this problem' – on the fiscal disadvantages and liabilities of separate customs and higher taxation for the North in any way tempered his resentment at this reopening of what he termed 'the final settlement' and 'supreme sacrifice' made by Ulster in the interests of peace. The question of area, he wrote, had been fully considered and what was decided upon formed no less an essential part of the Act than the powers conferred upon the Northern Parliament. He threatened a hypo-thetical – or was it? – new departure of his own. There should be not one but two Dominions in Ireland, the six counties being the second.[37] Lloyd George dismissed this as indefensible. Craig did not refer to it in his correspondence again. Yet, once made, it was not altogether lost to view as a possible ingredient in a restructured settlement. At the time one thing was clear – most of all to Ulster Unionists. The Coalition government which had sponsored the 1920 part of the settlement evidently did not regard it as 'final' in respect either of institutions or area. Captain Craig the preceding year had envisaged revisionist policies of Liberal or Labour governments as something to be guarded against, but not those of a predominantly Unionist Coalition, let alone the very one that had brought Northern Ireland into being.

For the Irish, the Ulster diversion of November 1921 marked the penultimate step on the road that led to concession on allegiance. The evidence now available points beyond question to the conclusion that Lloyd George would not concede association, that either he had dominion status with allegiance or he resigned, Chamberlain and Birkenhead pre-sumably with him. That would have opened the way to the awesome prospect of a diehard Bonar Law regime. Historians can afford to be dismissive of what did not happen, contemporaries not always so. In any event, the Ulster diversion, while ending in negation, opened up the possibility of a bargain in which the Irish would seemingly gain in respect of unity, which was their secondary aim, some compensation for failure to achieve their first, which was status. That compensation, given an Ulster refusal to enter into an all-Ireland parliamentary arrangement, would come through the appointment of a Boundary Commission which would, to quote Griffith, 'give us most of Tyrone, Fermanagh and part of Armagh, Down, etc.'[38] With these areas passing out of the jurisdiction of the Northern Ireland government, it was believed by Griffith and Collins that a devolved government for what remained would not prove a viable administrative or economic entity. It was because of that belief that Griffith indicated his comparative indifference to whether Craig accepted Lloyd George's all-Ireland proposition or submitted to the judgement of a Boundary Commission. In the longer run, Griffith thought, or persuaded himself, that it would come to much the same thing. In this he was ill advised.

The December Climax

The long-awaited, but at the last unexpected (by the Irish) break came, not on Ulster but on status. The members of the delegation on their return to London on 4 December after consultation in the Dáil Cabinet, restated the Irish position unmodified in essentials. The memorandum they drafted provided for association with the British Commonwealth for all purposes of common concern, including defence, peace and war, and political treaties, recognition of the British Crown as head of the association, an oath of allegiance to the constitution of Ireland and to the treaty of association of Ireland with the British Commonwealth of Nations and recognition of the King of Great Britain as head of the associated states.[39] But for Lloyd George, the days for debate were numbered. There was a settlement within the Empire or nothing. He made one concession on the fiscal question. In July, the British proposal had been that while the Irish people should enjoy complete autonomy in taxation and finance, the two governments should agree to impose no protective duties on trade and commerce between all parts of their islands. This was in accord with Lloyd George's insistence that fiscal autonomy should be reserved as a negotiating counter until a moment came when it might be conceded to clinch a bargain. He used it in precisely that way on the evening of 5 December 1921, 'with superb artistry',[40] in Tom Jones' reckoning. As a result, the Irish successor government was entitled under the Treaty to impose tariffs without restriction. From the Irish point of view that was a significant gain, however overshadowed by the political drama. For the rest, the alternative to a settlement was immediate and terrible war, the immediacy of which was deemed to preclude reference back to Dublin. This was the decisive factor★[41] in the Irish delegates' signing, without prior reference back to the Dáil ministry, as their instructions directed.

★ Frank Pakenham (*Peace by Ordeal*, London, 1935, p. 302) asked why the obvious question was not asked, let alone not answered: 'Why was no use made of the telephone to Dublin?' His own answer was that Lloyd George, if he had cast no other spell, had obsessed each delegate with a sense of inescapable personal responsibility. He had conjured Dublin off the map. But there is another question. Who was to be telephoned? The President? He was down in Limerick. He was staying with the Mayor, Stephen O'Mara, whose name was in the telephone directory. De Valera, however, at the vital time appears to have been in Ennis.

'The Irishmen', Churchill recalled in a phrase that corresponds so little with notions of what is appropriate to Commonwealth that many Commonwealth historians are disposed to discount or disregard it, 'gulped down the ultimatum phlegmatically'.[42] Though much had been gained, neither associate republican status nor unity had been won. In the shorter run the door was left ajar for the second, but not for the first: in the longer, for the first, but not the second. On that Bonar Law, not Childers, was right. Secession was implicit in dominion status.

Stack was in Dublin but telephone conversation between Griffith and Stack was as likely to result in discord as accord. There was also the near certainty that the line would have been tapped – we know Tom Jones on occasion spoke to Lloyd George in Welsh for that reason, even on one occasion from Bournemouth. Had any arrangements been considered in Dublin for circumstances requiring the President's availability for consultation and, if so, were they discussed with the delegates?

CHAPTER 8

The Treaty: Purposes and Provisions

The text of the Treaty reflected the skill and courage of those who drafted it almost as strikingly as the substance reflected the precise measure of accord that had been achieved. For illustration of that there is little need to look further than the title: '*Articles of Agreement for a Treaty between Great Britain and Ireland – December 6, 1921*'[1] indicative, as it is, of the degree of artifice needed to secure minimal acceptability of the whole.

To start with, there is the word 'Treaty'. The use of it was without precedent in the ordering of British dominion relations. But then the situation was without precedent. Where the overseas Dominions looked to a continuing progression, the Irish had in mind a rebellious past. Their first aim was to be rid of the Act of Union; Lionel Curtis coming to the conclusion that they wanted a repeal of the Union more even than a republic. In a memorandum submitted to the British delegation he advised that if the Act were repealed, the Renunciation Act of 1783 would be automatically revived, with an Irish parliament alone entitled to pass laws binding on the Irish people. The road to a republic would no longer be constitutionally barred. Amendment of the Act of Union as against repeal would, on the other hand, preserve the authority of the British government to confer a constitution on Ireland.[2] That would conform, moreover, to the constitutional precedents. The colonies which became dominions had acquired self-governing institutions through Acts of the British Parliament. In South Africa, self-government followed upon a period of Crown Colony government which was itself transmuted on Union in 1909 into dominion status. There was the South Africa Act 1909, but no treaty. This was a precedent. It ensured continuity in a British constitutional context and preserved imperial symmetry.

How was the use of the intrusive word 'Treaty' then to be regarded? A.B. Keith, an authority on colonial constitutional practice (although a professor of Sanskrit), took the view that the use of the word in 1921 implied recognition of Ireland as a sovereign entity.[3] Leo Kohn offered the refinement that *in statu nascendi*, that is until the Irish Free State had been established in law but not thereafter, the Irish state has been so recognised.[4] Churchill faced with diehard criticism in the House, deployed political argument, contending that the use of the word connoted the ending of an episode and had no effect on the actual British position. That being so, he thought it had been right to 'use the words most likely to help you to secure the goodwill, support, and agreement which you seek'.[5] That meant, *inter alia*, leaving two hypothetical questions un-answered: first, was the Irish Republic a party to the Treaty and would it therefore once again come into existence should be Treaty be abrogated? Secondly, if so, was the agreement an international Treaty or Common-wealth compact? Against an affirmative answer to either was interposed the qualifying 'agreement for' in the title; in favour of it was international usage, which came to give it the simple description of '*le traité de Londres*',[6] once the Free State government, despite British representations, had registered the Treaty as an international instrument with the League of Nations at Geneva on 11 May 1924.

In respect of status, however arrived at, there was no element of ambiguity. On 6 December 1921 Ireland became a Dominion. The first article of the treaty stated that she should have the same constitutional status in the community of nations known as the British Empire as the Dominion of Canada, the Commonwealth of Australia, the Dominion of New Zealand, and the Union of South Africa. The second and third articles of the Treaty defined the Irish position more closely by saying that her relation to the Imperial Parliament and government should be that of the Dominion of Canada and that the Governor-General should be appointed in like manner as Canadian Governors-General. The fourth article prescribing the terms of the oath made particular reference to Irish membership of the group of nations forming the British Commonwealth of Nations. In sum these provisions left no room for doubt about the fact that the status of the Irish Free State was to be that of a Dominion.

While the settlement in the form of a Treaty was an innovation and definition of status by analogy in accord with Commonwealth practice, the oath, as prescribed in Article 4, was neither. There was no new departure in prescribing an oath – that was uniform dominion practice – but there was in its formulation. True faith and allegiance was to be owed to the constitution of the Irish Free State as by law established and only then, derivatively, to the King, 'in virtue of the common citizenship of Ireland with Great Britain and her adherence to and membership of the British Commonwealth of Nations', the last in place of Empire at the suggestion of Michael Collins, a designation appearing for the first time in an official document. 'Subject' and 'subjecthood' were discarded: the oath remained. That so much ingenuity was reflected in its devising and defence serves most of all to underline its central position in a basic conflict over the symbols of sovereignty. Its wording was as far away from that of traditional allegiance as one could go, short of abandoning the concept altogether. But it was not, it could not, whether it was one, two or three removes from traditional formulation, disarm its Irish critics, moderates little less than extremists among them. It was the *existence* of an oath to an English King that offended. Lloyd George, resolute in his intention to preserve imperial symmetry, and ensure the survival of the Coalition which was conditional upon it, never wavered in his insistence upon its incorporation in the Treaty and constitution, while in Ireland no dialectical skill could save a settlement that embodied such an oath from engulfment in a groundswell of Irish resentment. It was perhaps as well such transcendent significance was attached on both sides to the concept of allegiance, lest otherwise the price in alienation might come to be too painful to contemplate.

When one turns from the symbols of sovereignty to its substance, one enters upon an area where ambiguities have no place. Three articles, 6, 7 and 8 are devoted to defence. The first, Article 6, which dealt with British responsibility for coastal defence, until the government of the Irish Free State was ready to assume this, is of transient importance. The second, Article 7, represents the outcome of the widely ranging discussions in London on provision for defence. It provided that (a) *in time of peace* the government of the Irish Free State should afford to the British forces such harbour and other facilities as were listed in the annex to the Treaty, while (b) *in time of war* or of strained relations, it should afford such harbour and other facilities as the British government might require. Both were formidable. The annex referred to in (a) listed Berehaven, Queenstown (Cobh), Belfast Lough and Lough Swilly, with facilities in the neighbourhood for air defence and oil storage depots at Rathmullen and Haulbowline. Article 8 fixed the relative size of forces, pending international limitation of armaments on the basis of notional (and quite unrealistic) figures for the Irish Free State, Lloyd George disclosing that an Irish army of some 700,000 men was the upper *limit* in mind.[7] The risk of 'domestic' warfare in Ireland was taken into account. What mattered, however, was not land but sea. Britain's security rested there, the bases on Irish soil being for the maintenance and support of naval forces. Because of British reliance upon the Royal Navy, so Lloyd George explained, 'we could not allow the ordinary working of Dominion status to operate'. There were lessons from experience in times past and from the First World War that could not be disregarded. 'We must leave nothing to chance.'[8] It had for the Irish the likely and unwelcome consequence that profession of Irish neutrality might, because of these facilities, be disregarded by an enemy of Britain. This meant that a principal aim of Griffith's Hungarian policy and of Irish republicanism alike was placed in jeopardy.

Article 5 of the Treaty disposed of financial questions arising from a breakdown of liabilities consequent upon transfer. The Irish Free State was to assume liability for her 'fair and equitable' share of the national debt and likewise towards the payment of war pensions, having regard 'to any just claims on the part of Ireland by way of set off or counter-claim'. The latter opened the door for enquiry into long-standing Irish allegations of over-taxation of Ireland under the Union as analysed and substantially con-firmed in the report of the Primrose committee on Irish finance in 1912. Article 10 of the Treaty recorded the agreement of the Irish Free State to pay compensation on terms that were judged equitable to public servants who retired, or were discharged, in consequence of the change of gov-ernment. This did not extend to members of the Auxiliary Police Force or, as it was diplomatically phrased, 'to persons recruited in Great Britain for the Royal Irish Constabulary during the two years next preceding the date hereof', that is 6 December 1921.

Finally, there are the Articles 11–15 relating to Northern Ireland and the machinery for putting the Treaty into effect – the first controversial and the second complicated. Unity was acknowledged in principle through-out. In the title the two parties to the Treaty were referred to as Great Britain and Ireland; in Article 1 it was Ireland, not the twenty-six counties or Southern Ireland, that was to be styled and known as the Irish Free State. Article 11 provided that for one month after ratification the powers of the Irish Free State would not extend to Northern Ireland and the status quo under the Act of 1920 be there preserved. Article 12 provided that before expiry of the Ulster month, an address from both Houses of Parliament of Northern Ireland might be presented to His Majesty asking that the powers of Irish Free State should *no longer* extend to Northern Ireland and that the provisions of the Act of 1920 should remain in force so far as they concerned Northern Ireland. Of first importance was the proviso that if such an address were presented, then a Boundary Com-mission of three persons, one representative of Northern Ireland, one of the Irish Free State, together with a chairman to be nominated by the United Kingdom government, would be appointed to determine: 'in accordance with the wishes of the inhabitants, so far as may be compat-ible with economic and geographical conditions the boundaries between Northern Ireland and the rest of Ireland'. Articles 13, 14, 15 and 16 dealt with Irish Free State as legatee of the Parliament of Southern Ireland for appointment of delegates to the Council of Ireland; the consequences if Northern Ireland did not opt out, and the prohibition in the Irish Free State and Northern Ireland of endowment of a particular religion or imposition of disabilities because of it. Of highest importance was the deferred decision on the boundary. 'Ulster', Lloyd George told the House of Commons, 'has her option either to join an All-Ireland Parliament or to remain exactly as she is'.[9] But if she was to be a separate unit, 'there should be a readjustment of boundaries'. It sounded sensible and simple. The second assuredly it was not and many would question the first.

The implementation of the Treaty was to be effected in two stages, once again with the procedures to be followed reflecting the British and more particularly Lionel Curtis' concern to preserve unbroken the line of British statutory authority.[10] With this much in mind, both arrangements, provisional and permanent, were made. Under Article 17 by way of making provisional arrangement until a constitution was drafted and agreed, a meeting of Members of Parliament elected for constituencies in Southern Ireland was to be summoned in order that it should constitute a Provisional government, to which the British government could transfer the powers and machinery necessary for the discharge of its duties. The arrangement was not to continue in force for more than twelve months.

Article 18, again devised to ensure continuity in British statutory succession, laid down that the terms of the Treaty should be submitted to Parliament at Westminster and to members elected to sit in the House of Commons of Southern Ireland. If approved, it should be ratified by enactment of appropriate legislation. Dáil Éireann had no role allotted to it in the process of ratification. It had authorised negotiations, had sent plenipotentiaries to London; and by majority had approved the Treaty and theirs was the decision that determined the outcome. The Dáil was asked neither to approve the Treaty nor to ratify it – those were responsibilities given to the House of Commons of Southern Ireland established under the Government of Ireland Act 1920. The Dáil, however, had a peripheral role as prescribed in Article 18: approving the process of ratification in which it had, at one remove and off-stage, the decisive role. Yet there was a break in British constitutional continuity. It arose because of the need for the institution of a Provisional government forthwith. The passage of the Bill through parliament was delayed until 31 March 1922. This has gone down in history as a 'moment of ambiguity', because for that period (14 January–31 March) there was no basis in law for the exercise of authority by the Provisional government. In circumstances later recorded, with the enactment of the Irish Agreement Act (to which the Treaty was appended) on 31 March 1922, constitutional sequence, in the British view, was restored.

In the making of long-term arrangements, no such complications arose. Dominion precedent was followed in the vesting of responsibility in an Irish parliament with powers of legislation and constitutional amendment, subject to one most important qualification: that fundamental authority was vested not in an Irish parliament but in the Treaty. 'Any proposal', affirmed Lloyd George, 'in contravention of this Agreement [i.e. the Treaty] will be *ultra vires*'.[11] He was making allusion to the repugnancy clause to be included in the constitution, to ensure that the Treaty would be invested with the highest legal status, its provisions overriding both constitutional and all subsequent legislation.[12] Nothing reflected the nature of the second part of the settlement more clearly than that. For the rest, it may be remarked that the transfer of authority from London to Dublin posed many questions, to which answers, provisional or otherwise, had to be given before the settlement could be established. That the Treaty did – many people did not like the way it did it, but no one could doubt the historical importance of how it was done.

CHAPTER 9
The Aftermath to the Treaty

British Reactions

In Britain the Treaty was acclaimed outside the ranks of the diehards as a political triumph without parallel in recent British history. Relief at the ending of a guerrilla struggle that by its very nature had brought little that was deemed creditable to British arms and, by reason of the inequality of the two parties, little but odium overseas, was a dominant reaction in the population at large. Profound was the satisfaction mingled with relief felt by the British delegates. 'No agreement', asserted the Prime Minister, 'ever arrived at between two peoples had been received with so enthusiastic and so universal a welcome as the Articles of Agreement'. The government, he claimed and Tom Jones echoed, had pulled off a settlement where Gladstone and Asquith had failed. Not only that, but the settlement made plain that the British had won on the two fundamental points at issue – status and unity. Jones went further still, saying that all the points listed in the basic document, Lloyd George's letter of 30 July 1921, had been settled on the lines therein proposed. In the light of all this, it came as something of a surprise that the British delegates, Lloyd George chief among them, were the target of denunciation of astonishing virulence both in the Lords and in the Commons.

Coalition triumphalism on the one hand and diehard acrimony on the other stemmed from that reversal – and not least its suddenness – in British policy towards Ireland in June 1921, which Churchill deemed to have been without parallel in modern times. The policy that was so abruptly jettisoned – namely the application and, if necessary, the enforcement of the Government of Ireland Act 1920 – still reflected one strand in Unionist thinking; it was now universally reinforced by another, very much of a minority, who believed that devolution on the 1920 model was not supplanted by dominion status on merit but from fear. On this view, it was not liberal thinking but a campaign of assassination and 'murder' that had decided the day. That in the view of the diehards was conclusively demonstrated by the course of the negotiations and the content of the Treaty. It was the 'suddenness' of the reversal in policy that touched a raw edge. Not surprisingly it was an Ulster Unionist Ronald McNeill (Member for Canterbury) who, in the debate on the Treaty on 15 December 1921, reminded the House of the very different note struck by Prime Minister and Chief Secretary, 'not so very long ago'. Then they had got 'murder by the throat. Murder was on the run.' Now it was the Chief Secretary who was 'on the run'. He did not blame Lloyd George for entering into negotiations with Sinn Féin, but he professed to have been shocked when in June he had first learned that instead of feeling humiliation and shame at the abandonment of its elementary duty to restore order, the government had relied upon the universal sense of relief at the prospect of ending the horrors in Ireland to disguise the fact that this was being achieved by a change of course that amounted to shameful and unconfessed failure.[1]

In the House of Commons debate on ratification of the Treaty, neither Churchill nor Lloyd George gave hostages to fortune, both keeping close to Lloyd George's letter of 20 July 1921 and arguing that British interests as listed there had all to be safeguarded in the terms of the Treaty.[2] Churchill vigorously defended the sudden change of course. That was how peace had been won with essential British interests preserved. 'Sinn Féin demanded an independent, sovereign republic for the whole of Ireland including Ulster. We insisted upon allegiance to the Crown, membership of the Empire, facilities and security for the Navy and a complete option for Ulster. Every one of these conditions is embodied in the Treaty.' To cries of 'No! No!' and 'What about allegiance?', Churchill rejoined that the oath was 'far more precise and searching' than that taken elsewhere.[3] The first was so, the second manifestly not. But there were more personal targets. Members of the Cabinet were denounced for having shaken hands with murderers, with having signed the Treaty with a revolver in their backs; Chamberlain was rebuked for always putting on 'the white sheet for Unionist policy', and more viciously denounced as a traitor, while in the Upper House, Carson stigmatised Curzon as a turncoat who had 'paid a generous and eloquent tribute to Michael Collins, the head of the murder gang'* and numbered Birkenhead with those 'of all the men . . . the most loathsome . . . who will sell their friends for the purpose of conciliating their enemies'. Yet in one respect Carson's resentments were his alone. He had believed in Union and it was for their 'betrayal' of the Unionist cause that he assailed them.[4] As was fitting, his was the despairing lament of Irish Unionism as Union was finally undone. 'For thirty years or more', cried Carson, 'the late Unionist

---

* Curzon complained to Birkenhead that evening that Carson's speech was an outrage on every convention of the House and on decency, the speech of a prosecuting counsel at the Old Bailey.

party has been fighting the question of modified Home Rule. . . . All of a sudden they say Home Rule is not good enough . . . the country must abandon Ireland at the very heart of the Empire to independence . . . I was in earnest . . . What a fool I was. I was only a puppet, and so was Ulster, and so was Ireland, in the political game that was to get the Conservative Party into power.' Words that 'would have been immature upon the lips of a hysterical school girl', rejoined Birkenhead, the 'galloper' and associate of other days, now Lord Chancellor. Others, however, may yet hear in Carson's outburst the authentic cry of Irish (as distinct from Ulster) Unionism at the last, with only oblivion before it.

More important than such philippics was the enigmatic attitude of Bonar Law, the Unionist leader emerging from retreat. To the surprise of many of his followers, he declared himself in favour of the Treaty. When it looked as if in fact there might be an attempt to compel Ulster to go into an all-Ireland parliament against her will 'it seemed a possibility that I might be one of those who would ask the country to condemn that policy'. But that had not arisen. He allowed that Ulster should be asked to make concessions, though not substantial, on area. The words of Article 12 taken in their obvious meaning made it impossible to think of throwing out counties; it was only a question of adjusting boundaries. What Ulster had been asked for were not concessions but surrender. As for Lloyd George's view that there was 'no harm in trying to persuade Ulster', Bonar Law pronounced: 'there is no greater defect in statesmanship than to propose something which in the nature of the fact is impossible'. While there was 'a feeling all through the Empire of rejoicing', he did not believe that in six months the Treaty would be a political asset to the Prime Minister, but he hoped that by 'the verdict of posterity' it would be a permanent triumph for him. In Ireland, North or South, it was unlikely to be so regarded.[5]

With Ulster safeguarded, Bonar Law no longer had any inclination to become embroiled in Anglo-Irish relations. In Ulster, however, it was not his discreet distancing but the more excitable mood of Ulster Unionism, stirred by an instinctive belief that they were about to be betrayed, that occupied people's minds.[6] In a dispatch of 14 December 1921, the day on which both parliament at Westminster and Dáil Éireann assembled to ratify the Articles of Agreement, the American Consul in Belfast reported that the people of the six counties awaited ratification as 'the condemned might await the headman's axe'. Their condemnation of the British government was not surpassed by the historic hatreds of the Germans in the war. Devoted subjects of the Empire, they regarded themselves as the victims of conscienceless statesmen, Lloyd George chief among them.[7] Ulster Unionist hopes, such as they were, were fixed upon the signs of dissension in Dublin. And what was the occasion of this near-hysteria? It was twofold: finance and the Boundary Commission, Articles 5 and 12 of the Treaty, both of which were held to be tantamount to coercion of Ulster with a view to regaining the six counties for the Irish Free State.

The reasons for such foreboding were as follows. Under Article 5, the Irish Free State had assumed liability for service of a fair and equitable share of the public debt and of payment of war pensions, having regard to any just counter-claim for over-taxation. No such proviso, however, applied to a Northern Ireland that seceded from the Irish Free State. It remained part of the United Kingdom and would accordingly continue to pay its allotted share of the Imperial Contribution as under the Act of 1920, while the Irish Free State might be able to offset its share by lodging a successful counter-claim for the same amount by way of past over-taxation. But both the continuing burden on Northern Ireland and the possible elimination of it in the case of the Irish Free State were consistent with their respective status. Northern Ireland remained in the United Kingdom and under its fiscal system or it did not. This could not be otherwise: other options did not exist. Yet the Boundary Commission to be set up under Article 12 held the possibility of far-reaching territorial adjustments. Certainly Unionist misgivings on that score, even if in the event not realised, were not groundless.

On the evening of the debate Lloyd George had felt not only aggrieved, but also puzzled, by the bitterness of Captain Charles Craig in the Commons, more so than he was by Carson's outburst in the Lords. Ulster, he felt, had 'nothing to complain about'. 'We have emancipated her and it was very unfair of Craig to talk of betrayal.' He recalled Ulster Unionist apparent interest in, though not endorsement of, the notion of a Boundary Commission – the possibility of which had been floated as early as 1917.[8] Sir James Craig the next day sent a letter to Chamberlain concluding with a rhetorical flourish to the effect that if the British government was unable to modify the Treaty and the people of Ulster took the matter into their own hands, would the British government 'withdraw all troops and allow us to fight it out ourselves?' Rarely can a letter so rasping in tone have been sent to a senior minister of the Crown. Chamberlain replied that he could not believe 'that men whose loyalty is their pride are contemplating acts of war against the King'.[9]

Irish Reactions

After signing the Treaty on 6 December, Collins wrote that day to John O'Kane: 'I tell you this – early this morning I signed my death warrant'.[10] He added that he believed Birkenhead might have said that in signing he (Birkenhead) had made an end to his political life. Perhaps Birkenhead's reflection provoked Collins' train of thought, but there seems no evidence for the more dramatic reconstruction in the form of a verbal exchange. Either way the inference was the same. The English signatories had jeopardised their political careers, Birkenhead not least; the Irish their lives. In that sense, the exchange was at once authentic and symbolic. The Treaty was divisive at Westminster, a source of death, destruction and alienation in the Irish Free State for the term of its existence and beyond.

In the Dáil debate on the Treaty, it has been remarked that partition figured little, only two deputies focusing attention on it.[11] In one sense this was not a matter for surprise. In the negotiations, a break on Ulster had been the tactical aim – and the tactic had not paid off. No one suggested it was the principal aim. Nor was it an issue in contention *within* the Dáil. Deputies for the most part were content to think of the Boundary Commission as likely to undermine Northern viability. The struggle had been waged for status – for the republic – and partition, subordinate to nothing else, was none the less subordinate to that. In a Treaty context it was Articles 1–4 that were at issue, not Article 12. It was when republican status was attained that partition became *the* principal preoccupation.

In the context of December 1921–January 1922, the concentration on status was heightened by one of the more potent of the images handed down from the past. It was that of the late eighteenth-century Irish Parliament that in 1800 had voted away its own independent existence. In 1921 there was once again such a parliament, Dáil Éireann, the fullness of whose independence was at issue in negotiations with Britain. If there was extreme sensitivity on questions of status, then there was all the more disposition to look behind the present and to conjure up an 'image', which ensured that proposals which touched upon status would be subjected to the sharpest scrutiny. No Irish parliament must ever tread that eighteenth-century path again. The perspective in which the provisions of the Treaty were viewed was, therefore, not how considerable was the advance on Home Rule, but rather how considerable might be the retraction concealed or open from the Republic.

Dominion Status

At the London Conference the Irish delegates were confronted with the problem of defining, or having defined for their own enlightenment, a concept, that of dominion status, of which it was to be remarked with satisfaction at the Imperial Conference of 1924 that it defied comprehension by foreigners. Curtis and Childers, it will be recalled, expounded and criticised, but did they enlighten? 'I was befogged by constitutional and legal arguments', Michael Collins told the Dáil on 15 December 1921, 'I did not understand them then. I don't now. I didn't care for them then. I don't now.'[12] He was unwise, as it proved, thus to expose a flank, but many must have shared his reaction. Yet for good or ill, dominion status brought the Commonwealth system right to the heart of Anglo-Irish relations for a generation. It was not the constitutional lawyers followed by political scientists who introduced these refinements of law or concept; it was the nature of the settlement itself: the bringing of the Commonwealth to the centre of Anglo-Irish relations.

The Commonwealth from the outset was spoken of as something not possessing final form at any given point in time. That indeed was claimed to be among its principal merits. Yet in negotiations that was a liability, uncertainties implicit in the status serving to accentuate mistrust and suspicion, not only of out and out republicans, but of moderate nationalists also, with the result that they came to think of Lloyd George as a master of the political arts deploying the liberal imperial vocabulary of Campbell-Bannerman and Smuts to disguise devices designed to retain the essentials of British power in Ireland. The problem at root was more than personal or tactical. At the time, and in an atmosphere of tense negotiation, it cannot have been easy to forecast what dominion status for Ireland would come to mean as the years went by. Yet an exact assessment of that rightly assumed critical importance either way, that is whether such status should be accepted or rejected outright.

In the post-Treaty House of Commons debate, Lloyd George came back to that very question. What, he asked, does dominion status mean? But he did not answer it. He talked instead of the dangers of definition of limiting development by too many finalities, of introducing rigidities alien to British constitutional thinking. He was prepared to say what dominion status did not mean. But not what it did. What the Treaty had done was to obviate the need for direct statement by saying that the status of the Irish Free State would be that of the other Dominions and more particularly that of Canada. This definition by analogy in effect placed the question at one remove. The British Prime Minister was prepared to go no further. Given that the Dominions were themselves engaged in resolving their own differences on status, Lloyd George had ready to hand convincing, even conclusive, reason for not embarking on such an enterprise.

At the 1921 Imperial Conference dominion opinion, moreover, was itself divided on whether or not the status of the Dominions should be defined so as to bring often anachronistic legal forms into conformity with more liberal contemporary practice. Smuts was foremost among those who wished to have that done. If it were not, he warned that the Commonwealth would be faced with other Irelands, with other examples of doing too little too late.[13] At the Imperial Conference, the issue was joined. Australia's Prime Minister, W.M. Hughes, did not like the idea of defining imperial relations. There was, he thought, no need for it. 'We were Colonies', he said, 'we became Dominions. We have been accorded the status of nations. . . . What greater advance is conceivable? What remains to us? We are like so many Alexanders. What other worlds have we to conquer?'[14] Let us leave well alone! Neither the South Africans nor the Canadians were persuaded. Because of this still unresolved debate it was hard for Lloyd George, even had he wished to embark on definition sufficently precise, to convince the sceptical or to convert the hostile. The Dominions were looking both ways. Collins and Childers could both adduce arguments to support their respective contentions, favourable and unfavourable as they were. What was to happen in 1923 and 1926 did not happen in 1921. In that sense, it could be argued that the question in its Irish context came up too soon.

There was another aspect. The anti-Treaty party were against dominion status, but not all for the same reasons. There were the fundamentalists for whom Austin Stack may serve as spokesman. He did not want dominion status in any form, and was therefore not concerned with whether or not Ireland would receive full or part dominion status or, for that matter, how it might be defined. For him the status itself was an irrelevance. What he wanted was Irish status, the 'isolated' republic. Let us assume, he said, full Canadian powers are given to this country: 'I for one cannot accept from England full Canadian powers, three-quarter Canadian powers, or half Canadian powers. I stand for what is Ireland's right, full independence and nothing short of it.'[15] At the least that lacked nothing in clarity. Erskine Childers' argument, while leading equally to the rejection of dominion status, rested on the quite different contention that dominion status could, and in this case would, have different meaning in different places. Britain would never in view of Ireland's proximity and her own security allow 'Canadian status'. Geography precluded that. The Governor-General would be the focus of British government in Ireland and recognised as such.[16] That would be inconsistent with Canadian usage but, Childers contended, it was not usage, it was law that would prevail in Ireland. To counter that, it was important to have an understanding of the Canadian position, of the direction in which Canada and the Commonwealth were moving, as well as of the interests that Britain deemed vital to her security. Judgement had thus to be exercised and a measure of faith one way or the other: there were few certainties and, on the dominion side, no conclusive precedent.

External Association – An Alternative Basis for Reconciliation

External association was first given form and some substance in August 1921 when, according to Robert Barton[17] and others, a means of reconciling English imperial and Irish republican aspirations was to be sought in the British recognition of the Republic at home, balanced by the Republic's association from outside with the British Commonwealth of Nations for the advancement of their common interest. Conceptually it was not the republican counterpart to dominion status: that was 'the

isolated republic'. On this de Valera was explicit. On 14 December he told
the Dáil in private session that 'I felt . . . in honour bound . . . to get an
isolated Republic'. But if he could not get it, it remained to devise a 'form
of association that would be consistent with the aspirations of the Irish
people'. External association appeared to offer a possible compromise.
Not for nothing did de Valera, in placing this on record, observe 'I have
been classed as moderate. So I am.'

With the Treaty signed and opinion flowing in its favour, de Valera
agreed, in late December 1921 on representations from members of the
Dáil, that the proper course was for him to reformulate what he had
described as hasty and incomplete earlier drafts with a considered version
of the concept.[18] The resulting revised draft became known as Document
No. 2 (the Treaty being No. 1) and it was circulated to members when the
Dáil resumed its sittings on 3 January 1922.[19] The document in this, its
final, form served to clarify matters in debate as between the Treaty,
Document No. 1 and External Association Document No. 2. The Treaty,
however, was the only matter for decision. Many deputies before voting
on the Treaty thought it desirable to determine first the relative merits of
the Treaty (Document No. 1) and Document No. 2 which was now
before them. This in turn was a source of some perplexity. On Northern
Ireland, defence and ancillary facilities and finance, the provisions were
identical or having insubstantial differences. That left the provisions of
Treaty and Document No. 2 on status the crucial feature in any comparison. The differences in this respect between them were fine but deep.

As centrepiece there was the conflict between the dominion status by
analogy in the first four Articles of the Treaty and the attribution in
Document No. 2 of legislative, executive and judicial authority in Ireland
to the people of Ireland. That would have opened the way to a republic by
constitutional means. It was as a republic that Ireland was to be associated
with the states of the British Commonwealth for matters of common
concern. When acting in its capacity as an associate state, Ireland's status
was to be no less than that enjoyed by the member states of the Commonwealth. The matters of common concern were duly listed as Defence,
Peace and War, Political Treaties, 'and all matters now treated as of common concern among the States of the British Commonwealth'. Allegiance
to the Crown was out but for the purposes of the association 'Ireland shall
recognise His Britannic Majesty as head of the Association'. For the rest
and remarkably, the defence provisions were the same as in the Treaty,
Article 7 of Document No. 2 being identical with Article 7 of the Treaty,
that is allowing Britain such facilities as she might require in time of
war or strained relations. An addendum on north-east Ireland indicated
willingness to grant to that portion of Ulster which constituted Northern
Ireland under the Act of 1920, 'privileges and safeguards not less substantial than those provided for in "The Articles of Agreement for a

Treaty . . ." signed on 6 December, 1921'. In sum, Document No. 2 offered a compromise which, as set out, was either more, or as, advantageous to Britain as the Treaty with the one qualification that it offered no compromise on what mattered most to Lloyd George as it did to de Valera: allegiance and an oath of allegiance. Neither the one nor the other was prepared to contemplate concession on these, the symbols of sovereignty. On that, de Valera's stand is written large on the page of history. But the more closely Lloyd George's position is studied, the more apparent it is that he, too, would not concede.

The Dáil Debate

In presenting the arguments for the Treaty, Arthur Griffith dwelt upon the magnitude of the problems that had confronted the Irish delegates. To reconcile Irish national aspirations with the British Commonwealth of Nations was an assignment 'as hard as was ever placed on the shoulders of men'. No demand had been made in the correspondence that preceded the London negotiations for recognition of the Republic. 'We knew it would have been refused.' Document No. 2 was suggested as an alternative that would go some way towards the Treaty. What it offered was a 'quibble'. It would result in a relationship half-in, half-out. He read out the Cabinet conclusion recording the decision that 'the President should not join the delegation in London at this stage in the negotiations'. The Treaty, perforce negotiated without him, gave equality and 'because of that I am standing by it'.[20] 'I signed that Treaty not as the ideal thing, but fully believing . . . it is a treaty honourable to Ireland, and safeguards the vital interests of Ireland'.

Michael Collins was more forceful and ranged more widely.[21] If the recognition of the Republic had been a prelude to any conference 'we could very easily have said so . . .', and then the oft-quoted words: 'it was the acceptance of the invitation that formed the compromise'. The aim was to rid the country of the enemy strength. That was achieved. 'Dublin Castle has fallen' was the phrase he was to use later in *Arguments for the Treaty*. 'I know it would be finer to stand alone . . . but if we find we cannot . . . what can we do but enter into some association?' and what better safeguard than the Dominions with whom an Irish Free State was constitutionally associated? 'The fact of Canadian and South African independence is something real and solid, and will grow in reality and force as time goes on.' 'We have got rid of the word "Empire". For the first time in an official document the former Empire is styled "The Community of Nations known as the British Empire"'. Non-coercion of north-east Ulster was agreed policy – 'I don't say it is an ideal arrangement', but what better alternative than that in the Treaty? It was not fair to quote 'the dead men . . . against us'. Did the living approve? That was the question before them. And the conclusion of the whole matter. 'In my opinion it [the Treaty] gives us freedom, not the ultimate freedom that all nations desire and develop to, but the freedom to achieve it.'

Kevin O'Higgins' approach was austerely rational.[22] He supported the Treaty but he did not wish 'to be forced into a stronger advocacy of the Treaty than I feel'. It was important to establish 'what remains between this Treaty and the fullness of your rights'. It offered internal freedom and a considerable degree of external independence. It gave the fullest fiscal freedom. Deputies ought not to reject it unless 'you have a reasonable prospect of achieving more'. 'The most objectionable aspect of the Treaty', he continued, 'is that the threat of force has been used to influence Ireland to a decision to enter this miniature league of nations. It has been called a league of free nations. I admit in practice it is so: but it is unwise and unstatesmanlike to attempt to bind any such league by any ties other than purely voluntary ties . . . I quite admit in the case of Ireland the tie is not voluntary . . . the status is not equal.' 'I hardly hope that within the terms to this Treaty there lies the fulfilment of Ireland's destiny, but I do hope . . . what remains may be won by agreement and by peaceful political evolution'. His overriding thesis was that there was no warrant for risking 'immediate and terrible war'.

De Valera's argument for the rejection of the Treaty is not readily dissociated from his view of what went wrong in its negotiation. In the Dáil,[23] he gave an account of the appointment of plenipotentaries and recalled the Cabinet's conclusion that the plenipotentiaries should have full powers to negotiate, coupled with an understanding that the Cabinet would decide policy in the light of negotiations and that any agreement would be submitted to the Dáil for ratification. He read out the instructions to the plenipotentiaries: point (3) read 'It is also understood that the complete text of the draft treaty about to be signed will be . . . submitted to Dublin and reply awaited'. Failure to ensure that this was done had resulted in an agreement less favourable in his view to the Irish position on status than would otherwise have been the case. The contention turns on the much-debated hypothesis that had the Irish delegates insisted on delaying their decision till they had consulted the Dáil Cabinet and in association rejected the British ultimatum, it would have been a fair risk that the threatened immediate and terrible war would not have followed and British concessions on status made. On that, the evidence suggests that, while the reaction might not have been immediate, Lloyd George would not have sacrificed his own credibility by conceding association with a republic in two stages as it would have been. Given the Unionist majority, he could not have done so and have remained in office. Neither, it may be assumed, though not with the same degree of confidence, would Bonar Law. With Northern Ireland's position secure, his attitude on Ireland had acquired an element of unpredictability. That there would have been great reluctance in Britain and the Dominions to see the armed conflict renewed has to be taken into the reckoning on the other side.

De Valera's substantive counter-argument was that the Treaty did not reconcile Irish aspirations with the British Commonwealth of Nations. He was against the Treaty not because he was a man of war,[24] but because it would not end the conflict of centuries. He conceded that the Treaty might win approval from a war-weary people. Yet the document signed under duress made 'British authority our masters in Ireland'. The Treaty was an 'ignoble document'. Its ratification would be 'inconsistent with our position' as guardians of an independent Irish state and members could no more vote it away than 'the ignominious House that voted away the Colonial Parliament that was in Ireland in 1800'.

The measure of difference on status between Britain and Ireland underlined by de Valera on the evidence appeared unbridgeable. Not even the boasted flexibility of dominion status was compatible in 1921 with a republic. On that point Lloyd George and de Valera were at one. And why? Because allegiance was an essential feature of dominion status. It was expressed in the form of an oath to the Crown. That oath was embodied in the Treaty; and it could not be removed without denouncing the Treaty of which it was an integral part. That was at the heart of de Valera's objection. More positively he said 'I am against the Treaty because it does not do the fundamental thing and bring us peace.' It did not recognise, as he claimed external association would have done, the separate, distinct existence of a republic. On the contrary, it gave away republican independence by bringing Ireland as a dominion within the British Empire and more precisely by insisting on the recognition of the English King as the source of executive authority in Ireland. So over against the substance, in part still prospective, of freedom there had to be placed the abandonment of the symbolism which represented Irish aspirations. That the division that ensued was deep and lasting is no matter for surprise. There are times when constitutional forms embody things that for most men matter most, and this was one of them. De Valera summed up his opposition to the Treaty in saying 'it is absolutely inconsistent with our position; it gives away Irish independence; it brings us into the British Empire; it acknowledges the head of the British Empire as the source of executive authority in Ireland'.

Erskine Childers was the principal proponent of the argument that dominion status for Ireland would never have the same application as in Canada. Geography had decreed otherwise. British security was involved. The British would not permit advances in status parallel with that of the Dominions. Equality of status could not and never would apply in the case of Ireland. That was the continuing relevance of forms of subordination. Custom and usage, Kevin O'Higgins had asserted, nullified law. Childers allowed this was so in Canada and South Africa. But he warned that every limitation – 'there are hundreds of them' – in the British North America Act would apply to Ireland and, while obsolete in Canada, they would not be so in Ireland. In Ireland the King would mean the British government and 'under the terms of this Treaty the British Government is going to be supreme in Ireland'. Ports and coasts would belong to it. So, by implication, would reponsibility for defence. 'Are we, by our own act to abandon our independence?' Not an advance in Irish status through association with the Dominions, but an actual retreat was what Childers envisaged.[25]

On 7 January, the division was taken: the voting – 64 in favour, 57 against. De Valera invoked the concept of limitation of the Dáil's authority. 'This', he said, 'is simply approval of a certain resolution. The Republic can only be disestablished by the Irish people.' Michael Collins appealed to the parliamentary analogy of majority and minority parties. Miss MacSwiney called upon example from time past. Cathal Brugha had a last word, and one not without its threatening overtone: 'I will see, at any rate, that discipline is kept in the army.' De Valera had spoken on 15 December, the second day of the debate on ratification of the Treaty, of Document No. 2 as his personal effort to try to get something 'which will enable us to keep . . . together'.[26] On the shorter view, it was rather a source of confusion. Nor was conciliation de Valera's forte. But his judgement was to be endorsed by time and the majority of the Irish electorate.

On 10 January 1922 de Valera resigned. Arthur Griffith was elected President of the Dáil Éireann. He left deputies in no doubt where he stood: 'I am in favour of this Treaty. I want this Treaty put into operation. I want the Provisional Government set up. I want the Republic to remain in being until the time when the people can have a Free State Election, and give their vote', which meant under the terms of the Treaty until the constitution was drafted and approved.

The Provisional Government and the Transfer of Powers

The procedures to be followed in the transfer of powers from the British to an Irish authority have already been outlined. The way to their application opened on 7 January when the majority vote in the Dáil was decisive for the Treaty. On the Irish view (from which the anti-Treaty party dissented), the Treaty had therewith been approved by the competent authority, namely, the Second Dáil. But the vote, as will be recalled, was not the formal act of ratification required in Article 18 of the Treaty. For that, not the Dáil, but members elected to the House of Commons of Southern Ireland, as established by the Government of Ireland Act 1920, was the designated body. Accordingly that assembly – with its four members for Dublin University, who were not members of the Dáil, but without the members for Northern Ireland, who were, was summoned to ratify the Treaty – therewith proceeded in accordance with the British view that transfer was being effected by authority of an Act of the British Parliament: the Government of Ireland Act 1920. On 14 January the majority of the Dáil favouring the Treaty assembled in the Mansion House, voted and approved the Treaty unanimously. Thereupon they proceeded to elect a Provisional government, every member of which was required to signify in writing his acceptance of the treaty, but did not in fact do so. On that day the Provisional Government, as contemplated in Article 17 of the Treaty, was duly constituted. It did not, however, supplant the Dáil Ministry under the Presidency of Arthur Griffith.[27] The two were to exist side by side with overlapping membership: the Provisional Government established on authority which stemmed from a British statute, the Dáil Ministry from the vote of the second Dáil on 7 January 1921. Griffith, Chairman of the Dáil Ministry, was not in the Provisional Government but Collins, Cosgrave and O'Higgins were in both. As Ernest Blythe put it from the Irish point of view, the Provisional Government would represent the majority in the Dáil; whether formally or informally, it would derive its authority from the Dáil. The Dáil and the Republic, Griffith had declared on election, would exist until the Free State government was set up. Continuity on the British side could be restored only by the passage of the Irish Free State (Agreement) Bill which, as already noted, was to give statutory sanction for the coming into existence of the Provisional Government. When this was completed, both the British and Irish established their ultimate source of authority – in the one case, 'by reason of the people's sovereignty vested in Dáil Éireann,'* and in the other by British statutory enactment.[28]

The Irish Free State (Agreement) Bill was not enacted until 31 March 1922 – a delay that caused concern at Westminster, since the Provisional Government had come into being on 14 January but its existence was not yet sanctioned in law. Churchill, as minister in charge, asked if it were 'not fatal to peace, social order and good government to have power wielded by men who have no legal authority? A provisional government unsanctified by law, yet recognised by H.M. Ministers was an anomaly unprecedented in the history of the British Empire.' He had cause to know the reason only too well. News of violence in the North, especially in Belfast, incidents and skirmishes almost daily along the Border, inflamed passions already running high at Westminster. The voting on the delayed second reading of the Bill was impressive – 302 to 60 in favour – but, as Churchill commented, 'most of the majority were miserable and all the minority were furious'.[29] Constitutionally, if not otherwise, all was again in order on 31 March 1922.

* 'the authority of the Irish government shall proceed from the people of Ireland alone' (stated at the head of all memoranda submitted by the Irish delegates).

The principal provision of the Irish Free State (Agreement) Act was the first. It stated that, as from the date of passing the Act, the scheduled Treaty should have the force of law – with the one reservation that this was not to be the Act of Parliament from which the Ulster month (Article 11 of the Treaty) was to run. It also provided that, within four months, the Parliament of Southern Ireland should be dissolved and elections held for a new House to which the Provisional Government would be responsible. These elections were held in June 1922 once again under dual mandate – in the British view on the authority of the Lord-Lieutenant acting in accord with the Irish Free State (Agreement) Act; on the Irish view on the authority of the Second Dáil. The new assembly, which was to serve as the constituent assembly for the Irish Free State as well as technically a legislative body, likewise owed its authority on the British view to an Act of Parliament, that of 1920; on the Irish, to the authority handed down from the first Dáil.

Constitution-making and the Constraints upon it

One feature, central to the settlement, remains to be considered – the form of goverment to be established in the Irish Free State. Aspects of it bearing on Anglo-Irish relations were the subject of negotiations, debate and differences in opinion. But as for the institutions themselves, they found their place, as it were almost by way of incidental consequence of dominion status, in Article 1 of the Treaty. There it was stated that Ireland was to have the same constitutional status as the Dominions, 'with a Parliament having Powers to make laws for the peace, order and good Government of Ireland' and an Executive responsible to it. Then Article 17 made provision for the administration of Southern Ireland during the interval that must elapse between approval of the Treaty and the constitution of a parliament and government of the Irish Free State consistent with the Treaty. The framing of the constitution, Lloyd George told Griffith in a letter of 13 December 1921 for communication to the members of Dáil Éireann, 'will be in the hands of the Irish Government, subject, of course to the terms of the Agreement . . .'.[30] The interpretation to be placed upon this letter was at the heart of the differences that followed.

On 14 December 1921, Hugh Kennedy, shortly thereafter to receive formal appointment as legal adviser to the Provisional Goverment and later to become Chief Justice of the Supreme Court in the Irish Free State, commented upon the latitude left to the Provisional Government by the general nature of these Articles. He interpreted their effect as 'blotting out' the Government of Ireland Act 1920 in so far as it related to the 'freak' Southern Ireland and leaving it mandatory for 'the Irish Free State to be constituted and to have a Parliament . . . and that such Parliament is to be fashioned on the democratic models of the other associated Nations'. For the rest, he thought it to be the spirit of the Treaty that 'the wishes of Ireland', subject to the Treaty, should prevail. If that were indeed to be accepted, then the constitution might extend the republican as against the monarchical basis of the Treaty.

In a subsequent memorandum, of 17 December 1921, Kennedy applied this interpretation to the most controversial issue of all – the oath to be taken by Members of the Parliament of the Irish Free State. He described it as twofold; in the first place, the swearing of true faith and allegiance to the constitution of the Irish Free State as by law established, and in the second the swearing of faithfulness to HM King George V and his heirs and successors, allegiance not being mentioned. With the constitution yet to be drafted, Kennedy further noted that 'there appears to be the freest hand as to the form the constitution is to take and . . . it is to be framed by our own representatives. An oath of allegiance to such a constitution cannot present great difficulty to the conscience of any Irish citizen . . .'. As for the Commonwealth aspect of the oath, he wrote of it as 'a solemn asseveration' made by reason of the Irish Free State's entering into the association of Commonwealth states. He concluded with reference to the contingency that should the Commonwealth of Nations be disrupted or dismembered as by secession, this allegiance would lapse.

As head of the Provisional Government, Michael Collins was responsible for the appointment of a committee to draft a constitution in due course to be submitted to the Irish Constituent Assembly. If Kennedy's advice were to be acted upon questions widely deemed to have been foreclosed by the Treaty might be reopened. To do so might imperil the settlement. Collins scorned the risk. At the first meeting of the committee, of which he himself was chairman with Darell Figgis – a man of varied gifts and colourful personality of whom it was said that he was apt to advise on everything having experience of executing nothing – as his deputy and Kennedy a member, Collins gave instructions that members were not to feel bound up by legal formalities, but to define and produce a true democratic constitution, short and easy to amend 'as the final stages of complete freedom were achieved'.[31] This approach produced results that startled some members of the committee, who were none the less well disposed to a republicanising of the constitution, by way of diminution of the notional standing of the Treaty in the Irish Free State that was to be. Thus, on Kennedy's advice to the effect that the Treaty did not require the inclusion of the oath in the constitution, Collins ruled that it should go. The Supreme Court was declared to be the Court of Appeal, so that the right of appeal to the Judicial Committee might lapse irrespective of overseas dominion practice. The Treaty clauses relating to the Governor-General were, on Collins' injunction, omitted altogether,[32] while in the committee's final draft – there were three – the Crown's representative was cut down to size by being styled 'Commissioner of the

British Commonwealth', and being appointed with the prior assent of the Executive Council.

Collins and other members of the committee were well aware that Kennedy's opinion would not be well received in London. He spoke of the committee and Provisional Government as having 'a fight on their hands'. But that was a prospect he was more than willing to face, partly by reason of his own conviction, but even more by near desperate political calculation. If the Republic could be shown to be the dominant influence on the constitution, might not the anti-Treaty party, and especially de Valera, whom Collins continued to consult, be persuaded to blunt the sharp edge of their hostility to the Treaty settlement? As late as 21 May 1922, Collins spoke as if it were a possibility that the draft might yet go forward as a Coalition paper. But it is important not to place more weight on this theory of motivation than it may reasonably bear. After all, Kennedy had tendered his advice before the vote on the Treaty in the Dáil was taken. Even if the draft were rejected outright by the British, it might prove of political advantage later to have tried and failed than to have acquiesced without contention. De Valera did in fact exercise restraint without, however, entertaining illusions about the nature of the British reaction.

In all these matters, the time factor was important. On 8 March the Constitution Committee submitted the three drafts on the basis of which Collins could assemble a final draft to be taken to London.[33] On 21 March the Irish Free State Agreement Act took effect providing, inter alia, for the dissolution of the Parliament of Southern Ireland; on 14 April, the republicans led by Rory O'Connor occupied the Four Courts: on 20 May, Collins and de Valera signed the Pact that has gone down to history by their names. It provided for a panel of Sinn Féin candidates at the forthcoming general election drawn from the pro- and anti-Treaty parties in proportion to their numbers in the outgoing Dáil. Yet it allowed that 'every and any interest is free to go up and contest the election equally with the Sinn Féin panel'. On 27 May Collins had his first meeting with British ministers on the constitution. They were affronted. The draft, they complained, was the Republic under 'the thinnest of disguises'. On 30 May the Lord Chief Justice, Lord Hewart, considered the possible bridging of the gulf in discussion with Kennedy, who additionally formulated Irish views in a memorandum. But there was no rapprochement. On 1 June Lloyd George wrote to Griffith that 'the draft constitution . . . is wholly inconsistent with the Treaty signed by the Irish Plenipotentaries and endorsed by their Parliament'.[34] There followed six specific questions: (i) Was it intended that the Irish Free State should be within the Empire?; (ii) Was the position of the Crown to be the same as in the Dominions?; (iii) Was the treaty-making power to be the same as that of Canada?; (iv) Were the courts to stand in the same relation to the Judicial Committee of the Privy Council as in Canada?; (v) Was the oath to be incorporated in the constitution?; (vi) Would all members of the Provisional Government be required to sign the declaration under Article 17 of the Treaty?

Behind the questions lay a resolve and a readiness to apply force, as the minutes of Churchill's Irish Committee amply confirm, should the Irish persist in seeking to subvert the Treaty in the constitutional provision drafted for that purpose. On 2 June, the Irish yielded. The constitution was accordingly to conform to the Treaty, not only in the particular issues raised by Lloyd George, but further by giving to the Treaty an authority over and above that of the constitution. This was achieved by rendering any provision of the constitution or any amendment thereto repugnant to the Treaty to the extent of such repugnancy being null and void. The concept of repugnancy therewith introduced was basic to the implementing of the Treaty, allegiance, oath and status being entrenched behind it.

Kennedy's advice may have been sound in law: politically it was unrealistic. In the light of what transpired in the October–December 1921 negotiations and the virulence of the Unionist assault on the Irish Free State (Agreement) Bill in February–March 1922, it could not be supposed that a Unionist-dominated Cabinet would allow provisions enforced by threat of war to be circumvented by constitutional sleight of hand. Collins, following Kennedy's advice, invited near humiliating withdrawal unless, indeed, Collins was contemplating resumption of hostilities. Of that there is no evidence. As it was, with formal agreement on the constitution, however unsatisfactory for the Irish, a milestone on the road to the completion of the settlment had been passed, with the public on this occasion knowing little or nothing of the issues, details of which were withheld from public scrutiny for some thirty years.

The Election

There was another long foreshadowed milestone ahead: civil war. Nomination day for the election was 6 June. The concurrence of the British signatories to the Treaty and the opinion of the British law officers that the constitution, as now revised to meet their objections, conformed with the Treaty was made known to the Cabinet on 15 June. The constitution was published forthwith, which meant that it became available to voters only on the morning of the election. It was the Treaty, little encumbered by the constitution, that was at issue. How much the panel affected the outcome remains debatable. The surprising feature was the extent to which independent candidates came forward, thereby ensuring a contest in most of the multiple proportional representation constituencies. The pro-Treaty party polled 491,542 votes, the anti-Treaty 134,165. In terms of seats, 68 were won by the pro- and 19 by the anti-Treaty party. The electorate, by a substantial majority of votes cast and seats won, thus accorded the Treaty the stamp of their approval. But they did not and could not ensure peace. On 22 June Field Marshal Sir Henry Wilson was assassinated in London by two members of the IRA[35] – an action widely, but almost certainly mistakenly, believed to be part of a larger conspiracy. There was no more critical moment in the aftermath of the Treaty than this.

On 26 June the full results of the election became known and also on that day the Irregulars, who had occupied the Four Courts since April, kidnapped two high-ranking Free State officers and held them there, an assault which the Provisional Government decided could not be disregarded. They launched an attack, and on 30 June, after repeated shelling and a series of explosions the Four Courts caught fire and the Irregulars surrendered. Many of Ireland's most treasured historical records were destroyed, eliciting from Churchill the felicitous but unfeeling comment: 'better a state without an archive than an archive without a state'. His own predisposition to and encouragement of strong action has lent colour to a belief that he had had some part in precipitating the Provisional Government's action. His own staff were concerned lest in this crisis his temperament should outweigh his judgement. Lional Curtis had remarked on 15 May that he had 'no great fears for the settlement in the long-run provided always that we can manage to keep clear of intervention'. It is not in doubt that Curtis had Churchill chiefly in mind, since he also canvassed the desirability of Churchill's taking a holiday.[36] But while London laid plans to storm the Four Courts if need arose, Collins ensured that it did not. Dr Lawlor concludes her detailed review of the episode with the comment that no evidence exists for the allegation that Collins acted under British pressure.[37] Hopkinson in his full and more recent account makes it clear that British intervention was closely planned, but was staved off at the last moment by Macready, who, however, did supply guns and ammunition at the request of the Provisional Government and with the encouragement of Churchill.

The challenge to the authority of the Provisional Government could hardly have been disregarded if the regime were to continue to have credibility. Yet reassertion of its authority inexorably led by stages, outside the range of this study, to civil war. The settlement which was the end product of the Anglo-Irish war thus came to be sustained only by a second and, this time, civil war in Ireland. In Britain the profit, in Ireland the price, loomed larger.

In August 1922 the Provisional regime was shaken by the death first of Arthur Griffith and then in an ambush at Beal na mBlath of Michael Collins. The impress of both lay deep upon the settlement. While analogies with the dual monarchy were swept aside as was the monarchy itself, Griffith's Magyar-modelled abstentionist tactics, his emphasis upon fiscal autonomy opening the door to tariff manipulation in the interest of small-scale industrialisation, his faith in parliamentary government and his balanced appreciation of the advantages and disadvantages of dominion status went far, indeed further than his critics have allowed, to determining the parameters of the settlement. Yet with so much by way of solid achievement, the American Consul felt moved to observe that fate had been kinder to Griffith than to most Irish leaders in removing him in the moment of victory, and before calmer reflection had enabled the people to realise the real nature of this achievement – the permanent partition of Ireland into two hostile camps.[38] If by the last the Consul meant the division on the Treaty, as presumably he did, then assuredly Griffith must share the responsibility with many others. As for Collins, his major contribution was in another field. In his lifetime, he was acclaimed as the man who won the war. As a negotiator he earned high regard from Churchill and Birkenhead, though he had his share of impetuosity in judgement, as was indicated by his sanguine overestimate of the changes in frontier likely to be effected by the Boundary Commission and the way in which he allowed himself to be diverted from a multitude of responsibilities to follow a constitutional will-o'-the-wisp in 1922. Yet beyond question he had the courage and ruthlessness that make for achievement in revolutionary times. Nor was there any very obvious limitation to his powers: he had all manner of qualities and with experience was deemed likely to acquire the great ones. Yet of him at the last it has to be written 'He died young.' A man may not be judged by the great things he might have done.

The death of these two leaders of the Irish delegation in August was followed on 19 October 1922 by the resignation of the Coalition Cabinet, basically as the result of a groundswell of Unionist misgiving about the way affairs were conducted under Lloyd George – shades of Inverness and Gairloch – and the fear among them lest, having destroyed the Liberal party, he might divide the Conservative. Stanley Baldwin identified him as 'a great dynamic force', and described it as 'a very terrible thing'. The Irish would have agreed. In the Treaty debate, Robert Barton, explaining and, in effect, retracting his signature to the Treaty, recalled how Lloyd George had persuaded him to sign by conveying 'with all the solemnity and the power of conviction that he alone, of all men I met, can impart by word and gesture – the vehicles by which one man oppresses and impresses the mind of another – ... that the signature and recommendation of

---

* S.M. Bruce, later Prime Minister of Australia, recalled breakfasting with Lloyd George in 1921 and far from impressing upon Lloyd George some matters of Australian interest, he found himself 'sucked dry' on matters about which Lloyd George wished to sound him out and came away, robust and youthful though he was, 'utterly drained and exhausted' (personal notes).

every member of our delegation was necessary or war would follow immediately'.[39] 'We know', said Michael Collins, taunted by his critics in the Treaty debate with falling under Lloyd George's influence, 'what it meant when John Redmond had breakfast with Lloyd George. If I had breakfast with Lloyd George I would tell you so.'[40]

The final draft of the constitution had been introduced in the third Dáil by the new President, W.T. Cosgrave, on 18 September 1922,[41] in the form of a Constitution Bill. It was conducted through its successive stages by Kevin O'Higgins with the mastery of detail it demanded. Deputies were advised that the repudiation of certain Articles would involve resignation of the Ministry, because repudiation, given the repugnancy clause, would be tantamount to repudiation of the Treaty itself.

Press reports suggested that Bonar Law, now in office, moved by the plight of the Unionist minority in the South and West – Lansdowne's once notional constituency – would seek further safeguards for them in the constitution, which in effect meant in the partly nominated Senate that was to be. President Cosgrave reacted by reminding Bonar Law on 24 November that the constitution as adopted by Dáil Éireann had been certified by the British government as being in full accord with the Treaty and could not in good faith be departed from. Bonar Law conceded that this was so.[42]

The Bill was passed and the constitution was brought into operation one year after the Treaty on 6 December 1922, by proclamation. This marked the last stage in the dual constitutional progression. On the Irish view, the constitution was finally enacted by the third Dáil sitting as a Constituent Assembly – it did not pass a single act of ordinary legislation, all matters of immediate importance being dealt with by decree or on orders of the Provisional Government – and deriving its authority from the people. The Constitution Act (No. 1 of 1922) was described as an Act to enact a constitution for the Irish Free State and for implementing the Treaty. In the preamble it was recorded that Dáil Éireann, sitting in this provisional Parliament, 'acknowledging that all lawful authority comes from God to the people . . . hereby proclaims the establishment of the Irish Free State (otherwise called Saorstát Éireann) and in the exercise of undoubted right decrees . . .'. This was an explicit assertion at once of popular sovereignty and of continuity of authority of successive Dála. But as for 'undoubted right', the United Kingdom government had no regard for it. In their view, the constitution derived its authority from 13 Geo 5 c1, Irish Free State Constitution Act 1922. Its preamble records nothing about the people or the Dáil, but about the fact that the House of Parliament 'constituted pursuant to the Irish Free State (Agreement) Act 1922 sitting as a Constituent Assembly for the settlement of the Constitution of the Irish Free State has passed the measure (hereinafter referred to as 'the Constituent Act') set forth in the schedule to this Act'. The measure was declared, subject to certain provisions, to be the constitution of the Irish Free State to come into force on being proclaimed by His Majesty. Indeed, on the British view, the Irish assembly had no authority to enact a constitution: it had not been authorised to do so and all along, if only to silence their critics, British ministers had acted in conformity with dominion precedent.

In sum, there was therefore a dual source of inspiration for the constitution, reflected in each successive stage in the process of ratification of the Treaty. On the British side, the sequence was approval of the Treaty by Parliament in December 1921, the Irish Free State (Agreement) Act 1922, and the Irish Free State (Constitution) Act 1922. On the Irish, there was approval of the Treaty by Dáil Éireann of the formal endorsement of the Treaty by the House of Commons of Southern Ireland, popular endorsement in a general election, and finally entrenchment of the Treaty in the constitution of Saorstát Éireann enacted by the third Dáil in the exercise of undoubted right. On 6 December 1922, the constitution with the entrenched Treaty came into force: on that there was agreement, but disagreement on how in legal terms it came about.[43] Finally in the British view, there had been an agreement on the Irish Treaty; both countries found a place in the title of this unusual political instrument.

The constitution was more important than its origins. Its style was post-war continental baroque: its working structure functional-parliamentary. The ornamental features, extern ministers, the initiative and, more surprisingly, the referendum on all legislation other than constitutional amendment were abolished in 1927–28. In the working part of the constitution there were features of more than Irish interest.[44] Here it suffices to remark that within a traditional framework the division between pro- and anti-Treaty parties became so deeply entrenched as to become part of the normal pattern of political life, little blurred at the edges with the passage of time. One consequence was that a change in government necessarily involved radical change in attitude to the Treaty settlement.

CHAPTER 10

'Elements of Dynamite':
The Rounding Off of the Settlement
1922–25

The Ulster Option

The Treaty was entitled 'Articles of Agreement for a Treaty between Great Britain and Ireland'. There was no third party in its negotiation but Ulster Unionists were waiting its outcome in the wings. Likewise there was no third party in its conclusion. It was a bilateral instrument. That was something Craig allowed neither Lloyd George nor the Free Staters to forget. He had an opening because of the provision made in the Treaty for the contingent recognition of a third party. Article 11, it will be recalled, stated that until the expiration of one month from the passing of the Act of Parliament for the ratification of this instrument, the powers of the Parliament and government of the Irish Free State 'shall not be exercisable as respects Northern Ireland' where the relevant provisions of the Act of 1920 'shall . . . remain in full force and effect'. While the 'Ulster' month ran its course, the Parliament of Northern Ireland might present an address to the King asking that the powers of the Parliament and government of the Irish Free State should not extend to Northern Ireland and that there the Act of 1920 should continue to be its Constitution Act. To the surprise of none, the option was exercised and an address presented on 7 December 1922, the day after the enactment of the ratifying Act, that is the Irish Free State Constitution Act 1922.[1]

As Sir James Craig explained, Members of the Northern Ireland Houses of Parliament had been summoned to meet 'at the earliest possible moment in order to make perfectly clear not only to Southern Ireland but to the world that . . . there is no use our holding out at the moment any hopes whatever of a desire on the part of the Ulster people to go in under a Dublin parliament'.[2] Six Nationalists and six Sinn Féiners had been returned at the first (May 1921) election as against 40 Unionists, but Sinn Féiners and Nationalists, otherwise deeply divided, were at one in repudiation of the new Northern parliamentary institutions from attendance at whose sittings they abstained, with the result that the Address was unanimously approved, as was never in doubt, by both Houses, concern being voiced only lest the severance from the rest of Ireland should be other than complete and final.

Here there was an element of paradox. In order to preserve the Union in six counties, Ulster Unionists judged it to be of first importance to sever all connection with the Dublin Castle administration by which the six counties with the rest of Ireland had been governed since 1801. On this Craig, with British Cabinet concurrence, had made moves in anticipation of the coming into effect of the Government of Ireland Act on 1 February 1921, by recruiting a cadre of administrators, the key appointment being, as already noted, that of Sir Ernest Clarke, who was to serve as Secretary to the Northern Ireland Department of Finance 1921–25,[3] as official in charge. Ulster Unionists, however, continued to express concern lest relics of Dublin Castle authority should surreptitiously continue to be exercised in the Six Counties. The Prime Minister was admonished that Northern Ireland must in no circumstances be brought into contact directly or indirectly with Dublin Castle. And why? Because, one member told him, 'there are two names we dread as we dread fire, and they are the names of Sir John Anderson and Mr. Cope'.[4] Did Dublin Castle deal with Northern Irish records, Craig was asked? He was altogether reassuring – indeed a Sinn Féiner could hardly have shown more zest for being rid of that stronghold of British administration in Ireland. Dublin Castle, Craig asserted, did not deal with their records. 'From yesterday [6 December] Dublin Castle ceases to exist, . . . and Dublin has nothing to do with a single inch of Ulster soil'.[5] There remained, however, the Boundary Commission. The Prime Minister alluded to one disturbing feature of it. Free State claims for Fermanagh and Tyrone he dismissed out of hand. He was 'not going to give away one inch of the soil' of either. But did not such confrontation – of the Free State claim and Northern Ireland's outright rejection of it – mean that the destinies of the two counties would rest in the hands of one man, the chairman of the proposed Boundary Commission? 'Was there ever such a preposterous suggestion?' he enquired.[6] But Craig had a way of disposing of notions he found un-welcome. In 1920 a correspondent had written to Carson that a Boundary Commission was a splendid means for delay.[7] Perhaps the thought was passed to Craig. More likely it was a consideration he already entertained.

The Crystallisation of Policies

It will be remembered that when first, on 14 October 1921, the question of partition had been discussed at the London Conference, Griffith had observed that partition, which he described as 'unnatural', could easily be settled if the British government were not behind the Ulstermen's 'unreasonable' demand. If it 'stood aside, if it did not throw its force behind those fellow-countrymen of ours in North East Ulster, we could come to an unanimous agreement with them'. What was an absolute priority was withdrawal of British support. But did that in itself suffice? When Lloyd George suggested direct conversation with the Ulster Unionists, Griffith demurred. 'No, it is you who made the position, and you must repair it.'[8] Evidently something more than standing aside was needed: there had additionally to be British remedial action. After all, division was effected by Act of Parliament at Westminster; only by that same authority could that Act be constitutionally amended. On that there could be no dispute; it was not in Ireland that ultimate responsibility, as the British would have been the first to assert, resided. But how, in the Irish view, given existing constraints, might it be realistically exercised? The answer was by British insistence on 'essential unity', which meant in practice either by the constitution of a Council of Ireland, or, as came to be widely canvassed by de Valera, the transfer to Dublin of Westminster's reserved powers over Northern Ireland with its local parliament continuing to be exercised additionally to the powers it already enjoyed. In such circumstances, the territorial status quo would remain undisturbed. But if the Ulster Unionists were adamant in their opposition to proposals and to all variants of them designed to preserve some semblance of a unitary polity, then given that the British government was pledged not to coerce Ulster, there remained the Boundary Commission provided for in Article 12 of the Treaty. Yet the constitution of such a body pointed as an immediate consequence, not to unity in any form but to a different partition.

The Boundary Commission: Terms of Reference and their Interpretation

The Commission's origins remain uncertain, except in as much as they were Unionist not Nationalist. Carson was evidently aware of such a proposal in 1916–17 and Craig alluded to the possibility in December 1919 when recommending exclusion of a six- as against a nine-county block from Dublin's jurisdiction. Thus far the proposal was intended to remedy illogicalities not to mention absurdities, along an artificial frontier taking into account the possibility that such adjustments might be made either way, allowing *inter alia* for the inclusion of small areas in east Donegal in Northern Ireland. But while certainly this was to be a Boundary Commission, it was conceived of in terms of carrying out a limited tidying up operation on both sides – hence Unionist consideration of it. Emphatically it was not of the kind Lloyd George said he had in mind on 7 November 1921 when looking for a way of making dominion status a negotiable proposition. What he then desired, so he told Tom Jones, was to find out from Griffith whether the Irish would support him in effecting a settlement on the basis of their taking a dominion parliament and Ulster retaining the 1920 status quo, subject to territorial revision by a Boundary Commission. The remit to a Commission thereupon underwent transformation in character and importance. It became a tactical device to be recommended to the Irish delegation as offering an alternative road to essential unity. Griffith, on learning later that Lloyd George was prepared to play the Boundary Commission on this basis as 'an absolutely last card' if Sinn Féin acquiesced, replied that it was not a Sinn Féin proposal, he could not give a pledge but that 'we [Sinn Féin] are not going to queer his [Lloyd George's] pitch . . .' while 'he was fighting the "Ulster" crowd'.[9] At that stage, the emphasis self-evidently was on tactical manoeuvre rather than substantive settlement. There was therefore little or nothing by way of precise definition, even to the extent of leaving unresolved doubts on whether the Commission would apply to nine counties or six. The purpose was to persuade the Irish to continue negotiations on status by allowing them to infer that the creation of a Boundary Commission would bring about 'essential unity'.[10] But would it? It was on this point that the wording of the subsequently embodied Article 12 of the Treaty came to assume critical importance.

Article 12 provided that if Northern Ireland exercised its option to secede from the Irish Free State a commission of three persons, one to be appointed by each of the three parties concerned – the Irish Free State, Northern Ireland and Great Britain, the British nominee to be Chairman – was to 'determine in accordance with the wishes of the inhabitants, so far as may be compatible with economic and geographic conditions, the boundaries between Northern Ireland and the rest of Ireland'; and 'the boundary of Northern Ireland shall be such as may be determined by such Commission'. There was no direction on procedural points, or on whether the Commission should seek to elicit preference by local enquiry or by a plebiscite (which Griffith favoured but Collins deprecated because 'it sacrificed unity entirely'),[11] or even the extent to which the wishes of the inhabitants should be basic, with economic and geographical conditions peripheral or whether frontier rectification was all that was in mind or something altogether more extensive coming close to a redrawing of the boundary.

The existence of so many loose ends is among the more striking features of a strange episode. Was it the result of inadvertence or design? There are two explanations. The first, to which Tom Jones gave credence, was that the article was hurriedly composed by the principal negotiators as opportunity offered and without officials (excluded because of Childers) and, as a result, despite the presence of the Lord Chancellor and other lawyers, by inadvertence imprecisely and ambiguously drafted. The second explanation was that the ambiguity was deliberate, indeed that it was the essence of the whole exercise. The first view was so generally entertained at the time as to lead a member of the House of Lords in

March 1922 to observe in passing that it was an 'admittedly' ambiguous clause. To this Birkenhead reacted sharply, 'It is not an admittedly ambiguous clause.' It laid down the essential distinction between a commission which dealt with boundary rectification, which was one thing, and a commission concerned with a transfer of territory, which was another. Later, Birkenhead was to elaborate on this. He told the House of Lords in 1925 there were articles in the Treaty 'which were so obscure as to be dangerous'. But, he continued, 'does anyone think so lightly of the capacity of those who signed that Treaty as to imagine that they were not alive to the dangers of Article 12 . . . there was no signatory of that Treaty but knew that in Article 12 there lurked the elements of dynamite'.[12] In other words, had it been clearly and precisely drafted, either way the Treaty, in Birkenhead's view, would not have been signed. Had rectification of frontier been indicated, Sinn Féin would have dismissed it as not deserving of consideration, while radical revision would have offended Unionist opinion, not only as beyond the limits of tolerance, but in breach of solemn assurance.

Within these parameters, the records of discussions between and within the delegations are illuminating but are short of being conclusive. There remain, however, inherent probabilities. In essence the Irish were being invited to make concessions on what to them mattered most, namely, status. They needed considerable persuasion. Had they been asked if adjustments in the existing boundary would suffice by way of counter-balance, the reply surely would have been a contemptuous negative. But no such limited proposition was made. As is clear from Griffith's October suggestion of plebiscites,[13] and the terms of Collins' dissent from it, what both envisaged was a redrawing by one means or another of the boundary in accordance with the wishes of the inhabitants. This was the assumption underlying Collins' otherwise incomprehensible remark to Lloyd George on 5 December 1921, the day before the Treaty was signed. He was, he is reported to have said, as agreeable to a reply from Craig rejecting as one accepting the essential unity of Ireland, the reasoning being that if unity were rejected 'we would save Tyrone and Fermanagh, parts of Derry, Armagh and Down by the Boundary Commission'. Such drastic re-drawing would mean that 'the North would be forced economically to come in'.[14] Lloyd George, on the record, neither countenanced nor dis-countenanced such an interpretation – seemingly he preserved a judicious silence. Chartres, who served as a legal adviser to the Irish delegation, later recalled that at a full conference at which the boundary issue was discussed there was no question of slight rectification, the discussion with maps being on the basis of substantial areas.[15] In Belfast – and here we have the testimony of the American Consul[16] – the expectation, dreaded or welcomed as the case might be, was that substantial change of frontiers would be recommended. But neither particular nor popular understanding amounted to conclusive evidence that this was so – only the words of Article 12 of the Treaty pact. It was, as Craig and Collins well understood, only the Commission, or more precisely, its chairman, who would have to give a ruling on the interpretation to be placed upon it. Until he had done so, even for a Prime Minister that remained a matter of conjecture.

In the Treaty debate, Collins contented himself with dismissing all thought of coercion of the six counties with the rider that while the Treaty arrangement was not ideal, it was hard to think of a better one.[17] Lloyd George's parallel statement in the House of Commons, without in any way underwriting Sinn Féin expectations, did not discourage them. He spoke on the no-coercion theme – no coercion of Ulster by Sinn Féin, but equally no coercion in Ulster of other units. Were Ulster to opt to remain a separate unit, then there should be a readjustment of boundaries. 'There is no doubt', he continued, '. . . that the majority of the people of two counties prefer being with their Southern neighbours to being in the Northern Parliament. . . . If Ulster is to remain a separate community, you can only by means of coercion keep them there, and although I am against the coercion of Ulster, I do not believe in Ulster coercing other units. Apart from that, would it be an advantage to Ulster?'[18] It was a question deserving more reflection than the familiar 'not an inch' response it received.

By late January 1922, the issue was more sharply defined. Collins, stung by Craig's 'no inch of Ulster's soil' being surrendered, spoke of the whole of Fermanagh and Tyrone over and above smaller areas elsewhere, notably South Armagh, being transferred to the Irish Free State. There were Unionist reactions. On 3 March 1922 Balfour, stimulated by Craig, sought reassurance from Birkenhead about the meaning of Article 12. Birkenhead supplied it with characteristic verve.[19] He pointed to innumerable European treaties of the nineteenth century which had some such provision, the example he quoted being that of the Treaty of Berlin, Article 2 of which set out in detail the territories to be comprised within the Principality of Bulgaria, just as those in Northern Ireland had been in the Act of 1920; this Act had, in his view – it was one from which the Irish dissented – to be read with the Treaty. Had large-scale change been contemplated, the Article would have had to have been otherwise phrased, and the Commission's responsibility extended to their determining in accordance with the wishes of the inhabitants the portions of Ireland to be included in the Irish Free State and in Northern Ireland and to fixing the boundary between them. Until Collins made the suggestion, 'no living soul in either House ever suggested that the clause was capable of the fantastic meaning of which Craig now professes himself to be apprehensive . . . I have no doubt that the Tribunal, not being presided over by a lunatic, will take a rational view of the limits of its own jurisdiction and will reach a rational conclusion'. Craig told Balfour on 16 March that the boundary question could only lead to civil war in view of Collins' assurances to his followers 'within our Borders' that he would not feel satisfied unless the Commission authorised the transfer of more than one-third of the province to the South of Ireland.[20]

For all the fundamental differences between Craig and Collins, there was no prospect of the early constitution of the Boundary Commission to resolve them. This was precluded by procedural requirements. Until the Treaty had been ratified by enactment of the Irish Free State Constitution Act on 6 December 1922, the Ulster option could not be exercised, and until it had been it could not be established how it would be. The necessity of delay on legal grounds was not, however, a source of complaint to either of the parties principally concerned. Given his 'not an inch' stance, Craig had reason to believe that time was on his side. The more securely he could establish six-county government and administration, the more unlikely that a commission would consider radical readjustment of area while, if it came to negotiating a settlement, a reasonably well-established authority would be at an advantage. But what of Collins? Surely he would favour an early reference to a tribunal while the situation was fluid? The answer is that he had serious reservations about a tribunal's handing down of judgement, as against a negotiated settlement between principals. This was partly because of the turmoil of the time, but chiefly due to reservations about the wisdom of committing the Irish Free State to acceptance of a commission award with no certain knowledge even of the principles which would determine the nature of its enquiry, let alone of what its conclusions might be. On that he was at one with Craig. Neither contemplated with equanimity the prospect of final arbitral delimitation which each was bound to respect. 'Preposterous', Craig had called it.

The state of Ireland in early 1922 had its Miltonic overtones – a Treaty in debate, power in process of transfer, a state to be established, a frontier to be rectified or redrawn, comrades in arms divided, a civil war impending and the hazards inseparable from confused and conflicting purposes:

> Chaos umpire sits
> And by decision more embroils the fray
> By which he reigns: next to him high arbiter
> Chance governs all

Surveying it, Bonar Law observed on 26 June 1922 that had he foreseen the sequel, he doubted whether he would have voted for the Treaty.[21]

The Craig – Collins Meetings

Much of the turmoil and most of the fray in those early months of the New Year were in the north-east, in Belfast itself and along the borders of

Fermanagh and Tyrone. In Belfast the latest phase of endemic violence was to be dated from the expulsion of Roman Catholic workers from shipyards and engineering works in July 1920; to this the Dáil responded, despite the counsel of Ernest Blythe, its one Protestant member, and others, by boycotting the city's Protestant firms. Faced with yet further violence in Belfast and its spread along the Border where IRA units were mobilising, Craig, Chairman of the Cabinet's Irish Committee, conveyed to Churchill his readiness to enter into discussions with the Provisional Government about relations with the North. Welcoming this initiative, Churchill brought Craig and Collins together on 21 January 1922.[22] The outcome was an agreement set out in what came to be known as the first of two Craig–Collins pacts, Collins *inter alia* agreeing that the Dáil's trade boycott of Belfast should end at once – it did on 24 January – while Craig was to facilitate the return of Catholic workers to the shipyards, which he did with limited effect.

But more remarkable was the agreement in anticipation of the Boundary Commission to seek a boundary settlement by direct negotiation, each of the two leaders, on Craig's proposal, appointing a representative to advise their respective governments on how the boundary between the two parts of Ireland should be fixed. The Ulster Unionist view was that as they were not a party to the Treaty, they were under no obligation to abide by its provisions, least of all Article 12, the interpretation of which might affect their very existence as a political entity, but which in their absence had been imposed upon them by arbitrary fiat of the British government and Sinn Féin. For Craig, therefore, this bypassing of Article 12 was consistent with his overall stance. But for Collins, who had set so much store by the Commission, the apparent readiness to act outside the Treaty conceded a point of principle, namely that the provisions of the Treaty were not deemed sacrosanct by one of its signatories. In the event nothing came of the *démarche*, claim and counterclaim soon being renewed.

On 2 February the two leaders met again, and again unprofitably to both, with Craig returning to his 'not an inch' position and Collins to his claim to the two counties plus. On 8 February there was superimposed upon violence within the six counties a series of raids and kidnappings by the IRA across the Border.[23] The British government lent assistance to the North by way of paying for special constables – a military under the guise of a police force – and allowing Field Marshal Sir Henry Wilson to prepare a 'scheme' of action. On 17 March, Tom Jones minuted the Prime Minister on his disquietude at what seemed to him a prospective breach of the spirit of the settlement,[24] and in May he sounded warning that 'the North (Henry Wilson and Co)' were seeking 'to embroil us on their side against the South'. On 30 March, Collins and Craig signed a further pact pledging the cooperation of both governments in restoring peace in the unsettled border areas.[25] 'Peace is to-day declared', the text began.

It was a demanding assignment. By midsummer 1922 there were nineteen battalions of British troops in Northern Ireland. With the outbreak of the civil war, pressure from the South was lessened and the Irregulars were drawn back to their own areas, thus easing a still tense situation on the Border.

From February onwards, Michael Collins, head of the Provisional Government, had become more and more preoccupied with developments in the north-east and concerned with the plight of Catholics there – he had now become their spokesman in intergovernmental exchanges with Churchill. When in London in June for the talks on the constitution, he was in a militant mood, thoroughly distrustful of the British and 'obsessed with the Ulster situation'. On the boundary, the records show how his opinion oscillated between high hopes of a Commission and a feeling that it were better settled by negotiation quietly and quickly. Where his judgement would finally have come to rest we do not know. What we do know is that Collins was psychologically committed to boundary revision; and it has been surmised by Dr Laffan that had he lived, a settlement of some kind would have been reached before 1925. For that, despite the constraints imposed by a triangular situation, a good case may be made. At the lowest reckoning, therefore, the bullet that ricocheted from an armoured car and killed Collins on the narrow moorland road near Beal na mBlath on 22 August[26] 1922 – at that moment, it seemed in the Irish countryside, where news passed from mouth to mouth, as if chance might govern all – changed the style and may have influenced the outcome of negotiations on the final stage of the 1920–25 Settlement.

The Formulation of Policies

Negotiation of the Treaty had been between two parties only, the British and Sinn Féin. Of the two, the British – given that they had conceded fiscal autonomy and retained control over defence in the area of devolved government over and above the Treaty ports – had two tangible long-term interests to which the boundary had relevance: first that the Border – as finally drawn – should commend itself as reasonable and just to public opinion at home and overseas, especially in the Commonwealth and the United States; secondly, that the excluded area, for the good government of which the Ulster Unionists would assume responsibility, was as well defined as circumstances allowed for those purposes.

To the British, the principal attraction of the whole settlement lay in the fact that it would, as the Chief Secretary had stated in introducing the 1920 Bill, 'give complete self-government to Ireland in all her domestic concerns'.[27] It was self-defeating on that basis to transfer an area to Northern Ireland with a range of responsibilities that its government might not prove well equipped to discharge without calling upon assistance from the Imperial government. Time and again Lloyd George and Austen Chamberlain alluded to the weakness of the Ulster Unionist case for retaining Tyrone and Fermanagh where elections had confirmed the existence of a Nationalist majority. The Southern Unionist Lord Desart, among others, had pointed to the risk of having such a local Catholic majority – in his view, the most irreconcilable in Ireland – perforce included within the Unionist enclave. Was any British interest thereby advanced? None, it would seem, given that British security interests were sufficiently safeguarded by the provisions of the Treaty. But besides long-term British national interests were domestic party pressures and political interests, which in varying degree conditioned the approach of successive governments. Dr Canning has made a systematic analysis of them in his *British Policy Towards Ireland 1921–1941*.[28] His unravelling of the evidence serves to dispel any notion that with the efflux of time, the winding up of the settlement was a matter detached from the passions of the past.

The Northern Ireland position was explicit at the least. The Ulster Unionists had secured 'almost everything', in Captain Craig's words, that they had campaigned for before the war. In so far as there was debate about area and boundary, it was not six counties or four, but six counties or nine, as can hardly be restated too often, that was at issue. Six was the minimum, 'not an inch' of which was to be surrendered. In democratic terms, this was not defensible. But then the Ulster Unionists at no point suggested that that was for them a consideration. The relevant question is surely: was it wise in their own interest? It assumed that the largest area consistent with a Unionist majority would be the most secure. In fact such security was more likely to be achieved by thinking in terms of an area in which the minority would be smallest. In the present and the middle distance, however, the six-county area was well devised to serve Ulster Unionist purposes: it was for a later generation to pay such price as might be exacted.

What of the Irish Free State? The aim was unity; on that conceptually there was no prospect of compromise. The three Home Rule Bills had been drafted on the basis of Ireland as one nation, not two. The Treaty also made acknowledgement of this, the Irish Free State being conterminous with Ireland. But with the Ulster option exercised, the state and nation were no longer coincidental. There was the six-county political entity, to use Lloyd George's terminology, excluded from the state. Unity accordingly was an aspiration to be achieved. That was an absolute, the realisation of which was thought of in terms of coercion or negotiated concession, not of a foreseeable change of mind on the part of the Unionist majority in the excluded area. From January until June 1922, Irish policy swung uneasily between the two. At the first January Craig–Collins[29] meeting, Collins had been prepared to contemplate a boundary settlement through bilateral negotiation dispensing with a Boundary Commission; on

2 February, he staked out an Irish claim for Fermanagh, Tyrone and Catholic/nationalist majority areas elsewhere not isolated from others of their community with the threat – and, not long after, the reality – of guerrilla warfare along the border and incursions across it by Sinn Féin supporters. At the third of the Craig–Collins meetings, on 30 March, the emphasis was once again on negotiation and agreement was reached that there should be a further meeting before any address in accordance with Article 12 of the Treaty had been presented with a view to ascertaining (a) whether a means could be devised to secure the unity of Ireland; and (b) failing that, whether agreement could be arrived at otherwise than by recourse to a Boundary Commission.[30]

All of this came to nothing, foundering as it did in the further deterioration of the situation first in Belfast, then along the Border and finally with the Collins–de Valera electoral pact on 20 May, which was interpreted comprehensively by Craig three days later as indicating a step towards a republic, a plan to destroy parliamentary institutions, carrying with it an implicit threat of Sinn Féin reunited in making common assault against the six counties.[31] Abortive once again as the last Craig–Collins meeting proved, it provided further evidence that both parties, and especially Collins, retained an interest in settling the boundary by means other than a commission. Why, it may be asked, was this so, when Collins with Griffith had expressed so much confidence in the substantial rectification of the boundary, even to a point that might render the six counties a non-viable unit?

The answer is to be sought in the constraints under which Free State negotiators laboured. It was not in doubt that two counties, with other areas including South Armagh and Derry City contiguous to the Border, would vote by small or large majorities for incorporation in the Irish Free State. At their meeting in July 1921, de Valera, to Lloyd George's relief, did not raise the question of Fermanagh and Tyrone. In this de Valera, in Lloyd George's view, had shown himself 'an unskilful negotiator'.[32] But had de Valera done so, it would necessarily have been on the point not of unity but of redefinition of area. That would have narrowed the issue. It would also have changed its nature. Such discussion would have made sense only on the understanding that a new border drawn with regard to the wishes of the majority was acceptable to both parties, that is that Sinn Féin and later the Irish Free State would have underwritten a partition in accord with the wishes of the people. More than that in practical terms they would have demonstrated *either* that the smaller area was non-viable *or* made partition virtually permanent. In such an excluded area the Protestant majority would have been overwhelming and its position vulnerable only in terms of criticism of a geographical imperative. Paradoxical though it may appear, it was not in Collins' interest to bring about such a situation; it was in Craig's – *unless* indeed Collins and others were to be persuaded that the reduced area was non-viable. On any balance sheet, the profit in reducing sharply the number of Catholics outside the Free State had to be counterbalanced by the consequent homogeneity of what would remain . . . in the excluded area. Craig would come close to having what he professed to desire – partition in perpetuity – with a Protestant state for a Protestant people.

Ernest Blythe as the one Protestant in the Free State government was among the first to question the assumptions conditioning Free State attitudes to the north-east, by analysis of the situation not as might be desired but as it was. This he did on 9 August 1922,[33] by which time he felt that the government's success in the June election and the progress of the offensive against the Irregulars enabled it for the first time to decide freely upon its policy on the north-east. His principal conclusions were (1) that there was no prospect of effecting unity by launching attacks against the north-east, the most likely consequence of which would be the extirpation of the Catholics there. All military operations in or against the north-east should, therefore, be brought to an end; (2) that economic pressure, for reasons analysed in some detail, gave promise of no more satisfactory results and 'nothing we can do by way of boycott . . . will bring the Orange party to reason'. The boycott might be ruled out as futile for the immediate future, while 'as for the widespread notion that it would be easy, should the North-Eastern counties opt out, to bring them in by use of regular and legal economic pressure, that was certainly not correct'. What then remained? In Blythe's judgement the abandonment of all thought of military force or economic pressure externally, coupled with no encouragement of any section in the North who refused to acknowledge the authority of the Northern government, would open the way to amicable relations and as a result over the years of the loss and inconvenience of the inland customs barrier, 'unification would come to be regarded as a wise and economical thing, by the majority in the six counties'. Few things might appear more improbable! But this was not the conclusion of the argument. It ended more persuasively that the Free State observing the Treaty in letter and in spirit could reasonably expect to be likewise done by. Its government should accordingly use every means to secure the last tittle of what the Treaty entitled it to. Here foremost there were at least two and a half counties to which the Free State had claim in a Treaty context. The border had been fixed 'where we cannot consent to its being fixed'. By standing on the Treaty, 'we shall put ourselves right in the eyes of any impartial arbitrator'.

On 17 October Kevin O'Sheil, assistant to the government's legal adviser with special responsibility for relations with Northern Ireland and shortly to be appointed director of a newly constituted North-East Boundary Bureau, set out in a paper circulated to all members of the Provisional Government the options open to them. At the outset, he noted that the members of the Commission were left free to arrange their own procedure. They might decide to sit together as a round table conference and determine the issue themselves, or they might decide the unit for inclusion or exclusion, leaving it to the inhabitants by plebiscite or election to indicate their wishes, or they might themselves make enquiries travelling from place to place to do so. O'Sheil advised the second, in close accord as it was with practice in post-war Europe, and he hoped that Free State views would be conveyed to the British government.[34]

On 2 December O'Sheil, in discharge of his responsibility for the preparation of the Irish case to be laid before the Boundary Commission, circulated a paper to ministers.[35] On aims, O'Sheil was emphatic. It was *not* the setting up of a Commission with the intention of wresting as much territory as possible from the North but 'a much more lasting thing than any temporary arrangement of purely arbitrary and utterly absurd boundaries, viz., *National Union.*' He conceded that there were permanent and temporary partitionists, the former including the vast majority of Northern Protestants and in the South individuals who saw in it 'a means of cutting out altogether a most objectionable social element' or feared 'brisk Northern trade rivalry'. But he was satisfied the overwhelming bulk of the people including many Northern Protestants were anti-partitionist. In this category, 'the extreme and uncompromising Anti-Partitionist people who would not accept Partition, even though they knew it would not endure longer than an hour, are to be found almost wholly amongst the Northern Catholic population'.

That section of the Catholic population was not only most closely concerned with the nature of the final boundary settlement but sensitive to the time factor. The greater the procrastination, the more difficult, with progressive consolidation of Northern authority, was major boundary adjustment likely to be regarded. Moreover the Free State administration had other preoccupations. Until the ending of the civil war and with it the reassertion of the government's authority in May 1923, the case for enlargement of its jurisdiction might be discounted. There were also major financial problems which imposed their own constraints, the resolution of which was seen as in part conditional upon the settlement of the oustanding financial issues provided for in Article 5 of the Treaty. Finally, and inherent in the nature of the case, was the implicit gamble – for it was little less. With lawyers divided on the inferences to be drawn from the wording of Article 12, governments could not foretell with assurance whether the outcome might be a transfer of allegiance for parishes or for counties and yet they were committed to accept the arbitral ruling whatever that might be and whatever the consequent popular reactions. It was the unknown that had decided Collins and Craig in January and again in March 1922[36] to think in terms of bypassing the Treaty and reaching a bilateral settlement.

It was when any such possibility had to be ruled out that the Free State had perforce to consider their position *vis-à-vis* the commission when constituted. When a settlement by agreement became self-evidently a non-starter, Craig had recourse to lobbying the English Unionist leaders about the choice of chairman of the Commission in whose hands, as he already discerned, would rest the 'preposterous' power of deciding how the boundary would run subject to a Treaty provision, the terms of which the chairman would himself interpret. The Free State suffered the same uncertainties without enjoying the same access to the corridors of power and its government moved by a great imperative to action because unlike the Ulster Unionists, not the status quo, or the status quo with boundary adjustment, but its subversion was in principle their aim. They were impelled therefore to maintain their demand for the implementation of Article 12, and to formulate their order of priorities.

In a memorandum of 17 May 1923 with three accompanying reports, Kevin O'Sheil addressed himself to *Our Territorial Demand at the Boundary Commission*.[37] He outlined three possibilities designated – the Maximum line, Minimum line and Middle line. The Maximum line would have given the Free State all of Ireland *except* Antrim, the north-east corner of Derry, part of Armagh (exclusive, however, of Armagh City) and all of Down, except the northern and middle portions. It represented the greatest possible amount of territory the commission could award and that award could only be supported on the basis of the wishes of the inhabitants. For the rest, O'Sheil allowed, it offended against 'every conceivable geographic and economic principle' and would have produced a frontier of some 148 miles. The Middle line was tactical, making allowance for salients that might be conceded. A submission resting on the Middle with contemplated withdrawal to the Minimum line, implied a pragmatic approach formulated so as to obtain a 'good' border and the maximum satisfaction to Northern Nationalists as against a 'bad' border devised by reason of its inconveniences and absurdities to discredit the concept of partition itself. The Minimum line was based on a balanced assessment of all three elements in the Commission's terms of reference, 'wishes of the inhabitants, geographic and economic considerations'. Derry City, part of the county, nearly all of Tyrone, South Armagh, the southern portion of Down and all of Fermanagh would be transferred. This would sharply reduce the number of Catholics living under a government not of their own choice and, while adversely affecting Protestants in some parts of the areas to be transferred, would be warranted under the terms of the Commission's brief. The length of the Border would be reduced to 124 miles. The stance recommended by O'Sheil was on the Minimum line. In this, members of the Executive Council concurred. Minimum Boundary lines, despite the deprecatory description, were unlikely to make any reassuring impression on the Ulster Unionists.

Certainly they involved much more than rectification of the existing boundary. The role of the Commission and its chairman seemed likely to be increased rather than diminished as time went by.

Another factor in the situation was the distancing of time, powerfully reinforced by the chances of war and politics. The assumption had been that those who negotiated the Treaty would implement it. Griffith would be able to get in touch with Lloyd George, Collins with Churchill – they had a common background of experience to ease consideration of matters in debate.* But the boundary Commission was delayed not only beyond the lifetime of the Irish leaders, but also beyond Lloyd George's prime ministerial span. If the Treaty in itself was not fatal to him, as Churchill judged but history now doubts, with Chanak and domestic discontents it was. In October 1922 Lloyd George fell from office, never to return. Bonar Law, then Baldwin, followed in short-lived succession with Ramsay MacDonald forming the first Labour government in January 1924. At the Colonial Office dealing with Irish affairs were other men – the Duke of Devonshire and then J.H. Thomas – and other responses. Those responses were more direct – in May 1924, Curtis spoke of J.H.T. (Thomas) as being 'under Craig's thumb[38] – and as usual it was 'Craig's word which carries most weight in Whitehall' – more committed to Ulster, and altogether less comprehending than Lloyd George – who on balance, as A.J.P. Taylor suggests, may be acquitted of fraudulent intent in respect of the boundary,[39] even though it should be added that had the last word rested with him, he would have paid no more regard to Irish understanding or misunderstanding than served his purposes best. However, the personal factor was not the crucial one. That remained the text of Article 12. Only the Irish Free State was anxious to subject it to early interpretation.

On 19 January 1923 Tim Healy, filling with idiosyncratic distinction the office of Governor-General that in other circumstances might have seemed an appropriate target for his coruscating wit,† wrote to the Duke of Devonshire to acquaint him with the fact that acting in accordance with Article 12, the Irish Free State had appointed Professor Eoin MacNeill as their representative on the Boundary Commission.[40] MacNeill was a scholar of the highest distinction. The conduct of great affairs was, however, not his talent. Alice Stopford Green had told Redmond in October 1914 that she had never seen 'a man less fitted for action'. His role in 1916 had underscored her judgement. Why then was he nominated?

---

* Austen Chamberlain however was present at the concluding Anglo-Irish talk in November–December 1925 and contributed from his earlier experience (CAB 55/21); and Jones, pp. 237–8, 245.
† Evidently he was to feel uninhibited in the case of the chairman of the Commission 'Feetham – cheat 'em'.

The answer, Dr Hand tells us in his admirable reconstruction of MacNeill's role,[41] was Cosgrave's view that the Irish commissioner had to be a minister, a Northerner and a Catholic. MacNeill, who held the Education portfolio, was at the time the only member of the government who satisfied all three desiderata. Where government and people had wanted and expected forthright political representation of their interests they learned too late that what was being given was detached, fair-minded appraisal without insistence upon a national standpoint and interest. For MacNeill, who took an elevated quasi-judicial view of his functions, the assignment led to 'personal obloquy and public resentment'. It was a saddening climax to a career outstanding in another field. He was not the only one to suffer such a fate.

The Free State's indication of its hope that other parties would take similar action in respect of the nomination of a Northern Ireland commissioner and a chairman, so that the Commission might be constituted, came up against British opinion in all parties, the Unionist most strongly, favouring further postponement. But the Free State government was known to believe that that would undermine Cosgrave's position at home. The British reply when this was indicated was a reluctant affirmative, coupled with the suggestion of preliminary tripartite discussion between representatives of Britain, the Irish Free State and Northern Ireland on the further steps necessary to give effect to Article 12. This was acceptable, Tim Healy laying emphasis in his reply on the Irish Free State's faithful and scrupulous fulfilment of their obligations under the Treaty, their reliance upon others doing the same and their gratification should any such discussions open up a prospect of remedying the unsatisfactory position in Northern Ireland.[42]

On 1 October, the Northern Ireland Cabinet reviewed their position. Craig had earlier counselled Baldwin that it would be inadvisable for the Imperial government to invite Northern Ireland to nominate a representative to serve on the Commission. On that there had been divided opinions in the Northern Ireland Cabinet, the Minister of Labour pointing out that even to enter into a conference would be liable to lead 'to considerable alarm and agitation'. But Craig on balance advised acceptance as the British government 'would not understand our attitude if we declined'. He was for once on the losing side among his own.

With the accession of Labour to office in January 1924, J.H. Thomas made his first appearance on the Anglo-Irish stage. The postponed exploratory conference took place on 1 February. What was under consideration were means, including a possible strengthening of the Council of Ireland, of getting round the need for a commission, or at the least deferring its constitution.[43] Irish demands for a resumption of talks foundered first on Craig's illness and then, following his unexpectedly early recovery, on Cosgrave's indisposition. During this period the British, as Tom Jones recorded,[44] sought to halt a discussion and to ensure that it remained halted so long as neither the Irish Free State nor Northern Ireland exercised its right to insist on the setting up of the Commission. The Free State, however, was not prepared to countenance indulgence in such tactics for domestic reasons, but only if convinced that it would materially advance Irish interests.

The resumed conference met on 24 April 1924 and as the records bleakly testify, 'after a prolonged discussion it was not found possible to reach an agreement'.[45] On 26 April the Free State formally requested that HMG take immediate steps for the constitution of the Commission. The British government asked the Governor of Northern Ireland to arrange for the selection of its representative. The Governor declined, observing that the decision conformed to an attitude Northern Ireland had consistently maintained.[46]

This negative response produced doubt and further delay. The first arose on the questions of whether, in the absence of a representative of Northern Ireland duly nominated by the government, the Commission would be properly constituted and, if not, whether it was competent for the Imperial government either to instruct the Governor of Northern Ireland to make such an appointment or, alternatively, themselves to advise the Crown to do so. There being no certainty about what the answer should be, the matter was referred to the Judicial Committee of the Privy Council. The Judicial Committee ruled that in each case the answer was in the negative. There was no way of proceeding constitutionally other than by supplementary legislation enacted by parliament and assented to by Dáil Éireann as a signatory to the Treaty. This, while duly accomplished, involved yet more delay.[47]

President Cosgrave, assailed by criticism at home, took the opportunity of voicing his dissatisfaction when introducing the resulting Treaty (confirmation of Supplemental Agreement) Bill in the Dáil on 12 August. He reasserted in the strongest terms his conception of the Treaty as a binding obligation on its signatories and one, moreover, which was properly and legally binding for the province of Northern Ireland with every other part of Ireland and Great Britain. This British governments had never hesitated to acknowledge. But each in turn sought for accommodation outside the Treaty. The panacea each time was yet one more conference with Sir James Craig. 'I went again and again to the conferences', President Cosgrave recalled, and at the end 'I had to confess that there was nothing offered which I could bring to this Dáil and say "Here is a working proposition", or, even, "Here is a hope of a working proposition". . . . Time after time Sir James has maintained the same attitude . . . he "will not budge an inch. He has never budged an inch."' The Free State desired the unity of Ireland, but if a piece of Ireland was to be cut off, then 'the metes and bounds of that piece shall be determined in accordance with the wishes of the inhabitants, so far as economic and geographic conditions allow'.[48]

Meanwhile the British government proceeded with the choice of chairman. Sir Robert Borden, Canada's wartime Prime Minister, was invited but was not prepared to serve unless both Irish governments indicated their willingness to nominate representatives. This Northern Ireland, consistent with its general attitude, would not give. Sir Robert cavalierly dismissed by Free State ministers as 'a rather silly man', was able to retreat honourably from an unwelcome assignment. That opened the way for the appointment of Mr Justice Feetham of the South African High Court, who was a member of the Round Table and when in England – which was rarely – attended gatherings of the Moot. He was known to have been in touch with Lionel Curtis and it may be assumed was influenced by him in accepting – beyond that is a matter for speculation. It is in any case immaterial. What mattered was Feetham's legalistic approach to his allotted task. In that he required no admonition from Curtis, or anyone else. The leader of the Labour party, Thomas Johnson, was quick to discern this. A forthright opponent of the Supplementary Bill to enable the Commission to be constituted, he inferred – so he told the Dáil – from a statement by Feetham that he (Feetham) was predisposed to a restrictive interpretation of Article 12 even before the Commission was in being. The statement was to the effect that Cosgrave and Craig had concurred in Feetham's proposal 'that I should make a tour on either side of the border in order to familiarise myself with the economic and geographical conditions, so that I may be able to follow the points raised in any discussion on the Boundary . . .'. The language, argued Johnson, was indicative of a predisposition in favour of a rectification or adjustment of the existing boundary. There was nothing, he contended, that would accommodate, let alone sustain, the Irish view that the wishes of the inhabitants should be taken wherever there was a *prima facie* case for so doing as in Antrim, Down and Belfast City as well as Tyrone, South Down and Fermanagh. But the statement of the proposed chairman 'precludes any such possibility from his mind'. That being so, Johnson argued, it would be wiser not to facilitate the British government in setting up the Commission. Given 'the mentality of the man who wrote that letter, far better not to attempt to implement Article 12 and so fix the Boundary and make partition absolute with Irish claims excluded from consideration'.[49] The argument was roughly rejected by Kevin O'Higgins yet Johnson was not mistaken in his assumption, questionable as may be the inference he drew from it. He rightly sensed also a developing predisposition little distinguishable from bias, stimulated by a propaganda campaign in the Unionist interest to the existence of which Tom Jones also testified. It was widely thought that the campaign drew sustenance from, and was given edge by the post-Treaty division and disorders in the Free State. If that indeed was so, Johnson's view that had the Commission been established within a year of the signing of the Treaty, the Irish interpretation would have been received with more balanced consideration does not carry much conviction.

The Agreement supplementing Article 12 was signed on 4 August 1924 and the Irish Free State (Confirmation of Agreement) Bill thereafter duly enacted by Parliament at Westminster and the Oireachtas.[50] The Act provided that if at the date of its passing, the government of Northern Ireland had not appointed a commissioner, its power to do so should therewith be transferred to, and exercised by, the British government. The government of Northern Ireland not having so done, the British government on 31 October appointed J.R. Fisher, a former editor (1891–1913) of the *Northern Whig* to serve. With Feetham having accepted appointment as chairman on 5 June 1924, the membership of the Commission was now complete. Its first meetings were held on 5–6 November; its concluding statement was dated 9 December 1925. Whatever else the Commission was or was not, there was no stinting on their part of time for enquiry and deliberation. But in fact, the outcome turned not on the conclusions to be drawn from representations or detailed submissions, but on what construction was to be placed upon the wording of Article 12.

In response to an enquiry from the Commission, the British government indicated that they did not wish to submit any statement or evidence. Likewise, though for different reasons, the government of Northern Ireland neither wished to lay any evidence nor to appear before the Commission by counsel. The government of the Irish Free State, however, availed itself of the opportunity to restate its opinion. At the heart of Free State representations was the contention that it was for the seceding areas to demonstrate their entitlement to secede. It was not to be contemplated that any area within Northern Ireland should have the right to withdraw permanently from the jurisdiction of the Irish Free State unless the majority of the inhabitants of such areas was in favour of such a course. The work of the Commission accordingly, on this view, should consist in ascertaining the wishes of the inhabitants of Northern Ireland with a view to determining, in accordance with such wishes, so far as might be compatible with economic and geographical conditions, what portions of that area were entitled to withdraw from the Irish Free State. In brief, the onus of proof rested with those who wished to secede – a view also to be entertained in 1947 by the Indian National Congress in respect of the partition of India.

The Free State claim implied acceptance of the argument that the drawing of a new frontier was not only within but a necessary part of the Commission's responsibilities – far from something they could rule out of consideration as exceeding the brief to which they were obliged to work. In Feetham's opinion, the Commission was not called upon to determine a boundary – that already existed – but only to make adjustments to it. In that the wishes of the inhabitants were the primary but not the paramount consideration. Such wishes meant, moreover, not bare majorities but a large consensus in favour of transfer.[51] What was at issue was not a question of simple majorities. Plebiscites Feetham in any event ruled out on the ground that the Treaty made no mention of them and silence on this point must be deemed to have been deliberate. As for the Free State contention that the onus of proof for the maintenance of the existing frontiers in disputed areas rested with the seceding counties, he rejected it out of hand. It was not the Commission's function to reconstitute the two territories. Northern Ireland, when the boundaries had been settled, must still be recognisable as the same political entity. Indeed he went further. He construed Article 12 as requiring parity of treatment on both sides of the Border so that areas that met the criteria laid down in Article 12 might be transferred equally either way. The Commission, accordingly, had power in either direction – it had no more and no less authority to take land from the Northern side of the existing boundary and give it to the Free State than it had to take land from the Free State and give it to Northern Ireland.

It was the last that proved Professor MacNeill's undoing. Erratic in his attendance, unpredictable in his attention to the Commission's business, and philosophic in his reaction to the ferment among the people along the Border whose future was at stake. MacNeill failed to register the sense of outrage that would be provoked in the Free State were the Commission's award, whatever its other recommendations, to rule that part, however small, of the area over which the Free State had jurisdiction was to be transferred to Northern Ireland. Yet precisely that was one of the features of the award on which agreement was reached on 17 October 1925. Overall, 183,200 acres with a population of 31,319 was to be transferred to the Irish Free State while Northern Ireland would acquire 49,242 acres and a population of 7,594. In the former areas there were 27,834 Catholics as against 3,476 others; in the latter, 4,830 others and 2,764 Catholics. The length of the boundary was shortened by 51 miles: 280 to 229.[52]

At this stage neither government had seen a draft of the award and both were evidently unaware of its recommendations. On 7 November a forecast was printed in the *Morning Post*. It was more than reasonably well informed – there is little remaining doubt that Fisher saw to that. Crisis ensued. On 19 November MacNeill acceded to Cosgrave's view that he should resign.[53] On 25 November James MacNeill, Eoin MacNeill's brother and Irish High Commissioner in London, wrote to Desmond Fitzgerald, Minister for External Affairs, expressing a belief that no British government would 'rush' the Free State into acquiescence in the publication of an award and 'risk' violent and continued resistance to the introduction of a new government in east Donegal. MacNeill further encouraged the thought of ministerial talks without the presence of mem-

bers of the Commission and without access by ministers to the award.[54]
Others likewise so inclined. A series of meetings was arranged and took
place in London and at Chequers under Baldwin's chairmanship in late
November and early December, the Free State being represented by
Cosgrave, Kevin O'Higgins, Vice-President of the Executive Council,
Patrick McGilligan and Desmond Fitzgerald.

The course of the discussions is recorded in some detail on the British
side in Cabinet papers and the lively supplement thereto provided by the
relevant entries in Tom Jones' *Diary*,[55] while for the Irish, the subsequent
exchanges in the Dáil at once confirm in outline the course of discussion
and bring out the dilemma in which the Irish government was placed.

On 28 November Baldwin put it to the Irish ministers, O'Higgins,
McGilligan and Fitzgerald, that the only alternatives were to accept the
award or to adopt the existing boundary. They elected to stand by the
existing boundary *if* the North would restore complete civic rights to
the Roman Catholic minority and release political prisoners. Cosgrave's
concern, so Baldwin reported to the Cabinet on 30 November, was to
obtain some concession from Craig in regard to the treatment of Roman
Catholics in the six counties so as to make a boundary settlement on the
basis of the status quo less unpalatable to opinion in the Free State. Craig
felt unable to give him any satisfaction. Cosgrave left for Dublin making it
clear that none the less there was no alternative to acceptance by the Free
State of the existing boundary. In the view of the Irish ministers, the most
likely sequel was that without concessions in regard to the Northern
Catholics, or even with them, they would be swept out of office and a
more uncompromising administration whose aim would be not to uphold
but to wreck the Treaty settlement would replace them.

At this stage in the talks, the documents and map relating to the award
arrived at Chequers. The Free State delegates were unwilling to see the
map but offered no objection to Baldwin's doing so. On inspection
Baldwin remarked on the respects in which the map differed from that in
the *Morning Post*. He also read out the figures (quoted earlier) on the extent
of the territorial and population transfers implementation of the award
would involve. Subsequent talks between O'Higgins and Craig resulted in
Craig telling Baldwin that he was satisfied that what was at the bottom
of the whole difference was Article 5. This on first hearing occasioned
surprise. Article 12 dealt with the boundary; Article 5 with finance. But as
Lord Birkenhead was to observe later, 'I have never in my experience and
recollection of politics discovered that there was anything imponderable . . .
between finance and any other subject known to human politics'.[56]

Article 5 of the Treaty provided that the Irish Free State, embracing the
whole of Ireland, should assume liability for the service of the public debt
and payment of war pensions 'in such proportion as may be fair and
equitable, having regard to any just claims on the part of Ireland by way

of set-off or counter claim'. The article, like Article 12, remained *de faire précisé*. Impending crisis lent an edge of urgency to British and Free State deliberations and their representatives were joined on 29 November by those from Northern Ireland who had secured the substance, but welcomed the prospect of further legislative buttressing of their position. This they obtained in a tripartite agreement,[57] signed on 3 December and subsequently approved by Parliament at Westminster and the Oireachtas. It confirmed the existing boundary, recorded the Free State's assumed responsibility for malicious damage done since 21 January 1919, and released it from its liability for its share of the national debt and certain war pensions.

These concessions were not so readily forthcoming as is generally supposed, Baldwin's initial reaction being that Irish debt liabilities could not be waived *in toto*. It was in the wider context of seeking to eliminate all outstanding points of difference that countervailing arguments were advanced and in the end prevailed.[58] The Council of Ireland, that 'fleshless' and 'bloodless' skeleton, was a first and at the time unlamented casualty, its powers, in so far as they related to Northern Ireland, being transferred to the government of Northern Ireland. In place of the Council there was an assurance that the representatives of the two governments in Ireland would meet to consider matters of mutual concern. There were many such matters – but no meeting – in the lifetime of the Irish Free State. And why? Because any such meetings would have been deemed tantamount to recognition of the legitimacy of the Northern government. If politics is the art of the possible, seemingly it had little to offer in the way of all-Ireland institutions.

Yet it has also to be recorded that the ministerial meetings in 1925 proceeded in an atmosphere of cordiality,[59] as is reflected in the warmth of the wording in the preamble to the Agreement – it spoke of the conclusion of outstanding matters that might impair or retard the growth of friendly relations between governments and peoples. On 3 December Cosgrave 'warmly welcomed' and Craig welcomed 'with enthusiasm' the outcome of the tripartite negotiations, Craig adding a word of appreciation for the statesmanlike attitude of the British government.[60]

Craig had reason for more than satisfaction, Cosgrave to prepare himself for protest and criticism. Challenged by de Valera to hold a referendum, Cosgrave reacted by declaring the passing of the Supplementary Agreement necessary for the immediate preservation of public safety – which, under the constitution, precluded a referendum being held. The debate in the Dáil lasted four days,[61] but in the absence of de Valera and his followers it lacked, as the United States Consul implied,[62] the edge of final conviction. How may this be explained? First, in retrospect, options seem open which contemporaries knew only too well were at that late stage foreclosed. Secondly, the Minister of Post and Telegraphs, who had direction of publicity in respect of the boundary, carried some conviction when arguing that economics and not heroics were going to settle the Border. At a meeting with British ministers on 1 February 1924,[63] J.H. Thomas being in the chair, Cosgrave contended that the division of the country was arbitrary – one side was unrepresented. Craig thereupon read out the text of Lloyd George's letter to Carson of 29 May 1916: 'We have', he said, 'nothing to give away after giving away three counties. We were asked "will you give up three counties and work the Act of 1920?"' (Actually he was asked whether he would take nine and replied asking for six.) That he implied was enough; Kevin O'Higgins reacted with some asperity, exclaiming 'we are not the political disciples or descendants of John Redmond, Joe Devlin, Stephen Gwynn', or in other words, they were not bound by concessions their discredited Nationalist predecessors were prepared to make to further Lloyd George's devious diplomacy in 1916. Yet how hard it was to escape from the constraints of the past! De Valera sounded one cautionary note for the future. As he was to tell J.H. Thomas in 1932, experience of one Commonwealth arbitrator was a conclusive argument against the appointment of another.

PART V

THE TESTING OF THE SETTLEMENT

CHAPTER 11
The Settlement in Being: Northern Ireland

Institutionally the settlement in its twofold formulation was a new departure. What was new was not, however, common to both. Devolution as a concept of general application had been the subject of intermittent discussion before the war and of conference enquiry after it; dominion status, well established overseas, was introduced into the British Isles not by way of natural evolutionary process, but by way of near-desperate resort to resolve the Irish question. Each therefore was experimental and for political scientists, a subject of interest in its own institutional right. Here, however, attention is confined to the Irish aspect only, with interest focused on what might be thought of as directly traceable to, or having had significant bearing on the working of the settlement. Were one to attempt to consider all that took place under it, not two chapters but a history would be needed. Within that wider range there are matters that were much debated in the making of the settlement, closely associated with its working, illustrative of its nature and to be reckoned among the causes of its undoing. It is to such aspects broadly conceived that this and the next chapter are addressed.

Devolution: the Institutional Factor

Until towards the end of the war, devolution had been discussed not in an Irish but an imperial context. It was put forward as a device to lighten the great volume of work falling on parliament at Westminster by devolving responsibility for regional affairs upon regional assemblies and administrative offices. By 1919 there was enough momentum behind the idea to persuade parliament to call a conference[1] representative of both Houses, and with the Speaker of the House of Commons as chairman, to explore the question further. The terms of reference were set out in a Resolution of the House of Commons dated 4 June 1919, requesting the conference 'to consider and report upon a measure of Federal Devolution applicable to England, Scotland and Ireland'. So it was not the responsibility of the conference to decide whether, in the words of the Resolution, 'the time has come for the creation of subordinate legislatures within the United Kingdom . . .' – that had been accepted – but to advise on how it might be done.

The conference failed, on the surface because of inability to reach agreement on the composition of the local legislatures and the allocation of financial responsibility between the Imperial and local parliaments, but basically, as the chairman, Speaker Lowther, later judged, because the discussions were 'academic rather then practical' and lacked 'the driving force of necessity'.[2] That was that so far as Great Britain was concerned, the conference had done what it was expected to do – namely, to offer a forum for debate and in so doing ensure that the question would be shelved for the foreseeable future. But in Northern Ireland the Speaker's comments did not apply. Acclaimed or condemned, devolution in the six counties rarely lapsed into the academical. On the contrary, reactions there, as reported by Carson to the House of Commons debate on the Resolution, diverted attention from the purpose it was designed to serve. Others might profess concern at the burden on central government. Carson used it to divert discussion to the implications for the future of Ulster. By way of tangential consequence of the conference's negative outcome, Northern Ireland was left to tread the devolutionary road alone.

The local self-government set up in Northern Ireland had one principal and one subsidiary purpose. The first was to provide a bulwark – the word was much used – for Ulster Unionists against Dublin, or Rome, rule; the second to effect a transfer of responsibility for the day-to-day government of the six counties from British to Irish hands. The Government of Ireland Act 1920, which was Northern Ireland's constituent Act, met both primary and secondary purposes. It was drafted for application in Southern as well as in Northern Ireland. That was of the essence. Principally it was because of its prospective extension to the twenty-six counties that the institutions of local self-government or devolution in the six were on so elaborate a scale.

The Northern Irish legislature was bicameral and in addition there was reduced, but continuing, representation (13 members) at Westminster; there was a Governor as Representative of the Crown to summon, prorogue and dissolve parliament in the name of the King and to withhold the Royal Assent to Bills when so instructed by the Imperial government;[3] there was a Prime Minister (not as might be expected a Premier, as in Canadian provinces and Australian states) and a Cabinet which in Sir James Craig's first government numbered six members, responsible for the work of seven departments. Much of this was planned on a scale that in the stringent years to follow came under criticism as over-elaborate, even by Unionists.

The division of powers between imperial and local parliaments was on lines made familiar in the Home Rule Bills.[4] The classes of government business specifically *excluded* from the competence of the local legislature were threefold: (1) matters of imperial concern called *excepted* matters all on conventional lines, that is the Crown, peace and war, foreign affairs and the Services; (2) certain matters *reserved* to the Imperial Parliament including postal services, land purchase, the levying of customs duties and the principal forms of taxation, on none of which the Northern Ireland Parliament had power to legislate; and (3) matters within the competence of the Council of Ireland until 1925, when, in so far as they related to Northern Ireland, they were transferred to Northern Ireland. The enactment of discriminatory legislation as between members of different creeds was debarred. The electoral system was entrenched on its existing proportional representation (PR) basis but only for three years.[5] The crucial factor, however, was the authority given to the parliament of Northern Ireland to make laws for the peace, order and good government of Northern Ireland. The phrase was used in a restrictive sense, yet its implications in a divided society were far-reaching. It was not Whitehall but Stormont that was to bear responsibility for community relations in a bitterly divided society.

Devolution: The Financial Factor[6]

Northern Ireland was not brought into existence for financial or economic reasons. There were economic interests to be protected but few or none to be advanced. In the deliberations that preceded Northern Ireland's creation, remarkably little attention was given to them. It was a political entity that the Ulster Unionists wished to establish, not an economic one. For that there was no case. It is otiose to say that with the six counties as an economic unit it has proved a near disaster. What was in mind was an arrangement, which would enable an admittedly artificial unit in economic terms to survive with a semblance of viability. So much even in stringent times could clearly be contrived – at a price which the United Kingdom exchequer quite reasonably would hope to meet.

In all schemes of devolution, the financial factor, by which in this context is meant principally the allocation of financial powers between the imperial and local parliament, is at once of fundamental importance and difficult to determine, if only because what appears equitable and practical in the abstract is likely to require stretching or foreshortening to fit the procrustean bed of local circumstances. In that Nothern Ireland was no exception. But it was not so much special problems as problems of special intensity that came to demand radical review. They arose from the disparity between Northern Ireland's living standards and those of the rest of the United Kingdom. This was associated with Northern Ireland's economic vulnerability consequent upon her traditional dependence on agriculture, linen and shipbuilding, the last two of which exposed its inhabitants to severe incidence of unemployment in years of depression. At Cabinet and Cabinet committee or conference meetings at the time of the settlement, allusions were made, notably by Lloyd George, to the potential wealth of Ireland in general and Northern Ireland in particular in terms which remain astonishing, even bearing in mind special and transient factors such as the post-war boom in agricultural products, the ready market for linen and shipyards working to capacity. As a result, particular financial provisions in the Government of Ireland Act 1920 were made on assumptions that were ill founded. It was a misapprehension to be corrected only by time and experience and which meanwhile imposed strain on Stormont–Westminster relations.

At the heart of the financial relationship at the outset was the Imperial contribution. This was a payment to cover Northern Ireland's share of the cost of the Imperial services. It was fixed in the Act of 1920 at the figure of £7.92 million. This proved quite beyond Northern Ireland's capacity to pay once harder times returned. A committee under the chairmanship of Lord Colwyn was therefore appointed.[7] In 1925 it recommended that the contribution should no longer be on a fixed but a fluctuating basis, the formula adopted for calculating its amount being based on relative taxable capacity. That was to be determined, so the Colwyn Report recommended, by the extent to which the total revenue exceeded the actual and necessary expenditure in Northern Ireland. In its turn, the amount of the necessary expenditure in Northern Ireland was determined each year by the Joint Exchequer Board. Negatively expenditure in Northern Ireland on any service providing its people with a higher average standard than was enjoyed in Great Britain would almost, if not quite, certainly be disallowed. On the positive side, the formula, resting as it did on the assumption that the same rates of taxation and of services should prevail in Northern Ireland as in Great Britain, was favourable to Northern Ireland. The fundamental change, which redressed an inequitable balance, was that the amount of its Imperial contribution was fixed in accordance with Northern Ireland's capacity to pay and *not*, as hitherto, in accordance with an assessment of Imperial needs. This was 'spelled out' statistically in the returns. The contribution, which was £1.35 million in 1926–27, dropped to the nominal figure of £10,000 for 1934–35 and 1935–36. In the war years it rose sharply to £36.3 million and thereafter fluctuated, the return for 1953–54 being £9.6 million.

While the Imperial contribution in earlier years constituted the centre-piece, there were further grants for particular purposes, which were of great significance later; among them were a contribution towards the building of Stormont, together with three subventions made by the Imperial exchequer to Northern Ireland each financial year; much the most important of these was that made under the terms of the Unemployment Insurance Agreement Act of 1926.

Northern Ireland for the greater part of its existence suffered from a percentage rate of unemployment considerably higher than that of the United Kingdom as a whole. This presented the Northern government with a problem of some complexity since in any event, heavy and growing expenditure on social services was necessary to keep such services in parity with those in Great Britain. Increased taxation in Northern Ireland, in itself undesirable, afforded no solution since, as already noted, it was not within the competence of the local parliament to impose taxation on a scale sufficient to meet the need. In 1926, an agreement was reached with the Imperial exchequer aimed at assimilating the burdens on the respective exchequers in respect of unemployment insurance. Under this agreement, the two funds were to be kept in a state of parity by the payment to the poorer exchequer of a grant equivalent to three-quarters of the sum required to equalise *per head of the total population* the payments out of the two exchequers into their respective unemployment funds. Even this provided a temporary respite, rather than a solution. In the years 1934–36 the Northern Ireland budget was balanced only by drawing on the reserve fund. The case for a new agreement more favourable to Northern Ireland was *prima facie* a strong one. In 1936 it was negotiated. Like the 1926 Agreement, its 1936 successor was reciprocal in form, identical in an assimilationist aim but with the method of calculation to be followed changed in one vital respect. The 1936 Agreement provided for mutual insurance against excess of unemployment on either side so as to keep the fund in a state of parity in both areas, though in practice Northern Ireland with its excess of unemployment would be the principal or only beneficiary. In 1935–36 Northern Ireland received a threefold increase in grant as against what it would have been due under the old Agreement: £722,000 as against £275,000.

Since the proportion of insured to general population was very much smaller in Northern Ireland, the new agreement provided a very welcome supplement to its financial resources. Under the older Agreement, for example, no grant was received from 1932 to 1935, whereas under the new, £1.2 million was paid in equalisation payment in 1937–38. 'The real outcome of the new arrangement', said the Minister of Finance, '. . . is that, in years of depression we will pay less Imperial contribution and receive a considerable sum for unemployment expenditure, in normal years we will receive less for unemployment and pay more Imperial contribution, while in prosperity we would receive nothing for unemployment and pay a still larger Imperial contribution'.[8] In fact a sceptic might observe that while reciprocity was to be the accepted principle, the Northern Ireland exchequer was the sole beneficiary. Given the differentials in social and economic conditions, this may be judged to be as it should. There is no doubt it was in accord with government policy in Belfast. As the Minister of Labour, J.M. Andrews observed on 25 March 1936, 'the

House has repeatedly endorsed the policy which the government has maintained for 15 years . . . that the same rates of benefit should be paid under the social insurance schemes for the same rates of contribution as obtain throughout the rest of the United Kingdom.'[9] The whole basis of Northern Ireland's relations with Britain, noted Major Sinclair, Minister of Finance, ten years later, could be summed up in one word – 'parity' – which meant that if they had the same taxation, that is taxation at the same rates irrespective of the amount per week, they were entitled as citizens of the United Kingdom to the same social services. But this had other and broader consequences, notably that of drawing Imperial departments further back into Northern Ireland financing and administration, and, by way of counterpart, of fostering Northern Ireland's social and economic development within a British context.

On Labour benches at Westminster there surfaced from time to time a feeling that the Ulstermen, like the Dutch, offered too little and asked far too much. The exchequer, it was contended, should turn the screw, they should not make payment to Stormont until they had received from Stormont the contribution which represented Northern Ireland's contribution to imperial services. A bit of home truth for its pantomime parliament, one Labour member ventured, would not be misplaced. At root what was at issue, however, was not particular extravagance on the one side or niggardliness on the other but the finding of a right balance in financial responsibility between Imperial and local parliaments such as the Act of 1920, with its contingent arrangements, had manifestly failed to provide. The conditioning factor was that Northern Ireland was not a viable economic entity.

Devolution: the Status Factor

The style of government, aptly symbolised by Stormont's granite pile, little reflected underlying fiscal exigencies. Stormont was the product of other less tangible considerations compounded as much of inner uncertainty as of triumphalist Unionism. Captain Charles Craig had told the House of Commons that the 1920 Act would give Ulster Unionists almost all the Covenanters had fought for before the First World War; his brother, Sir James, told Lloyd George than in accepting the 1920 Act Ulster had made 'the supreme sacrifice'. In consenting to the establishment of a separate parliament much against their wishes, wrote Craig, they had acted in the interests of peace and as 'a *final settlement* of the long outstanding difficulty with which Great Britain had been confronted'.[10] No government, he said, had ever had a more settled policy than that of Ulster: 'that policy is to retain a parliament of our own and not to come under a Dublin parliament'. To this end the importance of local parliamentary institutions must not be minimised.[11] 'There must', he said 'be a dignity about our Parliament . . . so that no opponents at any time dare come forward and say of that great structure . . . that is only a small affair, and we can easily sweep it to one side'.[12]

The frequency of assertions of this kind from the outset of Northern Ireland's existence as a political entity are customarily attributed to a concern to interpose literally and symbolically a barrier of Northern granite against nationalist claims, whether advanced by members of a resentful minority unreconciled to the six-county institutions under whose jurisdiction perforce they came or of Free Staters, or Sinn Féiners as they continued to be called, from South of the Border. Craig conceived of an Ulster fighting a dialectical battle, which at times became a good deal more, to ensure continued Unionist predominance in the six counties. But it was not only on an Irish front that he had to be on guard. Apart from Asquithian Liberals, an unreliable but fortunately declining force, there was in the 1920s emergent Labour, whose spokesmen in 1920 had deployed the language of self-determination and who, as they entered upon the struggle for power, were not likely to overlook the phalanx of Ulster Unionist MPs at Westminster – ordinarily 11 out of 13 – lined up against them. Only in the Baldwin–Neville Chamberlain years – and even here Chamberlain with his 1938 agreement with de Valera aroused uneasiness – did Ulster Unionists feel they might lower their guard. It may, however, be asked, were these not groundless, or at least much exaggerated fears? What British leader would contemplate 'betrayal' of Ulster? And if he did, was not Ulster's position assured even in respect of area by the 1920 Act itself?

The answer was that it was as secure in law, neither more nor less, than any provision or arrangement made by an Act of Parliament. As in 1912–14, the position remained that in the United Kingdom there was no written constitution or corpus of 'organic' legislation specially entrenched. It is true that this was questioned on the ground that with the coming into existence of Northern Ireland, in conjunction with subsequent enactments and growth of convention consequential upon its establishment, the United Kingdom had become a federal state. But the distinguishing characteristics of a federation were lacking.[13] There was, it is true, a written constitution in which the powers of the central and provincial governments are listed, as also separately concurrent powers shared between them. Where in a federation one would look for coordination of power with the imperial and provincial governments each sovereign in its own sphere, one finds assertion of a single sovereignty and not coordination, but subordination. On this Section 75 of the Act of 1920 could hardly be more explicit. It reads: 'Notwithstanding the establishment of the Parliament of Northern Ireland . . . the supreme authority of the Parliament of the United Kingdom shall remain unaffected and undiminished over all persons, matters and things in Northern Ireland.'

Neither the Ireland Act 1949, nor its 1972 sequel (enacted in circumstances to be described later) though giving an assurance that the Six Counties would remain within the United Kingdom so long as the majority of its parliament (1949) or its people (1972) desired, repealed the 1920 Act and accordingly Section 75 of that Act remains in full force.

It has been further contended that constitutions may at the least be modified in other than statutory ways, for example by judicial interpretation, custom or convention, and examples of this have been given. But if one returns to what is deemed to be the telling question – 'Where does power of constitutional amendment reside?'[14] – the answer, 'With parliament at Westminster', is inescapable.

The assertions of Craig and his successors in so far as they related to Northern Ireland's governmental institutions were contributions to another – a domestic – debate. At the time of the settlement, once it was conceded that the north-eastern counties might form a subordinate political entity, three possibilities in respect of its government were canvassed. They were that the excluded area should continue to be an integral part of the United Kingdom; that it should have its own local parliamentary and departmental institutions, and that it should become a Dominion or its near equivalent. The second was chosen, but the debate was never quite foreclosed. As a result, from time to time the Northern Ireland establishment found it necessary to discountenance signs of restlessness among their supporters at the limitations imposed by devolution on their freedom of action. In 1936 the Ulster Unionist Council were sufficiently disturbed to warn their members that the cry of 'Back to Westminster' was 'a subtle move fraught with great danger. Had we refused to accept a Parliament for Northern Ireland and remained at Westminster . . . we would be either inside the Free State or fighting desperately against incorporation. Northern Ireland without a Parliament of her own would be a standing temptation to certain British politicians to make another bid for a final settlement with Irish Republicans.'[15] J.M. Andrews spoke in similar strain, saying 'the Irish Free State people know in their hearts they can never reach the goal of an all-Ireland Republic, because Ulster blocks the way . . . we are . . . determined, to hold what we have got' and 'to maintain our Parliament'.[16] The implication was clear. Speculation among Unionists about whether they might fare better under direct Imperial governance incurred the risk of stimulating debate among British politicians and Irish republicans about the future government of the six counties. None the less speculation on whether devolution offered the best of all possible worlds was intermittently revived.

During and after the Second World War some influential Unionists drew attention to the advantages of moving in the opposite direction, that of consolidating the existing local institutions and investing them with wider responsibilities. Decentralisation was their theme, its formulation

prompted by reaction against wartime centralisation and the prospect of
more to follow in peace time with socialist policies in the ascendant at
Westminster. In March 1943 the Prime Minister, J.M. Andrews, was
urged to bring the Beveridge Report into operation in Northern Ireland
before it was given legislative effect in Great Britain.[17] In response, he
warned members that 'if we were to go on our own it would be folly'.
Northern Ireland was one of the poorer parts of the United Kingdom and
largely dependent on foreign trade and three great industries. It was not
well placed to sustain Beveridge welfare services without the support of
other areas more favourably circumstanced. 'Our claim', he concluded,
'here is that as part of the United Kingdom we have the right to expect the
same security'.

In 1945 difficulties in cooperation between a Unionist government at
Stormont, its electoral mandate reaffirmed in May 1945, and Attlee's
socialist administration, triumphantly returned two months later, were
widely anticipated. In that situation, would not greater local responsibility
on the dominion model have positive attractions as well as inbuilt safeguards? In November the Ministers of Labour and Commerce urged the
Northern Ireland Cabinet that Stormont should become a truly responsible parliament instead of one that would be reduced 'to the status of a
department of the imperial government'.[18] That would bring relief 'from
the constant anxiety as to what an unfriendly British Government might
be tempted to do in the way of pressing us to end partition'. In a long
memorandum to the Cabinet on 6 January 1946 Sir Roland Nugent argued
that there were two main dangers – one was that the Imperial government
would pass a measure Stormont could not accept, thus precipitating
an immediate crisis, and the other that they would 'whittle away our
independence piecemeal, not intentionally, but in the normal course of
developing their own plans'. It was the second that was the more serious
because each separate move would seem hardly worth fighting. Then
the temptation would arise that Northern Ireland should return to Westminster, restoring uniformity to the United Kingdom. It would be difficult to resist. And while *all* courses were dangerous, it would be wise to
balance out the dangers implicit in each lest the Union itself be imperilled.
His own balance sheet pointed to dominion status but not necessarily the
whole way. The exercise even of such a qualified dominion option invited
the question of who was to foot the bill for a welfare service in the six
counties on the mainland level short of subsidies unlikely to be granted
without Treasury or other central control.

In the event, misgivings about metropolitan attitudes proved groundless in the post-war years. Northern Ireland's wartime record and contributions left a substantial residue of good will on which Northern Ireland
could rely when problems arose. There were no reservations on aim, few
outward difficulties in collaboration and little evidence of political inhibi-

tions. The Unionist members denounced Labour's socialist measures at Westminster, while at Stormont pressing for their early extension to the six counties, so that they would keep in step with the provisions being made in Great Britain for hospitals, schools and state-subsidised housing, the allocation of the last of which touched upon one of the most sensitive of inter-communal issues.[19]

With every extension of state services the policy of 'step by step' became progressively more embedded in the Westminster–Stormont financial relationship. By stages the financial provisions of the 1920 Act withered away or, as Professor Lawrence phrased it,[20] became 'legal fictions', thereby partly disguising the erosion in practice of local powers over taxation and expenditure which had its natural counterpart in progressive concentration of policy determination in London. 'It is an exaggeration', wrote Professor Lawrence, 'to say that Northern Ireland has reverted to the position of Ireland under the Union and is part of a common Exchequer, but it is not a great exaggeration'.

In respect of finance and social welfare, one conclusion may also be drawn and one other consequence remarked upon. In the war years and after, Whitehall became committed to sustaining the Northern Irish experiment in devolution which had been devised to allow for progressive British extrication from the affairs of Ireland as a whole, and it may be remarked that progressive British involvement had in its turn introduced a new differential between North and South with the social services in the North at once of more extended application and higher standard than those of the South.[21]

Devolution: The Representational Factor

The last of the trilogy, devolution, finance and representation was from the outset a conditioning factor. On 12 February 1920 the editor of the *Spectator*, St Loe Strachey, in correspondence with Carson about the area to be excluded from the jurisdiction of an Irish parliament described the six-county area as 'the essential homogeneous area' adding, however, that the ideal plan would be to take Ulster as a whole and 'then cast out therefrom as many Catholic districts, unions and parishes as could possibly be eliminated' by an enlightened Boundary Commission 'intent upon getting nothing but the maximum of homogeneity for the North-East Ulster area'.[22] If, as seemed probable, this resulted in a 'jigsaw puzzle' of a Border line, it did not worry Strachey so long as the result was greater concentration of both Protestants and Catholics. He realised the time for such a solution was past but he underlined the need for principle – 'we must put ourselves right with the stupid, muddle-headed people of England by having a definite, clear and just scheme for partition'. Carson, in deprecating thoughts of a Boundary Commission, felt it must be six or nine counties.[23] This was something to be determined by practical consideration of what would best ensure lasting Unionist predominance. As already seen, Sinn Féin thought partition itself would be the more vulnerable, the less defensible on grounds of principle was the partition line. But Strachey was writing to Carson and not to Sinn Féin. It was in Carson's, not Sinn Féin's interest that if there was a boundary, it should rest upon a defensible foundation. By early twentieth-century criteria, that meant a minimal modification on practical grounds and otherwise respect for the wishes of the inhabitants. But despite concern expressed by some Liberal members of the Cabinet, such criteria were not to be applied. The Ulster Unionist leaders were given the choice between exclusion of a six- or nine-county area. Their option for the six was the largest area, so they judged, that they could hold indefinitely. No Unionist leader pressed the question, principle aside, of whether it would not be *wiser* in the Unionist interest to opt for a smaller area. That woud still have left the Northern Ireland government with a formidable assignment, but not one of the order of magnitude which they assumed.

It is a matter of some surprise that the Ulster Unionists, having obtained the balance in population they themselves desired, could not leave well alone. Yet having obtained an assured majority, they wanted more, regardless of minority fears as well as resentment. High on their list was the alteration of the prescribed electoral laws in parliamentary as distinct from local elections.[24] The Government of Ireland Act 1920 provided that all matters relating to the franchise, to the system of election, to the size of parliamentary constituencies and the distribution of members amongst them was to lie outside the jurisdiction of the Northern Parliament for a period of *three years*, dating from the first meeting of the parliament in Belfast. In addition, the Act ruled that in any new distribution sanctioned by the Northern Parliament after the lapse of this probationary period, the number of the members should not be altered and due regard should be paid to the populations of the constituencies.

The Belfast government, making no secret of its dislike for PR, proceeded with unseemly haste to abolish it when and where it could, in the first instance in local elections. Michael Collins on behalf of the Provisional Government entered forceful objections. It was not, he protested, a domestic matter. On the contrary, it was intended to sway the judgement of the Boundary Commission when appointed. It affected Article 12 of the Treaty and was an attempt to prejudice future action implementing it, notably by altering majority–minority representation on the Tyrone and Fermanagh County Councils. It was a matter affecting the minority and the moral obligation to seek at least their acquiescence had not been respected. The Lord-Lieutenant at the behest of Churchill as Colonial Secretary initially withheld his assent.[25] The Northern gov-

ernment countered by maintaining that the matter was within their jurisdiction and that they were in the position, so their legal adviser asserted,
of a Dominion and, were assent to have been withheld in a Dominion, it
would have provoked a constitutional crisis. Craig was prepared for one –
no election issue could be more popular in Northern Ireland than one
resisting the Imperial government's interference encouraged by Sinn Féin
in Ulster's domestic affairs which were 'our direct rights'. But while
Unionists were ready for the fray the British government was not. There
was compromise on deferment of legislation until after the Boundary
Commission, but no deflection of Unionist interest.[26]

Ulster Unionist leaders publicly proclaimed their further intention of
abolishing PR before the second general election held in Northern Ireland.
The surprise, therefore, lay not in the fact that the parliamentary electoral
law was amended but in that it remained unamended till 1929. For three
years, as already noted, the Northern Parliament had not the constitutional
power to alter the system of election, but that period elapsed on 7 June
1924. Craig was challenged by his supporters on the failure of his government to act forthwith. He replied that 'there are certain very grave
considerations that I am not at liberty to announce in the House, that
made it necessary to carry out the last election under P.R., much as I object to the system'.[27] These considerations took into account the earlier
exchanges on the abolition of PR in local elections, which had made it
abundantly clear that the abolition of PR was likely to be viewed with
disfavour in London – a consequence that could not be regarded with
equanimity in Belfast, so long as the boundary clause held out possibilities
of territorial readjustment. Meanwhile, however, Unionist denunciations
of PR had continued unabated, with as early as February 1924 the parliamentary draftsman, Sir Arthur Quekett, submitting the draft of a Bill
on redistribition of seats and method of voting.[28] A whole range of
possibilities for further strengthening Unionist political predominance
seemed to be opening up. The member for Enniskillen, James Cooper,
also in February 1924, adumbrated in a letter to Craig the thought that
with some little adjustments along the Border but without taking in pieces
so large as electoral divisions, it would not take very much chopping and
changes to make Fermanagh and Tyrone into two safe Unionist seats –
explicit in the proposition being the contention that the Irish Free State
had really 'very little claim to much of our territory', and 'we have one
quite as much'.[29] A Unionist deputation from the City and County of
Londonderry further proposed redistribution of seats as a result of which
City and County would return five Unionist members and so put an end
'to Nationalist aggression for all time'.[30] Neither bore fruit and on the
parliamentary in sharp distinction to the local level, there was partiality
but not on an exceptional scale. At the Orange celebrations in 1927,
Viscount Craigavon of Stormont announced the forthcoming abolition of

PR. But the timing needed to be right. On 19 September Herbert Dixon, Chief Whip (later Lord Glentoran) advised Craig that if they brought in the Bill at once they would have 'an uncomfortable time for the rest of the Session as of course the Nationalist and Labour people will oppose it bitterly and from the time we pass it, I do not think we will have very much peace or comfort in the House'. He advised leaving the draft in a drawer to be brought out 'at any moment when it suited us'.[31] The Prime Minister, however, noted, 'our own people might object to such tactics'.

Finally, on 25 October 1927, the Prime Minister introduced the Bill setting out the redistribution of seats and abolishing PR.[32] In so doing he pointed to the desirability of eliminating all minorities except that represented by the Nationalist party. This would mean that Ulster's political life would be confined to a straight fight on the traditional Protestant–Catholic, Unionist–Nationalist lines; and one in which, on a population basis, the Unionists were assured of victory. Craigavon, who kept the question of PR on the parliamentary side very much in his own hands, was explicit about the purpose he had in mind. It was the elimination of minorities, not least dissident Unionist minorities, and the consequent development of a stable two-party system in which the Unionists and the Nationalists, 'the two active, alert, vigorous, parties in Ulster', confronted one another in unchanging roles of victor and vanquished over the 'fundamental' issue of Unionism or Nationalism, the Union Jack or the Tricolour.[33]

While the likely consequences of electoral reform held obvious attractions for the Prime Minister, they could not be viewed with favour by the Labour party, whose political existence in Northern Ireland the measure was intended to terminate. In 1926 the Belfast Trades and Labour Council protested strongly against the declared intention of the government to abolish PR,[34] and in the autumn session of the Commons, 1927, the leader of the Labour party moved the appointment of a select committee to enquire into the authority of the government to carry out electoral reform on the lines proposed.[35] The debates both on this motion and subsequently on the government's Bill were marked with extreme bitterness. Kyle, the leader of the Labour party, allowed that in practice PR might not be perfect but held that it was not entirely its merits that were under discussion. There was also the question of minority rights guaranteed in the Act of 1920. 'It seems to me', he said, '. . . the abolition of PR is deliberately designed to favour the Unionist Party . . . and so make it the more difficult for minority opinion to be represented in this House'. Joe Devlin, leader of the Nationalists, thought much the same. 'I think', he said in the House, 'this is a mean, contemptible and a callous attempt by the majority which you now have to rob the minority . . . of the safeguard which was incorporated in this Measure . . . [as] an essential feature . . . in the task of national pacification'.[36] Outside the House equally vigorous protests were made. It is sufficient to refer to one of them. In January 1928, a manifesto addressed 'To the People of the Six Counties' was published under the signature of fourteen members of the House of Commons. The signatories included nine Nationalist MPs, three Labour MPs, an Independent Unionist and an Independent.[37] The manifesto protested against the 'glaring injustices' suffered by minorities in Ulster and specially condemned as the culminating Unionist triumph the proposed abolition of PR, 'an eminently fair system of representation', which the British legislature embodied in the Act of 1920, and which was intended for, and by the minority accepted as a safeguard of their meagre 'rights'.

The reasons given by the Prime Minister for the abolition of PR were such as are usually advanced by its opponents. He claimed that the cost was excessive, that the constituencies were far too large and as a consequence that members 'feel, as conscientious Ulstermen, that they are not able to give to the whole of those wide constituencies that meticulous care and attention that the electors are really entitled to receive'. In addition, he pointed to the menace of a multiplicity of parties such as PR is generally supposed to create, he argued that the system was bound 'in the end to result in confusion amongst the electors, who will hardly know whom they are voting for', and as 'loyal Ulstermen' they would prefer to vote under the same system as that in force in Great Britain.[38] 'How', he asked, 'would this little Ulster of ours like to be in the same position as Italy' with 'a Government trembling' and changing from year to year?

Some of the Unionist criticisms of PR were undeniably just. The introduction of PR did, in fact, involve a certain financial outlay, though the cost of subsequent elections could hardly be deemed a serious consideration. Certain of the constituencies were large and unwieldy; but then that might be remedied by reducing their size instead of by abolishing PR. The loss of the personal touch between members and their constituencies provided a familiar and legitimate ground for criticism. Once again smaller constituencies would have diminished its force. But there was no need to seek for complex reasons. There was a simple one. Patrick Buckland has put it in a sentence: 'PR was abolished and electoral boundaries redrawn in the interests of Unionism and the Unionist Party with scant regard for, or recognition of, the special interests and views of other sections of the community.'[39] Yet if that verdict be allowed to stand historically, the question arises: was it from the Unionist point of view worthwhile? They were secure in their Northern stronghold: their majorities in a sufficiency, or more than a sufficiency, of parliamentary seats were ensured whatever the electoral system for the foreseeable time. Why then revive at the parliamentary level all the criticism and obloquy abolition of PR provoked? Was it all an aberration of Craigavon's? Or of the Ulster Unionists, heedless on the longer term of one more unfavourable impression notched up in the British mind against this one time unconciliatory anti-Home Rule minority, now an oppressive majority? Or was he, and were they, well advised to perceive and guard against fissiparous tendencies likely to be nourished in the ruling party by long years of uninterrupted office, and in seeking to counter them by depriving minorities in his own party of favourable opportunity for effective political action? As against opinions formed fifty years ago,[40] there is reason now to concede that there was more substance in his misgivings on that score than was apparent then.

By June 1925 the electoral system in the six counties had in both its local and parliamentary manifestations come within Stormont's field of responsibility. With that the nature of devolutionary government and the range of its responsibilities was complete. As for its working, the British revealed no pronounced sense of continuing commitment. The experience of amendment of the local government PR electoral system in itself sufficed to confirm the wish on their part to retreat from this contentious field. The small Northern Ireland Office, unobtrusively housed and keeping a low profile in an outpost of the Home Office in London, sufficiently conveyed their sense of the little that was required of them. Dr Laffan has illustrated this state of mind with the story of a delegation of Northern Irish Labour MPs, who arrived unannounced in the office of Sir William Joynson-Hicks, the British Home Secretary, to protest against Craig's plan to abolish PR in parliamentary elections. Joynson-Hicks told them, according to the account he sent Craigavon, that 'of course this was a matter for the Ulster Parliament, and not for myself, but that I should feel in duty bound to tell you [Craigavon] of the Deputation'. Of Craigavon, the Home Secretary further enquired, 'I don't know whether you would care at any time to discuss the matter with me; of course I am always at your disposal. But beyond that I "know my place" and don't propose to interfere.' Dr Laffan comments, 'one can almost hear the splash of water as he washed his hands of any responsibility for protecting northern minorities'.[41] Quite so. But responsibility for that rested more widely than Dr Laffan implies. Had Joynson-Hicks intervened, he would have faced the wrath of Craig, something in itself formidable and all the more so when what was at issue was his pursuit of his own chosen course, along which he was authorised by statute to proceed, if he so wished, as he was doing. If there were to be appeals to the British government in respect of responsibilities that had been devolved, provision should have been made for them. The point was not altogether overlooked. In the course of the London discussions on the Boundary Commission Report on 1 December 1925, it was proposed informally by Lord Salisbury that there should be an acknowledged liaison officer appointed by the Catholics of north-east Ireland authorised to represent their grievances to the government of Northern Ireland. Cosgrave asked, 'Who is going to carry the baby?' Churchill replied, 'We've all got to carry a bit', by which he evidently had foremost in mind the two Irish governments but with the British not excluded. Cosgrave remarked that he was thinking of Tyrone and Fermanagh nationalists 'who have not got into the Free State'. O'Higgins added, 'restore Proportional Representation of 1920. It was designed to provide adequate parliamentary representation for minorities.' Craig demurred. PR was proving 'a failure all over the world . . . I can't stick PR. Does not seem to be British. Too Continental.'[42] That was that. And so it remained. In 1936 another deputation, this time pressing for an enquiry into the sectarian riots the previous year, received from Baldwin the uncompromising answer that it was entirely a matter for the government of Northern Ireland. Domestically no doubt it served, but in the world at large the damage, despite the shelving of responsibility, was to the reputation of Britain.[43]

In retrospect, the incident underlines a gap in the settlement, the result of some oversight in thinking about devolution in practice. In general, devolution had been the subject of enquiry, but in the context of devolution all round, without sufficient regard to the special problems of the bi-cultural, bi-communal political entity that was Northern Ireland. In sum it was a political device, but for situations other than this.

In the six counties distinctive considerations prevailed. They permeated almost every action and dominated life itself – with community calculation, and sometimes cheerfulness, breaking in. Of that one example may suffice, touching as it does on the graver questions of Northern Ireland's relations with Britain as they were (and are) and not as ironed out in textbook generalisations.

In May 1956 the British government decided to increase family allowances for the third and subsequent children by 2 shillings a week, with a view to easing the burden on poorer and larger families. In the ordinary way the Northern Ireland government in accord with the 'step by step' policy grounded in the concept of parity would have followed the same course. But in the Northern Ireland Cabinet what were deemed to be extraordinary considerations counselled departure from ordinary practice. At a Cabinet meeting on 9 May 1956, the Minister of Labour and National Insurance pointed out that these proposals, if adopted, would mean an increase of 12 per cent in the total expenditure on family allowances. It was not, as became clear as discussion continued, this that troubled him – or his colleagues. It was the size of Catholic families, something not to be encouraged by allowances without limit. The Minister of Finance had taken the precaution of sounding out the Treasury, where he was reassured to learn that the 'variations to suit local conditions' would not be regarded as a breach of parity. The Minister of Labour, thereupon, unfolded the occasion of their concern. It stemmed from representations from Unionist back-benchers that a scheme identical with Britain was unsuitable for Northern Ireland. The Minister of Education advised caution. He doubted the wisdom of any departure from 'strict parity', as it might be represented as a weakening of Northern Ireland's position as an integral part of the United Kingdom. Besides, the proposed departure from parity might not achieve the desired objective as members of the minority community 'would continue to have large families irrespective of the scale of family allowances'. Mr Hanna, the Member for Antrim, pointed out that the number, as well as the size, of large families had increased and felt that family allowances had been a contributory factor. Terence O'Neill warned that encouragement of large families would 'simply intensify the unemployment problem', and noted that in some areas there had been departures from British practice.

The upshot was a Cabinet decision to give allowances for second and third but not, as in Britain, for subsequent children. There was a storm of protest. The Nationalists had no doubt this was discrimination against Catholics with their traditionally large families, while Presbyterians and the trade unions denounced it as a blow against the poorest members of the community. By 31 May the Minister of Education was convinced they had made a mistake and should rescind it. The break with parity, he warned, would be regarded at Westminster as the abandonment of a basic principle, 'the consequences of which might be incalculable'. Others were sensitive to the difficulty in rebutting the charge of discrimina-tion against the minority. Moreover, some Unionist party members had deplored the 'deviation', as it was termed, from parity and felt that the Cabinet would incur greater discredit in adhering to a 'wrong' decision than in reversing it.

Despite the criticism, the Cabinet stood firm provided the 'deviant' Bill commanded sufficient back-bench support. That, however, was not put to the test. On 7 January the Prime Minister, Lord Brookeborough, told the Cabinet of the urgent representations that had been made to him by the Ulster Unionist MPs at Westminster and in particular the difficulties they were experiencing in refuting criticism not only from Labour but also from Roman Catholic members of the Conservative party. The informa-tion proved conclusive.[44] Withdrawal of the Bill followed and parity was preserved. The working of devolution in Northern Ireland illuminated at many points the working of devolved government, the relationship of imperial and regional authorities, the nature of parity, the dominance of finance and, on the Unionist side, the latent but not necessarily unreal fear of a demographic trend which one day might reverse the minority/majority roles.

CHAPTER 12

The Settlement in Being:
An Irish Dominion 1922–32

Political Perspectives at the Outset

The heritage the Irish Free State entered into was not in the short term an enviable one. The war of independence, the civil war, pogroms in Belfast, IRA incursions, with Provisional Government connivance,[1] across the Fermanagh border – layers of strife, alienation of comrade from comrade, all either associated with or partly attributable to the settlement – might well have instilled in the minds of contemporaries a fear lest, in the immortal phrasing applied by the doomed Girondist, Pierre Vergniaud, in the Paris of 1793, the revolution 'like Saturn might in turn devour each one of its children'.* This fearful prospect of predestined self-destruction lightened on 27 April 1923, when de Valera (with Frank Aiken) announced that offensive operations against the Free State were suspended and still more when on 24 May they issued an order to their followers to call off the armed struggle. Moreover, the scale of the Troubles,† even at the worst period, needed to be kept in perspective. The resilience of the market economy and of those who worked it provided one more illustration of the truth of Adam Smith's dictum that there was a lot of ruin in a nation. Despite disturbance, dislocation and destruction, foundations remained on which to build. But the scars of civil strife were not to be quickly healed: what had ended was not forgotten. As of Fouché, the regicide, it was said that to the end of a long life he looked at every event through the narrow window of Louis XVI's scaffold;[2] so of many of those who experienced the wounds, physical or psychological, of civil war, it might likewise be said that to the end of their days they related every

---

*Il a été permis de craindre que la Révolution, comme Saturne, dévorat successivement tous ses enfants.
†In the South, the war and the civil war were, and are, generally spoken of as the Troubles; often in the North as the Trouble. There is a certain logic in this; in the South, Anglo-Irish warfare was followed by civil war; in the North there was resistance to 'Rome rule'.

political issue to its place in the chronicle of national struggle or civil strife. What was significant politically, however, was less that their perspectives continued to be thus encased, as that for the great majority it conditioned not only their political allegiance, but also those of their children and their children's children. What divided parties in the Irish Free State and later the Republic of Ireland was not, therefore, social or economic aim or still less doctrine, but the national issue that was the Treaty. Cumann na nGaedheal (later Fine Gael) was the party for the Treaty; Fianna Fáil, launched by de Valera as a constitutional republican party on 16 May 1926, was that against it. For sixty years the two parties, Treaty-derived, continued to dominate Irish politics or, as party loyalists might prefer to put it, the national question retained its primacy over social, economic or ideological questions up to and into a period when this had generally ceased to be the order of priorities in the western world.

In the immediate post-Treaty period the developing division was spoken of as being between Free Staters and Republicans. This was in one respect misleading. In 1921, Dáil Éireann had sought a settlement on the basis of a republic, one externally associated with the Commonwealth if needs must, but a republic none the less. The majority of the Dáil Cabinet and of the Dáil itself had approved a status other than republican only when a republican goal was unobtainable without incurring the risk of a resumption of hostilities. A delegate, or a deputy, did not necessarily cease to be a republican because he thought that the best way to attain that goal was by stages. This was little understood in Britain and the misunderstanding led to mistaken assumptions, not least about the basis of support for dominion status. Indifferently grounded impressions served in turn to instil over-sanguine expectations of its becoming a lasting solvent. Yet the contrary signs were manifold – even the constitution itself with the openly republican provisions of the first draft, rejected out of hand by the British as inconsistent with the Treaty and duly withdrawn, still contrived to convey a republican image, so that in the final version it was not the republican, but the distinctively British imposed dominion provisions that appeared out of place. Article 2 declared that all powers of government and all authority, legislative, executive, judicial, are derived from the people of Ireland; for that reason J.A. Costello, as Attorney-General a member of the Irish delegation to the Imperial Conference in 1926 and 1930, reminded a Canadian audience in September 1948, these institutions derived none of their authority or validity either from any Act of the Imperial Parliament or the authority of the British government.[3]

While the constitution underlined national credentials at every point, those returned at the general election on 26 June 1922 composed at one and the same time the Houses of Parliament to which, in conformity with the Treaty,[4] the Provisional Government was responsible and also the Third Dáil Éireann, and it was as the latter that it was described in its own official publications. On both sides it was recognised as constituting the Irish Free State Constituent Assembly and by its members as that alone, and not as also a legislative assembly. It did not perform a single act of ordinary legislation. This concern to keep separate the constituent and legislative power was designed to emphasise the fact that, unlike dominion constitutions, that of the Free State emanated from a national Constituent Assembly.[5]

In introducing the Constitution Bill on 18 September 1922, W.T. Cosgrave informed the Assembly that certain articles,[6] namely, those implementing the Treaty and those introduced to safeguard the rights of minorities, were to be regarded as vital and rejection of any of them would involve the resignation of the Ministry. This was respected and the constitution was brought into operation by proclamation[7] on 6 December 1922.

The Balance of the Constitution

In the Preamble to the Constitution Act,[8] it was declared that 'Dáil Éireann sitting as a Constituent Assembly in this Provisional Parliament, acknowledging that all lawful authority comes from God to the people and in the confidence that the National life and unity of Ireland shall thus be restored hereby proclaims the establishment of the Irish Free State . . . and in the exercise of undoubted right, decrees' the enactment of the constitution. As Kohn remarked,[9] 'the sovereignty as well as the continuity of the native Parliament could not have been expressed more emphatically'. Even so ultimate authority did not rest there. The constitution was subordinate to the Treaty, the second article affirming that 'if any provision of the Constitution or any amendment thereof or of any law made thereunder is in any respect repugnant to any of the provisions of the Scheduled Treaty, it shall, to the extent only of such repugnancy, be absolutely void and inoperative'.[10] This was basic reality determining the constitutional balance in the Irish Free State. Final authority rested with the instrument that had called the state into being. The Treaty was thereby invested with the highest legal status and its provisions, in case of conflict, overrode those of the constitution itself and all subsequent legislation. It was, however, noted that while the assertion of the legal sovereignty of the Treaty was explicit, the powers of legal enforcement might prove less than adequate. Under the constitution[11] the question of repugnancy would be decided by the Irish central courts. While the latter might declare legislation inoperative because it conflicted with the Treaty, it was unlikely that they would be in a position or be willing to coerce 'the Parliament and Executive Council to pass such further legislation . . . as may be necessary to implement the Treaty'.

There was some anomaly that merits attention. There were instances in which provisions of the constitution themselves were in conflict with those of the Treaty. For example, under the Treaty the position of the Free State in relation to the Imperial Parliament and government was to conform to that of Canada. But in some respects it did not do so. The Governor-General of the Free State was not granted discretionary power in respect of the dissolution of parliament. An appeal from the courts of the Free State to the Judicial Committee of the Privy Council was not as of right, but only by special leave. Most important, the Free State Parliament was empowered to amend its constitution by ordinary legislation for a period of eight years (later extended for a further eight) and thereafter by a referendum, in which a majority of voters on the electoral register or two-thirds of the votes recorded were in favour, whereas amendments to the British North-America Act 1867 (which with amendments thereto was Canada's constitution) could be amended only by the Imperial Parliament until 1981. Since the Free State constitution had been shown to, and as amended approved by, the British Cabinet, it was to be inferred that a literal adherence to the practice of Canada had not been intended.[12] But while such deviations from Canadian practice were of interest, what mattered was that the two most deeply resented features of the constitution – those relating to the office of Governor-General and the oath – were protected by the authority vested in the Treaty by virtue of the repugnancy clause.

In various ways and despite the constraints imposed by the Treaty, the drafters of the constitution ensured that it should affirm as beyond question the indigenous republican-nationalist source of its inspiration. This was clearly to be seen in respect of government. 'The formal dualism which characterizes the Irish constitution is most evident', Kohn noted, 'in the structure of the Executive. Its framework is that of a constitutional monarchy, its substance that of a republic. Executive authority is "derived" from the people; it is "vested" in the King. It is "exercisable" by the Representative of the Crown; it is in fact exercised by an Executive Council – "nominated" by a popularly elected Chamber – which "aids and advises" him'.[13] By such device, the Provisional Government sought to counterbalance, and so minimise, authority vested in the King and thereby counter the conviction of republican critics that, in practice and through the Governor-General, the United Kingdom government would continue to exercise influence or exert pressure upon the Free State, where it did not in Canada. Thus in introducing the Constitution Bill in the Dáil, Kevin O'Higgins underlined that 'advice' to His Excellency was a signification of the decision of the Executive Council in matters of policy, no more, no less.[14] Then again in the appointment of a Governor-General, the Executive Council insisted on the finality of their own recommendation with an emphasis which Keith thought 'rather comic'. But would they have had Tim Healy otherwise? Article 3 of the Treaty had stated expressly that the representative of the Crown should be appointed 'in like manner as the Governor-General of Canada and in accordance with the practice observed in the making of such appointments' at that time. 'This means', so Lloyd George had conceded in a letter dated 13 December 1921, addressed to Griffith and read out by him in the Dáil on 19 December, 'that the Government of the Irish Free State will be consulted so as to ensure a selection acceptable to the Irish Government before any recommendation is made to His Majesty'.[15] The alternative of a statement in the constitution to the effect that the Governor-General was to be appointed with assent of the Executive Council did not commend itself to the Irish, on the ground that it spelled finality, whereas the Canadian analogy allowed of further advance.[16] Might not Canada, for example, elect some day its representative of the Crown?

The appointment of T.M. Healy as first Governor-General of the Irish Free State indicated Irish departure from convention hitherto followed in the overseas Dominions. That departure was reaffirmed with the appointment in December 1925 of James MacNeill, Irish High Commissioner in London, and as such an official of the Irish Free State government, as his successor. King George V was said to have been always prepared to regard the Irish position as a little different;[17] but in this respect at least, the flowing tide was with them. In 1930 Australian insistence upon the appointment of Sir Isaac Isaacs followed Free State precedent.

More important than procedures to be followed in the appointment of a Governor-General was his role in government. In the Irish Free State it was more circumscribed than in any of the overseas Dominions, with each function exercised being subjected to restrictive interpretation. For the summoning and concluding of sessions of parliament the dates were to be fixed not, as elsewhere in the Commonwealth, by the Governor-General in name but specifically by the Dáil. Likewise the President and members of the Executive Council were to be elected by the Dáil, not to be appointed by the Governor-General. In respect of discretionary powers, the limitations were striking. Most importantly, the Governor-General was expressly precluded from dissolving the Dáil on the advice of a defeated President of the Executive Council, a limitation in the first instance upon the range of options open to the President and then at one remove detracting from discretionary authority of the Governor-General; the phrase 'Governor-General in Council' never appeared in the Irish statute book, and where statutory powers were given to the Executive, it was to the Governor-General acting 'on the advice of the Executive Council', or some variant of the phrase. The Governor-General of the Irish Free State was not used as a medium of communication with, or regarded as, the agent of the United Kingdom government. 'No President of any Republic', Kohn concluded, 'is so limited in scope and function as the Governor-General of the Irish Free State'.[18] Did this diminish the hostility of the republicans to the office? Not in the slightest – its existence not its powers was the source of their objection.

The British connection apart, framers of the constitution of the Irish Free State shared the bias, common to many of the constitutions of re-emerging states in Central and Eastern Europe after the First World War, against the executive as such. Under Article 46 of the constitution, the Oireachtas was given the exclusive right to regulate the raising and maintaining of armed forces, both of which were made subject to its control. Here democratic principle, caution bred of revolutionary experience and the desire to subordinate the executive to the legislature contributed. More important and without counterpart in any other dominion constitution was Article 49, which declared that 'Save in the case of actual invasion', the Free State 'shall not be committed to active participation in any war without the assent of the Oireachtas'. This article was designed to meet two eventualities: (a) commitment to hostilities through association with the British Commonwealth of Nations; and (b) the Irish Free State government's taking any but defensive military measures.

Why did the United Kingdom government not register the dissent that might have been expected in this case in the light of the pre-Treaty discussions in London? The answer not explicitly formulated would seem to have been that they were satisfied, as they had reason to be, that the provisions of the Treaty, giving them control of the Treaty ports and other facilities required in wartime, sufficed to ensure British security, given the basic fact that Northern Ireland was part of the United Kingdom. Moreover, as was widely supposed, would not the use of such facilities by British forces alone expose the Free State to enemy counter-measures? And would not the Irish Free State then be committed to a war of defence which would give the Executive Council a free hand? Such considerations seemed academic in the 1920s, but no longer in the thirties.

The Oath and Politics

The oath prescribed in Article 5 of the Treaty was reproduced in Article 17 of the Irish Free State constitution with the injunction that it had to be taken by Deputies before they could take their seats. Because of this requirement, anti-Treaty Deputies refused to attend. In sharp reaction to the assassination of Kevin O'Higgins on 10 July 1927, the government forced their hand by passing an Electoral Amendment Bill requiring candidates to take the oath before their candidature was accepted. Confronted with a choice between enforced conformity or likely disintegration of a party unable to deploy its electoral muscle constitutionally, de Valera ruled that the oath might be deemed merely an empty political formula 'which deputies could conscientiously sign without becoming involved, or without involving their nation, in obligations of loyalty to the English Crown'.

Removal of the oath, however, remained the main political issue in the Irish Free State and one which mirrored the fundamental division between the parties. It was not in itself a source of controversy since the oath had few supporters. 'I have not heard anyone defend the Oath on its merits', noted Mr de Valera retrospectively in 1932. 'I have not heard anyone argue that it is right that an obligation of this sort should be imposed'.[19] It was retained because it was fundamental to the Treaty settlement. So long as any amendment of the constitution repugnant to the Treaty was deemed null and void, it remained. As Redmond had to secure the passage of the Parliament Bill before enactment of Home Rule, so de Valera had to remove the repugnancy clause before, or simultaneously with legislation to remove the oath. To do so, full and active participation in the politics of a state to which Fianna Fáil gave qualified recognition was deemed essential. It was, in the oft-quoted phrase of Seán Lemass,[20] a slightly constitutional party, and even more as he said in a neglected succeeding sentence – 'We are perhaps open to the definition of a constitutional party, but before anything we are a Republican party' – it was as a republican part that Fianna Fáil made its impact and opened the way to the advancement of its primary aim, that of removing the oath,[21] later to be described by de Valera 'as the cause of all the strife and dissension in this country since the signing of the Treaty',[22] and comprehensively as 'an intolerable burden, a relic of medievalism, a test imposed from outside under threat of immediate and terrible war'. So much for the greatest piece of pre-varication in history! But of course there was a longer-term objective; that of uprooting the settlement by concentration upon its most objectionable and therefore most vulnerable features. The assault left the British in the unenviable position of defending an oath, the principal effect of which was to alienate sentiment even among those otherwise in favour of sustaining the Treaty settlement.

In 1927 the Cosgrave administration survived two elections. But the returns showed that it was Fianna Fáil that by then was in the ascendant. In Professor Fanning's words, Fianna Fáil held 'the green card in the party politics of independent Ireland and, once in the Dáil, played it with devastating effect'. They were out to win power, something, as Fanning remarks, Cumann na nGaedheal had never had to do. The latter were in office before they founded the party.[23] They had always been responsible for law and order; the image of the policeman was not that far from them. Professor Hancock in his comments on the politics of the Irish Free State as viewed in a Commonwealth context, struck much the same note. He wrote of the pro-Treaty party over which Cosgrave presided with quiet distinction as a new state, seeking in domestic affairs as in its relations

with fellow members of the Commonwealth and of the League, to demonstrate 'the capacity of Irishmen to pass the most stringent tests of
political capacity and respectability'. They pursued political and economic
orthodoxies of the day 'with a proud resolution'. And he summed up his
impressions:

> The Irish Free State under Mr Cosgrave was the objective, the un-
> emotional scientific, intellectual State. Throughout Europe, and not
> least in Ireland, people were beginning to tire of this kind of state.
> They wanted more emotion and more drama. The political artists were
> pushing aside the political scientists. The party state was challenging the
> neutral state. In Ireland, people were getting weary of their Govern-
> ment's very virtues. They were tired of hearing Mr Cosgrave called the
> just.[24]

One might enter a caveat here. W.B. Yeats, briefly and improbably
ensconced in the Irish Senate for one, and the young Frank O'Connor and
Sean O'Fáolain among others, already skirmishing with the Censorship
Board, would have sharply repudiated the attribute 'intellectual', while
it is debatable whether the Irish electorate's weariness of Cosgrave had
much in common with the weariness of the Greeks for Aristides. But Dr
Fanning's observation to the effect that the just may and so often have a
touch of the policeman in them is on the mark. The law and order lobby is
apt to be popular only when out of office. More generally, that the Irish
people, ten years after an incomplete national revolution, wanted more
emotion and more drama also seems a right judgement.

In external, as in domestic affairs, Professor Hancock wrote of the pro-
Treaty administration as being logical in its thinking, straightforward in
its purpose. Did that imply a clearer sense of direction on the part of
the Cosgrave government than in fact it possessed? It was certainly the
impression made by the party leaders in the early 1930s. They had accepted the Treaty; they had fought for it; they were young. In the Treaty
debate they had argued, in the words of Michael Collins, that the Treaty
'gave freedom to achieve freedom' and they allowed, in the words of
Kevin O'Higgins, that even though Ireland had been forced into membership, the Commonwealth was in fact a 'league of free nations'. In external
policy the principal purpose of their government was to enlarge the area of
freedom by giving detailed practical effect to the conception of dominion
equality with Britain. Negatively, they had been concerned, so Patrick
McGilligan recalled when speaking in the Dáil on the passage of the
Statute of Westminster, to pull 'the old Colonial Empire . . . asunder'.[25]
They believed, and rightly, that they had played and were continuing to
play an important part in so doing. But, and here a certain ambivalence
creeps in, what was their ultimate purpose? Was it the case that they
were concerned to remodel the Commonwealth in accord with prevailing

dominion national 'orthodoxies' so as to make it acceptable to Irish opinion? Or were they out to weaken the ties of Commonwealth so as to ease the way for the Free State's secession from it? Or were the members of Cosgrave's government themselves uncertain of and divided on their goal and was this a contributory factor in their downfall?

The Irish Free State at the Imperial Conferences 1923, 1926 and 1930

At the outset it may be remarked that while the Irish Free State's impact on the Commonwealth has been the subject of detailed study, notably in Professor Harkness' *The Restless Dominion*, little has been done academically on the impact of the Commonwealth on the Irish Free State. The explanation is simple enough. Dominion status never really entered into the Irish body politic. It is with this that we are concerned.

The Irish government, well nigh engulfed in a sea of troubles at home, and unfamiliar with the imperial setting, played little part at the Imperial Conference of 1923. By 1926 when the next and most significant of conferences met, they were very much principals. The conference provided a memorable setting in which to establish their identity in London and, of greater immediacy, to present the Commonwealth in an acceptable light to the electorate at home. From the point of view of the Free State, timing and theme could hardly have been bettered. The government was well established and the dominant concern of the conference – definition of status – was of all topics nearest to the hearts of ministers. It was almost certainly a further advantage that another, the South African General Hertzog, should act as pacemaker.

For the Dominions who sought to have their status defined in terms of equality with Great Britain, there were two ways of proceeding – one by a declaration affirming that this was so and the other by removing inequalities where these existed. The first was the aim of the South Africans, the second of the Irish. The records of the meetings of the Conference Committee concerned, that on Inter-Imperial Relations, make it clear that the South African proposals for a formal declaration of dominion rights, coupled with a comprehensive definition of status in terms of dominion equality with Britain, set the substance and tone of the debate. Kevin O'Higgins indicated that the Irish Free State government, while sympathetic and understanding of the South African proposal, had another order of priorities. Where it was the South African Prime Minister's wish to proceed from the general to the particular, O'Higgins desired the reverse: to deal with the particular before the general, if indeed the latter were not by then rendered otiose.

Comparing the situation in the Irish Free State with that of the Union of South Africa, O'Higgins explained to the committee that while in both countries there was an intense and sensitive nationalism, the Irish took the view that a declaration such as had been suggested by Hertzog would be of little value if contradicted by the facts. There were certain anomalies and anachronisms which appeared to be a denial of equal status. They should first be removed.[26]

'Existing Anomalies in the British Commonwealth of Nations' was accordingly the title and theme of the principal paper submitted by the Irish Free State delegation,[27] the purpose of which was to identify inequalities in status to ensure their removal when identified, and then to establish equality with Britain, inequalities duly eliminated. The opening paragraph outlined the argument.

> The principle of the absolute equality of status and the legislative, judicial and constitutional independence of the members of the British Commonwealth of Nations is now admitted beyond controversy. It is accordingly thought that it would be opportune to direct attention to some of the more outstanding anomalies and anachronisms which appear most to detract from that principle with the object of abrogating anything which in form or substance interferes with its complete application in practice.

The memorandum proceeded to urge approval in principle and recognition in practice of the fundamental right of the government of each Dominion to advise the King in all matters whatsoever relating to its own affairs. For the Irish, this was the central political issue. Associated with it were proposals to delimit the functions of the Governor-General; to establish equal rights in territorial legislation; to ensure the repeal of the Colonial Laws Validity Act* (the very title of which implied subjection, in principle and in application, subversion of the principles of autonomy and constitutional co-equality); to amend the royal titles so as to place the Irish Free State in due dominion order after South Africa and before India; to ensure that appeals might lie to the Judicial Committee of the Privy Council only at the wish of the Dominion concerned (on this a separate memorandum was circulated); to remove restrictions on extra-territorial legislation by the Dominions; and to ensure direct correspondence between dominion Ministries of External Affairs and foreign countries.

The recital demonstrated, as did the recorded Irish contributions to the general discussion at meetings of the Inter-Imperial Relations Committee, the Irish resolve to concentrate on removing all elements of subordination. This tactical approach did not, however, necessarily disclose the Free State's strategic aim.

---

* Whether the Act applied to Ireland was questionable and the Irish courts were thought likely to rule that it did not.

It has long been known, one important source being T. de V. White's
biography of Kevin O'Higgins,★ that some members of the Irish delegation remained attracted by Arthur Griffith's notion of a dual monarchy.
But it has not hitherto been altogether clear how far this was a personal as against an official view. The conclusion to the memorandum on
'Anomalies' left the question unresolved. It read as follows:

> If the British Commonwealth of Nations is to endure as the greatest
> factor for the establishment of peace and prosperity throughout the
> world, its cohesive force must be real and permanent, whether viewed
> from within or without. It cannot be held together by a mere collective
> expression, which only serves to create doubt in the minds of Foreign
> Statesmen and discontent among the diverse nationalities of which it is
> made up.
>
> The King is the real bond, and forms used in international treaties
> will be devoid of all meaning so long as they do not give complete
> expression to that reality.
>
> The co-operation resulting from the bond of a common King will be
> effective only because it is free co-operation and to the extent to which
> it is free. Antiquated forms dating from a period when common action
> resulted from the over-riding control of one central Goverment are
> liable to make co-operation less efficacious, because they make it seem
> less free.

It would be possible but unwise to draw a broad political inference
from this conclusion to a technical submission, but it may be assumed that
the Irish Free State delegation, in thus underlining the significance of the
King as 'the real bond', at the least did not at that point in time wish to
rule out of consideration the appropriateness of the monarch for this purpose, given the essential element of free cooperation. The memorandum,
it will be noted, moreover, used the phrase, 'the bond of a common
King', wording which requires to be set in context. It was to be the basis
of Costello's argument in 1948 – he was Attorney-General in Cosgrave's
1926–32 administration and had advised the Irish Free State delegation at
the Imperial Conferences of 1926 and 1930 – that it was the Crown that
was the major cause of friction between Ireland and Britain from 1921
onwards. If so, why did the Irish memorandum in 1926 allude in such
terms to the possible role of a common King? The record suggests that
O'Higgins was thinking of a dual monarchy, two independent kingdoms
with a common King – a relationship, be it noted, without counterpart
in the Commonwealth. This is borne out retrospectively in a letter to
the author dated 10 September 1933 from John Hearne, Legal Advisor,

★ T. de V. White, *Kevin O'Higgins* (London, 1948).

Department of External Affairs, and a member of the Irish delegation at the Imperial Conferences of 1926 and 1929–30.

> The only juridical expression of the symbolism of the Crown', he wrote, 'is the expression "Personal Union". If the Union is not a Personal Union – it is certainly *not* a Real Union – it is juridically non-descript . . . in a Personal Union the States concerned are separate international persons. The notion of the Kingdom of Ireland is one of the big historical notions and it is a conception of an Irish Constitution in which there is a practical possibility of union amongst Irishmen themselves. Mr. O'Higgins built his policy upon the idea of the Kingdom of Ireland.

Hearne's restatement of O'Higgins' line of thought may be deemed to add a conclusive note as to O'Higgins' own views. What remains in doubt is whether any of the other members of the Free State delegation shared them. It rested upon an assumption that the Crown had no nationality and ran contrary to the notion of an indivisible Crown, favoured by Amery and other right-wing imperalists in Britain. It belonged to Anglo-Irish not Irish Commonwealth constitutional concepts. The sophistication of the concept apart from all else left them with little prospect even of minority survival in an atmosphere of emotive republicanism. They did not, moreover, belong to the realm of constitutional symbolism likely to appeal to Northern Unionist sentiment.

More generally, Free State contributions to the 1926 conference and its 1929–30 successor indicate a disposition to work within the Commonwealth conditional upon the Commonwealth ridding itself of all remaining imperalist stigmata. Externally, relations of the Irish Free State with the British Commonwealth dominated the decade that elapsed between the Anglo-Irish dominion status Treaty of 1921, and the Statute of Westminster, 1931. But they had a counterpart in Irish initiatives affirming the Free State's separate identity internationlly. The Treaty was registered with the League of Nations at Geneva on 11 July 1924. The first dominion diplomatic representative to be accredited to a foreign country was an Irish minister who presented his credentials to President Coolidge on 7 October 1924, and, while the Free State's candidature for election to membership of the Council of the League of Nations was unsuccessful, another Dominion, Canada, duly elected in the eighth Assembly (1927) established the precedent and the essential point was made. Canada's election was acclaimed by Patrick McGilligan (who had succeeded O'Higgins at External Affairs) as putting an end to Great Britain's pretence to represent the other states of the Commonwealth. Recognition of status internationally, McGilligan maintained, would come only by seizing every chance of exercising the powers of a sovereign state to achieve

concrete ends and, within the Commonwealth, by pressing for the reconstruction of dominion status in terms of equality as approved at the 1926
Imperial Conference and given detailed application by the 1929–30 co-
ordinated efforts of the Canadian, South African and Irish governments
to ensure the translation of the 1926 Report as required into legal terms.

Surviving inequalities were listed and submitted in a formal document
by the Free State representatives to the Operation of Dominions Legislation Conference 1929 and the Imperial Conference 1930. Relentless Irish
concentration at the two conferences proved decisive on many points.
Professor Harkness argues with cogency that earlier commentators (including the present author) by concentrating overmuch on 1926 and the
arresting imagery associated with the definition of dominion status in the
Balfour Report and by insufficiently regarding the detailed, often tedious
work of the 1929–30 conferences, diminshed unhistorically the Irish role
in the removal of often irksome and sometimes near incomprehensible
inequalities, without which definition would not have corresponded so
nearly in bringing detail into conformity with general assertions of principle. The point is well taken and assuredly Irish consistency in their view
of what needed to be done and their refusal, in minor as in major issues, to
be deflected from their course, were of the most impressive, if not the
most popular features of the Commonwealth Conference decade. The
Irish contention as their delegation put it was that harmony was eminently
desirable because of common interests between the governments of the
Commonwealth; that in the interests of such greater harmony the government had pressed for the elimination of anomalies, for extra-territorial
powers to be exercised as the sole right of the Dominion concerned, the
issue of exequaturs no longer on a mandate from a dominion government,
but with the King advised by the government, the King's title to be
amended so that for 'of Great Britain and Ireland' it should read 'Great
Britain, Ireland and the British dominions beyond the seas'. These were
important matters but some of them of recondite interest. In the Dáil there
were some who did not feel qualified and others who did not feel disposed
to offer constructive criticism.

Fianna Fáil deputies not having yet taken their seats, Labour constituted
the principal opposition in the debate that followed. Their leader, Thomas
Johnson, remarked upon the fact that the New Zealanders on their return
home were loud in their affirmation that New Zealand despite all that was
being bandied abroad had acquired *no* new status and were more than
content that this should be so. He allowed that had it been acknowledged
in 1921, as it was in the 1926 Conference Report, that each Dominion was
'the sole judge of the extent of its cooperation', many things could have
been more readily resolved. (Deputy Johnson was presumably aware that
the sentence in which it occurs had been adopted at the suggestion of
O'Higgins.) For the rest, the substitution of the comma – the 'O'Higgins

comma', as it came to be known – for an 'and' in the Royal Titles was received with some satirical comment.[28] The truth, unhelpful to the pro-Treaty party, was that such refinements, however significant in the context of an evolutionary progression from a familiar past to a foreseeable future, were regarded at best as a tedious, barely comprehensible, at worse as a dangerously seductive diversion from the onward march of an incomplete, republican-inspired revolution. O'Higgins was nearly if not quite alone among the Free State delegates in his readiness to contemplate a royal, dual monarchy nexus if it advanced Irish interests.[29]

With the entry of Fianna Fáil into the Dáil on 11 August 1927 there was more pressing demand for definition of policy on the two unresolved questions of unity and status. Of the first it was asked, as it had been in March 1928, what were the prospects of the emergence of a unified Irish State? Ernest Blythe replied. The position, he said, was much as it had been in 1922. It could only come by consent and 'not within this generation or perhaps within two generations . . . without the consent of Great Britain . . . never . . . against the opposition of Great Britain'. To the question whether the government was aiming at the establishment of an Irish republic, he returned a categoric 'we are not'. And he proceeded, 'we believe this country as a member . . . can enjoy greater freedom and greater security than she could outside the British Commonwealth of Nations and our policy within it is really to remove anomalies . . . between the members'.[30] Many had gone as a result of Irish efforts and the remainder he dismissed as neither numerous nor important.

The President of the Executive Council was challenged. Did he agree with his Minister for Finance? Cosgrave offered an oblique and incomplete reply. In the case of a Treaty signed under the conditions and circumstances of December 1921, it might, he said, without dishonour be repudiated by 'the majority will of the Irish nation' given that on balance it seemed advisable to do so. 'The majority will of this Nation is at all times sovereign . . . and we do not deny and we do not limit that sovereignty'. But as long as the Treaty in all its bearings and implications had the support of the majority, 'the Nation will stand honourably by that policy'.[31]

While the way ahead in the short term seemed clear, the more distant prospect was clouded. The British Commonwealth was to rid itself of anomalies and be thereby refashioned so as to be acceptable, or at any rate, less unacceptable to Irish opinion. On Blythe's view, this was an end in itself, not a device to ease the way to a republic; on Cosgrave's one to leave constitutional options open to be exercised in accord with the wishes of the majority of the nation, subject to a realistic assessment of national advantage. Clearly the government had in mind no hurried advance to a republic. Yet it was to be inferred from what the President said that he, given removal of the remaining inequalities, was content, even well content, with membership of a Commonwealth of autonomous states.

The last was not to be taken wholly for granted. In November 1929 amendments designed to exclude the Irish Free State from the general provisions of the Statute of Westminster were moved in both Houses of Parliament on the contention that the Treaty had frozen the status of the Irish Free State by making it analogous to that of Canada as it was in 1921. These amendments elicited a strong protest from Cosgrave to Ramsay MacDonald, reinforced by parallel representations from McGilligan to J.H. Thomas. Cosgrave trusted it was quite unnecessary for him to say that 'the Statute of Westminster in its present form' represented an agreement between all the governments of the Commonwealth, an agreement which had been considered at great length by the Irish representatives at the Imperial Conference and endorsed, as it stood, by Dáil and Senate. 'Any amendment', he concluded, 'of the nature now suggested would be a departure from the terms of the Imperial Conference Report and would be wholly unacceptable to us. . . . You will agree that this is a time when the interests of the peoples of the Commonwealth as a whole must be put before the prejudices of the small reactionary element in these islands.'

Cosgrave was on sure ground. It had been agreed at the 1930 Imperial Conference that no law enacted thereafter by the parliament of the United Kingdom should extend to a Dominion unless that Dominion had requested and consented that it should do so.[32] Yet to do precisely that was the purpose of amendments which had the backing of one signatory to the Treaty: Winston Churchill. McGilligan, who excepted Churchill from 'the rabid reactionaries' seeking on both sides of the Irish sea to undermine the foundations of the Free State, pointed out that they were trying to take away from the Treaty the one element that made it acceptable, or at any rate tolerable, to the pro-Treaty party – namely, the association of the Irish Free State with the Dominions in their advance to the status of 'autonomous communities', not only in practice but in law. If, so McGilligan wrote in his letter to Thomas, the belief of the Irish people in the Treaty 'as an instrument of the fullest freedom is now going to be shaken by a deliberate act of the British parliament, the consequences cannot but be of the gravest'. Ramsay MacDonald replied with justifiably confident reassurance about the rejection of the amendments – though not of the survival prospects of their respective governments. The incident ended by strengthening the impression of an Irish commitment, given respect by others for Imperial Conference conclusions, to think in terms of freedom within a developing Commonwealth system,[33] by demonstrating that there was no substantial body of opinion in favour of distinguishing the status of the Free State from that of the other Dominions.

On 9 September 1930 McGilligan listed the remaining anomalies in a dispatch to Thomas at the Dominions Office.[34] They were appeals to the Judicial Committee of the Privy Council, the right of direct access by dominion governments to the King, clarification of the position of the

Dominions in relation to treaty making and communications between dominion and foreign governments. The Irish contention was that the first should be abolished *tout simple*. The second was more complex, but less likely to stir emotions. It concerned the use of the Dominions Office and the Foreign Office as channels of communication with other governments. This was said to create an impression of British intervention in the conduct of dominion affairs, with the British government acting as a barrier between the King and his other Commonwealth governments and generally making it difficult for other governments to distinguish where the functions of the British government ended and those of their governments began. The Irish for the future desired the same relationship to be established with the King as in the United Kingdom and suggested the granting of a special position of dignity to High Commissioners to facilitate the new procedure. The remaining two items were again concerned with clarification, the first to ensure that foreigners understood that the Commonwealth was *not* a federal state, and the second, the ending of the system by which communication between members of the Commonwealth and foreign countries took place (with some exceptions) through the Foreign Office. All these things had their importance and the necessary changes were made, the Canadians being the first to abolish Privy Council appeals; but altogether more important was the prospective repeal, in what in 1931 became the Statute of Westminster, of the Colonial Laws Validity Act 1865, which *inter alia* declared that any colonial legislation which conflicted with the provisions of a British Act of Parliament was to the extent of such repugnancy null and void. Once that statute was enacted, new vistas of action by the Free State within the framework of British constitutional law opened up. If ever there were such a thing as a constitutional revolution, the Statute of Westminster in its Irish context merited that description.

Members of the Free State government were filled with a sense almost of awe at the measure of their own achievement and the correctness of their own Commonwealth prognostications in 1921. Writing from London in October 1930, Desmond Fitzgerald expressed it well:[35]

> Knowing the history of these last years as I do I am amazed at the way we have changed the situation... the Free State is (or will be in a couple of years – without even a vestige of any form even to mar it) just a constitutional monarchy – with only that to make the difference between it and an Irish Republic. In the matter of Independence and sovereignty there is no whittle of difference.... But accepting the Treaty we certainly are getting all that the most perfervid supporters were claiming for it – and more.

Patrick McGilligan was equally exultant. 'We had one purpose in 1926', he told the Dáil five years later, 'and that was that there must be uprooted from the whole system of this State the British Government; and in substitution for that there was accepted the British Monarch. He is a King who functions entirely, so far as Irish affairs are concerned, at the will of the Irish Government, and that was the summing up of the whole aim and the whole result of the conferences of 1926, 1929 and 1930.'[36]

That was July 1931; six months later – in February 1932 – the decade of Cumann na nGaedheal administration came to an end. Unlike Desmond Fitzgerald, their successors did not think of constitutional monarchy as a matter of small difference with the Republic. To them it was a denial of a fundamental right.

The period of Irish refashioning of the Commonwealth was to come to an end with de Valera's accession to power in March 1932.[37] On 20 January 1932 Berriedale Keith wrote to Patrick McGilligan,[38] congratulating him on having with the Statute of Westminster 'so successfully carried through your ideal', adding that while 'myself I should have preferred to see an Irish Republic as more consonant with the attitude of the Irish people towards the Crown, I fully appreciate the reasons which have resulted in the adoption of the present form of connection...', that is dominion status. The phrasing was less than felicitous; the reasons were clear enough. They were that in December 1921 the choice before the Irish representatives was dominion status or resumption of war. They opted in those circumstances by majority for dominion status. Had there been no ultimatum – this was Churchill's description★ – dominion status would hardly have become the source of corroding division that it did. But leaving speculation aside, was there not a psychological barrier? Dominion status was thought of at that time in terms of constitutional formulas. But it rested on more than them. It was a product of a particular history and, at a particular phase in its evolution, developed its own psychological outlook. As nationality is one identifiable politico-psychological phenomenon, so (for lack of a word) 'dominionality' also had its own recognisable features. The two, nationality and dominionality, are distinct and distinguishable. 'Ireland's right', as Stack put it, was 'full independence and nothing short of it'. Such was not, at that time, dominion assertion.[39] The differences were spelled out symbolically though in practical matters the line of division was overlapping and blurred. The Irish question was not a straightforward national or straightforward dominion question. Within it was another question, the Ulster minority Irish question. Consideration of the second might influence judgement on the right resolution of the first. But in practice status had its little-questioned priority.

There were complications stemming from history and difficult to weigh. While the Sinn Féin demand in 1921 had been for a republic, the pro-Treaty party, once in office, assumed or rather were enfolded by their critics in the mantle of dominion status. It was not something to which they aspired initially, but something they accepted *faute de mieux*. There was an Irish party committed to dominion status. It was the old Parliamentary party. Kevin O'Higgins had sharply rebuked British ministers who alluded to that party's dominion aspirations. 'We are not', he remonstrated, 'the heirs of Redmond and Dillon'.[40] They were not, they were the heirs of the Irish revolution. Yet here they were in office as the government of an Irish dominion: Redmondite, not Sinn Féin aspiration fulfilled. It was an unwelcome association. It was resented and perhaps in some measure reflected in the harsh judgements on dominion leaders, filling as they did an ungrateful third-party role. 'I'm told Borden is a stupid man', wrote James MacNeill to Cosgrave from London, 'I wonder if a Colonial is safer than an Englishman who is intelligent, straight and judicially minded'.[41] Feetham had every reason to have wished that MacNeill's feeling had been acted upon. Kevin O'Higgins' verdict on the 1926 Imperial Conference was unflattering – Hertzog talked too much and none too clearly, King was too complacent, the New Zealanders gave the impression that their country must be like Northern Ireland producing, as it did, 'the same type of Jingo reactionary',[42] while in the Dáil, one deputy, a professor at that, reflected that, unlike Australia, 'we had not evolved from a penal settlement for Great Britain into a self-governing State and member of the League of Nations'.[43]

Yet another side was shown when, after the 1930 Conference, the dominion leaders visited Dublin. The President of the Executive Council's welcome to R.B. Bennett, with its allusions to Canada 'as our guide and our example'[44] in the early years of the Free State's membership of the Commonwealth and more especially that to Hertzog, carried the impression of a developing relationship. Hertzog's reply was illuminating. 'How is it', he asked himself, 'that you feel different [here] from what you feel when with our friends in England . . . and the answer I gave myself was that I had but to talk to the Irish and feel at once that they and I understand one another. Our history has been very much a parallel.' Up to 1926 the word 'imperial' had had 'a very sinister meaning', but 1926 changed all that. Today 'we are free and independent peoples in voluntary association with others'.[45]

In the Irish case, the Commonwealth was still, despite 1926 and all that, thought of as *not* being a voluntary association. In Ireland, the pro-Treaty party had reached much the same position as General Hertzog's National-

---

★ Churchill showed the typescript of the Irish chapters of *The Aftermath* to Lionel Curtis before publication. L.C. replied at length and with concern at the disclosures it contained. W.S.C. replied on 18 December 1928 that he was 'under the impression that the ultimatum about the Treaty had already been made public . . . it is immaterial to history. The point can easily be made in a few harmless sentences.' However, what he had written remained as he had written it. Bodleian, Curtis, Ms.90.

ists, but the opposition remained unwavering in their rejection of 'full', as
of 'half Canadian status'. They held, in Dr Fanning's phrase, 'the green
card' with its tremendous emotional appeal to the republican tradition in
modern Irish history. And what had the pro-Treaty party by way of
counter? A Commonwealth remote and unfamiliar, for all the Irishmen
who had migrated there; a Commonwealth being defined or redefined in
ways some of which were meaningless to the average Irish voter. What to
him was an amended royal title or the limitation of the functions of
Governor-General? He was more likely to wish to be rid of them. As for
the repeal of the Colonial Laws Validity Act, rightly judged to be a
constitutional landmark, it was questionably applicable to Ireland and
either way less than ideal for exposition on the hustings as for exequaturs!

PART VI

THE UNDOING OF
THE SETTLEMENT

CHAPTER 13

The Dismantling of the
Dominion Settlement 1932–38

Broadly speaking, there had been two possible Commonwealth policies for Irish governments after 1921. The first was to refashion the Commonwealth in closer accord with Irish interests and outlook; the second to seek the first opportunity to unravel, or in dramatic revolutionary strokes to sever, Irish ties with the Commonwealth. These alternatives were pursued in turn by President Cosgrave's government from 1922 to 1932, and by President de Valera's administration from 1932 onwards. Behind them lay different assessments of Commonwealth potentialities, of Irish interests, not least in terms of national unity, and of personal temperament, political instinct and aspirations. The one had led to autonomy within the Commonwealth, the other aspired to independence outside the Commonwealth.

De Valera and the anti-Treaty Party in Power: the First Moves

The election of 16 June 1922 had given the imprimatur of popular approval to the pro-Treaty party and the dominion settlement; that of 16 February 1932, was to do likewise for Fianna Fáil and external association. In constitutional terms, the second election like the first was to mark a parting of the ways, to serve as a milestone in Irish history, its place signalled by a movement to the left, in conformity with familiar precedents – O'Connell to Young Ireland, Butt to Parnell, Redmond to Sinn Féin and now Cosgrave to de Valera. Yet while there was a consistent pattern, in each instance the leftward move inspired by concept was necessarily also conditioned by the existing politico-institutional circumstances through which it had to find, or force, its way to realisation. For de Valera the Treaty and dominion status were the constricting factors which had first to be moved out of the way.

The Commonwealth relationship was no longer that debated in Treaty days. It had been refashioned, not least by Irish hands, in terms of dominion equality in status with Great Britain, the Statute of Westminster enacted on 11 December 1931, giving legal affirmation to what had been achieved. It was an achievement by which the outgoing Cumann na nGaedheal administration set great store.

On 18 January 1932, with Cosgrave in his last month of office, J.W. Dulanty, the Irish High Commissioner in London, under instruction from the Department of External Affairs attended upon King George V for the purpose of receiving from him the Great Seal of an Sáorstat, as a symbol of the Free State's equal standing with Britain and the overseas Dominions. The striking of the seal had shown (so the High Commissioner advised the King) that the sovereignty of the Irish people and the development of their free institutions were not idle phrases but represented realities. 'The historians', he continued, 'not only of our countries but of others' would not fail to record the ceremony in which they had been participating. 'But', interjected the King, coming to a more pressing matter, 'what are we to do if Mr De Valera is returned?' Was he likely so to regard it? To this pertinent, if less than judicious enquiry, the High Commissioner replied with the altogether judicious observation that it would be 'most unwise . . . to adopt too aggressive an attitude' towards a Fianna Fáil government, since that might undo all the constructive work of the past decade.[1] In fact, when de Valera took office on 9 March, he was intent on carrying through, not a further advance on a dominion road, but a revolutionary departure from it.

On the eve of the Free State election, the Secretary of State for the Dominions, J.H. Thomas, had warned his Cabinet colleagues that should de Valera be returned 'a difficult position would be produced'.[2] In a memorandum laid before the Cabinet on 2 March, he outlined countermeasures to meet likely contingencies. By way of a guiding principle he advised that they should take no action 'which would enable Mr de Valera to say that we were forcing him out of the British Commonwealth'. Over the next five years, British policy was to be conditioned by this consideration. For the rest Thomas surmised 'time is on our side'.[3] On 22 March the Cabinet decided to reconstitute an Irish Situation Committee with the Prime Minister, Ramsay MacDonald presiding and Thomas, as Dominions Secretary, its principal adviser.[4] The British had surprisingly scant information about de Valera's intentions. This was partly because Britain – as Malcolm MacDonald was later to note and remedy – had no diplomatic representative in Dublin, only a Trade Commissioner, William Peters, on occasion seeking to fill a gap otherwise papered over by information or appraisal from unofficial and sometimes improbable sources.[5] Common to all apart from Peters was opposition to de Valera and the conviction that his minority government would soon be ousted from office.

In the election campaign, Fianna Fáil had singled out two immediate objectives: the abolition of the oath, symbol of all that was most resented in the dominion settlement, and the withholding from the British exchequer of the land annuities, paid by former tenant farmers in repayment of British government loans issued to enable them to buy out their farms under the terms of pre-war Land Acts. The monies were collected by the Irish tax collectors for transmission to the British exchequer.[6] If there were a competition to devise the most unpopular levy in an Anglo-Irish context this would be hard to beat. Nor did it help that to unpopularity was added an element of confusion. The land annuity payments had been the subject of two Financial Agreements, one in 1923, the other in 1926, the latter being envisaged as part of the final financial settlement referred to in Article 5 of the Treaty. Neither agreement had been ratified by the Dáil as both should have been – and it was this failure to conform to usual practice that allowed the dispute to arise in the first place.

The Free State government sought to keep the two issues, oath and land annuities, constitutional and fiscal, apart, de Valera being ready to submit the economic dispute to arbitration, with the one proviso that after experience of Mr Justice Feetham, the choice should not be limited to the Commonwealth. Thomas was equally agreeable that this should be so with the one qualification that the arbitrator *should be* from the Common-wealth. But there was rather more than that to the differences between them. Thomas was concerned to underline the contractual element in oath and annuities; de Valera to keep them apart as being different in kind. Neither dissented from the view that payment, or non-payment, of annuities was a fit subject for arbitration. On the Irish view the oath, and for that matter, the Governor-General, Privy Council appeals and related constitutional issues, all of which were to be raised, were not. They concerned the attributes of sovereignty and sovereignty, as de Valera time and again insisted, was vested in the people alone. But the argument did not rest there. Another and a larger dimension intruded. It had revolutionary implications, if it be not self-contradictory so to describe a parliamentary enactment. Did or did not the Statute of Westminster override provisions of the Treaty? If it did, what became of the sanctity of the Treaty? To seek an answer it is necessary to look at the Treaty setting once again in the light of this development.

Article 1 of the Treaty had declared that the Irish Free State should have the same constitutional status as the Dominions, and the third Article more particularly defined Irish status by reference to that of Canada, the oldest Dominion. The Treaty as a whole was vested with the force of fundamental law, both the Constituent Act and the Irish Free State constitution declaring that if any provision of the constitution, or any amendment thereof, or any law made thereunder was in any respect repugnant to any provision of the Treaty, it was to the extent of such repugnancy 'absolutely void and inoperative'. But was there not and had there not always been the possibility of conflict here? Canadian status was not fixed; Canada was foremost among the old Dominions in seeking and securing advances in it. If, as was the case, such advances were made, was it not also the cause that, under the earlier provisions of the Treaty, Irish status should likewise develop and advance? The answer was surely in the affirmative. But what if such advances were in conflict with other provisions of the Treaty? Was Irish status in such circumstances to be regarded to that extent as frozen and immutable? English diehard opinion, as earlier recorded, had taken this view, contending that the Irish Free State should accordingly be excepted from the Statute of Westminster on that ground. President Cosgrave had, as already noted, lodged his protest: the Irish Free State was not excepted. De Valera went further. Within three days of coming to office he announced his intention of removing the Oath of Allegiance from the constitution. It was mandatory under the Treaty – though President de Valera evidently entertained some reservations even about that. But was it mandatory under the Statute of Westminster? President de Valera, it is true, was wary in referring to the Statute: after all, it was a British enactment. Instead he deployed arguments grounded not in law but in natural right. He told Thomas that the constitution was the people's constitution; that the government had an absolute right to modify it as the people desired. The people had declared their will. There was no ambiguity about their resolve to remove the oath. It was a relic of medievalism and an intolerable burden. It made friendly relations with Britain impossible. It was a test unparalleled in treaty relationships between states, and it had been imposed under threat of immediate and terrible war.[7] It had to go and it was clear it was going, whatever the British government or Irish lawyers might say.

Was President de Valera in his assault upon the Oath about to challenge the sanctity of the Treaty settlement as a whole? Thomas, after some increasingly acrimonious exchanges, in which the area in dispute was widened both constitutionally and also economically by the decision to retain Irish land annuity payments, was persuaded that this was so. He maintained that the oath was mandatory under the Treaty, that it was an integral part of the 1921 settlement and that the Treaty as a whole was an agreement 'which can only be altered by consent'. In brief, he took his stand upon the twin foundations of constitutional law and contractual obligation. De Valera, on the other hand, as was evidenced by his rejoinder of 5 April 1932, continued to rest his upon indefeasible national sovereignty. 'Whether the Oath was', he said, 'or was not "an integral part of the Treaty made ten years ago" is not now the issue. The real issue is that the Oath is an intolerable burden to the people of this State and that they have declared in the most formal manner that they desire its instant removal.' Thomas deprecated the language of the communication. It was, he complained, that of a 'political manifesto addressed to Irishmen all over the world'. The de Valera of the early thirties had added a sharper edge and a more assured presentation than did the de Valera of the early twenties, when he had engaged in not dissimilar dialectical exchanges with an altogether more formidable adversary.

This time there was an additional interested party listening in – the Dominions. The constitutional issue was now clearly of concern to them. Should their governments be consulted? Initially the Irish Situation Committee of the Cabinet had been divided on the merits of so doing, but later decided the overseas Prime Ministers should have a direct communication encouraging them to express their views to de Valera.[8] In April they did so in terms of implied rebuke. De Valera regretted their failure to understand the situation. The outcome was counter-productive. Hertzog showed himself particularly sensitive to the possible implications for South Africa of a ruling on the constitutional issues involved. On 11 April 1932 Ramsay MacDonald noted, 'If we are not careful, we may get the Dominions up against us on the ground that we alone are dealing with a matter which is the concern of the Commonwealth as a whole.'[9] Yet undesirable as it might be to have the Dominions in, it was hardly possible on matters of status to keep them out.

Not all of the uncertainties were removed with the Irish publication on 20 April 1932 of the Constitution (Removal of Oath) Bill. It was drafted on the assumption that Article 17 of the constitution, that is the oath, was or might be deemed an integral part of the Treaty and that therefore it was at the least prudent to repeal Section 2 of the constitution (the repugnancy clause) and to delete the words 'within the terms of the Scheduled Treaty' from Article 50. 'The question', as de Valera put it to the Senate on 25 May, 'is can we do this without violating the Treaty of 1921? I believe we can.' And how? By taking into account the conclusions of subsequent Imperial Conferences. 'Whatever may have been the position in 1921', de Valera continued, 'there is no doubt that in 1926 and 1930 and the position today in so far as status is concerned the Irish Free State stands on the same level as Canada, Australia, New Zealand and Great Britain herself'. If they 'can do that . . . we can do it'. It was no use saying that the Irish Free State was precluded from so doing by the Treaty because that would mean the Treaty had fixed a position for all time. That was clearly contrary to Imperial Conference resolutions. When asked why he did not negotiate, de Valera replied there was no longer any point in so doing. He did not want to go through the pretence of asking permission. He held that this was 'a test, a real test, as to whether the declarations of 1926 and 1930 mean what they say or not'.[10]

As the President foreshadowed, there were further tests relating to the constitutional issue to come, chief among them being the place of the Crown in the constitution. The issue of advice had been disposed of by resolution of the Imperial Conference in 1930 – dominion governments thereafter each had its own exclusive right with direct access to the King to advise on the appointment of a Governor-General. But in effect, the government of the Irish Free State had enjoyed such entitlement since the state's inception. What de Valera sought was not more amenable or more congenial Governors-General, but to cut the office down to size before ejecting the person who occupied it.

Here the pace was not of the Valera's own making. The Governor-General was James MacNeill, politically unfortunate brother of the even more unfortunate Eoin and due to retire in 1933. Some of President de Valera's Cabinet colleagues resentful, not so much of MacNeill – though he was a Cumann na nGaedheal nominee – as of continuance of the office, offered discourtesies, which the President deprecated, but sought thereafter to anticipate and circumvent rather than openly discountenance. It was, however, only a question of time until MacNeill, deeply offended by ministers departing from diplomatic social functions as soon as the Governor-General arrived, decided enough was enough. On 10 July 1932, against the advice of the Executive Council, he released to the press the text of his acrimonious exchanges with de Valera about the discourtesies to which he had been subjected; on 9 September his appointment was terminated by King George V, acting on the advice of the Executive Council. It is not in dispute that, however much provoked, the Governor-General had acted unconstitutionally. None the less he appeared not dissatisfied with the course of events.[11]

With MacNeill's resignation, the question arose: who, if anyone, was to fill the office in the interval before de Valera was ready to foreclose on it? Rumour circulated that the Chief Justice was to be nominated. This moved Hugh Kennedy (who held that office from 1924 to 1936), to write to the President[12] on 6 October 1932 to say that the prospect of imposing the duties of the Governor-General upon the Chief Justice, or a panel of judges, was a course which would fill him with 'great anxiety' because of its effect upon the courts.

The Chief Justice further thought it well to advance counter-proposals and outlined them in a memorandum which in due course he submitted to the President. First Kennedy distinguished between Viceroys with their quasi-royal status and Governors-General, who were not quasi-royalty but officers of state. On social as well as political grounds, he thought it well to dispose of Viceroys and thus help to ensure that remnants of the former governing classes were discouraged in their attempts to create a sham court around the King's representative. As for the office of Governor-General, its responsibilities had been considerably narrowed by the Imperial Conferences. In the new order of things, the actual function of a Governor-General was that of an Agent or Attorney of the King 'as head of the Commonwealth of Nations', and as such he would have certain specific or ceremonial acts to perform including the formal sanction of the Crown to such acts. The title Governor-General was an anachronism and a distasteful one at that. Kennedy thought the holder of the office should be known officially as an *Agent* or *Attorney* of the King and should reside at some address in the city centre, for example Merrion Square.

Kennedy was advising on what might be done so long as the dominion position under the Treaty lasted. Though de Valera responded with detachment, the termination of MacNeill's appointment on 9 September was followed on 26 November 1932 by the nomination of Donal Buckley as Governor-General with an office in the outskirts of the city and agency duties. The diminution of status was effected forthwith, but proved of short duration. Not downgrading but abolition remained de Valera's aim. The removal of the King from the constitution was the next on the list.

In 1933 the Anglo-Irish debate acquired longer-term significance and a new dimension. The first came with President de Valera's seizure once more of the initiative, this time by dissolving the Dáil on 2 January. He was rewarded for his political courage by a gain of five seats giving him an overall, if slender, majority with the assurance of an extended term of office. It was with de Valera not Cosgrave, the anti- not the pro-Treaty party that agreement was, if at all, to be reached. That was a prospect the British government had been reluctant to face but could evade no longer.

The new dimension was reflected in the introduction of legislation for the dismantling of the Treaty settlement. It was embodied in three Bills[13] introduced in the Dáil on 2 and 16 November 1933 transferring from the Crown's representative to the Executive Council the power of appropriation under Article 37 of the constitution, foreclosing the Governor-General's power of withholding or resisting Bills and, a less technical matter, abolishing the right of appeal to the Privy Council – still regarded by Unionists at Westminster as a significant safeguard for ex-Unionists in the Free State, who, however, knew better.

In 1933 the Secretary of State surveyed the scene in the House of Commons on 4 May, and again on 14 November and 5 December.[14] The position of the British government remained that abolition of the oath would be in direct conflict with the Free State's obligations under the Treaty and that this was confirmed by the form of the Free State's legislation. In order to achieve its end, the Free State government had been compelled to include in their legislation clauses purporting not only to abolish the oath, but further to repeal the provisions of the Constituent Act and the constitution which set out the authority of the Treaty over the constitution. That was also to be the case with subsequent legislation transferring responsibilities from the Governor-General to the Executive Council. Its significance, Thomas told the House, was that it indicated an intention on the part of the Free State government gradually to eliminate the Crown from the constitution. 'Mr de Valera', he continued, 'has told us . . . that his ultimate aim is the recognition of a United Ireland as a Republic with some form of association with the British Commonwealth in some circumstances and for some reasons and the recognition of the King as the head of the association'. That was totally unacceptable to His Majesty's government. What they would like to see was 'the Irish Free State taking her full part as a member of the Commonwealth, not grudgingly, but of her own free will'.

To this last, de Valera reacted sharply. The Irish people, he said, had never sought membership, the Commonwealth on their side had never been a voluntary association but one entered into only under pressure of overwhelming material force. The alternative to the Treaty had been the threat of immediate war. For them it was not the final settlement. His government inferred from what the Secretary of State had said that the British govenment, recognising the evils of a forced association, would not treat a decision of the Irish people to sever their connection with the Commonwealth as a cause of war or other aggressive action. He asked for a direct and unequivocal statement to that effect. What he got after a lot of discussion in committee and Cabinet in Downing Street, was an expression of incredulity that the Irish Free State government contemplated the final repudiation of their Treaty obligations in that way. That being so, the British government did not feel called upon to say what they might, or might not, do in hypothetical circumstances. [15]

The negative response, as against one on Bonar Law lines, reflected at once the no-risks outlook of the government and regard for de Valera's dialectical skill. It indicated once again the British government's intention to maintain its stand on the sanctity of the Treaty and its overriding authority in Irish constitutional law. But with the enactment of the Statute of Westminster, new uncertainties intruded. They could be resolved only in the courts in the first instance, the Judicial Committee of the Privy Council on appeal.

It has been stated that the Irish courts continued to uphold the fundamental authority of the Treaty as set out in the constitution. This was nearly but not quite so. Where Canada had abolished the right of appeal to the Judicial Committee of the Privy Council in criminal cases in any judgment or order of any court in Canada, the Irish courts allowed that the Free State, consistent with the provisions of the Treaty, might follow – but otherwise they continued to uphold a restrictive view. What of the English courts? Was Irish abolition of appeals by the Free State government consistent with the Statute of Westminster? That had become the crucial question. It could be resolved only on appeal to the Judicial Committee of the Privy Council.

Such appeal was lodged in 1935, the Irish courts, basing themselves on the constitution of 1922 and the overriding authority given therein to the Treaty ruled, once again, as late as 1934, that the Irish government were acting *ultra vires* in their proposed constitutional reforms, because no power had been conferred upon them by which they were entitled to repeal the repugnancy clause in the constitution. On appeal the Judicial Committee of the Privy Council, in a judgment delivered in 1935 by *Moore and Others versus the Attorney-General*, concluded, however, that the effect of the enactment of the Statute of Westminster was to remove the fetter that lay upon the Irish Free State legislature by reason of the Colonial Laws Validity Act, and that consequently the Oireachtas had become free to pass legislation repugnant to imperial legislation and noted that they had in fact done so.[16] In British law, though not in Irish, the judgment therefore conceded that the Statute gave power to the Oireachtas to repeal or amend the Constituent Act and that accordingly the amendments which had been enacted were valid even though they did not fall within the terms of the Treaty. The repugnancy clause had ceased to be relevant, de Valera's action accordingly was not illegal. He had done in the constitutional field what under British law he was entitled to do after 11 December 1931. As he himself had contended, 'if they [the Dominions] can do that . . . we can do it'. This was precisely so.

The advance of the Dominions to equality in status with Britain co-incidentally in time almost certainly deferred the day of Irish departure to independence outside the Commonwealth, by diminishing the prospect of head-on confrontation. If the first wave of the Irish struggle had been memorable for its violence, the second was unprecedented in its exploitation of constitutional devices, which almost fortuitously lay ready to hand. In de Valera the moment had its man.

The Shredding of the Constitution

For the British government thereafter, gone were the days of affirmation, of standing 'absolutely by the Treaty settlement' in a position to which 'they most firmly adhere'. But continuing was the preoccupation with the constitutional position and associated with it an economic war viewed (despite mitigation by the coal–cattle pact of 1934) with increasing concern by the financial and trading departments of both governments. There was a sense of frustration to which the *Economist* gave expression.[17]

On 6 June 1935, the day after the Judicial Committee's ruling, the British Cabinet was reconstructed, Baldwin taking over from Ramsay MacDonald as Prime Minister on that day and Malcolm MacDonald succeeding J.H. Thomas as Dominions Secretary on 22 November that year. Dr McMahon remarks that in retrospect MacDonald's appointment is apt to seem 'like the arrival of the cavalry'. Even if the conjunction of events be deemed the decisive factor in ending the passivity of the immediately preceding years, Malcolm MacDonald's appointment supplied the personal impulse that got things moving again on the British side. After all, with de Valera's progressive pulling away the foundations of the 1921 Dominion Status Settlement could inaction any longer pass muster as a policy? (An Irish Nationality and Citizenship and an Aliens Act[18] came into force in April 1935 with British subjects exempted from the latter, not as of right but by decree of the Executive Council and the abolition of the Governor-General's office was promised.) De Valera had furthermore made public his intention to draft a new constitution. That stirred questions the British would have liked to let lie. Would the constitution conform in essentials to the Treaty? There were awkward questions also. Ought not the British government to convey a desire to be consulted, even though it was more than likely that de Valera, if asked, would rejoin that that was a matter of domestic concern? And how was he to be persuaded to adopt a less uncompromising stance now that he was riding, little in some respects as he liked it, in double harness with the Judicial Committee of the Privy Council?

These were questions which preoccupied the Irish Situation Committee in the spring and summer of 1936, by which time MacDonald had settled into his Dominions Office responsibilities. His first concern was to ensure that he had the backing of his colleagues, and especially of Baldwin, before venturing on the conciliatory moves to which he was predisposed. To this end he circulated a lengthy résumé of Anglo-Irish relations since 1932[19] rather as John Morley had done for Gladstone half a century before.[20] He followed up with an outline of the arguments that could be advanced for a comprehensive understanding between the two governments, retaining the essentials, but not more, of what remained of the 1921 settlement. MacDonald gave two reasons for favouring such an approach; the first that an agreement would enhance Britain's world status, the second that 'it had recently been established' that de Valera was preparing a new constitution in which the King would have no place in the Free State's domestic affairs. If de Valera's intentions were to be modified, MacDonald argued, it would be necessary to act quickly because 'as soon as a constitution of this nature was produced, all hope of keeping the Free State in the Empire would be at an end'. Not all of his colleagues were so persuaded, Lord Hailsham, the Lord Chancellor, dwelling on the hopelessness of approaching the problem without real prospect of success, while in the event of the likely failure the situation would deteriorate further. But from the outset it was apparent that this despairing, rather than hard-line stance lacked substantial support.

At a resumed discussion of MacDonald's proposition on 25 May, Baldwin enquired further of MacDonald whether there was ground for the impression that there had been a change in de Valera's attitude. MacDonald admitted there was none beyond a report that de Valera was 'tending to move to the right and more cooperative'. But to go further the British would have to give him something to which he would undoubtedly attach very great value. This, MacDonald suggested, might be a declaration, such as had already been a matter for debate in 1932, to the effect that the

Irish Free State was mistress of her own destiny, meaning that she could secede as and when she wished. The phrasing used by Bonar Law in 1920 he thought might suffice.[21] The Prime Minister was favourably disposed to an attempt to reach a new settlement, not least because the overseas Dominions would be critical of Irish secession without prior British attempts at reconciliation. He noted, however, that the British negotiators would have to adhere strictly to the principle that any satisfactory settlement would have to be on the basis that the Irish Free State continued to be a member of the British Commonwealth, which involves 'the recognition of the constitutional position of the King in the internal as well as the external affairs of the Irish Free State'.[22]

There was, albeit oblique, recognition of the fact that on the constitutional questions, on the fundamental importance of which both parties were agreed, the prospects of a meeting of minds were diminishing. The proposal for a declaration, commended by MacDonald as a counter to de Valera's contention on the political freedom of the Irish Free State, was deemed a non-starter, given that Britain did not contemplate the possibility of using force of prevent the Free State leaving the Empire. More specifically, the Chancellor of the Exchequer, Neville Chamberlain, assumed that any such declaration would not preclude the imposition of financial and economic sanctions, while the Secretary of State for India was disturbed by the thought of a precedent that might apply with equal force east of Suez, where he feared Bonar Law's doctrine would at the least have an unsettling impact.

The Cabinet also considered British attitudes to the office of Governor-General. In May 1936 the Dominions Secretary had reported to the Irish Situation Committee that it was unfortunately impossible to prevent de Valera from abolishing the office, and much time and ingenuity thereafter was spent on improvising other methods by which the Crown might be represented in the Free State, the most ambitious of which was for the King to perform the functions of the Crown in the Free State, thus acknowledging Ireland's position as a mother country. How would Northern Ireland react to that, enquired the Home Secretary? There was no need to stay upon an answer.

On 9 June 1936 a communication from President de Valera put an end to speculation on all save one of the constitutional issues. He confirmed his intention of introducing the new constitution in the autumn. The office of Governor-General would be abolished, and the Governor-General replaced by a President elected by the people. It was to be inferred that at this stage the position of the Crown in respect of external affairs was not to be changed.[23]

The President's communication was sent by courtesy and the Irish Situation Committee were left with the need to decide whether to send an acknowledgement only or to take soundings on the possibility of an early discussion of all outstanding issues. MacDonald continued to favour the second, the constructive course. But what were outstanding issues? Was the draft constitution one of them? The Home Secretary, Sir John Simon, thought not. Were that issue raised 'Mr de Valera would no doubt take the line that the Irish Free State was fully entitled to do what was proposed without anyone's leave and would quote from the Privy Council judgement the support of their contentions'.[24] What then was the point of doing so and courting de Valera's rejoinder that the provisions of the Irish Free State constitution were 'matters he would not discuss with anyone'. The Lord Chancellor had little doubt that de Valera's demands would remain exactly what they were in 1932: (a) he must have a republic associated with the King for external purposes only; and (b) he must have a republic of all-Ireland.

Even Malcolm MacDonald at that stage took the view, or deemed it a condition of progress to appear to do so, that if an elected President meant the displacement of the Crown, then the Free State would have to be regarded as outside the Commonwealth. On that seemingly now turned what remained of the Treaty of 1921 and the constitution of the Irish Free State. Nevertheless on the British side there remained a desire, despite the constitutional impasse, for an attempt at reaching an overall settlement.

After further soundings it was decided that Malcolm MacDonald should seek to elicit de Valera's views of the future of Anglo-Irish relations. The President was forthcoming. In a four-hour session MacDonald learned much that was fixed but little that was new. The Crown, de Valera told him, would have no function in the internal affairs of the Irish Free State but in matters of common concern the King would be recognised as Head of the British Commonwealth. He (de Valera) did not think allegiance a necessary condition of membership. The removal of the oath, and the Governor-General, and the abolition of Privy Council appeals from the constitution had not meant the Irish had gone out of the Commonwealth. If the British government thought his proposals inconsistent with membership, then 'it would have to turn them [the Irish] out' – a shrewd thrust that, being the one eventuality the British were specially concerned to avoid! What mattered, de Valera contended once more, was the will to cooperation in fields of common concern with particular allusion to finance, trade and, guardedly, defence in terms of maintenance and modernisation of installations at the Treaty ports and the purchase of equipment.

MacDonald proceeded to advise the Irish Situation Committee that if the Irish Free State were to remain in the Commonwealth, the abolition of the office of Governor-General would have to be accepted. There would have to be a declaration to the effect that the Free State was mistress of her own destinies if that enabled de Valera to draft his constitution in accordance with the fundamental principles of Commonwealth membership and in return for an understanding on defence should the British offer to transfer the ports to the Irish Free State and effect a financial and trading settlement. The list was wide-ranging but the items open to negotiation, with the one crucial exception – the drafting of the constitution in accordance with the fundamental principles of Commonwealth membership. As in 1921, allegiance to the Crown was declared to be an absolute. Any concession on this stirred misgivings, yet there were almost as many reservations about the consequences of insistence on it, if likely to result in Irish secession.[25] The upshot was agreement on negotiations with signs of some readiness on the British side to acknowledge that after all there might be a way out in the now somewhat less unfamiliar concept of external association. But, significant as that might appear in retrospect, at the time it proved impossible to get far in talks about any of the headings of a possible settlement without running into the question of allegiance. What was the point of discussing Treaty ports or trading preferences if it were unclear whether the Irish Free State were to be in or out of the Commonwealth?[26] All that could be said by November 1936 was that the balance of probability, given what de Valera and the British government had said about allegiance, was that the two were travelling on a collision course. If that indeed were so, then it was a King's abdication that opened the way to *de facto* Irish republican association with the Commonwealth for some thirteen years.

The External Relations Act

On 11 December 1936, Edward VIII, resolved to marry Mrs Simpson against the advice of his government, abdicated. Under the Statute of Westminster this required action on the part of all dominion governments to settle the succession. Was de Valera to be uncooperative? He was known to be occupied in drafting the new constitution and, while not ready to act, was more nearly so than was the British Cabinet, still undecided about the fundamentals, if any, on which to take a stand. Moreover, de Valera had the advantage of being in a position to decide these matters on his own.

It would have been at once more convenient and more logical to determine future Irish relations with the Commonwealth after, and not before the constitution was approved. This, de Valera explained to the Dáil, was not a situation of his making. He was taking action not because he cared about the succession to the Crown but to avoid the confusion that would result from inaction. Convenience and logic had been minor casualties of royal impetuosity. That meant in the Irish case that the determination of external relations had to come before the constitution was in final form.

On 11 December 1936, de Valera, rearranging his priorities, introduced two pieces of legislation: a Constitution Amendment and an External Relations Bill.[27] The first removed the King from the Legislature, the Executive and the constitution generally; the second, following from this elimination of the Crown in internal government, allotted to it a defined place with limited functions in the external field. Diplomatic and consular representatives thereunder were to be appointed and every international agreement to be concluded on the authority of the Executive Council, but so long as the Irish Free State was associated – and the precise wording was important –

> with the following nations, that is to say, Australia, Canada, Great Britain, New Zealand and South Africa, and so long as the King recognised by those nations as the symbol of their cooperation continues to act on behalf of each of those nations (on the advice of the several governments thereof) for the purposes of the appointment of diplomatic and consular representatives and the conclusion of international agreements, the King so recognised may, and is hereby authorised to, act on behalf of Saorstát Éireann for the like purposes as and when advised by the Executive Council so to do.

The External Relations Act (ERA) was permissive and conditional.[28] The procedure it outlined might be followed so long as the Commonwealth countries continued to cooperate and so long as they owed allegiance to the Crown. But it did not have to be so. On that de Valera was categoric. But permissive and conditional as it was, the Act acknowledged the role of the Crown in the Commonwealth without an explicit, or indeed implicit, recognition of Irish allegiance. The constitution when enacted in 1937 was to effect no change in the ERA, but it sanctioned the regulation of external affairs in this or other ways as national interest might require. In their formal aspect relations with Britain and the Commonwealth had thus been taken out of the constitution, where de Valera felt that they had no place, and had become matters of external policy for the government of the day.

President de Valera's declared purpose was to bring the law and the constitution of the Irish Free State into accord with existing political realities by removing the Crown from the Legislature, the Executive, and generally from the constitution. He assured Cosgrave that the Constitution Amendment Bill introduced on 11 December did not contain any proposition to sever 'our connexion with the states of the British Commonwealth'. Article 1 of the 1922 constitution, which provided that the 'Irish Free State is a co-equal member of the community of nations forming the British Commonwealth of Nations', remained untouched.[29] Nor did de Valera believe that the amending Bill would jeopardise Irish membership of the Commonwealth. While there would be no reference to the King in the new constitution, he pointed out that any relations which existed between 'our State and Great Britain, so long as the people willed to have that connexion, would be maintained by the fact of co-operation and would be regularised . . . by law'. He had not consulted other members of the Commonwealth about the terms of the legislation before the Dáil because he felt consultation to be inappropriate when the action to be taken by the Irish Free State was a matter to be determined by the Dáil and by the Dáil alone. He noted, however, that there had been 'a general desire expressed by the States of the British Commonwealth that there should be concerted action as quickly as possible' to dispose of the constitutional consequences of the abdication. While he was unprepared to give 'any countenance to the idea that the British Parliament can in any way legislate for us', and clear that 'if this thing has to be done it has to be done by our Parliament alone', he conceded that 'so long as there is any association at all . . . it is obvious that we ought to do our part to facilitate other countries in dealing with this situation'.[30]

In December 1936 the provisions of the Act were interpreted in the light of de Valera's statement that Article 1 of the 1922 constitution, (which declared the Irish Free State to be a member of the British Commonwealth of Nations), remained unaffected. But when the draft constitution of 1937 came to be approved by the people, no such provision appeared. Further it was specifically stated (Article 48) that any provision of the constitution of 1922 in its original, or current shredded form still in force was to be repealed on the day the new constitution came into effect. The implications of the External Relations Act as a result acquired a wider importance. An arrangement made while the Irish Free State was a member of the Commonwealth, by a provision of her own constitution, became within a year the one remaining link with the Commonwealth. It was not a link which, in the Irish view, acknowledged any allegiance to the Crown. It allowed an oblique recognition of the position of the Crown as the symbol of free cooperation within the Commonwealth. In that respect it conformed with the intention of and coincided almost exactly with what had been contemplated by the Sinn Féin leaders in 1921 and more nearly still by de Valera's Document No. 2 in 1922.

In the Dáil de Valera's first concern was to reassure his own followers that henceforward the King would act only in an external capacity so far as the Irish Free State was concerned, and that even in that capacity he would be only the instrument by means of which effect would be given to policies which were those of the Executive Council. It was in the Executive Council that authority was vested, and that was fully and formally stated to be so in the Act, so that there might be no possible misrepresentation or misunderstanding.

We propose [said de Valera][31] to continue the King for the functions which he in fact directly exercises and for these only. . . . We are providing for the continuance of these functions on the advice and authority – as in the past and in the future – of the Executive Council. We are clearing up the political, constitutional situation. . . . He [the King] is being retained for these [external] purposes because he is recognised as the symbol of this particular cooperation in the states of the Commonwealth. If the Irish people do not wish to continue him for these purposes, they can end that by legislation. They can end the whole situation by law or limit the exercise of these powers by law. What is given in the bill is permission to continue to use the same instrument.

It will be noted that this permissive element in the Bill would allow of its remaining indefinitely on the Statute Book as the symbol of Irish associa-tion with the Commonwealth whilst the actual use of the Crown in external affairs might be allowed to fall into abeyance.[32] De Valera as time passed was to give increasing attention to this possibility.

The External Relations Act was very much of de Valera's fashioning. It was received by his own supporters with a certain hesitancy by reason of its complexity and repudiated outright by the militant republicans, a small but politically dangerous group. The constitutional opposition, consisted of the Fine Gael party led by ex-President Cosgrave and a small Labour party led by William Norton, both of whom, albeit for different reasons, were highly critical. Norton felt that the Bill conceded too much. Adopt-ing the militant republican viewpoint, which held that if no action had been taken at the time of the abdication a republic would automatically have come into being, Norton argued such inaction was the course of wisdom now that the King had 'voluntarily relinquished his objectionable role here'.[33] The Fine Gael critique was more considered. James Dillon contemptuously referred to the Bill as yet one more exercise of the Presi-dent's 'admitted gift' for 'bewildering and misleading the people'.[34] Dr T.F. O'Higgins protested against this 'zebra legislation',[35] while Costello, Cosgrave's former Attorney-General, felt the Bill created 'a political monstrosity, the like of which is unknown to political legal theory, such a monstrosity as existed nowhere in any polity in the world'.[36] He doubted the value of de Valera's reassurances that the Act would not jeopardise the position of the Irish Free State in the British Commonwealth of Nations, and contended that the work which Cosgrave's government had done in securing a redefinition both of the practice and of the law of the Common-wealth had secured for the Irish Free State a satisfactory position within the Commonwealth. 'We have', he said, 'under the Treaty as a member of the Commonwealth of Nations . . . a greater security for the freedom of this country' and an arrangement 'that secures greater freedom for demo-cracy in this country than any other system that could be devised'.

He then went on to observe:

We heard talk today about striking the shackles from the feet of this nation. . . . There are not any such things as shackles on our freedom at present. . . . The sooner we recognise that fact . . . the better it will be . . . for . . . this country.[37]

Costello went on to ask did not the Act jeopardise the position of the Irish Free State in the Commonwealth? To which de Valera replied, that depended on British reaction, which in turn depended on their assessment of what had been done already and of what they could hope to attain. If it was allowed to fall into abeyance, that would be because the British had not been sufficiently compliant. It was up to them. His declared intention was to proceed by two stages, if that would help to conciliate the minority in the North. The External Relations Act represented stage one; stage two would be when the Act might be quietly allowed to fall into abeyance.

The British were reluctant to face the implications from their point of view of the new departure. De Valera, MacDonald noted,[38] in September 1936 (that is before the abdication crisis) 'has never, even in private conversation, gone beyond the point of saying he would recognise the King as head of the British Commonwealth of Nations. He has studiously avoided any admission that he might consider a new agreement with the United Kingdom in which the King was recognised as constitutional head of the Irish Free State government. Status was understood not to be for bargaining.'[39]

In January 1937 de Valera placed what had been done in perspective. He told Sir Henry Batterbee, the Permanent Under-Secretary at the Dominions Office, that he regarded 'the recent legislation as the end of the story'.[40] By this he meant the end of the status story which to him mattered most in 1937, as it had in 1921. Or in the perspective of this study, that the 1921 settlement was undone. Were the Cabinet to question that assumption of finality? Or were they to acquiesce with such semblance of consistency as they might contrive?

On 25 January the Cabinet had before them a report of the Irish Situation Committee on the interrelationship of the External Relations Act with the Constitution and two memoranda, both by Malcolm MacDonald, one summarising lengthy conversations with President de Valera, the other MacDonald's own recommendations on the attitude to be adopted in the light of the Irish Situation Committee report.[41] MacDonald's approach was cautious, one question to be resolved being how far he would be able to persuade his colleagues to travel along a road they did not wish to go. His principal recommendations were, first, that no final conclusion on de Valera's constitutional proposals could be reached other than in the context of Irish membership of the British Commonwealth of Nations, and therefore in consultation with the Dominions; secondly, that the British government would be prepared to regard the fundamental position of the Irish Free State as a Dominion as not altered by the Free State's constitutional legislation and, thirdly, that attempts should be made to persuade de Valera to subscribe to an Imperial Conference declaration, in the course of which the position of the Crown as the symbol of the free association of the Members of the Commonwealth was confirmed. To these was added a related resolution proposing an early resumption of talks on finance and trade.

In support of these recommendations MacDonald argued in Cabinet that the crucial point was that they should be able to regard the position of the Irish Free State as having been unaltered by recent Irish constitutional legislation and the proposed rewriting of the Irish constitution *only* if the position of the King as Head of the British Commonwealth of Nations and the Crown as the symbol of the association of its members was fully maintained. If it were not, foreigners might object and continued membership prove not to be possible – the last an oft alluded to but at all times improbable contingency.

Members of the Cabinet focused their attention on the position of the Crown. They thought it very inadequately and unsatisfactorily expressed in the Irish constitutional proposals, as indeed it was. They argued in favour of urging de Valera to provide for full recognition of Crown and Commonwealth membership. They felt that he might be prepared to accept a form of coronation oath and that the Free State might be re-presented at the coronation. The First Lord of the Admiralty at a less unrealistic level interjected that de Valera in some respects was moving 'back'. He instanced the fact that Article 1 of the 1922 constitution which had been alluded to by de Valera as indicating continued Commonwealth membership was after all not to reappear in the new constitution. As much was conceded. But dissatisfaction could be translated into action by representations that were likely to end Irish membership. At the prospect, the Cabinet once again drew back. It was not a desirable end. They were under constraint. The Dominions would be critical. The Prime Minister had said it all – he did not see what alternative there was to acceptance of the committee's recommendation subject to the concurrence of the Dominions. That was so because, short of grave provocation, the British government alone could not turn Ireland out; the dominion governments would not.

During the fifteen years 1922–37 the Ireland of the twenty-six counties had two constitutions. Both applied in principle to the whole of Ireland, neither in practice. That of the Irish Free State (1922) was drafted under constraint for a Dominion, that of 1937 for a sovereign, independent democratic state. The constitution of 1922 was drafted by a committee, that of 1937 effectively by the President of the Executive Council. The 1922 draft was submitted to the British government and perforce amended where it was deemed not to conform to the 1921 Treaty; in 1937 the President of the Executive Council let it be known that the constitution was his business and was not to be shown to the Secretary of State. How much had changed in those post-revolutionary years! And how important was the outlook and working practice of de Valera – not for him committee or conference! In such matters, he worked alone. He asked for preliminary drafts – which show de Valera from the outset favouring a radical republican constitution. It also shows his working practice.* It seems he had no constitutional conference or committee. De Valera consulted whom he willed. Again if the records on this are complete, on some of the principal articles he consulted no one. The constitution in a literal sense carried the stamp of his personality yet, social policy apart, it had the breadth that enabled it to serve as a basic document for countries, particularly in South Asia, on their gaining independence some ten years later. By contrast it had little or nothing to offer towards unity.

The Constitution and Status

The wording of the 1937 constitution[42] in relation to territory and status is categoric. Article 1 declared that the Irish nation affirmed its inalienable, indefeasible and sovereign right to choose its own form of government and to determine its relations with other nations; Article 2 that the national territory consisted of the whole island of Ireland and Article 3 that pending the reintegration of the national territory, the practical exercise of jurisdiction would be limited to the twenty-six counties without concession of entitlement. But while Articles 1, 2 and 3 were alike in allowing of no compromise on status or territory, what was written on status treated of issues that had been or were being tidied up; that on territory was a repudiation of the existence of the six counties as a political entity.

There was one surprising feature in the constitution which demonstrated the British dilemma. It was a republican constitution. Not one syllable or comma of it, de Valera explained, would require to be altered were a republic to be declared the next day. But it was not the omission that was deliberate. De Valera conceded at the time and later that he was reluctant so to describe the state, henceforward to be known as Eire, because to him the republic was sacred, and its application to a state comprising only twenty-six of the thirty-two counties of Ireland was akin to political sacrilege. Had not the martyrs of 1916 died for an all-Ireland republic? To sentiment was added, however, substantial reasons of policy. The declaration of a republic at that time would have further alienated the North and

---

* He had drafted the constitution without conference or committee for discussion or debate, but – and it is remarkable – with enquiry of individuals on occasion, as with John Hearne and also the Archbishop of Dublin on the position of the Church. But any such exchange was on a bilateral basis; save to that limited extent all remained in President de Valera's hands. The first two articles on Nation and State would appear to have been drafted without even minimal exchanges, or if there were, nothing of them remains on the files, at the drafting stage.

would thereby have effectively precluded thought of negotiations designed to modify or to end partition. It would almost certainly have jeopardised prospects of securing the return of the Treaty ports. More important even than either of these, it would have forced the issue of republican membership of the Commonwealth. Here the British government could hardly have waived the condition of allegiance altogether, if posed in a direct republican challenge. An oblique approach, non-committal in presentation, but republican in content, was unlikely to alienate dominion and for that matter, some British opinion. There might still be scope for negotiation on the basis of diluted Commonwealth membership. It would also indicate to the Dominions that the Irish Free State was not seceding as a result of British initiatives – in tactic as well as aim de Valera in 1937 was very different to Costello in 1949.

The Imperial Conference 1937 and Irish Membership

For the Prime Ministers assembling for the Imperial Conference 1937, MacDonald on 14 May added yet one more to the memoranda he had composed.[43] It gave a now familiar résumé of developments since 1932. In introducing it, MacDonald drew attention to the fact tnat the new Irish constitution, published on 1 May and to be submitted to the people in a referendum on 1 July 1937, was a republican constitution, even though not so described. He also underlined the fact that common allegiance to the Crown had been an essential part of the 1926 declaration and added 'we regard the position of the Crown as one of the things that must be maintained'. In the discussion that followed, the most notable feature was dominion, over and above continuing British insistence on the unique and indispensable position of the Crown, with Hertzog seeing no reason why even a republican Dominion need be ruled out so long as the symbolic position of the Crown in the Commonwealth was still acknowledged. The other feature of the note was the marked reluctance on every side to push Anglo-Irish estrangement to further extremes. 'What the British government does now as regards Ireland', observed Hertzog, 'is most important for the future of the Commonwealth'. Chamberlain explained that to the Irish mind there was nothing illogical in having a republic within a Commonwealth owing allegiance to the Crown and, in his concluding summary, he stressed in particular the disadvantages of taking any decision which would have the effect of pushing Ireland out when she wished to remain in. They were so obvious that such steps could only be justified if they were clearly necessary to save the Commonwealth 'from some worse fate'. Accordingly 'we do not propose to lay down any conditions, which if the Irish Free State were to transgress, she would put herself out of the Commonwealth'.

This conclusion, in which all of the dominion Prime Ministers concurred, conveys the essence of the British and dominion governments' response to the constitutional changes culminating in the External Relations Act 1936, and the 1937 constitution. They were determined to find technical evidence for adducing allegiance implicit in the former (and duly found it) and firm in their resolve to disregard the republican character of the latter. Yet, it will be noted, the *modus vivendi* was reached without conceding that a republic could be a member of the Commonwealth or taking advantage of Hertzog's passing allusion to explore the possibility of a twofold formulation of allegiance. This meant, and was probably bound to mean, despite the ingenuities of the External Relations Act, a postponement rather than a resolution of the problem of Irish/Commonwealth relations.

Taken together, the External Relations Act with the new constitution uprooted what remained of the dominion settlement of 1921, with one exception. The oath had gone, appeals to the Judicial Committee of the Privy Council had gone, the Governor-General had gone, the Crown had been taken out of the 1922 constitution, not to be reinstated in that of 1937, which, as an element in its republicanism had an elected President as its head. All that remained on paper of dominion status was the permissive procedure sanctioned by the External Relations Act, which was clean contrary to the relationship envisaged in the Treaty. What was the reaction of British and dominion governments to these revolutionary changes? Following MacDonald's advice, it was acquiescent and muted. They could not, however, altogether refrain from comment. The British government accordingly consulted with dominion governments and, in agreement with them, issued a statement. The statement said that the British government was prepared to treat the new constitution 'as not affecting a fundamental alteration in the position of the Irish Free State as a member of the British Commonwealth of Nations'. As a piece of understatement this has its place in history. Well might one ask, well may de Valera have reflected at the time, what then could effect a fundamental alteration? An invitation to irony, it came to be regarded as statesmanlike. It was not the end in constitutional terms of the Treaty story. The ports remained in British hands and the six counties were partitioned off.

The Ports

The ports and partition were, in one sensitive area, interrelated. That area was security. Had Britain not been assured of bases in Northern Ireland, it is hardly conceivable that its government would have been ready to contemplate the transfer of the ports to Eire on a basis other than that of an alternative defence arrangement. With that assurance, however, they felt no need in security terms to be inflexible. In the later twenties, they sought to interest Cosgrave in taking them over. He declined because of expense. Bonar law in the debate on the Treaty had explained the attitude of the Unionist party. In the House of Commons on 15 December 1921 he had put these points with characteristic force and observed, in reference to the defence article, that unless you got goodwill in time, nothing much else mattered. He believed the government were 'perfectly right . . . to put in that provision about the use of the ports and all the rest of it'. It was worth a great deal. There could never be any question of their using them, that being conditional on when they (the Irish) think it necessary. 'If the Southern Parliament and people are hostile, whether you call them a Republic or a Dominion will not make very much difference. We have always said that strategic considerations were of great importance but I say for myself . . . that Ulster, so large a part of Ireland, inhabited . . . by a population which is on our side in any struggle, would be worth more as a security in case of danger than any number of conditions in any Bill.'[44] All, or almost all, turned out as he surmised.

In any such negotiation de Valera's position was superficially ambivalent. He was categoric in his assurances that the Irish would not allow their country to be used for an attack on Great Britain.[45] His commitment to neutrality, however, remained down to the Munich crisis less than absolute. It was that ambivalence that kept negotiations alive.[46] Both sides accepted that there was a measure of common interest in defence, but it was the British alone who wanted a firm commitment. One possibility advanced by MacDonald was the return of the ports to Irish sovereignty coupled with an assurance that, in the event of war, the British by grace of the Irish government would be given use of them.[47] It was a proposal which, had it been adopted, was likely to cause the maximum of resentment with minimal advantage. The return of the ports was not an end in itself, but a means to an end, keeping Eire out of war. Without the ports the context of neutrality would thereby have been forfeited. Yet de Valera was concerned to keep MacDonald in play, by not excluding the possibility of some understanding related to defence, to keep negotiations for a return of the ports alive. In all this he moved warily, mindful of past precedent and experience.

Article 7 of the Treaty, it will be recalled, bound the Irish Free State in time of peace to afford the British forces extensive facilities in the Treaty ports and in time of war, or strained relations with a foreign power, such harbour and other facilities as the British government might require for the defence of the British Isles. In the 1930s the debate was resumed, this time in face of imminent reality. What would be the likely effect of the exercise of such rights by Britain in wartime? If exercised, would a belligerent be likely to respect Irish neutrality? In the 1921 negotiations, Griffith, Collins and Childers did not think so. It was hardly conceivable otherwise. The question in the later thirties was one with which de Valera, as may be judged by his speeches, was becoming increasingly preoccupied. He had been President of the Council at the League of Nations Assembly in 1932 and became convinced that the testing time of the League was approaching. When, following Japanese invasions into Manchuria, Mussolini decided to invade Abyssinia 'with Geneva, without Geneva, or against Geneva', de Valera warned the League★ – 'Make no mistake, if on any pretext whatever we were to permit the sovereignty of even the weakest state amongst us to be unjustly taken away, the whole foundation of the League would crumble into dust.' The Irish government supported sanctions, but opinion was troubled and divided. There were complaints, moreover, that Ireland was in this too closely associated with Britain. The League failed. Abyssinia was followed in March 1936 by German occupation of the Rhineland. All the portents were of approaching war. What was a small state to do? De Valera, who was throughout his own Minister of External Affairs, was convinced, once collective security had broken down and the League had self-evidently failed, that for a small state there was only one course – neutrality. This was the lesson from experience drawn not least from observation made from the vantage point of the League of Nations at Geneva. It was, on the evidence of the records, perception of approaching great power conflict, not abstract principle, as is retrospectively apt to be assumed, that so persuaded him. By June 1937 de Valera was said to be 'obsessed' with the dangers of the European situation. He was right to be. But could the British be induced, as part of a general settlement of the land annuities and other issues, to cede control of the ports at such a time? De Valera thought not. Some twenty years later, he recalled that he had little or no hope of success until Chamberlain made an allusion in passing to the advances being made in defensive devices and de Valera, who thought the reference was to radar, whether correctly or otherwise, was thereafter convinced that he would get the ports.

On 7 January 1938, the Irish Cabinet (for which one might read de Valera) authorised the sending of a delegation to London 'for the purpose of discussing the various outstanding questions', including finance and trade, it being ruled that 'any agreement which might be reached... would be subject to the approval of the Government as a whole'.[48] The sixth of December 1921 was one of the never to be forgotten days in Irish history! On the British side the role of conciliator was taken over by the Prime Minister, Neville Chamberlain, who was emotionally over and above politically, committed to Ireland, which for him was part of his family heritage. Writing to his sister on the opening of the conference, he wrote, 'in particular de V. himself and I get on excellently... I shall be grievously disappointed if we don't get all round agreement on everything

★ Speech in the Assembly of the League, 16 September 1935.

except partition. That is a difference that can't be bridged without the assent of Ulster.' And then the revealing aside: 'It would be another strange chapter in our family history if it fell to me to settle the Irish question after the long efforts made by Father and Austen.'[49]

In March the talks almost foundered – no doubt Chamberlain was right in thinking he had saved them.[50] His critics at the time and since have alleged that he was interested only in the appeasement of great and menacing totalitarian states. This does not, however, stand up to closer scrutiny. Neville Chamberlain kept up an extensive correspondence with members of his family throughout the negotiations and his letters are now in the possession of the Chamberlain archives at the University of Birmingham. He was passionately concerned to conciliate and by conciliation to end the bitterness of centuries.[51] Chamberlain was convinced that the return of the ports would further this broad political aim. Signed on 25 April, the 1938 Anglo-Irish agreement did precisely this. In the earlier phases of the negotiations Chamberlain was led on by hopes of a defence agreement that might be embodied in a Treaty. But de Valera, sensitive to the likely reaction of the IRA at home, withdrew from what Chamberlain deemed to have been a qualified assurance. Chamberlain was disappointed, but not as another might have been to the extent of abandoning his goal. The really important thing, he wrote, is to have a friendly Ireland, and that he accepted he would not get without the return of the ports. It was the big thing that mattered – he was sure Austen Chamberlain,[52] a signatory of the Treaty, would have approved. On the charge of neglect of British strategic interests, Chamberlain had the memorandum from the Chiefs of Staff[53] that did not on military grounds discourage a course of action, which for political reasons he was resolved to pursue. They argued that to hold the ports in wartime against a hostile hinterland would have imposed a drain on British resources when they were otherwise stretched to the uttermost. No one sensitive to the strength of republican nationalist anti-British sentiment in Ireland at that time would be disposed to discount that judgement. Indeed, it might plausibly be argued that within their own terms of reference, all were right – de Valera in thinking the return of the ports a condition of Irish neutrality; Chamberlain in concluding that it was a condition of good relations; and Churchill in asserting their retention essential to Britain's security. In the last resort, however, it is unrealistic to view the return of the ports in isolation from the larger whole where experience, instinct and temperament influenced judgement. In this wider perspective, MacDonald's 'pitiful cringe to de Valera' had been seen as merely encouraging 'a creature like Goering to ask for more', while Chamberlain foresaw a new era of peace grounded in appeasement,[54] and de Valera the liquidation of a substantive contingent liability imposed by the Treaty and likely to involve Eire in any major war in which Britain was engaged.

Northern Ireland: Constitution and Reactions to the 1938 Agreement

On Northern Ireland Neville Chamberlain from the outset of the negotiations declared he had nothing to offer. The fundamentals of British policy were and remained as set out in 1936. They remained recognition of the Crown in the Commonwealth and acquiescence by the 'Irish Free State Government in the present position whereby the consent of Northern Ireland is essential to the establishment of a United Ireland'.[55] No one would contemplate the making of an agreement, the Prime Minister had said, unless it was based on these two fundamental principles.[56] Both were at issue and to be sustained, albeit obliquely at times in the case of the first, and by constant reaffirmation in the case of the second.[57]

The Northern Ireland government, however, continued to indicate a twofold concern. On the one hand they feared lest in this subsidiary settlement Northern Ireland might lose out economically; and, more far-reaching, lest, despite Chamberlain's assurances, in the course of negotiations the British, in their desire for an overall settlement with the Irish Free State, should allow the future of Northern Ireland to be written into the agenda.

In the event, Northern Ireland had justifiable misgivings on the first count. They were real enough, and indeed an almost inevitable consequence of an artificial Border. The Northern Ireland government (having once again decided upon non-participation in triangular talks) complained that Irish tariffs had depressed natural outlets for Northern Irish goods. Chamberlain made representations to the government of the Irish Free State on its behalf. They were unrewarding. The Irish government declined, much to Chamberlain's chagrin, to make any concession whether by way of free, or freer, entry of the Northern Irish manufactured goods into Eire. The forebodings of those who in 1920–21 foresaw entrenchment of interest on either side of the border were fulfilled.

In respect of partition, Articles 2 and 3 of the constitution were well calculated to provoke the Ulster Unionists. Article 2 declared that the national territory consisted of the whole of Ireland pending the reintegration of which, Article 3 affirmed, the laws passed by the Irish Parliament should have the like area and extent of application as the laws of the Irish Free State. In conjunction, the two articles presented a frontal challenge to the existence of the Northern state. The same applied with equal force to the naming of the state 'Eire', or in the English language Ireland, in Article 4. In Belfast it was felt that at the least this last called for a rejoinder. Was not the appropriate one to call the six counties, Ulster?[58] The Northern Ireland Cabinet discussed the matter and, with evident regret, allowed it to lapse. And why? In the first place because, high politics apart, the government stockbroker advised against it. It would, he contended, reduce the status of government loans by suggesting they were only of local standing. In the realm of high politics the fear that the amendment in name might suggest other changes in the Government of Ireland Act of 1920 was well grounded. In the event the political entity that was the six counties remained Northern Ireland for all official purpose, with Ulster coming into its own for triumphalist Unionist occasions, while as for the Irish Free State, its nomenclature passed stealthily from the page of history.

Nomenclature was, however, of little importance. What signified in the longer term were political concepts as set out in the constitution. In October 1937, de Valera had explained them to Malcolm MacDonald, who was taken aback by the phrasing of Articles 2 and 3 of the constitution, of which he had had no forewarning.[59] De Valera sought to reassure him. The first four articles, he explained, were under the heading of the Nation. The Nation, as set out in Article 1, included the whole area of Ireland. The remaining Articles were listed under the State, which for the present was restricted to the twenty-six counties. As for Article 44 which affirmed the special position of the Catholic Church 'as the guardian of the Faith professed by the great majority of its citizens', de Valera upheld it as being in essence descriptive.

Anglo-Irish Relations on the Eve of War

Despite continuing differences in approach, a substantial improvement in Anglo-Irish relations was effected, one issue always excepted. In October 1937, de Valera had told MacDonald that he was strongly in favour of Ireland's continuing its association with Britain and the Commonwealth, not least because Irishmen were settled in every part of it. At one time he had favoured breaking the link, but no longer. He was in favour of a republic but now only in the context of association. But all of that would be at risk should partition continue indefinitely, such was increasingly his theme.[60] As other problems, and especially those of status, were eased or resolved, that of partition moved into the foreground. De Valera stood by his concession – as he deemed it – of a republic in name associated with the Commonwealth as the furthest he could go to meet the sentiments of the minority. After all in his view 'they were Irishmen: no nation had more definite and easily definable boundaries than the nation inhabiting the small island of Ireland'.[61] This was the assertion of a geographical determinant of nationality, which of its essence allowed of little or no scope for compromise.

What de Valera deemed a concession made negligible impact on Ulster Unionists. To the majority of them at that time acceptance of external association was inconceivable. If anything, attitudes had hardened since the 'not an inch' days of the early twenties. While de Valera, as the 1938 negotiations progressed, came to think to Neville Chamberlain as 'a sympathetic British Prime Minister', something he had never hoped to find,[62] this if anything enhanced his sense of the urgency of partition. How would they fare if they had to deal with an unsympathetic Prime Minister? In April 1939, he said that the feeling here and in the United States was becoming 'every day more and more bitter' over the continuation of partition.[63] And again 'If . . . efforts to find a solution are not made at once, it will be too late . . . and the appeasement of last year will be completely nullified. . . . It is vital that the temptation to our young people to try to cut this knot will be removed quickly . . . '.[64] How? The British government that made partition should undo it. Neville Chamberlain did not rule it out – if de Valera followed the advice he had given him, he wrote, 'I should not despair of ultimate agreement in unity'. The British government were pledged privately, if not publicly, to unity on conditions of assent from the two parts of Ireland. In the late thirties, indications of a readiness to cooperate at any level were hard to come by. In April 1937 Malcolm MacDonald, in the context of current changes, had sounded out Craig about a council meeting alternately in Belfast and Dublin to discuss technical subjects of common interest. Craig replied that of course there had been no change in Ulster's attitude: that they would never think of amalgamation with the Free State, that 'no representative of Northern Ireland would ever walk into a building to do official business unless that building were flying the Union Jack' and it would be 'impossible to confine the discussion to technical subjects because Irish Free State representatives could never keep off politics' or stop 'breaking agreements'.[65]

CHAPTER 14
External Association 1937–49

Belligerent and Neutral: a Tense Relationship

Some twelve years elapsed between the coming into effect of the new Irish constitution on 29 December 1937 and the final Irish secession from the Commonwealth on 18 April 1949. In those twilight years, Anglo-dominion relations with Eire were conducted on an equivocal basis, the Irish government proceeding on the assumption that Eire was a foreign country with a readily terminable relationship with the countries of the Commonwealth from outside, while Commonwealth governments concurred in the view that relations should be conducted on the assumption that Eire was not a foreign country, it was a member-state – albeit of a special kind. Neither was insistent upon its own interpretation – an element of fiction was understood to be a condition of cooperation. For six of those years, there was a world war in which the United Kingdom (including Northern Ireland) and the overseas Dominions were belligerents and Eire neutral, the period coming to be known in Ireland first in common parlance and then officially, as the 'Emergency'. De Valera allowed that the system was complicated but more than once asserted that it was well understood.

As for those who failed to understand, why most of them did not wish to succeed. Two questions have attracted the interest of historians – firstly, how the external association–Commonwealth relationship applied in peace and in the safeguarding of neutrality in time of war, and secondly, why its foreclosure was effected abruptly and seemingly with little close consideration after de Valera's defeat in the 1948 general election.

Modus Vivendi

Until September 1939 Irish–Commonwealth relations went on much as though Eire remained a conforming Dominion. But once war was unleashed, the instrumentalities of dominion status no longer sufficed, or indeed remained appropriate, for either party. As between belligerent and neutral distancing was inevitable and indeed generally prudent. There were bound to be misunderstandings; the modest aim was that of limiting them to the minimum. For that one innovation was deemed to have priority – the appointment of a British diplomatic representative in Dublin. De Valera agreed in principle, but in practice was reluctant to receive one. He was much concerned about the reactions of the more extreme republicans, he indicated to John Maffey, the recently retired Permanent Under-Secretary at the Colonial Office, who was sent to Dublin to negotiate the question. There was in particular the matter of nomenclature. 'British High Commissioner' and variants of it were put aside as being part of the vocabulary of Empire in the course of transformation into Commonwealth, while the British were unwilling to have Irish relations conducted by an Ambassador and, as would be implied, dealt with by the Foreign Office.[1] In September 1939 de Valera, though still reluctant, indicated his willingness to receive a 'United Kingdom Representative to Eire'. To the post Maffey was himself appointed; Dulanty, in London, however, continued to be styled Irish High Commissioner.

Until 1938 Maffey's experience had been imperial not Commonwealth – an erstwhile Governor-General of the Sudan, remembered on the North-West Frontier of India for the drawing of a 'Maffey' frontier line, and Under-Secretary at the Colonial Office. To all this far-flung Empire experience the practice of diplomacy in Dublin was a strange climax.

It was to be Maffey's responsibility to sustain such measure of understanding between de Valera, the nationalist leader *par excellence*, uncompromising in all that he sensed to touch on his country's rights, and the formidable and aggrieved imperialist Churchill protesting with demands to which de Valera said he would never accede. Now that more evidence is available, it becomes understandable how Maffey's reputation came to be earned. It was by his skill, not to mention balancing courage in tempering resentful injunctions from No. 10 Downing Street with some comprehension and concern to set out the conditions of Irish wartime cooperation. In addition he pointed out the problems arising from neutrality, despite the stormy reception this might provoke in Downing Street.

Survivors of the generation of the Treaty negotiations and more especially those on defence must have noted with satisfaction the transformation that had been effected in less than two decades between the Treaty debates and the testing years of the Second World War. On the Irish side, the first aim in 1921 had been to secure recognition of a sovereign Irish status which over and above its appeal to nationality would *inter alia* vest the choice between peace and war unequivocally in Irish hands; the second, closely related to it, was to avoid continuing or entering into an arrangement with Britain which in the event of war might prejudice Irish neutrality. Both, as earlier recalled, were achieved before the outbreak of the Second World War: the first by the advances in dominion status culminating in the Statute of Westminster; the second by the return of the ports under the 1938 Agreement. It has been alleged that de Valera did not disclose his intention to remain neutral in the event of war and that by his silence on the point he had misled Britain and other Commonwealth countries. This was not so. On that Maffey was explicit[2] that de Valera more than once had placed on record that, in the event of war, Eire would remain neutral unless attacked, in which case she would resist with such resources as were in her hands.

On the outbreak of war, 2 September, neutrality was approved in the Dáil without dissent.[3] This came as no surprise to those who had followed the formulation of Irish policy and de Valera's carefully phrased speeches. A large section of British opinion, however, which had little regard for and less understanding of the nature of abstractions, found it hard to reconcile with dominion status, let alone to take the further step of external association. Yet in fact on Commonwealth connection in international law, the Irish entitlement to decide on peace or war was established twice over in principle, once by virtue of Eire being a Dominion with the status of a Dominion and again after 1937, not as a Dominion, but as a sovereign state with final authority in the constitution approved by the people. This twofold basis derived from coincidence in *practice* of dominion and sovereign status on this point at this juncture in time. It was the dominion aspect that was a source of some difficulty. Nor did it apply to Eire only. In September 1939 two Dominions, Canada and South Africa, were concerned, as Eire was not, to establish their right to decide between peace and war, in their case within a dominion context. Mackenzie King underlined the Canadian doctrine he had made his own – namely 'parliament will decide'. To demonstrate this he delayed the taking of that decision till the Canadian Parliament could assemble,[4] the Canadian declaration self-evidently coming independently and later than the British.

In British eyes, Eire was a Dominion. Garner in his history of *The Commonwealth Office 1925–1968* entitled the chapter on wartime Anglo-Irish relations 'Neutral Dominion'.[5] It was as an externally associated state that Eire had decided on neutrality; it was as a Dominion that the British continued to regard it. Resentment in England at the climax of the battle of the Atlantic, in which the ports played the larger part, was the keener because Eire was deemed, not an externally associated state, but a Dominion acting out of character. There might have been some advantage all round had Britain and the overseas Dominions in 1937 taken the magnanimous course of inviting de Valera to make proposals, either for external association or for outright secession, as a final settlement of the status question. As it was on Commonwealth occasions between 1939 and 1945 acclaim for the Dominions at war came to be followed by reference to the 'one lamentable exception'.

Churchill, now back in office as First Lord of the Admiralty, felt aggrieved and resentful at being deprived of the use of the ports. He sought among other things to persuade his Cabinet colleagues that Eire was constitutionally not entitled to declare neutrality. In default of sufficient support Churchill turned his mind to the possibility of enlisting dominion association for backing a British demand for the return of the ports as 'essential to our security'. To this the objection was raised that there would be strong objections to any such representations by the Dominions.

Churchill had asked the Cabinet on 5 September 1939 to appoint a committee to report on questions arising from the 'so-called neutrality of the so-called Eire'.[6] On no account, he contended, should the government acquiesce in 'the odious treatment we are receiving'. Discarding Maffey's conciliatory line, which had been circulated to the Cabinet, what he had in mind was an enquiry into the likely effect of pressure on the government of Eire to accede to a British request for facilities in Eire, the use of the ports having first priority. Since his transfer of the ports, Chamberlain remained Prime Minister, while Churchill as First Lord of the Admiralty was responsible for the Royal Navy in its defence of the western approaches. These differences surfaced but the surprise was that there were no resignations – neither from Chamberlain, the proponent of appeasement of Eire, convinced of the long-standing advantages of the 1938 Anglo-Irish Agreement, nor from Churchill with his criticisms of Irish neutrality and his contention that the ports should be reclaimed forthwith by economic or psychological pressure, without in the last resort excluding force.

The debate came to a head at the Cabinet meeting of 24 October 1939. Dr Canning judges it to have been 'the closest the War Cabinet had yet come to an internal crisis'.[7] The views of Chamberlain and Churchill were 'diametrically opposed'; neither, however, Dr Canning argues, was in a position to afford an open break: Churchill because he had enjoyed nothing anywhere near the backing in the Conservative party needed for him to challenge for the party leadership, and Chamberlain because he was in no position to dispense with the most formidable of his colleagues. Had it come to implementation of a Churchillian forward policy in Ireland the evidence suggests that misgivings about it would have multiplied to the extent of rendering its implementation impracticable.

The actual outcome, a middle procrastinating course, was the appointment of two committees. The first with the Lord Chancellor re-elected as chairman, and the Law Officers as members, was deputed to sort out the legal and constitutional issues that would be involved in the termination of Eire's membership of the Commonwealth and the second with the Dominions Secretary, Anthony Eden, in consultation with other departments separately to advise on the financial, economic and political issues involved. The upshot was that in both cases, save life or death extremity, Irish neutrality should be accepted and worked to the best advantage with the Irish government or, as the interdepartmental committee put it, it seemed 'very doubtful whether any pressure which we could bring to bear upon Eire . . . would, in fact, induce the Government of Eire to accord us the facilities desired, while a hostile Eire would result in the loss of such cooperation, whatever it may be worth, as the Government of Eire are at present disposed to accord'. On this Garner commented retrospectively, 'This remained throughout the attitude of officials in the D.O.' It did not encourage dramatic interventions; it may indeed have preempted them. The official mind felt there had been a sufficiency of British enterprise in Ireland!

The critical phase of the war in the Atlantic opened with the fall of France and the German seizure of the Channel ports in May 1940. This brought neutral Ireland within distance of Nazi invasion about which Churchill was less perturbed than many, sensing that any such venture would offer opportunities for a telling rejoinder. Without a German invasion there would be no British intervention. That had become settled policy. There was, moreover, no Nazi intention to invade, as we now know, but Nazi intentions were not known in 1940 and the Battle of Britain still lay ahead. Yet there was felt to be a need for political action, reflected in a flurry of hastily composed diplomatic moves, which in calmer moments must have appeared more likely to rigidify familiar positions in the Anglo-Irish triangular interrelationship than open up resources for war.

The War Cabinet, seemingly without air of conviction, drafted proposals for an Irish bargain – unity of Ireland for de Valera after the war in return for Irish entry into the war or, failing that, concession of the ports forthwith serving as 'first step'. Chamberlain was nominated to take overall charge, with MacDonald and Cranborne to sound out Dublin and to put conditional proposals to Belfast for a deal.

On 5 June Chamberlain asked Craigavon to consider what conciliatory gesture the people of Northern Ireland might make at this, the great crisis of the war. Craigavon replied that de Valera's neutrality must needs be abandoned before he would meet for discussion with him. That meant no meeting. To Craigavon's counter of abandonment of neutrality and cooperation with Britain, de Valera returned an emphatic negative. Irish policy was resistance to any invader. Neutrality would not be abandoned even for unity. De Valera's aim was a united all-Ireland republic which would remain neutral; marking its own unfettered decision on neutrality or war.

The remarkable thing remains that it was thought first in London, as later in Washington, that neutrality might be a negotiable factor. In fact had de Valera contemplated any departure from neutrality, there was his Minister of Defence and former Chief of Staff of the IRA Frank Aiken at his side, at times literally, to remind him of the consequences of participation in the context of domestic division, shadowed by civil war memories. In the British draft there was the further proposal that unity was for the future, entry into the war immediate. Craigavon for his part was not consulted about the proposal for implementation extending to an Irish unity on the basis of a post-war federal constitution. When he learned by letter of it, his reaction was one of indignation. He telegraphed Chamberlain, 'profoundly shocked and disgusted by your letter making suggestions so far reaching behind my back'.

How should the War Cabinet proceed – persuasion deprecated, pressure precluded and force altogether excluded – to meet Churchill's resentful acquiescence in what he regarded as a wrongful and unwarranted situation, calculated to corrode relations between the two peoples? Only changes in time and circumstances could offer relief. On 6 December 1941, Roosevelt's 'day of infamy', the news reached Downing Street that the Japanese had struck at Pearl Harbour at 2 a.m. that morning. Churchill telegraphed de Valera – *'Personal Private and Secret. Now is your chance. Now or never! A nation once again!'*[8] There was later said to be some uncertainty as to textual meaning. Yet it seems clear enough in its general drift - unity for participation. De Valera delayed two days before replying. Henceforward it was not Britain, it was the United States that took the leading role in Allied policy towards Eire. That was as the British deemed best.

In the closing stages of the war de Valera as Taoiseach, with strict observance of protocol, called upon the German Minister in Dublin on 2 May 1945 to express official condolences on the death of Hitler as German Head of State. With neutrality underlined, this caused offence abroad rather than at home, where rigorous Emergency censorship obscured the infamy that was Nazi Germany. Churchill, in a triumphalist victory broadcast on 13 May, indulged his resentment in a lengthy passage on Irish neutrality and withholding of the ports. It was out of proportion and out of place and was in the perspective of the Cabinet debates of 1939–42. The Canadian High Commissioner in Dublin, J.D. Kearney, recorded in his Diary next day that it could redound to the disadvantage of Britain and of the Commonwealth by consolidating Irish national sentiment behind its leader and the policy of neutrality and, as a minor consequence, by undoing much of the endeavours of others on either side in less exalted positions, to create a new post-war climate in which Anglo-Irish relations might blossom. 'The final, crucial episode', writes Professor Fanning,[9] 'in determining popular perceptions of neutrality was the celebrated exchange of broadcasts between Churchill and de Valera when the war in Europe ended . . . Churchill's self-congratulation at his government's having refrained from seizing the Irish ports when her national interest demanded it', and de Valera's dignified rebuke . . . 'caught the public imagination and identified neutrality with national independence as nothing had done before'. It may, indeed, be so and that this dialectical confrontation may prove to be one of those examples of times past, which move men beyond comparison more than those of their own time.[10]

The Labour Government's Approach

The end of the war in Europe was followed in July 1945 by a historic Labour victory in the British general election. It was Attlee not Churchill who was to be confronted with the twofold problem – status and partition – of post-war Angol-Irish relations, now moving on to the centre of the politico-constitutional stage. What, it was increasingly asked, did external association amount to in nationalist thinking? What were its more general implications, especially in the context of unity? On the British side, Labour government and Conservative opposition were at one. Both would have liked to have deferred discussion indefinitely and, in the case of partition, ministers were content or rather more than content with its conceptual continuance, but without renewed debate on external association. To de Valera also this was acceptable in the existing circumstances, but not so to Fine Gael, Labour and others, notably Independents. This ensured that the problem, which had seemed to de Valera in the late thirties to have been settled, would surface again.

It will be recalled that when on 24 December 1937 the governments of the Commonwealth declared that they were prepared to treat the Irish constitution as not effecting a fundamental alteration in the position of the Irish Free State as a member of the British Commonwealth of Nations, de Valera had not felt it incumbent upon him to clarify the resulting constitutional position. It sufficed for him to indicate that he regarded Eire as being no longer a member. The debate was not further pursued during the war years. In 1945, however, he explained that the government did not feel called upon to make any comment. 'We could only accept the British Government statement as the expression of a view taken by them in full knowledge of our position here at the time.'[11] Thus he had placed and continued to place the onus of determining whether Eire was associated with the Commonwealth, and if so in what way, upon the governments of the Commonwealth. It was for them to say. That, however, was just what they wished to avoid doing.

Unlike their predecessors in the 1930s, Attlee's colleagues had no lack of information on the situation in Ireland after 1945, chief among them being the well-staffed office of the United Kingdom representative, with Maffey at its head, who surveyed the scene for the whole period of the war. Among the commentaries Maffey sent back to Downing Street, that of 3 August 1946 is of lasting interest. These were supplemented by reports from individual ministers, an unusual number of whom visited Eire. They included the Lord President, Herbert Morrison, the Prime Minister, Attlee, himself being there for three weeks from 30 July 1948,

Jowitt, the Lord Chancellor and Philip Noel Baker, Secretary of State for Commonwealth Relations, as well as others occupying less exalted positions, who disturbed Maffey by what he considered to be their uncritical reactions to what was told them by their hosts about the situation in the North. For his part Maffey felt the need for dealing aright with what he judged presently to be an insoluble problem. By that he meant partition. If nothing could be done about partition, it was best for little to be said. That was counsel that peregrinating ministers and particularly the Friends of Ireland found it hard to observe. On the other hand collectively the UK representative and interested Labour ministers did help to ensure that the Cabinet as a whole were more fully informed than in the thirties. Attlee, who was the first Prime Minister since Asquith to go there, contrary to widely credited impression sensed that 'much of the old bitterness between English and Irish had passed away'.[12]

In October 1946 the Secretary of State for Dominion Affairs, Lord Addison, a survivor of the Lloyd George era, recommended that British policy towards Eire should be quickly and unobtrusively to restore friendly relations by losing no opportunity of promoting intercourse and cooperation in practical matters.[13] Introducing his memorandum, Addison made two observations: the first was that it was 'unthinkable' in the light of wartime experience that 'we could or should persuade or force them [the inhabitants of the six counties] against their will' into any form of union with Eire, and the second, deriving from wartime experience, that without a base in Northern Ireland, the task of keeping open the shipping lanes would have been infinitely more difficult, if not impossible. In British eyes this was a crucial point. The Cabinet took note of the recommendation of the Secretary of State's memorandum with approval.

In an exchange of views he had had with de Valera on Northern Ireland,[14] Herbert Morrison, the Lord President, reported that de Valera had said that, if Britain as a first step indicated its acceptance of the principle of a United Ireland, he would for his part be ready to agree that Northern Ireland should retain her own parliament with its existing powers and that the powers reserved to parliament at Westminster be transferred to the new government of a united Ireland. De Valera had further indicated that any such united Ireland would remain within the Commonwealth as a republic. On this he was said to be insistent. In reply, Morrison restated the Cabinet view that precipitation of the partition issue should be avoided. That would lead to violent controversy. De Valera had replied that this meant difficult Anglo-Irish relations would have to continue. By way of general postscript, Morrison had to report on the Prime Minister of Northern Ireland's reactions to these ministerial proposals. If the issue of partition were raised there would be, Brooke had said, 'a storm in Ulster', with the Northern Ireland Parliament resolutely opposed to any discussion of any such indication. The Cabinet evidently had no difficulty in reaching the conclusion that 'we would be well-advised to avoid a revival of this controversy'.

In the early post-Emergency years, while the Irish government were engaged in restoring pre-war links and fixing post-war priorities, the British Cabinet were aiming at limiting their post-war involvement in Irish affairs. They had a social revolution and an Indian decolonisation on their hands. They asked Maffey whether he considered that, if ministers refrained from comment, the Irish spectre might pass away. The reply was not encouraging. In Maffey's view,[15] things were not and could not be the same as before the war. They had changed and become not less but more difficult. De Valera's 'stiffly held policy of neutrality has had a permanent effect on the relationship of Eire with the United Kingdom and the British Commonwealth'. The new relationship that resulted might appear 'to suggest nothing but regret and pessimism'. But viewed historically, there were countervailing factors to be taken into the reckoning. In the past, the slogan of Irish patriots had been 'England's difficulty is Ireland's opportunity'. 'This time that slogan was not heard.' It was replaced by a milder version – 'England's difficulty is none of Ireland's business'. The change in attitude reflected benefits accrued. Leaving aside the difficulty about the ports, a difficulty 'we created ourselves', 'and which at one time threatened disaster', 'the British Cabinet had been able to conduct a long war without any anxiety about Ireland'. There was cooperation on a scale not fully known, because of censorship, to the public in either country. But while much that was not discouraging had emerged from the war years, there was another and potent danger in growing agitation on the partition issue 'and its effect on the minds of a new generation of Irishmen indoctrinated with hatred and false history'. De Valera was not, Maffey observed, anti-British and there was no doubt of his wish to see Hitler defeated, despite concern to reinsure the Irish position in the event of a German victory, which had looked not impossible in the spring of 1940. But de Valera repudiated any suggestion that the service of Irish volunteers in the Allied Forces could be credited to him or his government. He stated plainly: 'This was not our victory and we had no part in it.' As for the future, there were anxieties about prospects facing Irish emigrants to Britain and other Commonwealth countries. Were they to become aliens, should Eire leave the Commonwealth? 'Anti-partition' propaganda, so Maffey reported, 'is being pressed to the utmost in Eire, in the United Kingdom, in the United States'.

No such commentary on the Irish side is available and, indeed, may not have been written. But if it had, on the balance of the two issues, partition and conduct of external affairs, it was the former that was the more dangerous and presented the more perplexing problem. So far as status was concerned, Eire had freedom of action. As for partition, the door was being kept open and de Valera was correct in saying that the relationship was understood by those immediately concerned in Britain and the Commonwealth overseas. By convention, Commonwealth governments referred to Eire as a member, or a quasi-member, of the Commonwealth. The Canadian and Australian records show that it was neutrality rather than constitutional refinements that made the points of difference, and even in Britain successive Secretaries of State sought to avoid the issue of whether the country was or was not a Dominion. There was little sense of an impending parting of the ways.

After the Emergency there were debates in the Dáil year by year on the departmental estimates of External Affairs, and the questions of the republicanism of the form of government and membership of the Commonwealth became recurrent features. For this there were two reasons – politics and an authentic uneasiness at the limitation, however, oblique, in full national sovereignty, deemed to be present in the provisions of the External Relations Act. The first derived from a conviction that the repeal of the Act might affect de Valera's national position unfavourably. On the second, the Crown, the Governor-General, allegiance, all had been swept away, independence had been vindicated in neutrality for all the world to see and still there remained the suggestion that even yet sovereignty might not be altogether without subtraction. When de Valera first explained the omission to designate the state a republic by reference to the precedent of the American constitution hearts were with him; but there was no precedent for the use of the signature of an 'external' King for the accreditation of representatives of a sovereign state to foreign countries. Did it not in fact mean that through membership of, or association with, the Commonwealth, the state was 'encumbered' by external forms and, over and above partition, could never be 'a complete republic' so long as an alien monarch was accepted by an Irish government as 'the one and only person entitled to accredit our representatives abroad or to sign international treaties for us'?[16] The question was raised by James Dillon in the Dáil. What did it mean? Was Eire a member of the Commonwealth? The Taoiseach replied that the situation was a bit delicate. There was some confusion, but no deception. Those who worked the system understood it perfectly.[17] The critics continued to argue and de Valera had no silencing rejoinder. He could, and did, underline the fact that the procedure was permissive under the Act and another might be substituted for it. But basically he had to rely on an appeal not to precedent or to emotion, but to reason. If, he argued in 1947, being in the Commonwealth implied in any way allegiance and acceptance of the King as King in Ireland, then Eire was not in the Commonwealth because she did not accept either of these things.

During the war years, the provision of the Act authorising the King's signature to letters of credence issued to Irish ministers and ambassadors on their appointment was allowed to fall into virtual abeyance, since to avoid embarrassment on either side, the Irish government appointed *chargés d'affaires* to fill new or vacated diplomatic posts. But thereafter use was made once again of the procedure authorised by the External Relations Act.

For a period, governmental restraint might serve its own purposes. But, the subject of persistent questions in the Dáil, could it provide a foundation for a lasting relationship? For that the agreement of the governments of the Commonwealth to a reinterpretation and/or restatement of Irish relations with the Commonwealth in conformity with existing political realities might be deemed essential. So much de Valera realised. By 1947,[18] he indicated that he was prepared to contemplate the adoption of alternative means for the accrediting of the Irish representatives overseas, one which might not necessarily involve a repeal of the Act but would allow of its falling into abeyance. 'If the method which we have so far used for indicating our association with the States of the British Commonwealth should not fulfill its purpose', he told the Dáil,[19] '. . . it is very easy, if we wish to do so, to transfer these powers to the President by an Act of this Legislature'. He had not himself deemed any such change desirable because he thought the existing arrangements a fitting 'external symbol' of Eire's association with the Commonwealth, but once convinced that it was creating confusion in the minds of the Irish people, he would, so he assured opposition deputies, reconsider his opinion. In any event, he argued, the External Relations Act would have served a useful purpose simply by keeping in suspense the question of Ireland's relations with the Commonwealth long enough to enable her government to see whether the post-war changes, arising from the transfer of power in India, would bring into being a Commonwealth so modified in structure and character as to be helpful in a fresh setting. The response was discouraging.

Fine Gael was critical, Labour hostile, Independents most in favour of its repeal. General Mulcahy, as leader of Fine Gael on W.T. Cosgrave's retirement, inclined to the view that Eire was still a member of the Commonwealth and argued briefly that the External Relations Act created 'a certain amount of doubt' which would be better dispelled in the interest of the people.[20] But his colleagues were more disposed to denunciation – McGilligan two years later spoke of people 'going about shamefacedly' because the country was 'living a lie',[21] and of their dislike of qualified association being so intense that, failing full membership, they came, whether by deliberate intent or not is difficult to determine now, to adopt the position that no association at all with the Commonwealth, even at the risk of further prejudicing future prospects of Irish unity, was to be preferred to an external symbol.

De Valera delayed his decision, seemingly continuing to hope that, if formal secession could be deferred, republicanism and unity might ultimately be reconciled, while his more conservative, traditionally pro-Commonwealth critics, with long years in the political wilderness behind them, insisted on an end to all prevarication and procrastination on the issue. In one thing assuredly they succeeded. They impaired de Valera's confidence in the continuing usefulness of his own constitutional devices, as he found it increasingly difficult to counter the attacks, and to tolerate the taunts, of his critics.

Republic in Association with Commonwealth. The Quest That Failed

It was not, however, the Fine Gael leaders, but two independent members (later both Fine Gael) who first broke through the barriers of de Valera's reserve. One was James Dillon, politically isolated as the solitary advocate of Irish entry into the war on the Allied side after Pearl Harbour; another was Oliver Flanagan, who as early as 1944 had become concerned to discover whether Eire was a part of the British Commonwealth or not. On 29 November 1944 he put the question to the Taoiseach. De Valera had referred him to section 3(1) of the External Relations Act and Article 29 Section 4(2) of the constitution, with the comment that he himself did not propose 'to try to paraphrase them or to give any definition to the relationship established by them save that contained in the words of the documents themselves.' Flanagan protested that his question had not been answered. Was Eire a part of the British Commonwealth or not? Yes or no? 'I think the Deputy will take some time to learn that you cannot always answer questions by "yes" or "no",' replied the Taoiseach. The relationship, he reiterated, was settled in 1936 and 1937 and, he added, 'we do not propose to change it at the moment'. 'Then we are a member of the British Commonwealth of Nations?' exclaimed Deputy Flanagan. 'Make up your own mind', rejoined the Taoiseach.[22]

But if in respect of membership of the Commonwealth de Valera proved reticent, an enquiry about the nature of the state from Dillon in July 1945 elicited more positive results.

> Deputy Dillon: Are we a republic or are we not, for nobody seems to know?
> The Taoiseach: We are, if that is all the deputy wants to know.
> Deputy Dillon: This is a republic? That is the greatest news I heard for a long time. Now we know where we are. . . . When did it happen, can anyone tell us? . . .
> The Taoiseach: You will hear all about it later.[23]

The following week de Valera was not as forthcoming as opposition deputies had hoped. He talked about the Republic with a fine impersonal detachment. Deputy Dillon, said the Taoiseach pretended that he (de Valera) was the only person who knew the answer to the question whether Eire was a republic or not, but the answer, in fact, did not rest with him at all. The state, constitutionally, was what it was, and to be qualified politically only by observation of its institutions and examination of its fundamental laws. To assist deputies, the Taoiseach quoted from the definitions of a republic contained in the *Encyclopaedia Britannica*, the *Encyclopaedia Americana*, the *Shorter Oxford English Dictionary*, *Webster's International Dictionary*, the *New Standard Dictionary of the English Language*, and *Chamber's Dictionary*. Perhaps the last, with its succinct statement that a republic was 'a form of Government without a monarch in which the supreme power is vested in representatives elected by the people', alone gave him the phrasing he required. At any rate he quoted it last, concluding with the warning that if anyone still persisted in maintaining that Éire was not a republic, he could no longer argue with him, for 'we have no common language'.[24]

Dr O'Higgins pointed out that the question had been addressed to the Taoiseach, not to Webster. The 'dictionary republic' invited witticisms.[25] Even with de Valera's backing it no longer looked like staying the Irish electoral course. It was too heavily handicapped. Irish nationalist opinion might have been persuaded that the declaration of the republic should be postponed until the country was united and might further, though with reluctance, have conceded that, at least for years to come, undisguised republicanism and unity were incompatible aims. But the retrospective definition of a republic by reference to standard dictionaries satisfied neither the Irish sense of politics nor their sense of drama. The one thing that had never been anticipated was its surreptitious advent. Even the more devoted of his followers shared in the widespread sense of unfulfilment, to which moreover was soon to be added doubts, which proved ineradicable, about the authenticity of the republic now said to have been in existence since 1937, though not as such proclaimed or declared.

The British Cabinet consistently maintained that allegiance was a condition of Commonwealth membership. Without allegiance, there could be no membership. But the statement issued by the United Kingdom government, with dominion concurrence in 1937 indicated that Commonwealth governments were satisfied that the text of the External Relations Act could be construed as evidence of Eire's continuing allegiance to the Crown, and despite Eire's affirmation to the contrary. If the British view was upheld under the 1937 constitution, Eire was not a republic, for no one suggested that a republic, least of all an Irish republic, could owe allegiance to a king, even an 'external' one. This had consequences both theoretical and practical. De Valera's opponents, once the Republic had acquired its dictionary imprimatur, were intent upon exposing the constitutional devices upon which the conclusions of the United Kingdom government alone could rest. Tacit acquiescence ceased to prevail, sentiment had hardened, and even those once disposed to admire de Valera's constitutional sophistication, as displayed in the framing of the Act, were now embarrassed by the authority it gave for the participation of the English King in the formal conduct of Eire's relations with foreign states. Dillon heightened feelings of *malaise* on the part of republicans by reading out in the Dáil the text of a letter of credence dated 19 June 1946, which was signed by King George VI and was presented by the Irish Minister to the King of Sweden.[26] The opening 'My Brother . . .' to the King of Sweden and the conclusion, 'Given at my court at Buckingham Palace, 20th day of June, 1946. I am, Sir, my Brother, Your Majesty's good Brother George, Rex Imperator, Countersigned – Eamon de Valera' conveyed all that was needed.

The point was made and it sufficed: the limited and particular significance or lack of it of the royal signature was conveyed. Such letters, Dillon explained, were signed by the King in accordance with the provision of the External Relations Act and as a matter of external policy. He emphasised the distinction that in consequence existed between the King's functions in Canada, South Africa and Australia, in each of which he acted as Head of State, and his functions in Eire where he 'is used by us as a mark of our association with these States'.[27] Dillon later alleged that Deputies felt a sense of humiliation on learning that the Irish Ambassador to the Holy See presented 'to the Papal Secretary of State letters of credence addressed to the Holy Father by His Majesty King George VI',[28] while McGilligan maintained that in all this the harm lay not in sending representatives abroad with letters of credence signed by the King, but in pretending that they were not so signed. In Eire there was no one to sign. They had no Head of State, for the President was not the head of the state. He had no relations internationally *vis-à-vis* other countries. The working of the system once disclosed bordered on the frontiers of credibility.

It was de Valera's belief that the republican constitution, balanced by the Republic's external association with the states of the British Commonwealth in the form sanctioned by the External Relations Act, reflected political realities, was the most that any Irish nationalist government could concede and at the same time preserve twenty-six-county unity at home. After the war, with mounting criticism from the right and also from the extreme left, the risk surfaced that it might imperil national unity in the twenty-six counties without making any, let alone appreciable, advance towards the reunion of the thirty-two. Yet repeal would evidently reopen the question of membership of the Commonwealth, which it had been the negative purpose of the device to avert, in case at some time it might help to ease the way to unity.

Whatever his own views, de Valera could not make further concessions because, as he judged, 'our people' might or would not tolerate them; ten years later he was forced into an exposed position by his opponents on the right, and ultimately was driven from office by a coalition between them and Labour and the new Republicans to the left. It might have been supposed that the Fine Gael party, which was to champion, albeit in muted tones, Commonwealth membership as late as the general election of 1944, would have preferred the maintenance of some link, however imperfect, with the Commonwealth rather than none. Yet impelled by its implacable hostility to de Valera and his External Relations Act, the party came to adopt a position which it might not have deliberately chosen. By sustained assault it compelled de Valera to expound and to define, and in so doing impaired that measure of acquiescence which enabled the ingenious and by no means unstatesmanlike experiment of external association to survive. But this was not to be. At the critical moment responsibility passed to other hands. By-elections in October 1947 in Tipperary and Dublin, both resulting in the victory of a new Republican party, the Clann na Poblachta, foreshadowed the close of de Valera's long tenure of power in the 1948 general election and with it the foundation of the experiment that was made peculiarly his own.

The Ending of External Association

The Irish General Election, 1948

It was with the challenge of the new republican party, the Clann na Poblachta that de Valera was principally preoccupied in the 1948 general election. Its leader, Seán MacBride, a barrister by profession and politically to the left of Fianna Fáil, was the son of John MacBride, executed in 1916, and Mme Maud Gonne MacBride,[1] the inspiration of Yeats' *Cathleen ni Houlihan*. He was also a militant champion of Irish nationalism. To an impeccable national background Seán MacBride added a charismatic personality, and an insistence on the need for enthusiasm and integrity in Irish public life. Characteristic was the listing among his party's aims of the need to end 'political corruption, quibbling, jobbery and graft'. He lacked experience of government. Like reforming and revolutionary parties before them, the new Republicans came forward as the 'sea-green incorruptibles'. In external policy it was their aim to carry the national revolution a stage further by the severance of the last formal tie with the Commonwealth.

There was no national issue in the strict sense of the word in the election campaign, but there was an all-pervasive national background heightened by MacBride's intervention. The parties were agreed in their desire to end partition, but it was MacBride who put forward the one positive suggestion, that members elected for Northern Ireland constituencies should take their seats in the Dáil. But if he obtained little support fot this particular and impracticable proposal, he succeeded in creating an atmosphere in which all parties felt that something must be done to end partition. That had its importance later. So, too, and for the same reason, MacBride's advocacy of repeal of the External Relations Act gave renewed prominence to an issue with which the parties rather than the people were much concerned. He had the open support of Labour, who had opposed the Act from the outset on the ground that it continued an association with the British Crown, which Labour's leader, William Norton thought should have been terminated at the time of the abdication crisis.[2] But on the other hand the principal opposition party, Fine Gael, however much they disliked the Act as such, remained to outward appearance sympathetic to the Commonwealth connection. 'The present position', General Mulcahy, the leader of the party, observed at Letterkenny in January 1948,[3] 'has been accepted by all members of the British Commonwealth as being in consonance with membership' and it was Commonwealth membership that the Fine Gael party had hitherto consistently championed.

The election took place early in February 1948, and the results showed that while Fianna Fáil with 68 seats remained by far the largest party in the new Dáil it had failed to secure an overall majority.[4] When the new Dáil assembled on 18 February, de Valera's nomination as Taoiseach was defeated by 75 votes to 70.[5] J.A. Costello, a leading member, though not the leader, of the Fine Gael party, and one who, in his own words, was 'detached from the controversial bitternesses of the past',[6] was then proposed and, with the support of all the opposition groups, was elected by 75 votes to 68.[7] Left and right had successfully combined to defeat the centre. The composition of the new government faithfully reflected the relative strength of the parties thus strangely united. Fine Gael received five portfolios, the party leader, Mulcahy, accepting a second-line post as Minister for Education. Norton became deputy Prime Minister, Seán MacBride Minister of External Affairs, and James Dillon Minister of Agriculture. MacBride, in supporting Costello's nomination as Taoiseach, allowed that while 'the reintegration of this nation as a republic, free from any association with any other country' remained the ultimate political objective of his party, it could not claim to have received a mandate that 'would enable us to repeal, or seek to repeal the External Relations Act and such other measures as are inconsistent with our status as an independent republic'.[8] The repeal of the Act was also presumably among those matters to which Costello referred when he said that 'any points on which we have not agreed have been left in abeyance'. Yet it was difficult for a government composed of such diverse elements, and which owed its accession to office very largely to the inroads that the new Republicans had made upon de Valera's traditional vote, to let the question lie. Confronted by so formidable an opponent, its survival seemed conditional from the outset on two things; first on the maintenance of interparty unity on essentials and secondly, on not allowing itself to be outbid on a national issue by de Valera. That Costello should declare the ending of partition to be the principal objective of his government was therefore to be anticipated, but though in the first months of office relations with the Commonwealth would appear to have little preoccupied the administration, ministers were constantly on their guard lest on this question too they might be outmanoeuvred.

The Interparty Government

The actions of the interparty government could be rightly predicted only by an assessment of the balance of forces within it at any given time. On paper the advantage lay with the conservative elements. Fine Gael was the predominant partner and in internal affairs its controlling influence was assured by the placing of the key posts of Prime Minister and Minister for Finance in the hands of leading members of the party,[9] and by the backing of the Farmers' party[10] and most of the Independents for their conservative home policies. But in external affairs the position of Fine Gael was by no means so strong. MacBride held the External Affairs portfolio, and, poorly though his party had fared at the election, its contribution to the overthrow of de Valera had been decisive. The appeal of the party and of Labour was to republican-nationalist sentiment and it was more cogent than that of Fine Gael's now tepid declaration of faith in continuing Commonwealth membership. In any appeal to public opinion on an external issue the verdict would assuredly come down on the side of the 'root-and-branch' republicans. This was well understood by MacBride's individualistic following. Few of its members were prepared to concede with their leader that the electorate had given no mandate for change in Eire's relationship with the British Commonwealth, and two of them, Con Lehane and Peadar Cowan, the latter of whom was expelled from the party in July 1948, embarrassed its leadership by skirmishing against what remained of the Commonwealth connection.

The first interparty government, which was formed on 18 February 1948, has a threefold place in Irish history: the first, by a new departure with the introduction of a coalition – because of the stigma attached to the term in other countries, notably Britain, ministers preferred the untarnished 'interparty'; second, by the severance of the last link with Commonwealth and Treaty settlement, and third, by health measures subsumed under the controversial 'Mother and Child' scheme, which was later to bring down the government. All were subjects of lively contemporary and subsequent historical interest; only the second of the three bears on this study. In the working of multi-party government, no member in this case had had experience of government since the early thirties, or of the demands for restraint or, in particular, of the compromises required to sustain an interparty administration in office.

In analysing the sequence of events, the politico-constitutional problems which had confronted de Valera need to be kept in mind. In 1945 he had restated his acceptance of the British government's assessment of Eire's relationship with the Commonwealth and had placed the onus on them. In the forefront of his mind was its bearing on the question of unity. The loyalty of the majority within the six counties to Crown and Commonwealth had to be recognised, and he felt that continued Irish association

with the Northern Unionists in a form consistent with national sovereignty was a concession properly to be made by the majority to minority
opinion. On this his expression of opinion varied little.

In November 1947 his classical formulation had been as follows:

> In dealing with this question of Partition . . . the problem is how far
> ought the people in this part of Ireland [to] go to meet the views of the
> people in the other part so that there will be agreement both here and in
> the North? I believe that the Constitution as we have it . . . as well as
> our association with the States of the British Commonwealth in the
> form in which it is at the moment, is the farthest that you can go to
> meet the views in the North and at the same time get agreement here.[11]

The device of external association was at all times dependent on its contribution as a compromise on status, with the ending of partition being
secondary and derivative.

In June 1948 a strong Irish delegation under Costello's leadership went
to London to negotiate a new trade agreement with Britain. The focus of
Costello's perspective, however, was on status and accordingly he noted
without satisfaction that at an official occasion at No.10 Downing Street,
Attlee proposed the toast of 'The King' as appropriate for the country of
his guests, thereby implying that in the British view Eire continued to
owe allegiance to the Crown and remained a member of the British
Commonwealth of Nations.[12] From the outset relations between the Irish
and British governments were constrained, little regard being paid on the
British side to Irish sensitivities. The contrast, at root impersonal, reflected
fundamental differences in attitude applying over a wide range. It was
made clear in an exchange of views that the Commonwealth setting was
not deemed appropriate. The title of the High Commission in London was
discarded as inappropriate for the representation of a republican state. On
that MacBride as Minister of External Affairs was categoric. The state was
a republic and had been since 1937.

Commonwealth Relations – the Last Stage

During the London talks Attlee had alluded to the forthcoming meeting of
Commonwealth Prime Ministers which was to be held in London in
October. This was to be a meeting of historic interest and importance,
being the first to which the three new Asian Dominions, India, Pakistan
and Ceylon, were to be invited. For that very reason it seemed to afford
the most propitious of opportunities for the reappearance of Irish representatives in the innermost councils of the Commonwealth, if only because
the enlargement of the Commonwealth by the addition of three strongly
nationalist members of non-British extraction might be expected to bring
into being a looser, and from the Irish point of view more congenial,

grouping than that of the former and predominantly British Commonwealth of pre-war years. The available evidence suggests that de Valera
alone of Irish leaders was aware of some of the wider implications of the
occasion.[13] The question of Irish representation was considered by the
Irish Cabinet. They informed the United Kingdom government that if
Eire were to be represented at the conference her representatives would
wish to have partition, and the basis of future Irish relations with the
Commonwealth, considered.[14] But in thus stating the conditions of Irish
participation, the Irish government returned no explicit answer to the
British invitation. Unfamiliar with Attlee's laconic style, Costello failed to
grasp that he was being sounded out about whether or not Eire would
welcome a formal invitation. Or so Dulanty interpreted what had
occurred.[15]

The most important consequence of discussion in the Cabinet about
Irish representation at the Commonwealth Prime Ministers' meeting was
to make the interparty government increasingly aware of the desirability
of defining more precisely their attitude to the Commonwealth connection. The case for so doing was further strengthened by the provisions of
the British Nationality Act,[16] which provided that in United Kingdom
law Irish citizens were no longer to be regarded as British subjects, though
equally they were not to be regarded as foreigners. This was a compromise
solution, worked out by a committee of Commonwealth nationality
experts on which Eire was represented and which met in London in early
1947. It came close to realising the Irish aim of reciprocal as distinct from
common citizenship, and in so doing removed the more startling of the
conflicts in the nationality law of the two countries and a long-standing
source of Irish grievance. MacBride spoke of the 'very serious effort to
meet our viewpoint . . . made by Mr Attlee's Government', and if the Act
did not go the whole way towards satisfying Irish claims, at least it
represented 'a vast improvement on the position that has existed hitherto'.[17] MacBride interpreted the new measure of accord which the Act
represented as an indication that henceforward those who desired to
promote better Anglo-Irish relations would pay attention to the substance
and not to the form. The difficulties in Anglo-Irish relations arose, he
argued, not from any outworn prejudice but from concrete obstacles such
as partition and short-sighted efforts to retain forms that could only serve
as a reminder of an unhappy past, and as irritants endangering and frustrating the relationship they were meant to express. 'The Crown and
outward forms that belong to British constitutionl history', he concluded,
'are merely reminders of an unhappy past that we want to bury, that have
no realities for us and only serve as irritants'.[18] By that test the External
Relations Act could not survive.

The provisions of the British Nationality Act, in so far as they substituted reciprocal for common citizenship on the lines contemplated by

the Sinn Féin leaders of 1921, in this one important particular tacitly
endorsed the Irish view that Eire was not a member of the Commonwealth, but a state externally associated with it. MacBride indeed went so
far as to say that the Labour government in Britain agreed that Eire was
not a member of the Commonwealth,[19] but in a formal sense this would
seem to have been an overstatement. On the other hand, MacBride's own
categoric assertion that Eire was not a member of the Commonwealth was
in significant contrast to his predecessor's guarded circumlocution. It
elicited in due course the inevitable enquiry from Captain Cowan: 'When
and under what circumstances', he asked on 28 July, did Ireland cease 'to
be a member of the British Commonwealth of Nations?' The process,
explained Costello, was one of 'gradual development'. But, like the
Minister of External Affairs, he too was satisfied that Ireland had ceased to
be a member of the Commonwealth, though she still remained associated
with it.[20]

    In the definition and the redefinition of Irish relations with the
Commonwealth, the ending of partition remained a very important, but
not always an overriding, consideration. When released from the cares of
office, de Valera embarked on a lengthy tour of the United States, Australia, New Zealand, and ultimately Great Britain in the hope of enlisting
the sympathy of their peoples for the cause of Irish unity. If the government deemed it necessary to compete with so formidable a figure on an
issue which he had made peculiarly his own it behoved it to move fast.

    The interparty government, whose strength numerically in the new
Dáil sufficed, was vulnerable in its lack of cohesion – or in the case of Fine
Gael and the new Republicans at each end of the Irish political spectrum,
near total incompatibility. Repeal of the ERA had not been an issue in the
election, but it appealed as something to which all might subscribe without the straining of some few tender consciences. MacBride again conceded
that, although repeal had been put at the top of the Republican programme, it remained for action to be taken after the next election, if the
electorate so ruled. He was accordingly not a principal advocate of repeal
forthwith, on the ground that Fine Gael was likely to favour some modification of the status quo rather than the breaking of the last Commonwealth
link. It was a case of the longest way round being the shortest way home.
So it emerged – but by different and unexpected procedure.

    By 1948 the External Relations Act was important, not by reason of
any diplomatic functions discharged, but because of the symbolic status it
had acquired as a surviving relic from past confrontations. It was unpopular and had been reduced to a device for leaving ajar the door to
unity. De Valera with John Hearne devised it; Maffey, UK representative,
personally came to think it the best arrangement yet contrived for the
ordering of Anglo-Irish relations; Costello, as heir to the pro-Treaty
party, now about to destroy it, thought that it was nationally self-

demeaning. There was paradox here: there was also electoral arithmetic
and the menace it conveyed. Costello, as Taoiseach, needed no convincing; Norton, the Tánaiste, had become well known for his forthright
opposition; MacBride, Minister of External Affairs and founder of the
Clann na Poblachta, who was strongly opposed to the Act (though prepared to contemplate deferring repeal till the succeeding election) opened
the way for repeal, while de Valera saw a balance of advantage in leaving
the way open, but favoured discarding an instrument that no longer had
its uses. There was a feeling that it might be best to reopen the question in
the interparty's second period of office, the crucial factor being sufficient
cohesion to survive.

At a Cabinet meeting on 10 August 1948 the new government turned
its attention to dominion affairs and the forthcoming Commonwealth
Prime Ministers' Conference, at which the Indian government, who were
committed to a republican constitution, were to explore the possibility of
continuing membership, Should the Irish government display contingent
interest or should they disregard it? Attention was concentrated on assessment of interest and disposition, allusion was made to the External Relations Act, but that apart nothing is on record. Discussion, however, was
wide-ranging and focus was on matters of immediate concern to Ireland.
Discussion of Northern Ireland was their highest priority,[21] but they also
wanted more and more discussion of Anglo-Irish developments, measures
to redress trade imbalances, and social problems, emigration high among
them. These were matters to be pursued in Anglo-Irish meetings. Debate,
however, was foreclosed by the Cabinet accepting MacBride's recommendation that Ireland should not go to the Commonwealth Conference.
This was the decisive step. Henceforward Ireland and India were destined
to go their different ways.

While Costello allowed that the successive steps taken by de Valera to
remove the formal bonds linking the Irish Free State to the Commonwealth were to be explained as part of the process of bringing Irish
political institutions into closer harmony with national sentiment, he was
highly critical of the Act through which his predecessor had sought to
symbolise the nature of Eire's new relationship with the Commonwealth.
Not only, in his view, did the provisions of the External Relations Act
contain 'inaccuracies and infirmities'[22] which of themselves caused confusion, but in principle the Act itself was misconceived.

Costello in Canada

On 1 September Costello went to Canada to deliver a lecture to the
Canadian Bar Association.[23] In it he indicated the intention of his government to amend, or more probably repeal, the External Relations Act,

irrespective of whether or not this would be done in such a way as to leave unimpaired Ireland's relations with the Commonwealth. He singled out the Crown as the embodiment of dominion national pride in Canada, but in Ireland as 'the symbol of centuries of civil and religious persecution and confiscation', which had become 'anathema to the vast majority of the Irish people. The harp without the Crown symbolised the ideal of Irish independence and nationhood. The harp beneath the Crown was the symbol of conquest.' And more particularly, he made unqualified assertion that with the enactment of the Statute of Westminster, 'the sovereignty of Ireland and the other members of the Commonwealth was beyond all question complete and absolute'.

In an informal exchange of view between Costello and the Canadian Prime Minister, Mackenzie King conveyed his own interest in defence cooperation and affirmed Canada's resolve to maintain full membership of the Commonwealth through a common allegiance to the Crown, but he conceded that in the Irish case a constitutional arrangement which acted only as an irritant could serve no useful purpose.

Thereafter the sequence of events is not without a Gibbonian, curious interest. On 4 September Costello dined with the Governor-General of Canada, Field-Marshal Lord Alexander. He was an Ulsterman. Discourtesies, including the placing on the table of a replica of 'Roaring Meg' – a cannon famed in Ulster for its role in the defence of Derry against the Catholic forces of James II – were seen as deliberate provocation to the Taoiseach and his wife by Alexander, the Governor-General, who seemingly neglected his duties to his guests as an official host. This appears to have inclined Costello further towards the ending of the ERA; he was now more than ever disposed to consider the continuing constitutional arrangement as intolerable. On 5 September the *Sunday Independent* in Dublin published as its front-page news story an article by its political correspondent carrying the headline 'External Relations Act to Go'. The writer recalled that all the parties in the coalition government had denounced the External Relations Act as a dishonest deception in the past, and he instanced MacBride's comments in the Dáil[24] to the effect that outworn political forms could act only as irritants endangering and frustrating the relationship which they were intended to express and preserve, and Norton's forcibly expressed conviction that Irish national honesty would rank all the higher if the External Relations Act were to go,[25] as signs that its repeal was contemplated. The correctness of this conclusion, argued the correspondent, was confirmed by Costello's address to the Bar Association in Montreal and therefore an early announcement was to be expected. 'It is open to question', a student of Commonwealth affairs had remarked, '. . . whether the one remaining constitutional link embodied in the External Relations Act any longer possesses practical advantages out-

weighing its psychological disadvantages'.[26] 'Who today', commented the
political correspondent, 'could say that it does. And that is why the Act
may already be considered dead.'

Precipitate Pronouncement

The quotation of the important parts of this article by Canadian news-
papers[27] prompted press enquiries which evidently impressed upon
Costello the desirability of an early pronouncement.[28] In any event, at a
press conference in Ottawa on 7 September he announced the intention of
his government to repeal the External Relations Act on the dual grounds
of its unsatisfactory character and of the impossibility of continuing Irish
association with the Crown in any form. He did not say in his original
statement whether repeal would or would not mean secession from the
Commonwealth. It was only when a correspondent asked that question
that Costello replied in the affirmative. Once he had done so, clearly there
could be no going back.

That the majority of Costello's Cabinet colleagues favoured the repeal
of the Act in principle was not in question and there was no occasion for
surprise in the decision itself. The Minister for External Affairs, the
Deputy Prime Minister, and finally the Taoiseach himself, had all made it
abundantly clear in the course of the summer that such was the intention
of the interparty government. Despite this, some Cabinet colleagues were
taken unawares by Costello's announcement and failed to conceal their
surprise when the news came. Not least among them was Seán MacBride.
As Minister of External Affairs he was entertaining the United Kingdom
representative at the Russell Hotel in St Stephen's Green, when the news
was conveyed to him. Unpremeditated has become the favoured gloss.[29]
It was the timing and not the event that was a matter of most speculation
and it was clear that umbrage was taken by Costello at several incidents
that had occurred in the course of the visit, all of which appear to have
been associated with the Governor-General.[30] Costello, an impulsive and
somewhat inexperienced leader on the highest political level, did not
dispute that there was one incident at which he had taken umbrage, but
consistently repudiated all suggestions that it was responsible for the
unexpected pronouncement. How then to explain the choice of time and
place? There was also the question of Cabinet responsibility.[31] It was
alleged to have been approved in June, but one member of the government claims the meeting was never held. This has been contested by
others, but no record of it is to be found in the State Papers Office. There
is, however, a comprehensive Cabinet minute in November, giving the
Taoiseach authority for all his statements while in Canada and the United
States.

Repeal of the ERA

More important were the implications of the decision and its timing. Had Costello not committed himself in Ottawa to the view that repeal meant secession, the nature of any future association between Eire and the Commonwealth might have been considered on its merits. As it was, an irrevocable decision was taken on this point before the outstanding question of republican India's relations with the Commonwealth had been settled. While Ireland had done much to pioneer the path herself and had shown Indians that it was possible to reconcile republicanism with Commonwealth membership and also to be flexible in respect of the monarch as symbolic head of the Commonwealth, she elected to travel other roads. At a deeper level, the Republic of India acceded to, and the Republic of Ireland seceded from the Commonwealth because of their respective governments' interpretation of their respective state interests. Some such continuing connection might indeed have seemed the more logical outcome of Costello's policy, for, as he later observed on many occasions, the repeal of the External Relations Act was intended, by removing the last vestige of alien authority, to cement relations with Britain and with the overseas members of the Commonwealth. But internal political considerations confronted him with the hard choice of acting precipitately or risking the break-up of the interparty government.

For the rest it must be said that there was no dispute, as in the 1930s, about a Dominion's right of secession and, therefore, on the British side, of Eire's right to secede. It is in the case of the Irish that possible ambiguity remained: did the impending repeal of the Act and the parallel decision to describe the state formally as the Republic of Ireland imply of necessity Irish secession from the Commonwealth? Costello had been asked that question, reputedly by a representative of the Tass agency at his press conference in Ottawa in September. He had replied in the affirmative and so disposed of what might otherwise have been deemed an open issue. It is not known if secession was the agreed purpose of the Cabinet in approving earlier the repeal in principle of the External Relations Act. However, to dispel any risk of misunderstanding, MacBride told Rugby that 'the decision to repeal the E.R.A. was not open to revision or modification'. For its part, the government of the United Kingdom, which was diplomatically represented in Dublin, appears to have been taken unawares, and it would seem from ministerial comments that it had given little or no consideration to the situation that might arise when the External Relations Act was repealed and to the subsequent conduct of Irish affairs.[32] No doubt it might have anticipated that any Irish government contemplating such a step would have forewarned it as a matter of courtesy. Yet it was not something on which any confident expectation could or should have been founded, for, as the Lord Chancellor, Jowitt, observed later, there was no reason why Costello should have informed the United Kingdom government and the United Kingdom government had not the smallest complaint on the ground that he had not done so.[33]

The situation that would be created by the repeal of the External Relations Act was not formally considered at the meeting of Commonwealth Prime Ministers in October 1948, but advantage was taken of their presence in London to arrange separate discussions with Irish ministers on the consequence of secession. These discussions were held at Chequers, and the Prime Ministers of the United Kingdom, Canada and New Zealand, the Australian Minister for External Affairs, and the Irish Ministers for External Affairs and Finance took part.[34] The countries of the Commonwealth which were represented were those whose populations included a large number of people of Irish origin, and the meetings were understood to have been arranged on the initiative of the dominion representatives.[35] While it was agreed on all sides that talks held at Chequers as also in Paris were helpful, what emerged most clearly from them was that in respect of future Irish relations with the Commonwealth, the Commonwealth was by no means of one mind. While the United Kingdom ministers indulged in discouraging forecasts of the possible effect of secession on trade preferences and citizenship, dominion ministers were resolved that the severance of formal constitutional ties should not be the occasion for a wider breach. In determining this, as in the case of citizenship, the influence of the overseas Dominions was decisive. It was pressure from them that deflected the United Kingdom government from the harder line it had at first contemplated. 'If we had taken a different line from the one we decided to take', admitted the Lord Chancellor,[36] 'we should have acted in the teeth of the advice of the representatives of Canada, Australia and New Zealand'. In this, the Commonwealth did play, not for the first, but presumably for the last time, a role – it may be thought not an unhelpful one – in Irish affairs.

Some attempts were made to dissuade the Irish government from the course of action on which it had embarked, but wholly without success. Had anyone spoken 'with the eloquence of Demosthenes and at greater length even than Mr. Gladstone', said the Lord Chancellor subsequently, 'I am convinced that he would have failed – as I failed'.[37] United Kingdom forebodings about the consequences of repeal were a test of nerve and resolution and at least served the purpose of indicating beyond possibility of dispute that the Irish mind was made up. Even had the severance of the last formal tie with the Commonwealth involved the ending of trade preferences and of reciprocal citizenship arrangements, the Irish government had no intention of allowing itself to be deflected from its course. The somewhat artificial air of crisis in fact served not to weaken but to strengthen the cohesion of the interparty government, while the opposition, though making legitimate fun of the somersault of Fine Gael – whose

sudden conversion to republicanism, in the words of MacEntee, was a
'skedaddle enough to make a skeleton merry' – could not oppose repeal
and were politically outmanoeuvred. Only Fine Gael Deputies in some
Dublin constituencies where the Protestant minority was strongly represented were embarrassed.[38] Some of them had made much at the general
election of their party's pledge to effect no change in constitutional relations, and after Costello's Canadian pronouncements they were left
explaining to a sceptical electorate that, strictly speaking, the repeal of the
External Relations Act, inasmuch as it involved no amendment of the
constitution, was not within the meaning of the phrase 'constitutional
change'. In a deeper sense there was less inconsistency in their purpose
than the critics allowed. The course Fine Gael had adopted was intended to
bring Eire closer, not to take her farther away from the Commonwealth.
That was something Costello deployed to some effect.

On 24 November Costello introduced the Republic of Ireland Act. The
purpose of the Act was to repeal the External Relations Act, to declare that
the description of the state should be the Republic of Ireland, and that the
President, on the authority and the advice of the government, might
exercise the executive power for any executive function of the state in
connection with its external relations. 'This Bill', said Costello,

> will end forever, in a simple, clear and unequivocal way this country's
> long and tragic association with the institution of the British Crown
> and will make it manifest beyond equivocation or subtlety that the
> national and international status of this country is that of an independent
> republic.[39]

The Act was not to be regarded as the product of unthinking or negative
nationalism, but was intended to clarify the position of the state and by so
doing to increase national self-respect and to lead to closer friendship with
the Commonwealth. The measure, the Taoiseach said, was not designed
or conceived in any spirit of hostility to the British people or to the
institution of the British Crown; on the contrary, one result of its enactment would be that Eire's relationship with Britain would be 'far closer
and far better, and will be put upon a better and firmer foundation than it
ever has been before'. It would be 'unthinkable' for the Republic of Ireland
to draw farther away from the nations of the Commonwealth with which
'we have had such long and, I think, such fruitful association in the past 25
or 26 years'.[40] Yet that was what, on one interpretation, he was proposing
the country should do. Commonwealth countries would not be regarded
as foreign by the Republic of Ireland, neither would the Republic be
treated as a foreign country by Britain and the overseas members of the
Commonwealth. Likewise arrangements would be made for a reciprocal
citizenship, on the lines indicated in the Irish Nationality and Citizenship
Act of 1935 and the British Nationality Act of 1948. Lastly, Costello

discounted the widely entertained view that the Republic of Ireland Bill would place a further, more formidable, barrier in the way of Irish unity as 'part of a foul press campaign'. This was debatable. It was, of course, true, as Costello observed, that no single approach had been made by the government of Northern Ireland towards either the dominion government of the Irish Free State or the externally associated government of Eire, with the object of promoting the reunion of Ireland. But was it correct to deduce from this that the case for the perpetuation of what he described as 'the national indignity' of the External Relations Act rested on nothing more than 'the vain vague hope that our ambiguous constitutional status . . . would prepare the way for cooperation from the Government of the six north-eastern counties of Ireland?'[41] While the majority in Northern Ireland were unlikely in the foreseeable future to take any initiative to end partition, the argument that no additional barrier should be placed in their way was not altogether insubstantial. The repeal of the External Relations Act, by taking the twenty-six counties outside the Commonwealth, ruled out the possibility of partition being resolved in a Commonwealth context. 'I hesitated about declarations of this sort', said de Valera, 'and I left a bridge for a long time, in the hope that by it it would be possible to bring about the unity of our country, that we were going to meet the sentiment of the minority . . . by means of association'.[42] Such from a nationalist standpoint was the essence of the case against the severance of formal ties with the Commonwealth by the proclamation of a twenty-six-county republic. It was twelve years afterwards that the Bill, introduced in 1936 to herald yet one more landmark in the onward march of national assertion in its institutional formulation, was discarded as a 'humiliating' relic of an earlier phase.

On 25 November[43] the United Kingdom government formally recorded that, while Eire would no longer be a member of the Commonwealth after the repeal of the External Relations Act, her government had 'stated that they recognise the existence of a specially close relationship between Eire and the Commonwealth countries and desire that this relationship should be maintained . . . The United Kingdom Government, for their part, recognise the existence of these factual ties, and are at one with the Eire Government in desiring that close and friendly relations should continue and be strengthened'. Accordingly the United Kingdom government declared that it would not regard the enactment of the Republic of Ireland Act as placing the Republic in the category of foreign countries or Irish citizens in the category of foreigners. On the contrary, the position of citizens of the Republic in the United Kingdom would be governed by the provisions of the British Nationality Act 1948,[44] while the Irish government for its part stated its intention of bringing its legislation into line with that in Commonwealth countries so that in Eire citizens of Commonwealth countries would receive comparable treatment.

In respect of trade, there was said to be a risk that the existence of preferential duties between Britain and Ireland would be challenged as conflicting with the most favoured nation clause in commercial treaties with foreign countries and with the General Agreement on Tariffs and Trade negotiated at Geneva in 1947. On this point, however, the Irish government were always and (it emerged) rightly confident.

The Republic Proclaimed

The Irish government decreed that the Republic of Ireland Bill should not take effect, and the Republic not be proclaimed, until Easter Day 1949, the thirty-third anniversary of the Easter Rising of 1916. Its choice of date was not welcomed by de Valera. It was not the republic for which Pearse and Connolly had died, and he declined to play any part in the formal inaugural ceremonies.

At midnight on 17–18 April, Eire accordingly left the British Commonwealth and the last constitutional tie with Britain was severed. From that moment the description of the state became the Republic of Ireland. The birth of the Republic was heralded by celebrations through-out the country which reached their climax in Dublin on Easter Monday. They were on a modest scale, but all had their republican credentials now. At the General Post Office, with memories of the 1916 Rebellion present in every mind, the tricolour was hoisted at noon and there followed a military parade watched by a subdued crowd. 'We believe', said the Taoiseach,[45] 'that what has been done today will ensure more cordial and closer cooperation between Ireland and Great Britain and the other members of the Commonwealth of Nations than could ever have existed under any conditions before'. It seemed as if Costello's hopes of closer, friendlier relations were to be fulfilled. But in fact, though the republican goal had been achieved on the domestic front, any price in terms of unity had yet to be paid.

CHAPTER 16
Stormont Undermined 1949–73

Old Antagonisms in a New Situation

The carving out of the six counties from the rest of Ireland was an awesome enterprise. Even had it not failed to bring better government, was it likely to endure in its current or even any devolutionary form? The area had little or no traditional sanction, its people were divided by layers of hostility, the Catholic minority deeply resentful of the Protestant position and inherited status and their unyielding resolve to keep what they possessed in social and political influence.

In the settlement years there was some conviction, over and above facile expression of belief, that partition might conceivably provide a way to unity. It was received with incredulity by much Labour and radical opinion in Britain and by individuals there, notably C.P. Scott, H.W. Nevinson and Hugh Martin, publicists grounded in the Ireland of the Troubles, all of whom saw partition leading on to entrenchment of vested interests building up either side of an indefensible Border line and resulting in progressive alienation. To a later generation, so much had manifestly come about that there was little disposition to seek the causes. It resulted, however, in a phenomenon familiar in triangular political situations, the aim of each to be *à deux* in a group of three. The 1925 Boundary Conference was the last occasion on which a *rapprochement* might have been pursued. The prospect of ministerial meetings was even debated and none had taken place by 1949. In place of mutual profit, the aim was particular advantage from such situations as arose.

The Irish Free State's contribution to the unfolding Commonwealth, which was a potentially significant factor, elicited little overall consideration in Whitehall and no enthusiasm in Belfast, where the Unionist stance was, and remained, less Commonwealth than imperialist. The division widened with each step forward in the republican programme, culminating in the repeal of the External Relations Act with a constitution republican in all but name, and a state identifiably Catholic with the enactment of the constitution professedly Catholic.* To this there followed the Agreement which resulted in the transfer of the Treaty ports to the Irish Free State and rejection of Northern Ireland requests for trading concessions. This last episode had shown that defensively the Ulster Unionist position was strong. As and when need arose, their well-placed English allies could be relied upon to deploy the strength to stifle any development that could reasonably be represented as a threat to the Unionist position, as had indeed been the case since 1920.

What is a matter for surprise is not the progressive distancing of Northern Ireland and the Irish Free State, the one from the other, but rather that by the late thirties there had been so little political movement. This could be explained by saying the stance that had been adopted left little scope for going further. Basically the judgement of the British official mind on the one post-Treaty question was invariably the same. It was that, given the United Kingdom government's pledge not to use force to undermine the position of Northern Ireland, nothing could usefully be done about partition. Only by the free will of the majority could unity be brought about. This, however, was not clearly recognised before the war. In 1939, with the question of status resolved, Malcolm MacDonald seems to have concluded that the immediacy and the sting of partition might have been removed. He appeared startled when de Valera sharply disillusioned him. The removal of objectionable status symbols rendered intolerable the continued vivisection of their country. The young men would not abide the continuation of such injustice. If not remedied in time there would be, de Valera continued, the unleashing of violence – and not only in Britain. Such, too, was the forecast of Maffey,[1] United Kingdom representative in Dublin throughout the war and till 1949. He sensed that 'the mutilation of the Motherland' would remain unacceptable and that, given the compulsive appeal of the blood sacrifice tradition, some military coup in the North might be attempted by a handful of hotheads in the 1916 manner, such as would stir worldwide repercussions of a character gratifying to Eire and humiliating to her traditional enemy.

With reaffirmation of the existence of a Republic of Ireland and its secession from the Commonwealth in 1949, the parameters of the Irish question once again had changed, though its triangular nature had not. In institutional terms what survived of the 1920–25 Settlement was partition

---

* De Valera greatly desired an expression of papal approval of Article 43 of the constitution. One condition of this, as emerged in detailed negotiations in writing and by the sending of an Irish emissary, J.P. Walshe to the Holy See, was that the special position of the Holy Roman Catholic and Apostolic Church should in its full title be there alone. With evident regret, but with deep conviction, de Valera indicated that this could not proceed without a qualification which would enable the Church of Ireland and other minority Churches to acquiesce in the provision.

of Ireland with devolution in Northern Ireland. That represented fundamental change from the primary purpose of the settlement, which was to
end with an Irish Dominion or derivative of it to provide its administration. The problem itself had been refined. The Dominion that was had
become a fully recognised international state. But it had been divided
against the wishes of the greater majority of its people. The difficulties of
the problem were underestimated. De Valera, however, saw them clearly
enough. He contended that as one by one the shackles on the Irish Free
State were removed, the resentment especially of Northern Irishmen
would be concentrated on a campaign against partition and by a majority
against Britain as the power responsible for the creation of Northern
Ireland and the maintenance of its administration by subsidies not contemplated at its origin. British governments, while reacting against oversimplification, became less insensitive to the problem, given the triangular
situation and the dominion relationship. On receiving an invitation to the
Prime Ministers' Conference in October 1948, the Irish Cabinet, as already
recorded, had ruled that partition would have to be an item on the agenda,
before it decided, in any event, to decline. In party politics the relationship
had become a liability, while in Anglo-Irish relations its contribution was
limited to keeping the door ajar. For whom? For the Ulster Unionists.
That they had indicated the strongest objections needed to be taken into the
reckoning. De Valera did not believe, as some of his critics professed to
think he did, that it would in itself predispose Ulster governments
towards unity.

In the six counties there was a majority to whom unity was anathema.
A redoubt had been established with the means of ensuring survival,
notably in an elaborate system of government to watch over its long-term
destiny. As a devolved region in the United Kingdom, Northern Ireland
had underscored its place and earned appreciation of its loyal services in
one of the most critical moments in the Empire's history. And yet, despite
all this, the Act of 1920 and the overall 1920–25 Settlement lacked an air
of finality. With the Treaty now dismantled, could the Act of 1920 be
relied upon to stay firm? The answer was in the affirmative. The six
counties were, and were likely to remain, assured of Protestant majority
rule. It was no minority like Southern Rhodesia, which was frequently
deployed by way of analogy. But with the tide of opinion running against
settlers watch had to be taken. Unionist leaders, even Craigavon himself,
needed to be reminded of this, as indeed he was during the negotiations
for the 1938 Anglo-Irish Agreement.

British attitudes in respect of policy for Ireland generally were not
optimistic. The Unionists sought fresh and formal entrenchment of their
position, vesting it with the semblance of permanence, as nearly as might
be contrived, subject always to the overriding authority of parliament. In
order to realise such an end, the Labour government had to be persuaded

it was a desirable step, especially in view of the violent reaction it would provoke. That the Northern government achieved their aim was attributed in large measure to Sir Basil Brooke, who had led a delegation from Northern Ireland to Whitehall in January 1949 and had obtained most, but not all, that he had sought. Writing on 30 March 1949[2] to thank Attlee for his assurances on the constitutional position and territorial integrity of Northern Ireland in the debates on the forthcoming Ireland Bill, he sought to reopen the question of the designation 'the Republic of Ireland'. In his opinion this suggested not the Southern Irish, but endorsement of national claims, and usage of it would connote British acquiescence in republican claims. But on this repeated representation Attlee stood firm. Even for Brooke it became a minor matter. On 28 April the entry in his Diary reads 'we have got what we wanted . . . Ulster is safe'.[3]

On Easter Day 1949 the Republic of Ireland Bill took effect and the Republic was proclaimed. Account of the changed situation was taken in Britain with the introduction of the Ireland Act 1949,[4] which was enacted on 5 June. The Act recognised that as from 18 April 1949 Eire ceased to be part of his Majesty's Dominions and it confirmed that 'in no event will Northern Ireland or any part thereof cease to be part of His Majesty's dominions and of the United Kingdom without the consent of the Parliament of Northern Ireland'. It was this latter provision that provoked an angry outburst in Dublin. At a special session, Costello, with the support of all the parties, moved that the Dáil should solemnly reassert the indefeasible right of the Irish nation to the unity and integrity of the national territory and reaffirm the sovereign right of the people of Ireland to choose its own form of government and through its democratic institutions to decide all questions of national policy free from outside interference. The claim of the United Kingdom Parliament to enact legislation affecting Ireland's territorial integrity was repudiated and the Dáil recorded its indignant protest against the introduction in the British Parliament of legislation 'purporting to endorse and continue the existing partition of Ireland'.[5]

The vehemence of the Irish reaction was sharpened by a sense of grievance on a matter of comparative detail. The Irish government felt that it had at the least been insufficiently forewarned by United Kingdom ministers of the nature of the renewed pledge they would feel it necessary to give to Northern Ireland when the Republic of Ireland seceded. On 28 October 1949 Attlee had stated that the United Kingdom government had always entertained, and continued to entertain, the view that no change should be made in the constitutional status of Northern Ireland without Northern Ireland's free agreement,[6] but it appears that at the meeting at Chequers on 17 October, and at the subsequent meeting in Paris on 17 November with the Irish ministers, the question of partition, though raised by the Irish representatives, was not discussed on the ground that it was outside the scope of the topics under review at these conferences. Neither, so Costello asserted, had there been suggestion of any kind made by British ministers that the Republic of Ireland Act would necessitate United Kingdom legislation relating to partition. It might be that had the United Kingdom government been earlier forewarned of the intention of the Irish government to repeal the External Relations Act, Attlee would have felt bound to indicate British intentions about legislation affecting the position of Northern Ireland in advance. But in any event lack of prior consultation did not affect the substance of the dispute. The protest of the Irish government against an Act of the United Kingdom Parliament involving 'the further tightening of the ligature which was fastened round the body of Ireland by the Government of Ireland Act, 1920'[7] was addressed to that provision of the Ireland Act which specifically transferred the right of self-determination to the parliament, not even to the people, of Northern Ireland. The Act of 1920 had paid lip service to the unity of Ireland, but the Act of 1949, by confirming that the United Kingdom Parliament itself could not, without the consent of the subordinate parliament in Belfast, even adjust the boundary so as to transfer minorities to the Republic of Ireland, in fact meant that the boundary acquired an air of permanence and of rigidity in law which it had not hitherto possessed. Since the area to be excluded from the Irish national parliament in 1920 had in fact been favoured by the Ulster Unionist party, who, on the admission of one of their own leaders, claimed an area in which Unionists might be assured indefinitely of a safe majority, the reaction of republican Ireland was understandable, even though its leaders had themselves taken the initiative in bringing about the sequence of events which led to the enactment of the Ireland Act 1949. In the exchanges between Attlee and Costello, which had a personal edge, neither conceded any ground on the failure to give advance notice, though it is debatable how much this might have achieved. To outward appearance, the Ireland Act 1949 marked the high point of Ulster Unionist influence in Anglo-Irish relations. The weakest numerically of the three and self-evidently the most vulnerable, it had not only held, but had further consolidated its position.

Erosion of the Unionist Position

This may seem an exaggerated assessment, but resting upon the assurances by which the Ulster Unionists set most store, it did not lack substance. In 1949 there was a boundary declaration underwriting the Act of 1920 with its ringing phrases about Northern Ireland, nor any part of it, ceasing to be part of His Majesty's Dominions without the consent of the Northern Ireland Parliament. Given the political loyalties of the Unionist majority, what more lasting guarantee might have been devised? Yet in fact it was to endure for little more than twenty years. In 1949 an observer might well have concluded that the Ulster question could be shelved until a new generation might approach it in the light of a changing climate of opinion. Yet appearances might have been deceptive, particularly in a triangular situation, for the remarkable fact is that the advantages of the Unionist position had seemingly been dissipated in little more than two decades. How had this come about?

In the passage of the years since 1920 some aspects of the settlement itself, as well as the way in which it was worked out, played a corrosive part. One of these was the basic factor of responsibility for law and order, which the Coalition government in London had seen to it was transferred to the regional authority, while retaining sefeguards for security and mutual fiscal advantages on a basis that, by way of concession, might best ensure the acquiescence of Unionist Ulster and Nationalist sentiment elsewhere in Ireland. During the thirties, the Belfast pogroms had exposed the British government in a technically correct stance, pointing out that law and order was a transferred responsibility which they could only discharge on the inevitably unconvincing plea of *ultra vires*. But this was a reaction less than satisfying to some departments including the Dominions Office. In retrospect, the question was did the British government ensure that sufficient resources would be placed at the disposal of Stormont to administer justice with impartiality? It was the duty of parliament to provide supporting, supplementary resources and to continue this on a regular basis to meet necessity. But their apparent indifference and failure to do so was a serious misjudgement of what the situation required, so that when disruptive forces came from several quarters, the state crumbled. Given the religious and social antagonisms which existed in the community, it was an awesome charge that was laid upon them.

As for the minority, whose allegiance lay and is likely always to lie, elsewhere, the 1925 Boundary Commission's draft report noted that

> in the course of their evidence witnesses gave various reasons for their wishes to be in one or other of the States.[8] In general, it appeared that the primary reason for wishing to be on one side or the other of the border lay in the desire . . . to be in "their own country", that is, in the country in which persons of their own religious or political complexion were in a majority, and in the case of the Nationalists, where they could satisfy their national aspirations under the most complete form of self-government.

That satisfaction Stormont could not offer, and it is hardly open to criticism because it did not, in the face of disruptive and sometimes violent opposition, achieve the impossible. Where criticism may justly lie is on the score of needless affront: for example, the almost immediate abolition of proportional representation, discrimination in respect of housing and jobs,

other local services and gerrymandering in electoral boundaries, and, overall in long years of quiescence, a lack of the magnanimity that is becoming
to those entrenched in power. In respect of education, Dr Buckland has
noted that during the inter-war years, 'discrimination became an integral
part of government policy'. Of the acquiescence of Whitehall and Westminster he observed that it derived partly from a reluctance to be drawn
once again into Irish affairs, partly from unwillingness to undermine the
authority of the devolved government by appearing to intervene in that
government's area of responsibility (which included law and order), ultimately from an awareness that either there was a Unionist government in
office at Stormont or the experiment in devolution had failed, there being
no conceivable alternative.[9]

However one assesses the grievances of the Northern Ireland minority,
their politico-dialectical campaign was not and could not be on a scale to
imperil the six-county administration. Only Collins in 1922 seemed reluctant to acknowledge that it was not feasible, other than by first gaining
international good will. There remained the members of the Provisional
IRA, generally known as the Irregulars. They refused to accept the Irish
Free State government as the lawful authority of the Irish Republic. They
were hostile to the Cosgrave administration, accorded it intermittent
recognition and helped to bring about its downfall. They were an embarrassment to de Valera. He indicated his intention to take steps against
them. Above all he rebuked them – he had been regarded as one among
them. Like Cato in ancient Rome they asked, 'Quis tulerit Gracchi de
seditione quaerentes?' Who indeed could tolerate the last of the 1916 rebels
complaining of acts of sedition? Few indeed. His credentials were un-
challengeable in the later thirties when the IRA campaign in Britain was
foreclosed.

In the seventy years since the settlement was made, partition has been a
central part of it and the Act has gone down in history as the 'Partition'
Act. That it remains. With the 1960s came a broader range of secondary
issues and protagonists with mounting tensions and disturbances, but
there was great hesitation about the expediency of intervention. In the
course of the next few years the Troubles came to be identified with a
series of violent outrages.[10] The thinking belonged to its own time and
place, but to return to de Retz's imagery, it drew prototype and inspiration from other times. In the early days some among the Provisionals
thought of modelling themselves on the historic figures of half a century
earlier, discounting the extent to which it was not realistic or attainable.
At a deeper level, the partition of the six counties offered little parallel to a
revolution on a national scale with the great majority in protest, as had
been the case in the South, where the evidence had indicated that the
majority could rely on the support of a nationwide movement – whereas
within the six counties the insurgents were a minority.

344   THE UNDOING OF THE SETTLEMENT

Here a cautionary note may be sounded. In the 1960s the later descent
to bloodshed and destruction did not monopolise the scene. There was a
glimpse of another canvas: the hope expressed by members of the
Boundary Commission that the Prime Ministers of the Irish Free State and
of Northern Ireland should meet from time to time to consider matters of
common concern – a hope reiterated, though without avail, by Seán
MacBride in 1948[11] – was fulfilled by the exchange of visits in Belfast and
Dublin: in January and February 1965 between the Taoiseach, Seán Lemass
and the prime Minister of Northern Ireland, Terence O'Neill and, some
three years later, between O'Neill and Jack Lynch. As a result of the first
of these meetings, the Nationalist opposition abandoned their abstention
from Stormont and there was a slowing down of the advance of the
Northern Ireland Labour party. Such accord as was achieved, however,
may have lost more Unionist than it gained Catholic support and so may
have contributed to O'Neill's fall from power.

O'Neill's premiership from 1963 to 1969 occupies a pivotal position in
the turmoil of the sixties. In 1966 the Ulster Volunteer Force was refounded
and it declared war on the IRA, new in method maybe, but traditional in
aims and purpose, while in 1967 the Northern Irish Civil Rights Association was formed. Among its members there were some who had experience of student unrest in America and France, where policies of the
established authority, which was vulnerable, had been successfully over-
thrown. By the summer of 1968 the protest marches followed by confrontation and rioting had begun and when on 5 October 1968 the People's
Democracy stepped in with a Belfast–Derry march, the floodgates were
opened. O'Neill countered this quasi-revolutionary movement by
enunciating a set of reforms, including housing allocation, the franchise
and local government. There was some support for his reforms and the
Civil Rights Association declared a truce and an interlude on marches and
demonstrations. Despite support from the New Ulster Movement,
O'Neill decided upon an election, which he lost; Chichester-Clark succeeded him on 1 May. There was abdication at one or more remove. By
July–August, British army units were operating in Northern Ireland
and the IRA had acquired their best recruiting sergeant. Why was a
reformist Unionist regime prepared to let a chance slide with inability to
take a stand? The combination of civil rights and IRA was formidable –
possibly too formidable for a devolutionary local government. But in the
winter of 1969 the ground was not tested. The main answer suggested by
John Cole was that it was the 'lack of grass roots support in the Unionist
Party itself' which finally overwhelmed him [O'Neill], at the end of
April.'[12] Beckett takes this a stage further and, as a historian, suggests the
problems for the rank and file of altering course. They tended to see
O'Neill's policies as a threat to their own monopoly of power.

In the meantime there was preoccupation with survival on the part of the six counties' administration. Responsibility for law and order had became the major question and during the period of outrages, with Bloody Sunday, 30 January 1972 and the reactions to it, it rested unequivocally with Stormont under the 1920 Act. The burning of the British Embassy in Dublin on 2 February was evidence of the frustration of the Northern Catholics' inability to deliver more than a telling propaganda counter.

Suspension of Stormont and the Framework of the Settlement Finally Broken Up

On 24 March 1972, Edward Heath, after his own one-day visit to Northern Ireland two days after Bloody Sunday and the reaction and sequel to it, sought permission to make a statement agreed with the opposition leaders. It marked a parting of the ways forward, which were fraught with unusual foreboding. The Prime Minister had three proposals to lay before the House: the first made in the hope of taking the Border out of politics by the reassurance that there would be no change in the Border without the consent of the majority by a system of regular plebiscites on the issue – in 1920 a plebiscite was favoured, but was deemed too provocative for the defining of the excluded area in the first instance. The Prime Minister's second proposal was the phasing out of internment, which it was seen retrospectively would have been better not brought in. The third was fundamental to virtually all community problems in Northern Ireland. In a classic understatement to the effect that it would be an advantage if responsibility for law and order were transferred from Belfast to Westminster, the government recommended that this should be done and Brian Faulkner, as Prime Minister of Northern Ireland, was told that transfer of responsibility was deemed essential; it was 'an indispensable condition for progress in finding a political solution in Northern Ireland'. That, so Heath reported, meant the resignation of the government and with it suspension of the parliament at Stormont; that very symbol of the Ulster Unionist polity and bulwark against hostile Liberal or Labour forces was dismantled and ceased to exist. Northern Ireland was placed under the rule of a Secretary of State, a diminution of status imposed against the will of the Unionist majority. On resignation, ministers in Belfast were said to be unanimous.[13] It was a decision that came as a shock rather than a surprise. William Whitelaw, the Lord President, was appointed as Secretary of State, the first holder of what came to be regarded as the least attractive post in Her Majesty's Service. The outcome for Northern Ireland was direct rule under its own Secretary of State but not, as many older Unionists favoured, integration.

Most of the signs conveyed the impression of unease in Whitehall at what it had been thought necessary to effect. Perhaps, it was suggested by Harold Wilson, had they been introduced earlier, these proposals might have had a better chance and 'history, perhaps, will have a view'. As things were, the Bill was described as 'inevitable'. Direct rule had always been regarded by both Labour and Conservative governments as the very last resort. As 'there will not be a Government in Stormont', Harold Wilson suggested a conference of all parties. The Prime Minister, who had little regard for members of the Northern Ireland administration, with the qualified exception of Brian Faulkner, took a robust, insensitive and seemingly unrealistic view, thinking of their action as giving 'an opportunity for a breakthrough to lower tension and make a fresh start'. Far from being any such thing, it represented a return to direct rule.

Within a few days Whitelaw took up his position as Secretary of State for Northern Ireland and this was followed by the Constitution of Northern Ireland Act 1973, which declared that Northern Ireland should not cease to be part of the United Kingdom without the consent of the majority of the people expressed in referendum. It was this declaration which provoked further protests from Dublin on the ground that by this procedure support for the status quo would be ensured for an indefinite period.

PART VII

PERSPECTIVES

CHAPTER 17
Some Reflections

Whatever happened to the Act of Union – the statute that transformed the Anglo-Irish relationship from a dual to a unitary monarchical system on 1 January 1801 and which lasted for just over a hundred years? With the Home Rule Bill enacted in 1914, but suspended until the end of the war, what happened to it then? The question was put to three eminent jurists in 1987. They suggested that the Union had been repealed in the Act of 1920, the Irish Free State Constitution Act and the Agreement Act 1925. But the effective repeal dated from 1953, when Article 7 of the 1920 Act, redefining the area of its application, was repealed by the Statute Law Revision Act of that year and finality was confirmed in 1973. To the layman it had, with due account of the amendment, long outlived its time. To the historian it might serve as a reminder that revolutions are generally untidy in their conclusion and require familiar tidying-up operations. In a successful revolution, institutional continuity can be of critical importance to the outcome.

A striking feature of the settlement was its division into two parts: the Government of Ireland Act 1920, and the Anglo-Irish Treaty 1921. At that time no other transfer of power in British history had been so phased and in an analogous Indian situation some quarter of a century later, partition and autonomy were both provided for in one Act, the India Independence Act 1947. In resolving the Irish question, disposing of Ulster Unionist claims was a preliminary condition to the making of concessions to Irish nationalist demands.

The dominating theme running through the history of the settlement was a fundamental imperialist–nationalist confrontation. In the search for a structural arrangement to bring about a *modus vivendi* acceptable to the two at the outset, there was no assurance that effective and, to those concerned, acceptable institutions could be negotiated and devised. If there was not absolute failure, equally there was not success. Those faced with both have generally concluded that success surpassed that of failure or, in the vocabulary of the settlement, status meant more than unity. It would be reasonable to concede that on a small scale there was to be seen one of the most cruelly destructive conflicts of post-war decolonisation. In the aftermath of such experience, it was unrealistic to appeal for friendship. The most on offer was an adjustment in attitude – the protagonists standing side by side instead of face to face.

The settlement reflected the duality of British policy towards Ireland as a whole during 1920–25. The first part was designed to entrench and satisfy the minority; the second to bring an Irish Dominion into being. But these were not consistent aims. Dominion status for Ireland, as earlier overseas, had been thought of as a device for preserving unity. But it came to be associated with division. Further, the natural supporters of such status were outside the Irish Dominion. It could be argued that the inconsistency at root derived from British reluctance to abandon the concept of unity. No one who wished to ensure the permanence of partition would have included in Northern Ireland so large a proportion of those whose natural allegiance lay elsewhere. But if the aim were unity, as the Cabinet records reaffirmed, the arguments might run otherwise. A strict delimitation of frontier, such as later took place in India, on the basis of the wishes of the inhabitants down to district level, would in Ireland have produced a Unionist/Protestant enclave which, if economically viable, would have had about it an air of permanence.

The three successive experiments in the ordering of Anglo-Irish relations are recorded on settlement lines in the three different names which have been given or are commonly attributed to the sovereign state which comprises twenty-six of the thirty-two counties of Ireland. Between 1921 and 1937 she was known as the Irish Free State. In the constitution of 1937 the name of the state was declared to be Éire or, in the English language, Ireland. Since the jurisdiction of her government extended only to twenty-six of the thirty-two counties, this created confusion, and outside the twenty-six counties the name Éire was commonly, if incorrectly, used as though it were a synonymous successor title to the Irish Free State. In 1948, contrary to general belief, the name of the state was not changed by the Republic of Ireland Act.[1] Any such change would have necessitated an amendment of the constitution. The Act declared that 'the description of the State shall be the Republic of Ireland'.[2] Evidently this refinement was too much for British draftsmen, for the Ireland Act 1949 speaks wrongly of 'The Republic of Ireland' as the name 'attributed thereto by the law thereof'.[3]

Yet the fate of these experiments in dominion status and external association, while final in the sense that neither could be repeated, determined the nature of what remained. Characteristic of Irish relations with the Commonwealth since 1921 had been an approach towards a finality that was never quite attained. Even the declaration of the Republic and secession did not effect the final break which in fear or in hope had been awaited for so many years. What was most remarkable after April 1949 was not how much but how little had been changed. But with secession, the commitment to the postures of the 1920s was rigidified. Attlee's response was the introduction of the Ireland Bill, the passing of which provoked impassioned protest in the Dáil,[4] and which to this day continues to be interpreted as reflecting a shift in British policy from a bias in favour to a bias against unity, as shown by the interposition of a third party with statutory entitlement to withhold consent to change.

The Sinn Féin leaders attributed responsibility for the creation of Northern Ireland, as distinct from special treatment for Ulster, to the backing, many would allege incitement, given by English to Ulster Unionists in the critical decade 1912–22[5] under Bonar Law's leadership. Robert Blake, Bonar Law's biographer, concurs in this view to the extent of concluding that without Bonar Law's uncompromising support, 'without his much criticized decision to pledge the whole of the English Conservative Party to the Ulster cause, it is very unlikely that Ulster would stand where she does today'.[6] What is apt to be overlooked is that the pro-Treaty party were no less insistent on British responsibility than their republican critics.

With Éire's secession from the Commonwealth in 1949, followed by the dismantling of the Stormont government in 1972, both parts of the Anglo-Irish Settlement in 1920–21 have passed into history. It is asked of Stormont, 'Why did it fail?' But it might be better to pose the open-ended question: did it fail? The answer to that may be conditioned by perspective. From the point of view of Ulster Unionists, for the safeguarding of whose interests it was established, it gave for half a century most of what they had campaigned for: exclusion from an all-Ireland parliament, uninterrupted Unionist government in an area they themselves reckoned to be within their capacity to hold, and partnership within the United Kingdom. In practical terms the working of the experiment in devolution was less predictable. Judged in those terms, the verdicts pronounced at various times have been of uneven rather than altogether discouraging achievement. None the less, in perspectives other than that of Ulster Unionists and possibly even in theirs, the sequel to Stormont has left an imprint of overall failure so bleak as to suggest that the explanation must needs be sought against a wider background and at a deeper level.

One last impression may be deserving of mention. From the summer of 1914, certainly from that of 1916, it needed no great gift of political perception to see, whatever Carson or influential Southern Unionists might say about the maintenance of the Union, that the issue was fined down to the exclusion of Ulster or some part of it. What remains surprising, that being so, is the subsequent protracted uncertainty, the going backwards and forwards at the highest level, on fundamental issues. Rarely in politics, it may be thought, have so many questions, so long debated – integration, area, institutions, the nature of the 'link' between the two parts of Ireland – remained seemingly so open, as if they might be settled either way, right up to the moment of decision. For the rest, political leaders might reflect, 'We had the experience but missed the meaning.'[7] But historians, mindful of the price of improvising institutions and maintaining a judicial system, may prove less disposed to judgement.

NOTES

Introduction

1. 10 and 11 Geo. V, Ch. 67.
2. The Irish Free State (Agreement) Act, 1922. 12 Geo, 5, Ch. 4.
3. 15 and 16 Geo. V, C, 77: Irish Free State Act No. 40 of 1925 scheduled to the Treaty.
4. N. Mansergh, *The Irish Question 1840–1921* (London, 1965).
5. Frank Pakenham, *Peace by Ordeal* (London, 1935).
6. *Speeches by Lord Macaulay* (London, 1935), pp. 111–12; see also Parl. Deb. 1833, H. of C. Vol. XV, Col. 262. Macaulay for good measure further remarked on 26 February that 'He would far rather live in Algiers, in its most despotic day than . . . in the county of Kilkenny at the present time'; *ibid.*, Col. 1335.
7. See *The Nationalist* (Clonmel), 25 January 1919, for a report of the inquest and 29 January for the Archdeacon's premonition, for such it reads.
8. W.S. Churchill, *The World Crisis: The Aftermath* (London, 1929), p. 307.

Chapter 1

1. Jean François Paul de Gondi de Retz, *Memoirs* 2 vols, trans. P. Davall, ed. Ernest Rhys (London, 1917), Vol. I, p. 155.
2. Oliver MacDonagh, *States of Mind. A Study of Anglo-Irish Conflict 1780–1980* (London, 1983), p. 101.
3. Michael MacDonagh, *The Life of Daniel O'Connell.* reprinted in Thomas and Valerie Pakenham, *Dublin – A Traveller's*

Companion, (London, 1988), p. 196. F.S.L. Lyons, *The Fall of Parnell 1890–91* (London, 1960), p. 177.
4. Dáil Éireann, *Debate on the Treaty between Great Britain and Ireland, December 1921–January 1922*, pp. 25 and 347.
5. Rt Hon. J.T. Ball, *Historical Review of the Legislative Systems operative in Ireland 1172–1800* (Dublin, 1889), reproduces these extracts in his summary of the principal contents of the speech, pp. 116–23.
6. See *The Parliamentary Register or, History of the Proceedings and Debates of the House of Commons of Ireland* 3 vols, Vol. I, 9 October 1781–27 July 1782, pp. 278, 283, 290 and 334–46 for extracts, and also Ball, *op. cit.*, pp. 131–2, for the extract from Grattan's speech of 16 April 1782.
7. Cf. J.C. Beckett, *Confrontations. Studies in Irish History* (London, 1972), Chapter 7. This is a brief but important contribution to the understanding of a period that is pivotal in Irish history. See also J.L. McCracken, *The Irish Parliament in the Eighteenth Century* (Dundalk, 1971); E.M. Johnston, *Great Britain and Ireland 1760–1800, A Study in Political Administration* (Edinburgh, 1963) and G.C. Bolton, *The Passing of the Irish Act of Union; a Study in Parliamentary Politics* (London, 1966).
8. Ball, *op. cit.*, pp. 114–42, offers a concise record of Grattan's parliament.
9. Quoted *ibid.*, p. 165.
10. *Thoughts on Ireland: Its Present and Its Future*, trans. W.B. Hodgson (London and Manchester, 1868), pp. 18–19. See also N. Mansergh, *The Irish Question 1840–1921* (London, 1965), p. 70.

11. *Home Rule Problems* (London, 1911), quoted in F. Eyck, *Gooch* (London, 1982), p. 118.

12. A. Griffith, *The Resurrection of Hungary: A Parallel for Ireland*, 3rd edn (London, 1918), pp. 118–19 and 86–7.

13. As reproduced in Charles Phillips, *Specimens of Irish Eloquence* (London, 1819), p. 399.

14. Griffith, *op. cit.*, p. 87.

15. H. of C. Deb., 1912. Vol. XXXVI, Col. 1488.

16. Text as supplied by Government Information Services, 16 April 1982.

17. H. of C. Deb. 21 February 1905, Vol. CXLI, Col. 860.

18. R.B. McDowell, *The Irish Administration* (London, 1964), p. 62.

19. Should the Viceroy accept an invitation from the Rotary Club, should he receive a deputation or send an address to the Galway District Council – these are examples from his early 1916 correspondence with the Under-Secretary in the Castle, Sir Matthew Nathan. Nathan Papers (NP) Bodleian Library, 449, ff.251–3.

20. Leon Ó Broin, *The Chief Secretary, Augustine Birrell in Ireland* (London, 1969), p. 1. The author is probably right to note this in the third sentence of his biographical study.

21. McDowell, *op. cit.*, pp. 27–31.

22. H. of C. Deb. 21 February 1905, Vol. CXLI, Col. 853.

23. *Ibid.*, 7 May 1907, Vol. CLXXIV, Col. 104.

24. *Ibid.*, Col. 155.

25. H. of C. Deb., 1905, Vol. CXLI, Col. 651, Vol. CLXXIV, Col. 83 and 104. McDowell, *op. cit.*, opts for 40 in 1914.

26. H. of C. Deb., 1905, Vol. CXLI, Col. 626.

27. F.S.L. Lyons, *John Dillon, A Biography* (London, 1968), pp. 229–36.

28. There was a similar dialogue between Gandhi and Jawaharlal Nehru in the India of the late 1920s. See S. Gopal, *Jawaharlal Nehru* 3 vols (London, 1975), Vol. I, p. 129.

29. H. of C. Deb., 3 February 1904, Vol. CXXIX, Col. 202.

30. Lyons, *John Dillon*, pp. 274–6; also H. of C. Deb., 1904, Vol. CXLI, Cols 788–98.

31. H. of C. Deb. 21 February 1904, Vol. CXLI, Cols 803–4. MacDonnell however stood firm on the assent to his

action given, albeit casually, by George Wyndham, and Wyndham thus became the unsuspecting victim of an odd episode even by Anglo-Irish standards of the time and resigned. See J. Biggs-Davison, *George Wyndham, A Study in Toryism* (London, 1951), pp. 160–73.

32. Report of Sir Warren Fisher to the Chancellor of the Exchequer, 12 May 1920; Lloyd George Papers (LGP) House of Lords Record Office, F/31/1/32 and see below, pp. 149–50.

33. Oliver MacDonagh, *op. cit.*, pp. 56–7.

34. B. Holland, *The Life of Spencer Compton, Eighth Duke of Devonshire*, 2 vols (London, 1911), Vol. II, p. 94.

35. D. Gwynn, *The Life of John Redmond* (London, 1932), p. 596.

36. John Wilson, *CB, A Life of Sir Henry Campbell-Bannerman* (London, 1973), pp. 108–9. See below, pp. 27–8.

37. Holland, *op. cit.*, Vol. II, p. 68.

38. Lyons, *Dillon*, Chapter 10 is entitled 'The Liberal Alliance'; also J.C. Beckett, *The Making of Modern Ireland* (London, 1966), pp. 420–1.

39. The story is told in Ulick O'Connor, *Celtic Dawn. A Portrait of the Irish Literary Renaissance* (London, 1984), pp. 162–3.

40. H.A.L. Fisher, *James Bryce* 2 vols (London, 1927), Vol. I, p. 341; Ó Broin, *op. cit.*, p. 82. The Bryces did not in fact leave for the US until 13 February 1907.

41. *A Report of the Debate in the House of Commons of Ireland on the Subject of a Legislative Union with Great Britain*, 5–6 February 1800.

42. Quoted in Patricia Jalland, *The Liberals and Ireland. The Ulster Question in British Politics to 1914* (Brighton, 1980), p. 80. See also p. 18 and *passim* for her contention on the pronounced elitist nature of politics at this time.

43. *Debate in the House of Commons of Ireland*, p. 58.

44. Gwynn, *op. cit.*, p. 15.

45. See Ball, *op. cit.*, pp. 293–5, note 00.

46. The sequence of events from 1848 is outlined in the commentary by Griffith, *op. cit.*, pp. 6–60. For a historian's account, see J. Redlich, *Emperor Francis Joseph of Austria* (London, 1929), Chapter 10 for an account of the *Ausgleich* and more especially Chapter 11, Dualism in Action.

47. See also Holland, *op. cit.*, Vol. II, p. 83. The 'experience' was brought into discussion also as a possible model for the

ordering of Indo-Pakistan relations on independence in 1947.

48. Griffith, *op. cit.*

49. G.A. Birmingham, *An Irishman Looks at His World* (London, 1919), pp. 186–7. As quoted in R.F. Foster, 'History and the Irish Question', *Transactions of the Royal Historical Society*, 1983, 5th Series, Vol. 33, pp. 169–92.

50. D.P. Moran, 'The Battle of Two Civilizations', in Augusta Gregory (ed.) *Ideals in Ireland* (London, 1901), p. 40; and F.S.L. Lyons, *Ireland since the Famine*, (London, 1971), p. 247.

Chapter 2

1. J.A. Spender and C. Asquith, *The Life of Lord Oxford and Asquith*, 2 vols (London, 1937), Vol. I, p. 144.

2. Herbert Gladstone Papers (HGP), British Museum, 45989, f.131.

3. *Ibid.*, 45988, f.196.

4. Ripon Papers, Add. Ms 43518, f.42; and HGP, 45989, f.184. Letters dated 9 September and 20 October 1905.

5. Redmond Papers (RP), National Library, Dublin, 15161.

6. *Ibid.*, Ms 15171 (2).

7. Quoted in F.S.L. Lyons, *John Dillon. A Biography* (London, 1968), p. 279.

8. RP, 15193 (8).

9. Ripon Papers, Add. Mss 43518, f.50.

10. RP, 15174.

11. Austen Chamberlain Papers (ACP), Birmingham University Library, 30 January 1925.

12. H.A.L. Fisher, *James Bryce* 2 vols (London, 1927), Vol. I, Chapter 18 and pp. 220–1. Also, personal information from Professor W.G.S. Adams.

13. *The Holy Roman Empire* (London, 1904) had concluded that with the unification of Italy and Germany, 'the triumph of the principle of nationality was complete' (p. 498). The Irish might have drawn his attention to its incomplete application in practice.

14. Ruth Dudley Edwards, *Patrick Pearse, The Triumph of Failure* (London, 1977), p. 73.

15. HGP, Add. Ms 46065, f.54. Campbell-Bannerman Papers (CBP), British Museum, Add. Ms. 41240, ff.127–32; Leon Ó Broin, *The Chief Secretary, Augustine Birrell in Ireland* (London, 1969), p. 217.

16. RP, 15215 (1) and 15189.

17. Lyons, *op. cit.*, p. 292.

18. H. of C. Deb., 7 May 1907, Vol. CLXXIV, Cols 78 and 102.

19. J.A. Spender, *The Life of Sir Henry Campbell-Bannerman* 2 vols (London, 1923), Vol. II, pp. 339–40.

20. A.G. Gardiner, *Prophets, Priests and Kings* (London, 1908), p. 303.

21. For an account of the complex manoeuvres that were involved first in formulation and then in amendment of the Bill, see from their respective points of view, Denis Gwynn, *The Life of John Redmond* (London, 1932), pp. 141–50; Lyons, *op. cit.*, pp. 290–8; Ó Broin, *op. cit.*, pp. 13–16 and John Wilson, *C.B. A Life of Sir Henry Campbell-Bannerman* (London, 1973), pp. 114–16.

22. For the letter offering resignation see CBP Add. Ms 41239, f.250.

23. *Ibid.*, ff.209–210–212. The restoration of an Irish parliament was stated to be a matter of vital interest and urgent necessity and the only solution of present difficulties was to be found in giving to the Irish people full legislative and executive control of all purely Irish affairs.

24. H. of C. Deb., May 1907, Vol. CLXXIV, Col. 158.

25. Irish Universities Act (1908), 8 Edw VII C 38, created the National University of Ireland comprising, in a federal structure, the University Colleges in Dublin, Cork and Galway. Birrell contributed much to its enactment and the National University decided for this reason to confer an honorary degree on him in 1929. He was prevented from receiving it in person because of a 'Great Storm' in the Irish sea. Ó Broin, *op. cit.*, p. 213. The Irish Land Act (1909), 9 Edw VII C 42, supplemented that of 1903 (Wyndham Act) which had opened the way to tenant ownership of land.

26. For the 'magnanimous gesture' see N. Mansergh, *South Africa 1906–1961 – The Price of Magnanimity* (London, 1962), pp. 17–23. For the final stages of India's journey to independence see N. Mansergh, *Survey of British Commonwealth Affairs – Problems of Wartime Co-operation and Post-War Change 1939–1952* (London, 1958), Chapter 4.

27. H. of C. Deb., May 1907, Vol. CLXXIV, n.26, Col. 114.

28. Lloyd George's exposition of the rele-

vant new or increased taxation is in H. of C. Deb., 29 April 1909, Vol. IV, Cols 525–6; see also Lyons, *op. cit.*, pp. 263–4.

29. RP. 15161 (2).

30. *Ibid.*, 15207, for Morley's reply, dated 6 December 1910.

31. Gwynn, *op. cit.*, p. 169; and Spender and Asquith, *op. cit.*, Vol. I, pp. 268–70.

32. Asquith Papers (AP), Bodleian Library, Oxford, V, ff.190–1. See also, Spender and Asquith, *op. cit.*, Vol. I, pp. 273–4, and generally, Chapter 21; and Roy Jenkins, *Asquith* (London, 1964), pp. 206–7.

33. H. of C. Deb., 29 March 1910, Vol. XV, Cols 1162–82; see esp. 1179–81.

34. *Ibid.*, Vol. XVI, Cols 1526–47, for voting on the resolutions and Cols 1547–8 for the Prime Minister's statement on future procedure.

35. *Ibid.*, Vol. XVI, Cols 462–530.

36. Lyons, *op. cit.*, p. 319; Gwynn, *op. cit.*, p. 181.

37. RP, 15215(2).

38. Ensor, *England 1870–1914* (Oxford, 1936), p. 424. Lansdowne, as Foreign Secretary, was architect of the Anglo-French Entente, 1904, and by no means inflexible on issues other than Irish policy. He was Anglo-Irish, a landlord with large estates at Derreen near Killarney in Co. Kerry.

39. 1 and 2 Geo. V, c. 13.

40. Irish votes in pursuit of Irish aims had tangential effects on English politico-constitutional developments at this time. Without the pressures they exerted, the Parliament Bill if introduced would presumably have had a more relaxed passage and the abortive constitutional conference would have been freed from the incubus of Lansdowne's Irish interests.

41. Dillon Papers (DP), Trinity College, Dublin Archives, Correspondence with Lloyd George 6 November 1910.

42. Ensor, *op. cit.*, pp. 418–19. Ensor, a member of the Fabian Society in its early days, was a remarkably well-informed contemporary historian in the strict sense – as becomes apparent on perusal of the archives, personal and public.

Chapter 3

1. J.D. Kestell, *Through Shot and Flame* (London, 1903), p. 285.

2. Macaulay, *Selected Speeches* (Oxford, 1935), pp. 107–8.

3. Nassau Senior, *Journals, Conversations and Essays relating to Ireland*, 2 vols (London, 1868), Vol. I, p. 22.

4. Hansard, Parl. Deb., 3rd series, 8 April 1886, Vol. CCCIV, Cols 1053–4.

5. *Ibid.*, Cols 1200–1.

6. *Dictionary of National Biography (DNB) 1922–30*, p. 579.

7. *Ibid., 1931–40*, p. 147.

8. For their membership and organisation, see P. Buckland (ed.) *Irish Unionism 1885–1922, A Documentary History* (Belfast, 1973).

9. See P. Buckland, *Ulster Unionism and the Origins of Northern Ireland 1886–1922* (Dublin, 1973), pp. 20–1 and 52–3 for genesis of the Ulster Unionist Council.

10. E. Marjoribanks and I. Colvin, *Life of Lord Carson*, 3 vols (London, 1932–6), Vol. II, p. 104.

11. Chamberlain Papers, (ACP), Birmingham University Library, 22 August 1910.

12. *Ibid.*, Lansdowne to Chamberlain, 2 September 1910.

13. Balfour, a hardliner, contributed to the formulation of Cabinet policy on Ireland in 1916 and again in 1919–21.

14. Robert Blake, *The Unknown Prime Minister* (London, 1955), p. 85. Three Canadians, Hamar Greenwood, the last Chief Secretary, being the third, played a part in the shaping of Anglo-Irish relations in the period of the settlement. The two who held office, Bonar Law and Greenwood, were notable for the inflexibility of their views. Aitken and Bonar Law were both from New Brunswick, Greenwood from Ontario.

15. *DNB 1922–30*, p. 519.

16. Blake, *op. cit.*, pp. 26–32, 125 and 129–30.

17. Law to Asquith, 10 October 1913, Bonar Law Papers (BLP) House of Lords Record Office, 33/6/73 and Law to Lansdowne, 8 December 1913, *ibid.*, 33/6/109.

18. Lord Newton, *Lord Lansdowne* (London, 1929), pp. 501–2. The biography relegates Lansdowne's Irish policy to an uncritical and incomplete survey in an appendix.

19. Blake, *op. cit.*, p. 149–53.

20. BLP, 33/5/61.

21. *Ibid.*, 33/5/57.

22. Patricia Jalland, *The Liberals and Ireland: The Ulster Question in British Politics to*

1914 (Brighton, 1980), pp. 49 and 56.
23. Asquith Papers (AP), Bodleian Library, Oxford, 7 February 1912, Box 6, ff.95–6.
24. Roy Jenkins, *Asquith* (London, 1964), p. 279.
25. W.S. Churchill, *The World Crisis 1911–1914*, 6 vols (London, 1923), Vol. I, pp. 181–2.
26. Jalland, *op. cit.*, pp. 65–77. The 6 February decision is central to an argument which if not altogether convincing is cogent and illuminating. See also Spender and Asquith, *The Life of Lord Oxford and Asquith*, 2 vols, (London, 1932), Vol. II, pp. 14–15; and Mansergh, *The Irish Question* (London, 1965), pp. 219–20, which shows a change of view possibly influenced by later Ulster Unionist imperviousness to English Unionist views.
27. H. of C. Deb., 11 April 1912, Vol. XXXVI, Cols 1400–1 and 1426.
28. *Ibid.*, Col. 1406.
29. John E. Kendle, *The Round Table Movement and Imperial Union* (Toronto, 1975). Chapter 6 analyses the views of Round Tablers and other federalists, most if not all of whom were unsympathetic to the Irish national claim.
30. The Government of Ireland Act 1914, 4 and 5 Geo. V, Ch. 20. Sections 1–3 deal with the establishment of an Irish Parliament and its legislative powers. The Prime Minister's exposition of them may be read in H. of C. Deb., 1912, Vol. XXXVI, Cols 1407–23.
31. *Ibid.*, Cols 1442–3.
32. *Ibid.*, Cols 1425–6 and 1441.
33. *Ibid.*, Col. 1484 and Vol. XXXIX, Cols 771–3.
34. *Ibid.*, Col. 780.
35. *Ibid.*, Col. 790.
36. *Ibid.*, Cols 1119–20 and 1083.
37. Buckland, *Irish Unionism, op. cit.*, pp. 217–18.
38. On 5 October 1912.
39. ACP, Lansdowne to Chamberlain, 22 August; Chamberlain to Lansdowne, 26 August 1912.
40. A.J. Balfour, *Nationality and Home Rule* (London, 1913).
41. See above p. 55.
42. Jenkins, *op. cit.*, p. 208, where Asquith's uses of the phrase are listed.
43. ACP, letter from Lloyd George to Chamberlain, 15 May 1914, A.C. 11/1/62.
44. R.B. McCallum, *Asquith* (London, 1936), p. 12.
45. ACP, 11/1/21.
46. Denis Gwynn, *The Life of John Redmond* (London, 1932), p. 232.
47. F.S.L. Lyons, *John Dillon* (London, 1968), pp. 330–9.
48. *King Henry IV, Part I*, Act III, scene i, line 53.
49. ACP, 11/1/4, letter from de Broke to Chamberlain, 21 November 1913.
50. A.M. Gollin, *Proconsul in Politics* (London, 1964), pp. 184–8.
51. Kendle, *op. cit.*, Chapter 6.
52. Law and Lansdowne joint memorandum, BLP, 39/E/10.
53. Cf. Jenkins, *op. cit.*, pp. 283–7; and Spender and Asquith, *op. cit.*, Vol. II, pp. 29–31, where Asquith's memorandum is reprinted.
54. *The Times*, 11 September 1913, and Denis Gwynn, *The History of Partition, 1912–1925* (Dublin, 1950), p. 59.
55. BLP, 33/5/54 and 33/5/56.
56. Spender and Asquith, *op. cit.*, Vol. II, pp. 31–4.
57. AP, 38, ff.198–201.
58. *Ibid.*, ff.202–9.
59. Lyons, *Dillon, op. cit.*, pp. 330–1.
60. Redmond Papers (RP), National Library, Dublin, ff.15181 (3).
61. Gwynn, *Redmond, op. cit.*, pp. 229–32.
62. AP, 38, ff.232–7; BLP 33/6/80 with covering letter to Lansdowne, 15 October 1913.
63. ACP, 11/1/48.
64. BLP, 33/6/93.
65. Lloyd George's proposal set out in Asquith's letter to the King, 14 November 1913, AP, 7, ff.71–2.
66. RP, ff.15161(2) for Redmond's account of his meeting with Asquith on 17 November and also Asquith's, AP, 39, ff.23–6. For Redmond's meeting with Lloyd George on 25 November, see Gwynn, *Redmond, op. cit.*, pp. 237–8.
67. RP, 15165(3).
68. ACP, 11/1/21.
69. AP, 39, ff.97–8.
70. Law to Stamfordham, 4 October 1913, BLP, 33/5/66.
71. BLP, Law to Stamfordham, 26 January 1914, 34/3/16.
72. RP, 15165(4).
73. M. and E. Brock (eds) *H.H. Asquith: Letters to Venetia Stanley* (Oxford, 1982), No. 29, p. 44.
74. RP, 4 February 1914, f.15165(4).
75. *Ibid.*, 15169(4), Birrell to Redmond, 9 February 1914.
76. H. of C. Deb., 11 February 1914, Vol.

LVIII, for Bonar Law's and Carson's speeches, Cols 270–84 and 169–79 respectively.

77. Jenkins, *op. cit.*, pp. 300–2.
78. Lloyd George Papers (LGP), House of Lords Record Office, C.20.2.6, RP, 15257(2) and Gwynn, *Redmond, op. cit.*, pp. 256–9.
79. RP, *ibid.*; AP, 39, ff.134–41.
80. AP, 39, ff.118–21; RP, 15165(4).
81. Jenkins, *op. cit.*, p. 303.
82. RP, 15165(4).
83. H. of C. Deb., 9 March 1914, Vol. LIX, Cols 906–18.
84. Asquith, *Letters, op. cit.*, p. 53.
85. H. of C. Deb., 9 March 1914, Vol. LIX, Col. 933.
86. *Ibid.*, Col. 941.
87. *Ibid.*, Cols 929–30.
88. Cabinet Papers, Vol. CXX, 15 June 1914, substantially reformulated in Leon Ó Broin, *The Chief Secretary, Augustine Birrell in Ireland* (London, 1969), pp. 99–102.
89. H. of L. Deb., 23 June 1914, Vol. XVI, Cols 377–88.
90. *Ibid.*, Cols 390–1.
91. *Ibid.*, Col. 1174.
92. BLP, 39, f.4 and RP, 15257(4), 15520, f.261.
93. R.S. Churchill, *Winston S. Churchill*, Vol. II, *Young Statesman 1901–1914* (London, 1967), p. 505; and Spender and Asquith, *op. cit.*, Vol. II, p. 55.
94. Asquith, *Letters, op. cit.*, p. 123.
95. ACP, 11/1/90.
96. *Ibid.*
97. *Ibid.*, ACP, 11/1/44.

Chapter 4

1. M. and E. Brock (eds) *H.H. Asquith: Letters to Venetia Stanley* (Oxford, 1982), p. 111: Patricia Jalland, *The Liberals and Ireland: the Ulster Question in British Politics to 1914* (Brighton, 1980), p. 259.
2. Cf. Piaras Béaslaí, *Michael Collins, Soldier and Statesman* (Dublin, 1937), p. 19; Bonar Law Papers (BLP) House of Lords Record Office, 34/4/53.
3. W.B. Yeats, *Collected Poems* (London, 1933), 'Easter, 1916', p. 202–5.
4. Asquith, *Letters, op. cit.*, p. 111.
5. H. of C. Deb., 3 August 1914, Vol. LXV, Cols 1828–9.
6. *Ibid.*, 15 September 1914, Vol. LXVI, Cols 911–12.
7. P.S. O'Hegarty, *A History of Ireland*

under the Union 1801–1922 (London, 1952), p. 693, and F.S.L. Lyons, *John Dillon* (London, 1968), pp. 354–7.

8. Redmond Papers (RP), National Library, Dublin, 15164, Redmond to Asquith 8 August 1914. H. of C. Deb., 18 October 1916, Vol. LXXXVI, Cols 581–94; see also, Cols 632–4, 645–6.
9. Asquith, *Letters, op. cit.*, p. 233; also pp. 163 and 239.
10. H. of C. Deb., 31 August 1914, Vol. LXVI, Cols 438–40 for Redmond's speech; and for the Prime Minister's appeal for restraint, Col. 453.
11. *Ibid.*, 15 September 1914, Cols 882–905 for the Asquith–Bonar Law exchanges on 15 September; for Royal Assent given on 18 September, Col. 1017; see also D. Gwynn, *The Life of John Redmond* (London, 1932), p. 383.
12. W.S. Churchill, *The World Crisis: The Aftermath* (London, 1929), p. 285; D. Gwynn in *The History of Partition 1912–25* (Dublin, 1950), writes that the Suspensory Act 'imposed an indefinite delay', p. 143.
13. H. of C. Deb., 15 September 1914, Vol. LXVI, Col. 892.
14. *Ibid.*, Cols 906–7.
15. O'Hegarty, *op. cit.*, p. 692.
16. Asquith, *Letters, op. cit.*, p. 337.
17. Gwynn, *Redmond, op. cit.*, pp. 423–6.
18. Nathan Papers (NP), Bodleian Library, Oxford, 449, 242 and 244.
19. See Leon Ó Broin, *The Chief Secretary, Augustine Birrell in Ireland* (London, 1969), pp. 110–24.
20. NP, 449, ff.348, 350, 352.
21. Ó Broin, *op. cit.*, Chapter 5, suggests in a dramatic reconstruction of events how Birrell's judgement was at fault by a narrow margin in timing.
22. NP, 477, f.247, where there is a collection of relevant press cuttings (including *Irish Times* editorial, 5 May 1916).
23. Asquith Papers AP, Bodleian Library, Oxford, 8 ff.157/8 and 161.
24. Dillon Papers (DP), Lloyd George to Dillon 9 June 1916.
25. Roy Jenkins, *Asquith* (London, 1964), pp. 403–4.
26. W.B. Yeats, *Last Poems and Plays* (London, 1940), pp. 25–6.
27. Jenkins, *op. cit.*, pp. 397–8.
28. CAB. 37/148/18.
29. For an account of the negotiations that followed as recalled by Lloyd George, see *War Memoirs*, 2 vols (London, 1938),

Vol. I, pp. 418–25, and as interpreted by Asquith's biographers, see Jenkins *op. cit.*, pp. 397–402 and Spender and Asquith, *The Life of Lord Oxford and Asquith*, 2 vols (London, 1937), Vol. II, pp. 215–24.

30. CAB. 37/150/11 and 15.

31. H. of L. Deb., 29 June 1916, Vol. XXII, Col. 506.

32. Ronald McNeill, *Ulster's Stand for Union* (London, 1922), pp. 247–9; I. Colvin, *The Life of Lord Carson*, 3 vols (London, 1932–6), Vol. III, pp. 164–79. Lloyd George's letter to Carson dated 29 May 1916 is reproduced on p. 166; D. Gwynn, *Redmond, op. cit.*, Chapter 14 and *History of Partition, op. cit.*, Chapter 5.

33. RP, 15189.

34. CAB. 37/150/17.

35. CAB. 37/150/18.

36. CAB. 37/150/21.

37. CAB. 37/150/23. See also Jenkins, *op. cit.*, pp. 399–401.

38. CAB. 37/151/8.

39. AP, 46, f. 217, dated 12 July 1916.

40. H. of L. Deb., 11 July 1916, Vol. XXII, Cols 645–9.

41. CAB. 37/151/37.

42. CAB. 37/151/38.

43. CAB. 37/151/42.

44. CAB. 37/152/1.

45. CAB. 37/152/22.

46. A.J.P. Taylor, *English History 1914–1945* (Oxford, 1965), pp. 71–2, Note B.

47. Quoted in Trevor Wilson, *The Downfall of the Liberal Party 1914–1935* (London, 1968), p. 74, from *Manchester Guardian*, 26 July 1916.

48. RP, Correspondence.

49. Cf. F.S.L. Lyons, *Ireland since the Famine* (London, 1971), pp. 368–9.

50. RP, 15189.

51. LGP, Adams to Prime Minister, 1 March 1917, F63/1/1.

52. *Ibid.*, 63/1/2.

53. Lyons, *op. cit.*, pp. 388–9.

54. RP, 15215.

55. H. of C. Deb. 7 March 1917, Vol. XCI, Col. 459.

56. Cd. 8573, and also reprinted in *Report of the Proceedings of the Irish Convention* Cd. 9019, pp. 50–1. See also, R.B. McDowell, *The Irish Convention 1917–18* (London, 1970), and John Turner, *Lloyd George's Secretariat* (Cambridge, 1980), Chapter 5.

57. RP, 15169.

58. Turner, *op. cit.*, pp. 108–11 and generally.

59. Gwynn, *The History of Partition, op. cit.*, p. 165.

60. CAB. 23/14. 28 March 1918.

61. CAB. 37/155/8 and 37/155/40.

62. CAB. 24/5.

63. CAB. 37/157/8.

64. Thomas Jones, *Whitehall Diary*, ed. K. Middlemas, 3 vols (London, 1969), Vol. I, p. 57 and Vol. III, p. 4. See also, D.G. Boyce, 'How to settle the Irish question: Lloyd George and Ireland 1916–21' in A.J.P. Taylor, *Lloyd George – Twelve Essays* (London, 1971), pp. 143–5 and generally.

65. CAB. 23/14. Sir Henry Robinson was Vice-President, Local Government Board for Ireland.

66. H. of C. Deb. 10 April 1918, Vol. CIV, Col. 1364.

67. Jones, *Whitehall Diary, op. cit.*, Vol. I. p. 56.

68. Churchill, *op. cit.*, p. 283.

69. Lyons, *John Dillon, op. cit.*, p. 447.

70. *Ibid.*, pp. 73–4.

71. *Ibid.*, pp. 380–4.

72. *Ibid.*, p. 104.

73. *Ibid.*, p. 484.

74. Jones, *Whitehall Diary*, Vol. I, p. 61.

75. *Ibid.*, p. 63 and CAB. 27/46.

76. CAB. 27/46 and Churchill, *op. cit.*, p. 281.

77. Jones, *Whitehall Diary*, Vol. III, pp. 5–6, and CAB. 27/46.

78. CAB. 24/5, 14 July 1918.

79. Jones, *Whitehall Diary*, Vol. III, p. 9.

80. *Ibid.*, p. 11.

81. Lloyd George Papers (LGP) House of Lords Record Office, F/68/22, 4 June 1918.

Chapter 5

1. Winston S. Churchill, *The World Crisis: The Aftermath* (London, 1929), p. 319.

2. W.B. Yeats, *Collected Poems* (London, 1933), 'Easter 1916', p. 205.

3. D. Macardle, *The Irish Republic* (Dublin, 1951), pp. 919–20.

4. This copy is now in the author's possession.

5. Richard Holmes, *The Little Field Marshal: Sir John French* (London, 1981).

6. Rex Taylor, *Michael Collins* (London, 1958), pp. 111–13; David Fitzpatrick, *Politics and Irish Life 1913–21; provincial*

experience of war and revolution (London, 1977), Chapter 5, 'Revolutionary Administrators', is an important pioneering case study of what actually happened and why, in the attempted Sinn Féin administrative take-over, and unravels the often haphazard relationship with the centre, when the theory of a separate and rival administration was in process of realisation in County Clare.

7. The results of the election are reviewed in A.J.P. Taylor, *English History 1914–1945* (Oxford, 1965), pp. 125–8; and Trevor Wilson, *The Downfall of the Liberal Party* (London, 1968), pp. 135–83. Because of difficulties in identifying allegiance in a few cases, the figures do not exactly coincide. See also, *Lloyd George – Twelve Essays*, ed. A.J.P. Taylor (London, 1971), VIII; K.O. Morgan, Lloyd George's Stage Army – The Coalition Liberals 1918–22.

8. J.M. Keynes, *The Economic Consequences of the Peace* (London, 1920), p. 133. R.B. McCallum made the suggestion about photographs and wills.

9. Cmd. 692.

10. H.A.L. Fisher Papers (HFP) Bodleian Library, Diary 10 and 14 April 1918. Wimborne reported that the Nationalists would accept the Committee solution and Lloyd George that Carson wanted it. T. Jones, *Lloyd George* (London, 1951), pp. 188–9.

11. Reprinted in CAB. 27/68, CP 56, 4 November 1919.

12. Sir Laming Worthington-Evans' Papers (LWEP) Bodleian Library, c. 908.

13. H. of C. Deb. 29 March 1920, Vol. CXXVII, Cols 980–1; 1122–3 and 976.

14. CAB. 27/68, CP 56, 33.

15. CAB. 27/69, CP 20, 23, 8 October 1919.

16. CAB. 27/68, CP 56, 4 November 1919.

17. CAB. 23/18, 11 November 1919.

18. CAB. 27/68, CP 103, 11 November 1919.

19. *Ibid.*, 13 November 1919.

20. CAB. 27/70 C.I.87 29 September 1920.

21. CAB. 27/69 C.I.41 22 November 1919.

22. *Ibid.*, C.I.37 26 November 1919.

23. *Ibid.*, C.I.48.

24. CAB. 23/18 3 December 1919.

25. *Ibid.*

26. *Ibid.*, 10 December 1919.

27. *Ibid.*

28. *Ibid.*

29. *Ibid.*, 15 December 1919.

30. *Ibid.*, 19 December 1919.

31. *Ibid.*, 19 and 22 December 1919.

32. H. of C. Deb. 22 December 1919, Vol. CXXIII, Cols 1168–82.

33. CAB. 27/69 C.I.54, 6 January 1920.

34. CAB. 27/69 C.I.58, 4 February 1920.

35. CAB. 27/68 CP 565.

36. *Ibid.*, CP 564.

37. In fact Bonar Law wrote two reports, one for the Prime Minister and one for the Committee. CAB. 27/68 CP 564.

38. Craig had so advised Fisher, CAB. 27/68, 13 November 1919, see note 19.

39. Enacted as 10 and 11 Geo. 5 ch. 67.

40. H. of C. Deb., 30 March 1920. Vol. CXXVII, Cols 1112–3.

41. See above.

42. H. of C. Deb., 31 March 1920, Vol. CXXVII, Cols 1288–99.

43. *Ibid.*, Cols 986 and 990.

44. *Ibid.*, 29 March 1920, Col. 1019.

45. *Ibid.*, Cols 984–5.

46. *Ibid.*, Cols 1005–12.

47. *Ibid.*, Col. 1023; see also J.H. Clynes, Cols 944–56 for Labour views.

48. *Ibid.*, Cols 979–81.

49. *Ibid.*, Col. 1331.

50. *Ibid.*, Col. 1333.

51. F.S.L. Lyons, *Ireland since the Famine* (London, 1971), p. 412.

52. A.J.P. Taylor, *op. cit.*, p. 156.

53. Birkenhead, *F.E. Smith, 1st Earl of Birkenhead* (London, 1959), p. 361.

54. D.G. Boyce, 'British Conservative Opinion. The Ulster question and the partition of Ireland, 1912–21', in *Irish Historical Studies*, vol. XXII pp. 89–112 provides an analysis of developments in Conservative opinion down to the Treaty.

Chapter 6

1. Lloyd George Papers (LGP), House of Lords Record Office, F/16/7/61.

2. *Ibid.*, F/31/1/32.

3. E. Burke, *Reflections on the Revolution in France* (London, 1790).

4. Pádraic H. Pearse, *Political Writing and Speeches* (Dublin, 1922), pp. 224–5.

5. Dan Breen, *My Fight for Irish Freedom*, new edn (Tralee, 1964), p. 37 and D. Macardle, *The Irish Republic* (Dublin, 1937), p. 317.

6. Dáil Éireann, *Official Correspondence relating to the Peace Negotiations June–*

September 1921 (Dublin, 1921), pp. 16–17; see also Cmd. 1539.
7. Dáil Deb. Vol. 2, 1921–2, p. 15.
8. W.K. Hancock, *Survey of British Commonwealth Affairs*, 2 vols, Vol. I: *Problems of Nationality 1918–1936* (Oxford, 1937), p. 113.
9. H.A.L. Fisher Papers (HFP), Bodleian Library, Oxford, Box 8A Diaries, 20 April 1919.
10. CAB. 27/69, 26 November 1919.
11. CAB. 23/18, 3 December 1919, section 4, and 22 December 1919.
12. *Ibid.*, 19 December 1919.
13. H. of C. Deb., Vol. CXXVII, Col. 1324, 30 December 1920.
14. *Ibid.*, Clynes, Cols 944–56; Parkinson, Cols 994–8; Wedgwood Benn, Cols 1017–28.
15. *Ibid.*, Col. 1124–5.
16. Austen Chamberlain Papers (ACP), Birmingham University Library, 30/1/22, letter dated 29 September 1920.
17. H. of C. Deb. 31 March 1920, Vol. CXXVII, Col. 1332.
18. *Ibid.*, Cols 1322–3.
19. Midleton to Chamberlain 25 September 1920, ACP, 30/1/23.
20. CAB. 23/37.
21. CAB. 23/21.
22. *Ibid.*, 12 May 1920. Both part and supplementary memorandum were circulated to the Chancellor of the Exchequer, the Lord privy Seal and the Prime Minister.
23. *Ibid.*, F/31/1/33, 15 May 1920.
24. CAB. 23/37 and Thomas Jones, *Whitehall Diary* ed. K. Middlemas, 3 vols, Vol. III, *Ireland 1918–1925* (London, 1971), pp. 16–23.
25. CAB. 46 c, Fisher Diary and Jones, *op. cit.*, pp. 25–31. Jones' record as printed omits to summarise Wylie's opening observations, with the result that what follows is not always intelligible.
26. CAB. 23/38; Jones *op. cit.*, pp. 39–41.
27. CAB. 23/38 Government of Ireland Bill.
28. CAB. Conference 49 and 50.
29. John McColgan, *British Policy and the Irish Administration 1920–22* (London, 1983).
30. Winston S. Churchill, *The World Crisis: The Aftermath* (London, 1929), p. 290.
31. H. Nicolson, *King George V* (London, 1952), pp. 346–9.
32. Churchill, *op. cit.*, p. 288.
33. Charles Townshend, *The British Campaign in Ireland, 1919–1921: The Development of Political and Military Policies* (Oxford, 1975).
34. C.E. Callwell, *Field Marshal Sir Henry Wilson: His Life and Diaries*, 2 vols (London, 1927), Vol. II, p. 252.
35. *Ibid.*, Vol. II, p. 263.
36. *Ibid.*, Vol. II, p. 273.
37. Churchill, *op. cit.*, pp. 288–9 and Macardle, *op. cit.*, Chapter 43.
38. LGP, F. 107; see also CAB. 35(20)
39. Jones, *op. cit.*, p. 49; see also pp. 44–5 on Clune's mediation.
40. *Ibid.* See also Jones, *op. cit.*, p. 68 for Lloyd George's dismissive references to de Valera, and HFP, 23 May 1921 for Greenwood's.
41. Craig Papers (CP), Public Record Office Northern Ireland (PRONI), D/1415/13/32.
42. Jones, *op. cit.*, pp. 63–71.
43. *Ibid.*, p. 68.
44. Sir Laming Worthington-Evans Papers (LWEP), Bodleian Library, c 909 CP (2945), State Department, Washington, from the American Consul Dublin, 16 April, 4 May 1921 and from the American Consulate, Belfast, 25 May.
45. CP 3075.
46. Anderson to Chief Secretary, 18 June 1921, ACP, 31/2/3.
47. Churchill, *op. cit.*, p. 290.
48. W. K. Hancock, *Smuts*, 2 vols (Cambridge, 1968) Vol. II, *The Fields of Force 1919–1950*, pp. 51–5, also *Selections from the Smuts Papers* (Cambridge, 1973) Vol. V, pp. 89–91.
49. CAB. 23/35 ff.349–50.
50. Jones, *op. cit.*, pp. 74–6.
51. Hancock, *op. cit.*, Vol. II, pp. 51–5; Nicolson, *op. cit.*, pp. 348–54.
52. Jones, *op. cit.*, pp. 79–82.
53. To Secretary of State, Washington, July 1921.
54. Jones, *op. cit.*, pp. 82–4. Personal recollections. President de Valera to the author. See also Longford and O'Neill, *Eamon de Valera* (Dublin, 1970), p. 133.
55. Jones, *op. cit.*, p. 105.
56. As told by President de Valera to the author, 1956. The exchange tallied closely with that of Miss Stevenson, which de Valera had not seen.
57. The exchanges are reproduced in Dáil Éireann, *Official Correspondence relating to the Peace Negotiations, June–September 1921* and Cmd 1470, Cmd 1502 and Cmd 1539.

58. LGP, F/45/9/50. De Valera felt aggrieved at the publication of this letter before his own reply to Lloyd George had been sent. On his return to South Africa Smuts wrote to Lloyd George making suggestions which showed the limitation of his sensitivity to Irish aspirations. Smuts to Lloyd George, 30 August 1921 F/45/9/53. See also *Selections from the Smuts Papers* ed. W.K. Hancock and J. van der Poel, 7 vols (Cambridge, 1966–73), Vol. V, pp. 48–63 for Smuts' correspondence.
59. ACP, 31/2/7 and 8.
60. Nicolson, *op. cit.*, pp. 356–8.
61. Dáil Deb., 16 August 1921–8 June 1922, pp. 13–15.
62. Jones, *op. cit.*, pp. 102–3. Cmd 1539.
63. ACP, 31/2/19.
64. *Ibid.*, 31/2/18.
65. Cmd 1539.

Chapter 7

1. W.S. Churchill, *The World Crisis: The Aftermath* (London, 1929), p. 296.
2. Dáil Éireann, *Debate on the Treaty between Great Britain and Ireland*, 14 December 1921, p. 32.
3. Charles Townshend, *The British Campaign in Ireland, 1919–1921* (London, 1975), p. 202.
4. D.G. Boyce, *Englishmen and Irish Troubles 1918–1922* (Cambridge, Mass., 1972), p. 180.
5. Cmd. 1474.
6. Cf. Churchill, H. of C. Deb. 15 December 1921, Vol. CXLIX, Col. 171. on how British interests all over the world especially in the Dominions and the US were prejudically affected by policies of repression in Ireland.
7. W.K. Hancock, *Survey of British Commonwealth Affairs*, Vol. I, *Problems of Nationality* (London, 1937), pp. 1–4.
8. Cmd. 1539.
9. Dáil Deb. (Private Session) 1921–22, 14 September 1921, pp. 94–6 and 103; Dáil Éireann Files, Griffith to de Valera, 3 December 1921, University College Dublin Archives (UCDA) Richard Mulcahy Papers (RMP); Treaty Debate, p. 8.
10. Robert Blake, *The Unknown Prime Minister* (London, 1955), p. 531; and Thomas Jones, *Whitehall Diary*, Vol. III, *Ireland 1918–25* (London, 1971), p. 156.
11. The Childers Papers are in the Archives, Trinity College, Dublin (TCD); Jones, *op. cit.*, Vol. III. Lionel Curtis' (LC) in the Bodleian Library, Oxford.
12. Jones, *op. cit.*, p. 171.
13. *Ibid.*, pp. 184–6.
14. Dr S. Lawlor, *Britain and Ireland 1914–1923* (Dublin, 1983), a complementary study based on primary sources providing detailed critical analysis of the contributions and aims of the principal protagonists; J.M. Curran, *The Birth of the Irish Free State 1921–1923* (Alabama, 1980) is an authoritative study and suggests how the new state came into existence and established its authority.
15. Dáil Éireann, *Treaty Debate*, p. 11.
16. Cmd. 1502.
17. Hancock, *op. cit.*, p. 133.
18. Lloyd George Papers (LGP), House of Lords Record Office, F45/9/51 for de Valera's letter: Dáil Deb. 26 August 1921, p. 82.
19. Dáil Éireann, *Treaty Debate*, p. 32.
20. Frank Pakenham, *Peace by Ordeal* (London, 1935), p. 90.
21. Cmd. 1502.
22. Dáil Deb., 17 August 1921, p. 12.
23. UCDA, RMP, Minutes of Proceedings of Committee on Defence, 17 October 1921.
24. Jones, *op. cit.*, p. 140.
25. *Ibid.*, pp. 120–3.
26. Childers Papers, 7849, letters of 22, 23 and 24 April 1921.
27. Jones, *op. cit.*, p. 122; see also, *Treaty Debate*, p. 32, for Collins' recollections.
28. F.M.A. Hawkins, 'Defence and the role of Erskine Childers in the treaty negotiations of 1921', *Irish Historical Studies*, vol. XXII, no. 87 (March 1981), p. 259.
29. Memorandum of the Proposals of the Irish Delegates to the British Representatives, 24 October 1921, State Paper Office (SPO) and UCD P7/A/72. For Griffith's exposition, see also Jones, *op. cit.*, pp. 140–3.
30. LGP, F45/9/51 and Jones, *op. cit.*, pp. 127–31.
31. UCDA, RMP, 17 October 1921. Cf. Jones, *op. cit.*, pp. 129–37.
32. *Ibid.*, Griffith to de Valera, 24 October 1921.
33. Jones, *op. cit.*, pp. 146–7.
34. Austen Chamberlain Papers (ACP) Birmingham University Library; note initialled by Birkenhead, 3 November 1921.

35. UCDA, RMP, 2 November 1921.
36. Sir Laming Worthington-Evans Papers (LWEP), Bodleian Library, Oxford, 8 November 1921, c.910, f.194–5.
37. Correspondence between HMG and the Prime Minister of Northern Ireland relating to the Proposals for an Irish Settlement, Cmd. 1561.
38. UCDA, RMP, Griffith to de Valera, 8 November 1921.
39. Dáil Éireann files, Amendments by the Irish Representatives to the Proposed Articles of Agreement, 4 December 1921.
40. Jones, *op. cit.*, p. 183.
41. Earl of Longford and T.P. O'Neill, *Eamon de Valera* (London, 1970), pp. 164–5, makes clear the extent of de Valera's isolation and how it would have been virtually impossible to get in touch with him.
42. Churchill, *The World Crisis, op. cit.*, p. 305.

Chapter 8

1. The text of the Treaty is annexed as the Second Schedule to the Irish Free State Constitution Act 1922, 13 Geo 5, CI, Sess. 2, as also to the Constitution of the Irish Free State (Saorstát Éireann) Act No. 1, 1922.
2. For memorandum see CAB. 21/243 and J. McColgan, 'Implementing the 1921 Treaty: Lionel Curtis and constitutional procedure', *Irish Historical Studies*, vol. XX, no. 79 (March 1977), an admirable essay in detailed historical reconstruction of a neglected topic.
3. A.B. Keith, 'Notes on imperial constitutional law', *Journal of Comparative Legislation and International Law*, vol. IV (1922), p. 104. The Act acknowledged the exclusive right of the Irish Parliament to legislate for Ireland.
4. L. Kohn, *The Constitution of the Irish Free State* (London, 1932), p. 59.
5. H. of C. Deb. 2 March 1922, Vol. CLI, Col. 602.
6. For example, *Nouveau Petit Larousse*, 1968, p. 1293, Col. 1, under *de Valera*.
7. H. of C. Deb. 14 December 1921, Vol. CXLIX, Cols 33–4.
8. *Ibid.*, Col. 36.
9. *Ibid.*, Cols 39–40.
10. McColgan, *op. cit.*, p. 314.
11. H. of C. Deb. 14 December 1921, Vol. CXLIX, Col. 42.
12. *Ibid.*, Col. 43.

Chapter 9

1. H. of C. Deb., 15 December 1921, Vol. CXLIX, Cols 187–8.
2. *Ibid.*, Cols 27–8 and 36–7.
3. *Ibid.*, Cols 176–7.
4. *Ibid.*, Cols 192–6 and H. of L. Deb. 14 December 1921, Vol. XLVIII, Cols 36–53 and 204.
5. H. of C. Deb. 15 December 1921. Vol. CXLIX, Cols 196–209.
6. See also I. Colvin, *The Life of Lord Carson* 3 vols (London, 1936), Vol. III, pp. 410–15.
7. Department of State, Washington. Dispatch from American Consulate, Belfast, 14 December 1921.
8. Thomas Jones, *Whitehall Diary*, Vol. III, *Ireland 1918–1925* (London, 1971), p. 189.
9. *Ibid.*, pp. 189–91.
10. Frank Pakenham, *Peace by Ordeal* (London, 1935), p. 342; *F.E. The Life of F.E. Smith, First Earl of Birkenhead* by His Son (London, 1959), p. 388; and Rex Taylor, *Michael Collins* (London, 1958), pp. 188–9.
11. Cf. Michael Laffan, *The Partition of Ireland 1911–1925* (Dublin, 1983), p. 87.
12. Dáil Deb. (Private Session), 15 December 1921, p. 172; and for Lloyd George, H. of C. Deb. 15 December 1921, Vol. CXLIX, Cols 27–8.
13. Colonial Office 886/10. See W.K. Hancock, *Smuts*, 2 vols (Cambridge, 1967), Vol. II, pp. 38–49 and N. Mansergh, *The Commonwealth Experience*, 2nd edn (London, 1982), Vol. I, pp. 209–14.
14. Cmd 1474. Reprinted in A.B. Keith, *Speeches and Documents on the British Dominions 1918–1931*, p. 56.
15. Dáil Éireann, Debate on the Treaty between Great Britain and Ireland, p. 27. See also, the Private Sessions of the Second Dáil, 14 December 1921–6 January 1922. The exchanges in Private Session 14–16 December 1921 convey the strength of feeling on the pro- and anti-Treaty sides. It was such as to preclude considered comparison of the respective merits of the Treaty (Document No. 1) and Document No. 2. A

number of deputies admitted to being in a state of confusion.

16. *Ibid.*, p. 40; see generally pp. 36–42.

17. Dáil Deb. (Private Session), 14 December 1921, pp. 101–3.

18. Treaty Debate, pp. 43–5.

19. Dáil Deb. (Private Session), 14 December 1921, pp. 104–9. Document No. 2, see *ibid.*, Appendix 17, pp. 317–20.

20. Treaty Debate, pp. 20–3. For Michael Collins' arguments for the Treaty see pp. 30–6 and for Robert Barton's account of why he signed the Treaty, see p. 49. The text of the Treaty is reproduced in Dáil Deb. (Private Sessions), Appendix 15 pp. 312–15 and in revised form as alternative Treaty proposals in Appendix 18, pp. 321–4. For an appraisal of de Valera's attitude, see John Bowman, *De Valera and the Ulster Question 1917–1973* (Oxford, 1982), pp. 64–9.

21. Bowman, *op. cit.*, pp. 30–36.

22. *Ibid.*, pp. 45–7.

23. *Ibid.*, pp. 6–8.

24. *Ibid.*, pp. 7–14; 24–7.

25. *Ibid.*, pp. 36–42.

26. Dáil Deb. (Private Session), 15 December 1921, pp. 149–50; Treaty Debate, 7 January 1922, pp. 345–7.

27. For the voting on his election, see Treaty Debate, pp. 378–9, for Blythe's observation, p. 366; for the controversy about Griffith's status, see p. 399, where Griffith contended that de Valera had been President of Dáil Éireann, not the President of the Republic, whilst de Valera retorted that as President of Dáil Éireann he was President of the Republic. Griffith said that if he was elected, he would occupy whatever position de Valera had occupied and leave it at that.

28. Reference has already been made (see pp. 190 and 194) to Dr McColgan's article 'Implementing the 1921 Treaty: Lionel Curtis and constitutional procedure' (*Irish Historical Studies* vol. XX, no. 79, (March 1977) pp. 312–33). It provides an instructive guide to the aims of Curtis and his colleagues.

29. W.S. Churchill, *The World Crisis: The Aftermath* (London, 1929), p. 320.

30. University College Dublin Archives (UCDA), Hugh Kennedy Papers (HKP) P4/VII/25 for text of paragraph in Lloyd George's letter of 13 December 1921.

31. See *ibid.*, P4/III/15: 14 December 1921, Replies to Queries; and 17 December 1921 for Memorandum on Oath.

32. There are two complementary accounts of the drafting of the constitution. The first, by D.H. Akenson and J.F. Fallin, is subtitled, 'The Irish Civil War and the Drafting of the Free State Constitution, Parts I–III', in *Eire-Ireland, A Journal of Irish Studies* (Minnesota, 1970), Vol. v, nos 1, 2, 4, pp. 10–26, 42–93 and 28–70. This reproduces the texts of drafts A and B and part of Draft C, together with relevant comment on the course of the consultation with members of the Provisional Government Committee of the British Cabinet and also with Lloyd George. The second, a comparatively brief analysis, is in J.M. Curran, *The Birth of the Irish Free State 1921–1923* (Alabama, 1980), Chapter 14, where the drafting of the constitution is given its place in the overall context of Anglo-Irish negotiations 1921–22. In association, the two have illuminated an episode which threatened the Treaty settlement.

33. For the official British account see 1 May 1922, CAB. 43/3, also CAB. 32/22. Jones, *op. cit.*, Vol. III, see entries for 27 May–1 June, pp. 202–6. For the Irish side, see especially UCDA SFB 60; also Curran, *op. cit.*, pp. 201–10.

34. CAB. 43/3.

35. On the assassination of Sir Henry Wilson see Michael Hopkinson, *Green against Green. The Irish Civil War* (Dublin, 1988), pp. 112–14.

36. Jones, *op. cit.*, Vol. III, pp. 200–1.

37. S. Lawlor, *Britain and Ireland 1914–1923* (Dublin, 1983), pp. 191–4, also Hopkinson, *op. cit.* Chapter 15.

38. American Consulate General to Secretary of State, Washington. 18 November 1922. The dispatch is a report on the political situation in Southern Ireland for the Secretary of State, Washington.

39. A.J.P. Taylor, *English History 1914–1945* (London, 1965), p. 192; Treaty Debate, p. 49.

40. Treaty Debate, p. 381.

41. Dáil Deb. Vol. I, September–October 1922.

42. See also H. of C. Deb., Vol. CLIX, 22 November 1922, Cols 327–33.

43. See Chapter 12.

44. K.C. Wheare, *The Statute of Westminster and Dominion Status* (Oxford, 1938), Chapters IV and XI, provides an analy-

sis of an intricate episode. Students of the politico-constitutional origins and early development of the Irish Free State are greatly indebted to the contribution made by two Australians of international reputation; Professor Wheare as a political scientist and Professor Hancock as a historian.

Chapter 10

1. 13 Geo. V, Sess. 2 c. 1.
2. Northern Ireland (NI) H. of C. Deb. 7 December 1922, Vol II, Cols. 1147–8.
3. See pp. 153–4.
4. NI, H. of C. Deb. 7 December 1922, Vol. II, Col. 1157.
5. *Ibid.*
6. *Ibid.*, Col. 1152.
7. Public Record Office Northern Ireland (PRONI) Fred H. Lawford to Carson 14 February 1920; Carson Papers, D. 1507/1/1920/10.
8. University College Dublin Archives (UCDA). P7/A/72, 14 October 1921. For Lloyd George's allusion to Carson's initial suggestion of a Boundary Commission, see Thomas Jones *Whitehall Diary*, Vol. III (London, 1971), p. 161.
9. John Bowman, *De Valera and the Ulster Question, 1917–1973* (Oxford, 1982), pp. 62–4; Jones, *op. cit.*, pp. 156–7; F.S.L. Lyons, *Ireland since the Famine* (London, 1971), p. 432; Frank Pakenham, *Peace by Ordeal* (London, 1935), pp. 216–20. See also Pakenham's later comment in T. Desmond Williams (ed.) *The Irish Struggle 1916–1926* (London, 1966), pp. 107–15.
10. Jones, *op. cit.*, pp. 164–5.
11. Jones, *op. cit.*, p. 156.
12. H. of L. Deb. 21 March 1922, Vol. XLIX, Cols 684–6 and 9 December 1925, Vol. LXII, Cols 1230–2.
13. UCDA. P7/A/72, 17 October 1921.
14. Memorandum by Collins of interview with Lloyd George 5 December 1921, UCDA. P7/A/72.
15. Letter from Chartres to General Mulcahy, 5 February 1924, Richard Mulcahy Papers (RMP), UCDA, P35/B/137.
16. Consul to State Dept. 14 December 1921.
17. Dáil Éireann, Debate on the Treaty between Great Britain and Ireland 19 December 1921, p. 35.

18. H. of C. Deb. 14 December 1921, Vol. CXLIX, Cols 39–42.
19. Chamberlain Papers (ACP), Birmingham University Library, 30/1/27 Birkenhead's letter of 3 March 1922 to Balfour was copied to Austen Chamberlain.
20. *Ibid.*, ACP,30/1/33, Craig to Balfour, 16 March 1922, copied to Chamberlain.
21. H. of C. Deb. 26 June 1922, Vol. CLV, Col. 1744.
22. Churchill, *The World Crisis: The Aftermath* (London, 1929), pp. 316–17 and Martin Gilbert, *Winston S. Churchill* 8 vols (London, 1977), Vol. IV, pp. 1732–3.
23. *Annual Register*, 1922, pp. 9–12 and 42–4. An extract from the Agreement of 21 January 1922 and the agreed statement of 2 February are reproduced in Cmd 2264, pp. 41–2.
24. Jones, *op.cit.*, pp. 194–5 and 202.
25. *Ibid.*, pp. 196–8. For text, see Dorothy Macardle, *The Irish Republic*, 1st American edn (New York, 1965), pp. 966–8.
26. Rex Taylor, *Michael Collins* (London, 1958), pp. 241–50. See also E. Neeson, *The Life and Death of Michael Collins* (Cork, 1958). Michael Laffan, *The Partition of Ireland 1911–25* (Dublin, 1983), pp. 95–8, speculates on what would have happened if Collins had lived, because he cared more about Northern Catholics and was more prepared to help them by violent means than any of his Cabinet colleagues.
27. H. of C. Deb. 29 March 1920, Vol. CXXVII, Cols 927–8.
28. Paul Canning, *British Policy towards Ireland 1921–1941* (Oxford, 1985).
29. See above, p. 224.
30. See 7(a) and (b) of the Agreement. For an account of the negotiations, see Conferences of the Irish Committee with Representatives of Northern and Southern Ireland, March 29–30, 1922 (CAB. 43/5).
31. NI H. of C. Deb. 23 May 1922, Vol. II, Cols 595–612.
32. Jones, *op. cit.*, p. 110.
33. UCDA, P24/70, Blythe Papers (BP), 9 August 1922.
34. *Ibid.*, Assistant Legal Adviser 'to Each Minister', P24/77.
35. *Ibid.*, P4/V/2.
36. Agreement reprinted in Cmd 2155.
37. UCDA, McGilligan Papers (McGP), P4/V/3.

38. Jones, *op. cit.*, p. 231.
39. *English History 1914–1945* (London, 1965), p. 158 and Note B on p. 162. The record is in Jones, *op. cit.*, pp. 181–2. Note summarises adjustments – that seems the right word here – in the views of Chamberlain; also of Churchill and Birkenhead, where there was a good deal more adjustment. The assumption remained this was a matter of personal understanding rather than of interpretation of a document.
40. Cmd 2155.
41. See F.X. Martin and F.J. Byrne, *The Scholar-Revolutionary: Eoin MacNeill 1867–1945 and the Making of the New Ireland* (Shannon, 1973). Chapter by G.J. Hand, 'MacNeill and the Boundary Commission', pp. 199–276.
42. Cmd 2155 and PRONI, CAB. 4/87/18.
43. Jones, *op. cit.*, pp. 227–8.
44. *Ibid.*, p. 228.
45. Cmd 2155, p. 91.
46. *Ibid.*, pp. 92–3.
47. Cmd 2166 where the relevant papers are assembled. The Report of the Judicial Committee of the Privy Council is in Cmd 2214.
48. Dáil Deb. Vol. VIII, 12 August 1924; Cols 2414–15 for an exposition of the government's policy and problems, see generally Cols 2407–18; Lyons, *op. cit.*, p. 486 remarks that the Commission while perambulating the Border gave no inkling of how it was going to report. But in view of Thomas Johnson's inference, this requires some qualification.
49. Dáil Deb. Vol. VIII, 12 August 1924, Cols 2425–31; see also G.J. Hand, *Report of the Irish Boundary Commission 1925* (Shannon, 1969), p. 9.
50. 14 & 15, Geo. V, Ch. 41.
51. See *Report*, ed. G.J. Hand, Part I, Chapter 3 (pp. 25–32) which treats of Article 12 'Interpretation and Principles of Application', and Annex to Chapter 3.
52. *Ibid.* For maps, see Appendices 6 and 7.
53. For an account of the resignation set out in its dramatic detail by Dr Hand see *The Scholar Revolutionary, op. cit.*, pp. 254–9.
54. UCDA, P35B/141. High Commissioner to Desmond Fitzgerald 25 November 1925.
55. CAB. 55/25, 30 November 1925; Jones, *op. cit.*, pp. 240–6, Dáil Deb. Vol. XIII, Cols 609–41 and 795–818.

56. H. of L. Deb. 9 December 1925, Vol. LXII, Col. 1236.
57. The text of the 'Agreement amending and supplementing the Articles of Agreement for a Treaty between Great Britain and Ireland, December 3, 1925' (15 and 16 Geo. V, c. 77 and Irish Free State Act, No. 40 of 1925) is reprinted in A.B. Keith, *Speeches and Documents on the British Dominions 1918–1931* (London, 1932), pp. 137–9.
58. CAB. 56/25, 2 December 1925.
59. See especially, Jones, *op. cit.*, pp. 244–6.
60. CAB. 56/25, 3 December 1925.
61. Dáil Deb. Vol. XIII, 7–10 December 1925. Treaty (Confirmation of Amending Agreement), Bill was passed by 71 votes to 20, Col. 1767.
62. Dispatch to Secretary of State Washington on Irish Political Situation 17 December 1925. The commentary as a whole provides an interesting external view.
63. PRONI, Londonderry Papers, D3099/2/7/82.

Chapter 11

1. Cmd 692. Letter from Mr Speaker to the Prime Minister. See R.V. Vernon and N. Mansergh (eds) *Advisory Bodies. A Study of their Uses in relation to the Central Government 1919–1939* (London, 1940), pp. 67–72.
2. H. of C. Deb. 3–4 June 1919, Vol. CXVI, Cols 1873–2127. J. Lowther, *A Speaker's Commentaries* 2 Vols (London, 1925), Vol. II, p. 271, see above p. 187 for Craig's letter to Lloyd George of 11 November 1921, which is reproduced in Cmd 1561.
3. Government of Ireland Act, 1920, 10 & 11 Geo. V, Ch. 67, Sections 11–14; Northern Ireland (NI) H. of C. Deb. 6 June 1929, Vol. XI, Col. 300.
4. *Ibid.*, Sections 4–7.
5. *Ibid.*, Section 14 (5).
6. *Ibid.*, Sections 20–36.
7. Report of the Special Arbitration Committee, 1923, Cmd 2073, Final Report 1925, Cmd 2389.
8. NI H. of C. Deb. 20 February 1936, Vol. XVIII, Col. 229.
9. *Ibid.*, 25 March 1936, Col. 704.
10. NI H. of C. Deb. 20 September 1921, Vol. I, Cols 48–9.
11. See above, p. 246.
12. NI H. of C. Deb. Vol. I, Col. 174.

13. K.C.Wheare, *Federal Government*, 3rd edn (Oxford, 1956), is the standard authority; see especially pp. 30-1.
14. W.S. Livingston, *Federalism and Constitutional Change* (Oxford, 1956), pp. 13-15.
15. N. Mansergh, *The Government of Northern Ireland* (London, 1936), p. 237.
16. *The Irish Times*, 9 February 1936.
17. NI H. of C. Deb. 16 March 1943, Vol. XXVI, Cols 293-7.
18. D. Harkness, *Northern Ireland since 1920* (Dublin, 1983), pp. 106-7 and *The Irish Jurist*, Summer 1977, pp. 176-86.
19. Cf. NI H. of C. Deb. 6 November 1945, Vol. XXIX, Cols 1090-3 on parity in farm prices and social services.
20. Cf. R.J. Lawrence, *The Government of Northern Ireland - Public Finance and Public Services 1921-1964* (Oxford, 1965), p. 88.
21. See generally, K.S. Isles and N. Cuthbert, 'Ulster's economic structure', in T. Wilson (ed.) *Ulster under Home Rule* (Oxford, 1955), pp. 91-114.
22. Public Record Office Northern Ireland (PRONI), Carson Papers D 1507/1/1920/6.
23. *Ibid*. D 1507/1/1920/9A.
24. 10 & 11 Geo V, Ch. 67, Section 14.
25. P. Buckland, *The Factory of Grievances: Devolved Government in Northern Ireland 1921-1939* (Dublin, 1979), pp. 267-73.
26. PRONI, CAB. 9B/40/1. There is a balanced appraisal of the reactions to the hasty abolition of PR and its consequences in Buckland, *op. cit.*, pp. 231-46. See also Mansergh, *op. cit.*, Chapter 7, for a near contemporary account.
27. NI H. of C. Deb. 21 April 1925, Vol. VI, Col. 146.
28. CAB. 9B 13/1-2, Quekett to Spender 18 February 1924.
29. *Ibid.*, 23 February 1924.
30. *Ibid.*, 12 May 1924.
31. *Ibid.*, Dixon to Craig 19 September 1927 and reply, 21 September 1927.
32. Representation of the People (Equal Franchise) Act, 18 &19 Geo. V, Ch. 12, Section 8(4) and Ch. 24, Section 2(3).
33. NI H. of C. Deb. 25 October 1927, Vol. VIII, Col. 2271.
34. *Belfast Newsletter*, 7 April 1926.
35. NI H. of C. Deb. 25 October 1927, Vol. VIII, Cols 2262 and 2268.
36. *Ibid.*, Col. 2280.
37. *Irish News*, 30 January 1928.
38. NI H. of C. Deb. 25 October 1927, Vol.

39. VIII, Cols 2275-7.
39. Buckland, *op. cit.*, p. 229.
40. The author's *The Government of Northern Ireland* was published in 1936.
41. M. Laffan, *The Partition of Ireland* (Dublin, 1983), p. 114.
42. Thomas Jones, *Whitehall Diary*, Vol. III, *Ireland 1918-1925* (London, 1971), p. 244.
43. *The Annual Register*, 1936, p. 115.
44. *The Irish Times*, 1 and 2 January 1987, reprints extracts from PRONI Cabinet minutes 9 and 31 May and 7 June, 1956.

Chapter 12

1. See above, pp. 223-4.
2. L. Madelin, *The French Revolution*, trans. (London, 1916), p. 453.
3. The Taoiseach, John A. Costello, 'Ireland in international affairs', Lecture to the Canadian Bar Association, Montreal, 1 September 1948.
4. Proclamation of 27 May 1922.
5. B. O'Brien, *The Irish Constitution* (London, 1929), p. 54.
6. These Articles were: Articles 12, 17, 24, 36, 40, 41, 50, 58, 65, 67, 77, 79.
7. As prescribed in Article 83 of the constitution.
8. No. I of 1922.
9. L. Kohn, *The Constitution of the Irish Free State* (London, 1932), p. 97.
10. 13 Geo. V, c. I, Session 2.
11. Article 65.
12. A.B. Keith, *The Sovereignty of the British Dominions* (London, 1929), pp. 209-15, takes a contrary view. On the Irish amending procedure see Article 50, the Constitution of the Irish Free State (No. 1 of 1922) and N. Mansergh, *The Irish Free State. Its Government and Politics* (London, 1934), pp. 48-9.
13. Kohn, *op. cit.*, p. 263.
14. *Dáil Deb.* Vol. 12, Col. 2154.
15. Dáil Éireann, Debate on the Treaty between Great Britain and Ireland, p. 21.
16. *Dáil Deb.* Vol. I, 19 October 1922, Cols 1775-9.
17. H. Nicolson, *King George V* (London, 1952), pp. 480-1.
18. Kohn, *op. cit.*, p. 270, and letter dated 10 September 1933 from John Hearne to the author. Mansergh, *op. cit.*, pp. 148-55.
19. See *The Annual Register 1927*, pp. 137-9, for a near-contemporary account, also

R. Fanning, *Independent Ireland* (Dublin, 1983), pp. 95–9; The Earl of Longford and Thomas P. O'Neill, *De Valera* (London, 1970), pp. 254–5.
20. Dáil Deb. Vol. XXII, Cols 1615–16.
21. Cmd 4056.
22. *Ibid.*, reprinted in A.B. Keith, *Speeches and Documents on the British Dominions 1918–1931* (London, 1932), pp. 460–4; and N. Mansergh, *Documents and Speeches on British Commonwealth Affairs 1931–1952*, 2 vols (Oxford, 1953), Vol. I, pp. 300–1.
23. Fanning, *op. cit.*, pp. 100–3.
24. W.K. Hancock, *Survey of British Commonwealth Affairs: Problems of Nationality* (Oxford, 1937), pp. 322–4.
25. Dáil Deb. 16 July 1931, Vol. XXXIX, Col. 2290.
26. E (I.R./26), p. 3: CAB. 32/56.
27. See N. Hillmer and P. Wigley (eds) *The First British Commonwealth* (London, 1980), p. 114, for the impact made by the Irish memorandum as recorded by Hankey for Baldwin.
28. Dáil Deb. Vol. XVII, 15 December 1926, Cols 714, 728–34, 737.
29. D.W. Harkness, *The Restless Dominion* (London, 1969), pp. 105–6.
30. Dáil Deb. 22 March 1928, Vol. XXII, Cols 1645–6.
31. *Ibid.*, Cols 1728–9.
32. State Paper Office (SPO) for correspondence dated 21–4 November. Keith, *op. cit.*, pp. 213–14 and p. 302, where the President's letter to the Prime Minister, dated 21 November 1931 is reprinted. For the debates, see H. of C. Deb. Vol. CC and H. of L. Deb. Vol. LXXXIII, Cols 231–45.
33. S6009/4.
34. University College Dublin Archives (UCDA), P. 35B/106. D5829/4 Dispatch No. 233, 12 September 1930.
35. Quoted in Harkness, *op. cit.*, pp. 226–7.
36. Dáil Deb. 16 July 1931 Vol. XXXIX, Cols 2306–8.
37. N. Mansergh, *The Commonwealth Experience* Vol. II. *From British to Multiracial Commonwealth* 2 vols (London, 1982), p. 34.
38. UCDA P35B/111, Keith to McGilligan 20 January 1932.
39. Treaty Debate, p. 27, see above p. 180.
40. See above, p. 239.
41. UCDA P24/129, McNeill to Cosgrave, 3 May 1924.
42. T. de V. White, *Kevin O'Higgins* (London, 1948), pp. 220–2.

43. Dáil Deb. 15 December 1926, Vol. XVII, Col. 758.
44. S6009/4, 17 November 1930.
45. *Ibid.*, 1 November 1930.

Chapter 13

1. University College Dublin Archives (UCDA) Richard Mulcahy Papers (RMP), P35B/115. D. Harkness, *The Restless Dominion* (London, 1969), pp. 235–9, gives a comprehensive account of the place of the Great Seal in Irish thinking.
2. CAB. 23/70, 17 February 1932; Memorandum by Thomas, CAB. 24/228, CP 86(32), February 1932.
3. CAB. 16(32), 2 March 1932.
4. The proceedings of the Committee (ISC) are recorded in CAB. 27/523 and provide a chronological record of the considerations influencing British policy. The committee held 25 meetings between 7 April 1932 and 17 June 1936. For initial membership, see CAB. 27/523, 7 April 1932.
5. Dr McMahon in her analysis of Anglo-Irish relations at this time has drawn attention to Peters' reports. Since they were outside his duties, they were in the nature of an uncovenanted mercy but no substitute for a diplomatic representation. D. McMahon, *Republicans and Imperialists, Anglo-Irish Relations in the 1930s* (New Haven and London, 1984). On Peters, see pp. 29–30, 80, 123 and 144.
6. Irish Situation Committee (ISC) 25 & 26 October 1932. For an 'inside' exposition of the Land Annuities dispute, see R. Fanning, *The Irish Department of Finance 1922–1958* (Dublin, 1978), Chapter 7. For a more general account, see James Meenan, *The Irish Economy since 1922* (Liverpool, 1970).
7. The statement of 22 March 1932, here summarised, and the subsequent exchanges referred to below were reprinted in a British White Paper, Cmd 4056, an Irish White Paper P. No. 650 and are reprinted in A.B. Keith *Speeches and Documents on the British Dominions 1918–1931* (London, 1932), pp. 460–76.
8. CAB. 20 (32) 6 April 1932.
9. Quoted in McMahon, *op. cit.*, p. 49.
10. Seanad Éireann Deb. 25 May 1932, Vol. XV, Cols 675–82.
11. To the author.

12. UCDA Hugh Kennedy Papers (HKP) P4/vii/12.
13. The Constitution Amendment Acts Nos 20, 21 and 22, No. 22 being entitled 'An Act so to amend Article 66 of the Constitution as to terminate the right of appeal to His Majesty in Council'.
14. H. of C. Deb. 14 November 1933, Vol. CCLXXXI, Cols 726–8. Reprinted in N. Mansergh, *Documents and Speeches on British Commonwealth Affairs, 1931–1952*, 2 vols (London, 1953), Vol. I, pp. 300–5.
15. H. of C. Deb. 5 December 1933, Vol. CCLXXXIII, Cols 1457–9.
16. Moore and Others *versus* The Attorney-General for the Irish Free State. Law Courts – Appeal Cases, 1935. Petition and Judgement are reprinted in Mansergh, *op. cit.*, Vol. I, pp. 305–14. The presentation of the Petition and the reasoning in the Judgement are of more than legal interest. They reflect many of the complexities and niceties influencing Anglo-Irish relations in the thirties.
17. CAB. 27/523, ISC (32) Meeting 7 April 1932. For negotiations in November and December 1934 and announcement of the Anglo-Irish Coal-Cattle Pact in January 1935, see D. McMahon, *Republicans and Imperialists, Anglo-Irish Relations in the 1930s* (New Haven and London, 1984), pp. 151–2. See generally *The Economist*, July 21 and September 15, 1934.
18. 13 & 14 Geo. V, 1935. The exemption mitigated without removing British regret at loss of common citizenship.
19. CAB. 24/262, Cabinet Paper (CP)124 (36).
20. Philip Magnus, *Gladstone* (London, 1954), p. 352.
21. H. of C. Deb. 30 March 1920, Vol. CXXVII, Col. 1125. See above, Chapter 7, pp. 175 and 179–80.
22. CAB. 24/262, CP/124 (36), para. 9.
23. CAB. 27/523, ISC (32), 17 June 1936.
24. CAB. 27/527, ISC (32) 107, 10 July 1936.
25. McMahon, *op. cit.*, pp. 179–88.
26. CAB. 27/527 ISC (32) 118, 12 November 1936.
27. Constitution (Amendment No. 27) Act 1936 and the Executive Authority (External Relations) Act, 1936. Reprinted in Mansergh, *op. cit.*, Vol. I, pp. 321–2.
28. A. Berriedale Keith, *The King, the Constitution, the Empire and Foreign Affairs* (London, 1938), pp. 53–8.

29. Dáil Deb., Vol. LXIV, Cols 1232 ff.
30. *Ibid.*, Cols 1233–4.
31. *Ibid.*, Cols 1279–80.
32. *Irish Press*, 18 April 1949.
33. Dáil Deb., Vol. LXIV, Cols 1249–50.
34. *Ibid.*, Col. 1254.
35. See also *ibid.*, Cols 1268–70 for Dr O'Higgins' comments.
36. *Ibid.*, Col. 1293.
37. *Ibid.*, Col. 1438.
38. Malcolm MacDonald Papers (MMP), Durham University Library, 10/1/6, 16 September 1936.
39. *Ibid.*, 10/1/8.
40. *Ibid.*, 10/3/29–31.
41. CAB. 23/87.
42. Bunreacht na h'Éireann. Enacted by the People, 1 July 1937. On the drafting of the 1937 constitution see in *De Valera's Constitution and Ours* (The Thomas Davis Lectures, Dublin, 1988), ed. Brian Farrell, the essays by Ronan Fanning, No. 3, 'Mr de Valera drafts a constitution', and No. 8, 'Church, state and society', by Dermot Keogh.
43. CAB. 32/130. E. 37, No. 12.
44. H. of C. Deb. 15 December 1921, Vol. CXLIX, Cols 204–5.
45. CAB. 24/262, CP 124 (36), May 1936.
46. MMP, 11/11/50, 10/2/8 for retrospective comment.
47. *Ibid.*, 5 February 1937, 10/3/45–57.
48. Cabinet Minutes, 7 January 1938, S. 10389.
49. Neville Chamberlain Papers (NCP), Birmingham University Library, 18/1/1036.
50. *Ibid.*, NCP 18/1/1041.
51. See K. Feiling, *The Life of Neville Chamberlain* (London, 1970), pp. 309–11; and Lord Chatfield, *It Might Happen Again* (London, 1947), pp. 125–8.
52. NCP, 18/1/1036.
53. CP 124 (36), Appendix II, memorandum by Chiefs of Staff, February 1936.
54. Martin Gilbert, *Winston S. Churchill* 6 vols (London, 1976), Vol. V, p. 1027.
55. CAB. 27/523.
56. *Ibid.*
57. There is a detailed account of the negotiations in McMahon, *op. cit.*, pp. 264–80 on partition; see also John Bowman, *De Valera and the Ulster Question 1917–1973* (Oxford, 1982), pp. 160–85.
58. C.P. 228(37), October 1937.
59. CAB. 24/271.
60. MMP, 10/4/1; CP 228(37), October 1937.

61. *Ibid.*
62. NCP 18/1/1041.
63. MMP, 10/1/87.
64. *Ibid.*, 10/1/56.
65. *Ibid.*, 10/5/28.

Chapter 14

1. J. Garner, *The Commonwealth Office 1925–68* (London, 1978), pp. 235–8. See also the Earl of Longford and T.P. O'Neill, *Eamon de Valera* (London, 1970), pp. 350–1.
2. PREM 8/1222, Pt 1, XC/A0244900, 3 August 1946.
3. Dáil Éireann, Deb. Vol. LXXVII, 2 September 1939.
4. Canada, H. of C. Deb. 1939, 2nd Session, pp. 25–36. South Africa, H. of A. Deb., Vol. XXXVI, Cols 17–23.
5. Garner, *op. cit.*, Pt II, Chapter 7.
6. *Ibid.*, p. 234.
7. CAB. 65/1, 24 October 1939.
8. Paul Canning, *British Policy Towards Ireland 1921–1941* (Oxford, 1985), pp. 250–3. Winston S. Churchill, *The Second World War* (London, 1950), Vol. III, p. 539.
9. Ronan Fanning, *Independent Ireland* (Dublin, 1983), p. 126.
10. See above, Chapter 1, p. 1.
11. Dáil Deb., Vol. XCVII, Col. 2574, 17 July 1945.
12. C.R. Attlee, *As It Happened* (London, 1954), p. 190.
13. PREM 8/1222, Pt I, Cabinet Paper (CP) (46) 391, 18 October 1946. Memorandum by the Secretary of State for Dominion Affairs.
14. CP (46) 381.
15. PREM 8/1222, Pt I, Note by Sir J. Maffey, United Kingdom Representative to Eire, dated 3 August 1946.
16. Dáil Deb. Vol. XCVII, Col. 2649.
17. *Ibid.*, Vol. CVII, Col. 87.
18. Personal information.
19. Dáil Deb., Vol. CVII, Col. 93, 24 June 1947.
20. *Ibid.*, Vol. XCVII, Col. 2575.
21. *Ibid.*, Vol. CVI, Cols 2322–3.
22. *Ibid.*, Vol. XCV, Cols 1024–5, 29 November 1944.
23. *Ibid.*, Vol. XCVII, Cols 2116–17.
24. *Ibid.*, Col. 2572.
25. *Ibid.*, Col. 2607.
26. *Ibid.*, Vol. CI, Cols 2181–2.
27. *Ibid.*, Col. 2246.
28. *Ibid.*, Vol. CVI, Col. 2326.

Chapter 15

1. She founded in 1904 the 'Inginidhe na h'Éireann' which later developed into the better known Cumann na mBan.
2. Norton's speeches in Dáil Deb. 11 December 1936, Vol. LXIV, Col. 1249, and 18 July 1945, Vol. XCVII, Cols 2637–49.
3. *Irish Times* and *Irish Press*, 28 January 1948.
4. General election 1948: Fianna Fáil 68, Fine Gael 31, Labour (including National Labour) 19, Independents 14, Farmers 5, Clann na Poblachta 10.
5. Dáil Deb. 18 February 1948, Vol. CX, Cols 41–2.
6. *Ibid.*, Col. 47.
7. *Ibid.*, Cols 45–6.
8. *Ibid.*, Col. 25.
9. Mr Norton, the Labour party leader, who was An Tánaiste (Deputy Prime Minister) and Minister for Social Security, was persuaded to restrict the scope of the social security legislation he sponsored after receiving public admonition from Mr McGilligan, the Minister for Finance, on the paramount need for economy in social services.
10. Clann na Talmhan.
11. Dáil Deb. 24 June 1947, Vol. CVII, Col. 86.
12. Michael McInerney, 'Mr John A. Costello Remembers', in *The Irish Times*, 8 September 1967.
13. He had visited Delhi on his way back from New Zealand and Australia.
14. See Costello's speech, 10 May 1949, Dáil Deb. Vol. CXV, Cols 796–7.
15. Personal information.
16. 11 & 12 Geo. VI, c. 56.
17. Dáil Deb. 20 July 1948, Vol. CXII, Col. 908.
18. *Ibid.*, Col. 910.
19. *Ibid.*, Col. 1019.
20. *Ibid.*, Cols 1555–6.
21. See Costello's speech, 10 May 1949, Dáil Deb. Vol. CXV, Cols 796–7.
22. Costello was justified in this criticism. The Act spoke of the King as the symbol of the 'cooperation' of the members of the Commonwealth instead of their free 'association', and while it dealt with the appointment it made no provision for the reception of diplomatic representatives.
23. Published as *Ireland in International Affairs* (Dublin and Bray, Monument Press, 1948).

24. Dáil Deb. 24 July 1948, Vol. CXII, Col. 909.
25. *Ibid.*, 6 August 1948, Cols 2440–1.
26. N. Mansergh, 'The implications of Eire's relations with the British Commonwealth', *International Affairs*, January 1948.
27. E.g. *Montreal Gazette, Ottawa Citizen*, 6 September 1948.
28. The Irish High Commissioner had earlier stated that no further pronouncement was to be expected, which suggests that Costello changed his mind in view of the interest stimulated by the article in the *Sunday Independent* (see *Ottawa Citizen*, 6 September 1948).
29. Attlee in his autobiography noted with his usual studied understatement, 'He [Costello] made a speech in Canada – which was, I believe, not premeditated' *As It Happened* (London, 1954), p. 190.
30. This was borne out in official circles in Ottawa. See also J. Garner, *The Commonwealth Office 1925–68* (London, 1978), p. 320.
31. The record is still in dispute even among members of the interparty government. See in particular, Noël Browne, *Against the Tide* (Dublin, 1986) and Seán MacBride, 'The making of the Republic', published posthumously by *Magill*, April 1989. In this article MacBride answered every question except the one he was asked.
32. See the Lord Chancellor's comment, 15 December 1948, H. of L. Deb., Vol. CLIX, Col. 1089.
33. *Ibid.*, Col. 1087. Costello may have feared that if informed of Irish intentions in advance, the United Kingdom government would commit itself to a course of action from which, later, it might find it difficult to depart, even if it so desired.
34. On 17 October 1948. No official advisers were present at them.
35. *The Times*, 18 October 1948. Neither the Asian Dominions nor South Africa were represented at the Chequers meeting.
36. H. of L. Deb., 15 December 1948, Vol. CLIX, Col. 1090.
37. *Ibid.*, Col. 1089.
38. Costello was among them.
39. Dail Deb. 24 November 1948, Vol. CXIII, Col. 347.
40. *Ibid.*, Cols 351 and 353.
41. *Ibid.*, Col. 385.
42. *Ibid.*, Col. 413.
43. H. of C. Deb. 25 November 1948, Vol. CDLVIII, Cols 1413–15.
44. 11 & 12 Geo. VI, Ch. 56, 30 July 1948.
45. *Irish Times*, 19 April 1949.

Chapter 16

1. PREM 8/1222 Pt 1.
2. *Ibid.*, Pt 2.
3. Brian Barton, *Brookeborough, The Making of a Prime Minister* (Belfast, 1988), p. 232.
4. 12 & 13 Geo. VI, c. 41.
5. 10 May 1949, Dáil Deb., Vol. CXV, Col. 786.
6. H. of C. Deb. 28 October 1948, Vol. CDLVII, Col. 239.
7. Dáil Deb. 10 May 1949, Vol. CXV, Col. 788.
8. *Report of the Irish Boundary Commission 1925*, introduction by Geoffrey J. Hand (Shannon, 1969), p. 72.
9. Patrick Buckland, *The Factory of Grievances–Devolved Government in Northern Ireland 1921–39* (Dublin, 1979), pp. 206–75.
10. In the absence of availability of official records, there are some near contemporary studies: Martin Wallace, *Drums and Guns: Revolution in Ulster* (London, 1970); John Darby, *Conflict in Northern Ireland: The Development of a Polarised Community* (Dublin, 1976); D.G. Boyce (ed.) *The Revolution in Ireland, 1879–1923* (London, 1988).
11. PREM 8/1222 Pt 2.
12. Terence O'Neill, *Ulster at the Crossroads* (London, 1969), introduction by John Cole, p. 26. See also J.C. Beckett, *A Short History of Ireland*, 4th edn (London, 1971), pp. 180–1.
13. H. of C. Deb. 24 March 1972.

Chapter 17

1. No. 22 of 1948.
2. Section 2.
3. Section 1, subsection 3.
4. Dáil Deb., Vol. CXV, Cols 786–95, 10 May 1949.
5. See D.G. Boyce, 'British Conservative opinion, the Ulster question, and the partition of Ireland 1912–21', *Irish Historical Studies*, March 1970, vol. 17, no. 65.
6. R. Blake, *The Unknown Prime Minister* (London, 1955), p. 531.
7. T.S. Eliot, 'The Dry Salvages' (1941), in *Four Quartets* (London, 1944), p. 28.

APPENDIX

The Implications of Eire's Relationship with the British Commonwealth of Nations was the title of an address given by the author before an audience, which included Ministers, government officials and diplomats, at Chatham House on November 25, 1947. It is published in full in the quarterly journal of the Royal Institute of International Affairs, *International Affairs*, January 1948, vol. XXIV, No. 1 and has been reprinted as Chapter VIII in Mansergh's book, *The Commonwealth and the Nations* (R.I.I.A., 1948).

In respect of Commonwealth membership, the author emphasised

a real need for some considered assessment of the concept of 'external association'; of its history in the general context of Anglo-Irish relations, and of the lessons to be drawn from it for application in other fields . . . The phrase 'external association' was interpreted by the Irish delegates [at the 1921 peace conference] as meaning absolute sovereignty in all internal affairs for an Ireland associated with the British Commonwealth for purposes of common external concern . . .

In 1921 Mr Lloyd George asked the question, how best can Ireland's national aspirations be reconciled with the community of nations known as the British Empire? The question to be asked today is, can the interests of India, of Pakistan, and in a rather different context, of Ceylon be reconciled with those of the community of nations known as the British Commonwealth and if so, how can this best be done? Tomorrow the same question will be asked in Africa and in the West Indies, and they will be profoundly influenced by the Asian precedents, whatever they may be. It is quite certain that in answering this question Irish experience has a significance all of its own . . .

The implications of Eire's relationship with the Commonwealth . . . suggest a Commonwealth of the future, in which there are both member States and associate States, the distinction between them being one, not of status, but of history, tradition, and cultural background. By such a development the Commonwealth could only be strengthened, for it would mean that political and constitutional realities would once again be brought into harmony . . .

INDEX